S0-AIQ-763

Women, a Modern Political Dictionary

For Shane Anderson, whose love, support
and friendship has enriched my life

Women, a Modern Political Dictionary

CHERYL LAW

I.B. Tauris *Publishers*
LONDON • NEW YORK

Published in 2000 by I.B.Tauris & Co Ltd
Victoria House, Bloomsbury Square, London WC1B 4DZ
175 Fifth Avenue, New York NY 10010
Website: http://www.ibtauris.com

In the United States and Canada distributed by St. Martin's Press
175 Fifth Avenue, New York NY 10010

ISBN 1 86064 502 X

A full CIP record for this book is available from the British Library
A full CIP record for this book is available from the Library of Congress

Library of Congress catalog card: available

Typeset in Ehrhardt by Dexter Haven, London
Printed and bound in Great Britain

CONTENTS

Preface   vii

Acknowledgements   xi

PART 1: 1914–67   1

   Biographical Sketches Summary   3

   Biographical Sketches   9

   Organizations   162

PART 2: 1968–84   187

   Biographical Sketches Summary   189

   Biographical Sketches   192

   Organizations   227

Appendix 1: Chronology of UK Emancipatory Legislation 1918–84   245

Appendix 2: Clubs   250

Bibliography   252

Glossary   262

PREFACE

Personally, I am a feminist... while the inequality exists, while injustice is done and opportunity denied to the great majority of women, I shall have to be a feminist...

Winifred Holtby, *Feminism Divided* (1926)

How do people come to a new consciousness of themselves in the world? How does a new concept of what it is to be female come about? How are new ideas made social through the practical activities of a movement? How is social transformation communicated to the individual psyche?

Sheila Rowbotham, *Women's Liberation and the New Politics* (Wandor, 1972)

Although an increasing number of biographical dictionaries of women are being produced, there is still substantial ground to recover before the reference shelves of our national libraries contain anywhere near a gender equity. The arguments concerning the historiographical process of women 'hidden from history' have been well rehearsed and do not need reproducing here (see Rowbotham 1973, Lerner 1979, Offen et al. 1991). The obstacles to feminist research reflect the impediments to equality that women have encountered for generations and that persist in the resistance of many academics to acknowledging the veracity and place of women's history in the Academy. Pervasive attitudes which still seek to portray women throughout history as the dead force of reaction deny feminism its success as a significant and sustained challenge to modernist conceptions of power.

Women, A Modern Political Dictionary provides biographical sketches of women involved in the Women's Movement in the last century in two phases: the first part travels from the outbreak of the First World War in 1914 up to the eve of the British Women's Liberation Movement (WLM) in 1967 and Part 2 covers the years from the WLM's inception in 1968 to that point in the early 1980s where political tides had turned to usher in increasing darkness in Britain. Contextualization of the women's campaigning is provided with outlines of the organizations in which they worked, which enables the networks established in both phases to be traced by the reader. The intention in Part 1 is to reveal women from the past whose contribution to women's emancipation has been lost or obscured, together with women whose stories are more familiar, to capture the diversity and intermeshing nature of their contribution. More problematic are Part 2's entries, women who are for the most part still living and working. Nevertheless, the work of the theorists and activists of the WLM needs some retrospection and this is a brief, initial attempt at cohering some of their work by way of an introduction for those unfamiliar with that period.

This book started life as a by-product of the doctoral research which became, *Suffrage and Power: The Women's Movement 1918–28* (1997). To keep track of the multiplicity of events, organizations and women participants during that research, I compiled an alphabetical record, noting the circumstances in which each woman activist made an appearance. The women were divided into two categories according to the frequency with which they occurred. By the end of the research that record included 133 women in the most frequent category and over 800 in the second. This record formed the point of departure for further extensive research.

During the First World War, much of women's war-work provided an opportunity for the first time for women from all social positions to make serious challenges to the social, economic and psychological position of women. This extended provision of employment for women also engendered new areas for the active defence of women's rights (see Law 1997, p. 13). By 1928, the campaign for the extension of the vote to all women on the same terms as men, which had acted as the cement of the Movement throughout the 1920s, was a reality and the Women's Movement regrouped to consider its priorities for the future redress of outstanding inequalities. During the 1930s, the restrictions on married women's lives were to the fore, together with spreading awareness of the need for the international defence of women and children against the growth of Fascism. With the advent of the Second World War, conflict with regard to the government's utilization of women, their representation in wartime agencies and their subsequent employment position, sustained the need for various forms of action. After the war, campaigning continued to extend and refigure the rights of married women, together with the perennial struggle for equal pay. The need for a seemingly endless assault on a panoply of social, economic and political disabilities fuelled a demand for a more comprehensive anti-discrimination legislation. The rise of state welfare provision fostered the emergence of a public demand for contraception and abortion rights. Far from being a fallow period, the 1950s and early 1960s provided propitious ground for the advent of the WLM's storming revolution. Seeds planted in the previous period for equal pay, anti-discrimination legislation and contraceptive rights were brought to fruition by the direct action of a new generation. Back on the streets, women's demands were substantiated by the emergence of feminist theory, which explored and challenged preconceptions about the role and nature of women. The advent of the WLM caught the echoes that reverberated from the women of the nineteenth century. The women's movement was, in Millicent Fawcett's analogy, 'like a glacier... ceaseless and irresistible' (Law 1997, p. 226).

The 'new politics' of the Women's Liberation Movement – characterized by the process of women coming together in consciousness-raising groups (see entries), an immersion in feminist theory and participation in direct action – evolved new methods of organization where power was in the hands of collectives, not individuals. Unlike their predecessors, their 'revolution' was not in claiming legislative equality on the same terms as men, they wanted to revision the world in a feminist image. But the radical departures in analysis and operation give credence to Smyth's observation that 'No social movement is static – indeed, if and when it reaches a point of stasis, if it is ceases to *move*, it fades away and dies' (Smyth 1993, p. 249).

The question of what constitutes feminism, therefore, can be a vexed one. Many of the women in Part 1 affirmed their identity as feminists engaging in work that clearly demonstrated a commitment to women's equality; others protested their disavowal of such a label. These protestations were often couched within the context of a belief that a designated feminist stance would alienate women from the mainstream and that such alienation would result in further ruptures in the process of accommodating women into a position of equality and increased power. Many other women fought for women's rights on a justice platform – what we might now recognize as a women's-rights-as-human-rights agenda – fighting against injustice and inequality using a class analysis. In common with many feminists, some women believed such struggles should be waged in partnership with men as a means of benefiting the whole of society. It was thought that the battle of the sexes was sterile ground on which to build a better world; that to estrange men, many of whom supported the Cause, would hardly provide a solid basis for equality and continuing progress. Isolation and antipathy were never a goal, political representation and power were. Matters of consistency in political performance, and the question of change and development in ideas and allegiances, is also crucial in this debate. Further considerations arise in relation to the schools of feminism to which women in Part 2 were aligned, reflecting the development of WLM feminist theory with liberal, socialist, radical, lesbian, and black feminists seeking to embrace women's diversity.

Women have been included on the basis of Banks' inclusive definition of feminism as 'Any groups that have tried to change the position of women, or the ideas about women' (Banks 1981, p. 3) and 'At its simplest level it [feminism] represents a criticism of the position of women in relation to men and a desire to change that position' (Banks 1985, p. vii). These reflections can be supplemented by Alberti's belief that 'The definition of feminist has been that their activities were informed by an understanding of the role and position of women in society which saw them as oppressed' (Alberti 1989, p. 6).

Shirley Summerskill's (see entry) position that 'We've all got to play our different roles in feminism' is an apposite acceptance of the immense amount of capital invested in women's struggle for freedom which the lives of the women in this book represent.

ACKNOWLEDGEMENTS

Many people have enabled the women represented here, particularly those in the first section, to come into the light. It is heartening to encounter so much cooperation and shared enthusiasm. Firstly, I would like to thank my Research Assistant, Dr Shaun Milton. Although limited resources meant that he was only able to work briefly on the project, his tenacity, passion and good humour made a significant contribution. Not only did he reveal new sources and information on individual women's lives, but his conviction as to the importance of the work provided considerable reassurance. Despite the financial restrictions placed on this country's reference libraries, they still manage to provide an excellent service due to the dedication of their staff. I would like to thank all those people in the libraries noted in the sources, for their patient persistence in tracing information about these women. Without their generosity this work could not have been completed so rapidly. It comes as no surprise to see that I owe a debt to David Doughan of the Fawcett Library, especially for his constant warm welcome and wonderful anecdotes. Financial assistance was generously contributed in the way of several research grants, together with a short sabbatical, by my college. But it was most fitting that the first grant made towards this project came from the Scouloudi Foundation which was founded by Miss I. Scouloudi. Other women have kindly given time from their overloaded schedules to assist me. I wish to thank: Christine Coates at the TUC Collection at the University of North London, who has such a valuable and extensive knowledge of the trade union movement; also, my predecessor at Birkbeck, Mary Kennedy, for kindly sharing her considerable WLM experience, knowledge and contacts with me; Professor Maryann Valiulis of the Women's Studies Centre, Trinity College, Dublin, for setting me on the road toward discovering Irish activists and subsequently, Dr Kate (Caitriona) Beaumont of South Bank University; Professor Lynne Segal of Birkbeck, for her suggestions on Australian women; and Professor Judith Glazer Raymo of Long Island University, for adding to my list of American women and for her friendship when she was recently a visiting Fellow to the Institute of Education in London. Special thanks to Phil Tomlinson at Birkbeck for last-minute sanity-saving on the computer front. Finally, I want to recognize the continued support of my Birkbeck colleague, Verity Barnett, whose understanding and friendship I very much value.

Cheryl Law, Birkbeck College, University of London, March 2000

PART 1

1914–67

BIOGRAPHICAL SKETCHES

Summary

Abbott, Elizabeth	(women's rights campaigner)
Aberdeen and Temair, Marchioness of: see Gordon, Ishbel	
Adam, Nancy	(trade unionist)
Adamson, Jennie	(Labour politician)
Adler, Nettie	(social work/local government)
Aldridge, Olive	(women's rights organizer)
Allen, Mary	(women police/women's rights)
Anderson, Adelaide	(industrial pioneer)
Anderson, Louisa Garrett	(physician/surgeon)
Archdale, Helen	(journalist)
Archdale, Helen Elizabeth (Betty)	(barrister/teacher)
Ashton, Margaret	(suffrage/peace activist/local government)
Astor, Nancy	(Conservative politician)
Auerbach, Helena	(rural welfare)
Ayrton, Hertha	(mathematician/physicist/inventor)
Bacon, Alice	(teacher/Labour politician)
Baker, Hannah (Jennie)	(health lecturer)
Balfour, Francis	(women's rights campaigner)
Bamber, Mary	(trade unionist)
Barlow, Anna	(moral welfare campaigner)
Barrett, Florence	(obstetric/gynaecological surgeon)
Barry, Florence	(women's rights campaigner)
Barton, Eleanor	(Co-operative/Labour organizer/pacifist)
Beaumont, Florence	(women's rights campaigner)
Beilby, Emma	(engineering employment)
Harrison-Bell, Florence	(teacher/Labour activist)
Bennett, Louie	(trade unionist/pacifist)
Bennett, Victoria Evelyn May	(doctor/public health)
Bentham, Ethel	(doctor/industrial)
Bethune-Baker, Edith	(welfare campaigner)
Bideleux, Hilda	(health/social services)
Bondfield, Margaret	(Labour politician)
Bonham-Carter, Helen Violet	(Liberal activist)
Bosanquet, Theodora	(literary)

Boucicault, Nina	(actress)
Bourne, Adeline	(actress)
Boyle, Nina	(journalist/lecturer/children)
Brereton, Maud Cloudesley	(public health)
Bright, Edith	(industrial women's rights)
Brittain, Vera	(writer)
Brocklehurst, Nellie	(health worker)
Burton, Elaine	(teacher/Labour politician)
Butler, Joyce	(Labour politician)
Cadbury, Elizabeth Mary	(social reformer)
Campbell, Janet	(women/child health reformer)
Carlin, Mary	(trade unionist)
Castle, Barbara	(Labour politician)
Cazalet-Keir, Thelma	(Conservative politician)
Challoner, Phyllis	(women's rights campaigner)
Chance, Janet	(sexual/abortion law reformer)
Chesterton, Mrs Cecil	(social worker/writer/philanthropist)
Clark, Hilda	(peace activist)
Coates, Alice Schofield	(Labour activist)
Collisson, Marjorie Chave	(moral law reformer)
Colville, Helen Cynthia	(women's health campaigner)
Corbett, Marie	(local government)
Corbett-Ashby, Margery	(international feminist campaigner)
Courtney, Janet	(international relations)
Courtney, Kathleen	(writer)
Cousins, Margaret	(suffragist)
Creighton, Louise Hume	(writer)
Crewe, Margaret	(employment campaigner)
Crosby, Edith	(teacher)
Crowdy-Thornhill, Rachel	(international diplomat)
Cullis, Winifred	(physiology professor)
Dane, Clemence	(writer)
Davidson, Frances	(Conservative politician)
Davies, Margaret Llewelyn	(Co-operative Movement activist)
Davies, Mary	(sanitary inspector/welfare)
Dawson, Agnes	(teacher)
Dawson, Mrs Boyd	(sanitary inspector)
Deakin, Evelyn	(teacher)
Despard, Charlotte	(leader militant suffrage group/socialist activist)
Douie, Vera	(librarian)
Durrie Mulford, Rosetta	(public health)
Eliott-Lynn, Sophie	(aviator)
Elliott, Dorothy	(trade unionist)
Emmet, Evelyn	(Conservative politician)
Emmott, Mary	(welfare camapigner)
Eustace, Violet	(artist)
Evans, Dorothy	(barrister/trade unionist)

Evans, Dorothy Elizabeth	(women's rights campaigner)
Eve, Fanny Trustram	(social reformer)
Fairfield, Josephine	(barrister/doctor)
Fawcett, Millicent Garrett	(leader constitutional suffragists)
Fawcett, Philippa	(educationist)
Frampton, Rosina	(trade unionist)
Franklin, Henrietta	(education/religious reformer)
Fraser, Helen	(women's rights campaigner)
Friel, Sophia Seekings	(doctor/maternity/child welfare)
Froud, Ethel	(teacher)
Glasier, Katharine Bruce	(Labour activist)
Godwin, Beatrice Anne	(trade unionist)
Goodered, Gladys	(public health)
Gordon, Ishbel	(women's rights campaigner/philanthropist)
Gould, Barbara Ayrton	(Labour activist/politician)
Griff, Cleone	(engineer)
Gwynne-Vaughan, Helen	(academic)
Hadow, Grace	(academic)
Halpin, Kathleen	(civil servant)
Hamilton, Mary	(writer/economist/Labour activist)
Hancock, Florence	(trade unionist)
Hardie, Agnes	(Labour politician)
Harraden, Beatrice	(novelist)
Harris, Lilian	(Co-operative activist)
Hart, Judith	(Labour politician)
Hartley, Christiana	(public servant/philanthropist)
Haslett, Caroline	(engineering/electricity employment)
Hayden, Mary	(academic)
Head, Mildred	(trade unionist)
Hewitt, Annie	(teacher)
Higgs, Mary	(social worker)
Hill, Eveline	(Conservative politician)
Hobbs, Mrs	(industrial welfare)
Hodge, Esther	(teacher/editor)
Holmes, Verena	(engineer)
Holtby, Winifred	(writer)
Hood, Eleanor	(Labour activist)
Horsburgh, Florence	(Conservative politician)
Hoster, Constance	(women's employment)
How-Martyn, Edith	(birth control reform)
Howse, Edith	(trade unionist)
Hubback, Eva	(educationist/social reform)
Huffinley, Beryl	(trade unionist)
Hughes, Margaret	(trade unionist)
Innes, Kathleen	(writer/peace activist)
Jewson, Dorothy	(Labour politician/activist)
Kent-Parsons, Jessy	(public health)
Kitson-Clark, Georgina	(welfare worker)

Knight, Elizabeth	(doctor/moral reform)
Lane-Claypon, Janet	(cancer researcher)
Lawrence, Arabella Susan	(Labour politician)
L'Estrange Malone, Leah	(social welfare)
Le Sueur, Violet	(employment)
Lewin, Octavia	(physician)
Lockwood, Betty	(Labour activist/EO)
Loughlin, Anne	(trade unionist)
Lowe, Eveline	(teacher/Labour activist)
Macadam, Elizabeth	(social work/women's rights activist)
Macarthy, Mary	(trade unionist)
McDonald, Edith	(trade unionist)
Macmillan, Chrystal	(lawyer/women's rights activist)
Maguire, Christine	(trade unionist)
Manicom, Kate	(trade unionist)
Mann, Jean	(Labour politician)
Manning, Leah	(teacher)
Martindale, Hilda	(industrial welfare)
Martindale, Louisa	(surgeon)
Mason, Bertha	(social welfare)
Matheson, Hilda	(broadcasting)
Mathews, Mabel	(electrical engineering)
Mathews, Vera Laughton	(women's services)
Mayo, Winifred	(actress)
Moir, Margaret	(employment)
Moore-Guggisberg, Lilian	(actress)
Murray, Flora	(physician)
Murrell, Christine	(doctor)
Neilans, Alison	(moral law reform)
Nettlefold, Lucy	(industrialist)
Nevinson, Margaret	(writer/lecturer)
Normanton, Helena	(lawyer)
Nutting, Helen	(women's rights campaigner)
Ogilvie Gordon, Maria	(geologist)
O'Kell, Lizzie	(public health)
Palmer, Beatrix, Countess of Selborne	(Conservative activist)
Pankhurst, Emmeline	(leader suffragettes)
Parnell, Nancy	(internationalist campaigner)
Parsons, Katherine	(employment)
Parsons, Rachel	(engineer)
Partridge, Margaret	(electrical engineer)
Pethick-Lawrence, Emmeline	(women's rights campaigner)
Phillips, Juanita	(local government)
Phillips, Marion	(Labour activist)
Phillipson, Hilton, Mabel	(Conservative politician)
Phipps, Emily	(teacher)
Picton-Turbervill, Edith	(social reformer/writer)

Power, Jennie Wyse	(politician)
Quaile, Mary	(trade union)
Rackham, Clara	(women's rights campaigner)
Rathbone, Eleanor	(Independent politician/social reformer)
Rhondda, Viscountess: see Thomas, Margaret Haig	
Rolls, Eleanor Shelley	(engineering/aviation)
Royden, Maude	(minister of religion/preacher)
Rust, Tamara	(Communist women's organizer)
Ryland, Beryl	(regional women's activist)
Scharlieb, Mary	(gynaecologist)
Seear, Nancy	(academic/Liberal politician)
Selborne, Countess of: see Palmer, Beatrix	
Simm, Elizabeth	(regional Labour activist)
Skeffington, Johanna Sheehy	(suffragist/pacifist)
Smith, Constance	(factory inspector/labour campaigner)
Snowden, Ethel	(Labour activist/lecturer)
Soddy, Winifred	(women's rights campaigner)
Solomon, Daisy	(women's rights campaigner)
Soloman, Mrs Saul	(moral welfare camapigner)
Spurgeon, Caroline	(academic)
Stocks, Mary	(economist/writer/broadcaster)
Strachey, Philippa	(women's rights campaigner)
Strachey, Ray	(women's rights campaigner/writer)
Streatfeild, Lucy	(factories inspector/welfare activist)
Summerskill, Edith	(doctor/Labour politician)
Summerskill, Shirley	(doctor/Labour politician)
Sutherland, Mary	(Labour activist)
Swanwick, Helena	(journalist/peace activist)
Symons, Madeleine	(trade unionist)
Tate, Mavis	(Conservative politician)
Tavener, Grace	(Labour activist)
Tennant, Winifred Coombe	(social work)
Thomas, Margaret Haig	(industrialist/journal proprietor/women's activist)
Thompson, Edith	(public service)
Tuckwell, Gertrude	(trade unionist)
Turner, Ethel	(moral rights campaigner)
Tweedy, Hilda	(welfare activist)
Underwood, Florence	(women's rights campaigner)
Varley, Julia	(trade unionist)
Veitch, Marion	(trade unionist)
Vickers, Joan	(Conservative politician)
Walker, Jane	(doctor/tuberculosis pioneer)
Ward, Irene	(Conservative politician)
Watson, Alexandra Chalmers	(physician)
Whately, Mary Monica	(local government)
White, Amber Blanco	(civil servant/writer)
White, Eirene	(Labour politician)

Whitty-Webster, May	(actress)
Wilkinson, Ellen	(Labour politician)
Williams, Ethel	(doctor/public health)
Wilson, Emelye	(regional/industrial/health)
Willson, Laura	(engineer)
Wintringham, Margaret	(Liberal politician)
Zangwill, Edith	(writer)
Zimmern, Elsie	(welfare)

BIOGRAPHICAL
SKETCHES

ABBOTT, Elizabeth Wilhelmena Hay (née Lamond) (22 May 1884–17 October 1957) equalitarian feminist campaigner; *b.* Scotland; *do.* Andrew Lamond & Margaret McIntyre; *e.* City of London School for Girls, Brussels, University College London; *m.* George Frederick Abbott, 1911; one son; *r.* poetry, music; *c.* International Women's Franchise Club; *a.* 48 Lambolle Road, London NW3 (1907), 96 Church Street, Chelsea, London (1913), 2 Airlie Gardens, London W8 (1927).

Trained as a secretary and accountant, 1903–06; studied Ethics, Modern Philosophy and Economics at UCL for the Summer Term, 1907; NUWSS organizer Edinburgh National Society for Women's Suffrage, 1909; Executive Committee SFWSS, 1910; Scottish Committee (Glasgow) Minority Representative on Poor Law Reform, 1910; toured India, Australia and New Zealand for the Elsie Inglis Scottish Women's Hospital, raising £60,000, 1916–18; Secretary IWSA; Editor of *Jus Suffragii*; IWSA representative Conference of Women, 1921; member NUSEC; founded the ODC with Chrystal Macmillan (see entry), 1926; member NUSEC's sub-committees on Trade and Commerce and Health Services, 1926; spoke on Factories Bill legislation for NUSEC; member Sub-Committee Social Insurance; NUSEC delegate IAWSEC's Congress, Paris, 1926; NUSEC speaking tour, Scotland, 1926; spoke at an Edinburgh school event organized by the Education Secretary of Glasgow SECWCA, sharing a platform with Lady Beilby (see entry) and Eva Hubback (see entry), 1926; one of the 11 resigning members of the Executive Committee of NUSEC over protective legislation, 1927; took part in a debate at SPG, 'Protective Legislation for Women', with Dr Marion Phillips (see entry), 1927; a passionate campaigner for the rights of prostitutes during her 40 years of work for the AMSH, for which she was its Chairman for ten years; according to Katherine Bompas, she 'had that passion for justice' and, for Vera Laughton Mathews (see entry) 'was also warm-hearted and lovable'.

p. Women and Factory Legislation (with Mrs Aldridge); *Women in Industry: A Study of American History* (1911); pamphlet, *Women and the Right to Work in Mines* (1929); *Women's Present Economic Struggle The Inevitable Outcome of the Whole Feminist Movement* (1933).

s. Women's Who's Who, 1913; *The Times*, 31 October, 11 November 1957; *Catholic Citizen*, 15 November 1957; UCL records.

ADAM, Nancy (1895–6 May 1982) trade unionist; *b.* Glasgow.

Organizer of the NFWW, 1917–20; resigned from the NFWW to take up a scholarship at Ruskin College, Oxford; secretary to two MPs in the House of Commons in the 1920s; travelled in Europe studying social conditions; private secretary to A J Cook, General Secretary of the MF, 1924; joined the TUC in 1932; Secretary of the TUC NWAC, 1932–51; Chief Woman Officer of the TUC GC, 1937; appointed by the TUC as a representative on the CWP during WW2; awarded MBE, 1945; retired in 1951.

s. Industrial Newsletter for Women, July 1951; *TUC report*, 1982.

ADAMSON, Janet (Jennie) Laurel (née Johnston) (pen-name 'Laurel') (9 May 1882–25 April 1962) Labour politician; *b.* Kilmarnock, Ayrshire, Scotland; *do.* Thomas Johnston, railway porter and coachman & Elizabeth Denton; *m.* William Murdoch Adamson, Trade Union organizer, Labour MP, 1902; two daughters, two sons; *a.* 26 Sancroft Street, London SE11 (1927), 20 Woodcome Crescent, London SE23 (1938).

The poverty of her childhood, and her experiences of low-paid work as a dress-maker, factory worker and as a teacher, influenced her course in life; joined the LP, 1908; member WU, 1911; living in Manchester she was involved with the women's suffrage campaign, also working with her husband in the WU, and assisted in the Black Country strike, 1915; when her husband was moved to Belfast, she continued as an activist and became involved with the Co-operative Movement; they moved to Lincoln, 1921; member Lincoln Co-operative Management Committee; Midland Section WCG; served on the Lincoln Board of Guardians for three years; her husband became an MP and supported the suffrage extension campaign and the birth control movement, 1922; member Women's National Strike Committee, 1926; member LP NEC 1927–43 and 1945–7; member Executive Committee SJCIWO and Chairman, 1928–9; member LCC 1928–31; London LP; Chairman of the London Labour Women's Advisory Committee and the Labour Women's National Conference, 1929; represented the LP on the SWIC at conferences across Europe throughout the 1930s; Chairman LP, 1935–6; active campaigner against the exclusion of civilian women who were working in the home and their entitlement to wartime compensation in the Personal Injuries (Civilians) Scheme passed in 1939; PPC LP Dartford, 1935; successful LP candidate in the Dartford by-election, 1938–45; when an MP, she and her husband served in the Commons together until his retirement, 1938–45; PPS to Minister of Pensions 1939–45; member of the War Service Grants Commission, supporting work for war orphans; known for her struggles for working mothers and spoke in support of the Family Allowances Bill, 1945 which had been inspired by Eleanor Rathbone (see entry); supported campaigns for women's civil service and industrial promotion and equal pay; re-elected as LP candidate for Bexley, 1945; Parliamentary Secretary, Ministry of Pensions, 1945–6; resigned to become Deputy Chairman of the National Assistance Board, 1946; at a lunch to mark her retirement from the WWO, she spoke of the responsibility that subsequent generations of women owed to their predeccesors to sustain campaigning work for women, 1947; retired in 1953.

s. Ladies' Who's Who (1927); *Ladies' Who's Who* (1938); Brookes (1967); Stenton and Lees, vol. 4 (1981); *Dictionary of Labour Biography*, vol. 4; Banks (1990); Pugh (1992).

ADLER, Henrietta (Nettie) CBE, JP (1 December 1868–15 April 1950) social worker and local government; *b.* Kensington, London; *do.* Chief Rabbi, Dr Hermann Adler & Rachel Joseph; *e.* private school and classes; *r.* weekends in the country, reading; *c.* Pioneer, Writers'; *a.* 6 Craven Hill, London W2 (1902), 121a Sinclair Road, Addison Gardens, London W14 (1929).

Adler began her social work in Jewish working girls' clubs in the East End of London, before becoming a London School Board manager; Joint Honorary Secretary for the Committee on Wage-Earning Children, 1899–1946; co-opted member London Education Committee, 1905–10; Chair Central Industrial Committee Central Bureau Employment of Women, 1906; member Council National Association for Women's Lodging Homes, 1910; Liberal member LCC Central Hackney, 1910–25, 1928–31; Deputy Chair LCC, 1922–3; co-opted LCC Public Health Committee, 1931–4; member governing bodies Dalston Community School, Hackney Downs School, Hackney Technical Institute; member Departmental Committee on Charity Collections, 1925–7; speaker at the Conference of UJW, 1927; member LCC for Juvenile Employment; magistrate attached to the Islington Juvenile Court and member London Advisory Council for Juvenile Employment; awarded CBE, 1934; member Council Anglo-Jewish Association; Vice President Butler Street Jewish Girls' Club; Council member UJW, 1921; Vice President UJW, 1923; member Jewish Board of Guardians; member Jewish Religious Education Board; she died in Fulham, London.

p. articles on children as wage earners; on women's work during and after the war; the early treatment of young offenders; boy and girl labour since WW1 in the *Contemporary Review*; chapter on Jewish life and labour in East London, in the *New Survey of London Life and Labour*, vol. vi; article on Juvenile Courts for the *Encyclopaedia Brittanica*; regular contributor to the *THES*; 'Child Employment and Juvenile Delinquency' in *Women in Industry from Seven Points of View* (1908); *Sermons (Jewish)* (with A.A. Green, 1935).

s. Hutchinson (1934); *Who's Who*, 1934; *Who's Who*, 1929; *The Lady's Who's Who*, 1938–9; *The Times*, 17 April 1950; *Who Was Who*, vol. 1; archive UJW University of Southampton MS129/AJ73/21.

ALDRIDGE, Olive M., equalitarian feminist organizer.

A nurse with an English unit in Serbia, during part of WW1; Honorary Secretary WTUC, Manchester, for nine years; appointed by NUSEC as research worker into the effects of lead paint and heavy lifting of weights for men and women, 1926; addressed over 50 meetings on protective legislation, 1926; in the NUSEC Annual Report 'Special Thanks' recorded for all her speaking; ODC Organizer, her position being terminated when due to financial considerations they were forced to stop employing paid staff, 1927–32; ODC Executive Committee member, 1933–7; ODC Honorary Secretary from 1937.

p. The Retreat from Serbia: through Montenegro and Albania (1916); *Women and Factory Legislation* (with Elizabeth Abbott).

s. NUSEC Annual Report, 1926; ODC Annual Reports, 1927–37.

ALLEN, Mary Sophia, OBE (12 March 1878–16 December 1964) women's rights/women police; *do.* Thomas Isaac Allen, manager Great Western Railway & Margaret Carlyle; *e.* privately and Princess Helena College, Ealing, London; *r.* flying, motoring, gardening; *c.* Ladies' Carlton, Forum, Woman's Auto and Sports. *a.* 46 Hurlingham Court, London SW6 (1913), 7 Rochester Row, London SW1 (1924), 51 Tothill Street, London SW1 (1934), 1 Morpeth Terrace, SW1 and Danehill, Lympne, Kent (1935), 68 Victoria Street, London SW1 (1938), 4 Birdhurst Road, Croydon, Surrey (1964).

Allen was a WSPU Organizer; she was imprisoned three times and, as a hunger-striker, she endured force-feeding, 1909; co-founder and Sub-Commandant, with Commandant Margaret Damer Dawson, of the WAS and Women's Reserve, 1914; she and Damer Dawson trained and supervised approximately 1000 women for the Ministry of Munitions, 1916–18; succeeded Dawson as self-styled Commandant of the WAS, 1919–38; supplied 50 trained women for duty with the Royal Irish Constabulary in 1920; founder of the *Policewoman's Review*; travelled abroad to speak on the employment and training of women police; according to Lilian Wyles of the Metropolitan Women's Police, Allen had nothing to do with the official police force; member WFL and AMSH, active throughout the Women's Movement; represented WAS at the CCWO, 1921; stood as an Independent Liberal PPC St George's, Westminster, 1922; visited Cologne for the War Office in order to submit recommendations to deal with the problem of the Occupied Area, she recommended that a squad of British women police be instituted for duties, which would be outlined by her, and that a group of German women should be trained along the same lines to work together – these recommendations were accepted, 1923; she attempted to gain a seat as LCC representative London Unit of NUWT, 1923; member NUSEC deputation to Home Secretary for EWMC Bill, 1925; NUSEC delegate IAWSEC's Paris Congress, 1926; member Committee on Women Police to establish training procedures, NUSEC HQ, 1926; lecture to SPG on 'The Present Position of Women Police in This and Other Countries', 1927; visited Germany and met Hitler and Goering, 1930s; supported Franco; joined the BUF, denied being a Nazi, despite speaking on platforms with Oswald Mosley, the BUF's leader, and writing articles for that cause; this activity coupled with the WAS's involvement in civil defence, and her living on the Cornish coast, gave rise to questions being asked in the Commons and Allen being under threat of internment as a security risk in 1940; suspended her organization; became a Roman Catholic, 1953; died in a Croydon nursing home.

p. Pioneer Policewoman (ed. J.H. Heyneman, 1925); *Woman at the Crossroads* (with J.H. Heyneman, 1934); *Lady in Blue* (1936); ed. *Policewoman's Review*.

s. Women's Who's Who, 1913; *The Lady's Who's Who*, 1938–9; *Daily Herald*, 26 April 1940; *The Times*, 18 December 1964; *Daily Telegraph*, 18 December 1964; Bank and McDonald (1998).

ANDERSON, Dame Adelaide Mary, MA, DBE (1863–28 August 1936) industrial pioneer; *b.* Melbourne; *do.* Alexander Gavin Anderson, Scottish shipowner & Blanche Emily Campbell; *e.* privately, at home, schools in France, Germany, Queen's College in Harley Street, London, Girton College, Cambridge; *r.* music; *c.* University for Ladies and Albemarle; *a.* 21 Allen House, Allen Street, London W8 (1929).

Her grandfather was Dr Alexander Anderson, principal of the Gymnasium of Old Aberdeen and she was sent from Australia to Britain as a child; took a second-class degree Moral Science tripos, 1887; won the Gamble Gold Medal, 1893; when she left Cambridge she coached girls for examinations, and her concern for working women's hardship developed through contact with the Women's Co-operative Guild to whom she lectured in philosophy and economics; began work in the civil service as a temporary clerk under the Royal Commission on Labour, 1892–4; these investigations into industrial conditions carried out for the first time with women investigators led to workers and employers demanding the creation of women factory inspectors; Anderson was appointed Lady Inspector of Factories (the first two such women inspectors had been Miss Abraham, later Mrs H.J. Tennant, and Miss Mary Paterson), 1894; promoted to HM Chief Lady Inspector of Factories, on Abraham's marriage, 1897–1921; during her career she extended the scope of the women inspectors' work; she was still two years away from official retirement age when her enforced 'retirement' was brought about by a reorganization within the Home Office, which abolished the women's branch together with the post of Principal Lady Inspector, creating a new post of Deputy Chief Inspector (Women) at a higher salary, 1921; at the same time, the prime minister recommended her for the award of DBE; but the CWCS expressed their surprise and concern at this sequence of events, as well as wanting to ensure that adequate pension provision had been made for Anderson; on her retirement a celebratory dinner was held in her honour, hosted by Lady Rhondda (see entry), attended by hundreds of prominent women campaigners, with Julia Varley (see entry), Lady Astor (see entry) and Mary M. Paterson as speakers, 1921; in retirement, Anderson worked on child labour issues for the Shanghai Commission, visiting China, 1923–4; Vice President SPG, 1925; worked for the Foreign Office on the Boxer indemnity fund, going to China 1926, 1930–31; also with the ILO in Egypt on the same issue, 1930; she died in a London nursing home.

  p. Factory and Workshop Law in *Women in Industry* (1908); *Women in the Factory: An Administrative Adventure 1893–1921* (1922); *Humanity and Labour in China: An Industrial Visit and its Sequel 1923–1926* (1928); articles for *China Review*.

  s. The Times, 22 October 1921; *Manchester Guardian*, 21 August 1936; Banks (1990); *DNB Missing Persons* (1993).

ANDERSON, Dr Louisa Garrett, MD, CBE, BS, FRSM, JP (28 July 1873–15 November 1943) physician, surgeon, suffrage worker; *b.* London; *do.* James George Skelton Anderson, shipowner & Dr Elizabeth Garrett Anderson; *e.* St Leonard's School, St Andrews, Bedford College for Women, London School of Medicine for Women, further study Paris/USA; *r.* gardening; *c.* University Women's; *a.* Paul End, Penn, Bucks (1934).

  Niece of Millicent Garrett Fawcett; MB London, 1897; joined the BMA, 1898; MD, 1900; house surgeon at the RFH; house surgeon, house physician at the New Hospital for Women (later the Elizabeth Garrett Hospital); surgeon to outpatients at the Women's Hospital for Children, Harrow Road; on qualifying, became consulting physician in private practice in London; assistant surgeon at the New Hospital for Women, 1902–15; Honorary Secretary for Obstetrics and Gynaecology at the BMA's Annual Meeting, 1905; chief surgeon, Women's Hospital for Children; WSPU member, present at the infamous WSPU Black Friday Demonstration, when hundreds of women were assaulted by the police, 1910; imprisoned for militant action; went to France as joint organizer and chief surgeon to the Women's Hospital Corps, Voluntary Unit, establishing a hospital at

Wimereux, near Boulogne, with Flora Murray (see entry), in 1914; subsequently set up home with Murray; when this hospital was disbanded, Garrett Anderson was appointed chief surgeon at the military hospital, Endell Street, London, 1915–18; retired from professional duties after WW1 to live in Buckingham; JP for the county of Buckinghamshire; Honorary Secretary Penn Branch Mid-Buckinghamshire Conservative Association, 1924–35; Vice President SPG, 1925; during WW2, donated her house for war service, although she continued to live in London throughout the Blitz doing voluntary work; she died in Brighton from cancer.

p. The Life of Dr Elizabeth Garrett Anderson (1930); article on peritonitis, *Encyclopaedia Medica*; numerous contributions to medical journals.

s. The Times, 16 November 1943; *Manchester Guardian*, 16 November 1943; *British Medical Journal*, 27 November 1943; Bank and McDonald (1998); Alberti (1989);

ARCHDALE, Helen Alexander (née Russel) (25 August 1876–8 December 1949) journalist; *b.* Nenthorn, Roxburghshire; *do.* Alexander Russel, *Scotsman* journalist & Helen de Lacy Evans; *e.* St Leonard's School, St Andrews, St Andrew's University; *m.* Theodore Montgomery Archdale, DSO, Lt-Colonel Royal Artillery, 1901; one daughter (see below), two sons; *c.* Provisional; *a.* Stonepitts, Seal, Sevenoaks, Kent (1930), 15 Chelsea Court, London SW3 (1934), 3 rue Butini, Geneva (1934), Stilestone, Crouch, Sevenoaks (1939).

Episcopalian; lived in India immediately after her marriage, but her husband was subsequently killed in WW1; joined the WSPU, imprisoned twice, a militant activist until 1914; worked on the WSPU paper, *Britannia*; initiated a training farm for women agricultural workers, 1914; clerical worker QMAAC, 1917–18; Women's Department, Ministry of National Service, 1918; secretary Ministry of Health Watching Council; Honorary Secretary Women's Political and Industrial League; went to the same school and was a close companion of Lady Rhondda (see entry) with whom she and her children lived when Archdale became the first editor of the *Time & Tide* publishing company, 1920–26; she and Rhondda's close relationship suffered when Rhondda took over the editorship of the paper in 1926, and it gradually deteriorated as Rhondda became involved with Theodora Bosanquet (see entry); member Executive Committee SPG; International Secretary SPG until 1933; member board of directors WPH; member of and present at the first meeting of the ODC, 1926; member Executive Committee ODC, 1927–32; member ODI; member IFBPW; member British Institute of Journalists; member WEA; she was a specialist in international women's movements and was co-opted as a member on the Liaison Committee of Women's International Organizations; Vice Chairman, then Chairman, of the Equal Rights International, 1926–34.

s. Hutchinson (1934); *Who's Who*, 1929; St Leonard's School Archive; Eoff (1991); David Doughan's entry for the *Dictionary of National Biography* (2000).

ARCHDALE, Helen Elizabeth (Betty) MBE, BA McGill, LLM Lon. (21 August 1907–11 January 2000) teacher and barrister; *b.* London; *e.* Bedales School, Petersfield, St Leonard's School, St Andrews, McGill University, Canada, University of London; *do.* Theodore Montgomery Archdale & Helen Alexander Russel; *r.* cricket, hockey, gardening, reading, music; *a.* 25a St Peter's Square, London, W6, Northis, Crosslands Road, Galston, NSW, Australia (1980).

Strong emancipation influences on maternal side, her grandmother was one of the first women medical students at Edinburgh University and her mother was a suffragette (see above); Adela Pankhurst acted as her governess one summer; Betty remembered collecting stones in the back garden for her mother to take on a suffrage demonstration and visiting her mother in Holloway Prison; when her mother became the editor of *Time & Tide*, the family moved in with Lady Rhondda in Chelsea, spending school holidays in Kent with prominent women visitors from the movement, such as Winifred Holtby (see entry), Vera Brittain (see entry) and Rebecca West (see entry); Honorary Secretary WIL, 1919; she spoke at the LN, Geneva on equality for men and women; Honorary Political Secretary SPG; Honorary Secretary ERC; member Executive Council SPG, 1925; toured America publicizing SPG, 1928; spent three years in Canada at McGill University with her brother, and took first-class honours in Economics and Political Science, returning in 1929; read Law at the University of London, taking an LLB; the influence of WW1 and her father's death gave her an interest in peacekeeping, specialized in International Law for her LLM; the level of unemployment led her to become a socialist; SPG representative on a NUSEC/ERGECC deputation to Ramsay MacDonald, 1929; worked as part-time private secretary to Labour MP, Ellen Wilkinson (see entry), during the 1930s; took an Intourist trip to Russia, 1932; member ODC Executive Committee 1932–6; member BCL, NCL, BFUW; Honorary Secretary Equal Rights Committee working on an Equal Rights Treaty, 1933–5; captained English Women's cricket team's Australian tour, 1934–5; attended the first the meeting of BUC; the sole woman and top candidate in International Law in Britain, 1934; compiled a report on all discriminatory legislation against women existing in the common and statute law of England for the Women's Consultative Committee to the League of Nations, 1935; described as a 'brilliant young lawyer' by Emmeline Pethick-Lawrence (see entry), called to the Bar (Gray's Inn), 1937; deeply committed to equal pay and the equal status of women; drafted the British Nationality and Status of Aliens (Amendment) Act, 1937; Vice Chairman of the ERI; the director of the WRNS was her mother's friend, so Betty joined WRNS in WW2, serving overseas and ending up in Australia, 1940–46; became the principal of the Women's College, University of Sydney, 1946–57; returned to England for her mother's funeral, 1949; previously a Presbyterian, she was confirmed into the Church of England, 1957; established the Australian branch of the International Law Association, 1958; headmistress Abbotsleigh Church of England Girls' School, Wahroonga, NSW, 1958–70; held progressive ideas about education and discipline, which provoked controversy; the first woman to be elected Fellow of Senate of University of Sydney, 1959; Chair of the NSW branch of the Australian Institute of International Affairs, 1960–62; government adviser, serving on educational councils and on the New South Wales Privacy Committee, 1975–8; elected as one of the first ten women honorary life members of Lords by the Marylebone Cricket Club, 1999; died in Sydney.

p. Girls at School (1970); *Indiscretions of a Headmistress* (1972).

s. Indiscretions of a Headmistress (1972); *Who's Who in Australia*, 1980; *Monash Biographical Dictionary of Twentieth Century Australia* (1994); *Independent*, 18 February 2000.

ASHTON, Margaret (19 January 1856–15 October 1937) suffrage/peace activist and local government worker; *b.* Didsbury; *do.* Thomas Ashton, cotton manufacturer & Elizabeth Gair; *e.* at home, Manchester University; *r.* reading, fine needlework, gardening; *c.* Dartmouth House; *a.* 8 Kinnaird Road, Withington, Manchester (1920–21), 12 Kingston Road, Didsbury, Manchester (1937).

Ashton came from a Liberal nonconformist tradition; Elementary School Manager, 1875; began service on the Women's Trades and Labour Council Lancashire, 1895; first woman chosen to arbitrate a dispute on women's wages in the cooperative laundries; instigated girls' trade schools in Manchester; member Withington Urban District Council, 1900; first Chair of such a body working on health and education, particularly teachers' conditions; Chair Lancashire and Cheshire Union of Women's Liberal Associations; left Liberal Party on their refusal to enfranchise women, 1906; joined the NUWSS, becoming chairman of the NESS, and moved into a smaller house in order to have the money to fund the party, 1906–14; the first woman to be elected on to Manchester City Council, 1908–21; awarded honorary MA for her civic contribution; awarded Medaille de la Reine Elizabeth, Belgium; one of the ten to resign from the NUWSS Executive Committee to found the WILPF, 1915; worked at WILPF HQ during WW1; Chairman WIL, Manchester Branch; politically, she moved to the Left during WW1, joining the LP; Chairman Maternity and Child Welfare Committee, Manchester; Vice President Manchester Association BFUW; member ESU; member Executive Committee WIL, 1927; despite blindness and heart trouble in later life, she continued her interest in WIL, Manchester University and the High School for Girls; in acknowledgement of her work to improve housing, the first municipal boarding house for women was named after her; died suddenly at her home in Didsbury, Manchester.

s. List of Women Nominated for Service in Connection with the League of Nations (NUWT Archive, nd 1920–21?); *Hutchinson* (1934); *Manchester Guardian*, 16 October 1937; *The Times*, 18 October 1937.

ASTOR, Viscountess Nancy Witcher (née Langhorne) (19 May 1879–2 May 1964) MP, women's rights campaigner; *b.* Danville, Virginia, USA; *do.* Chiswell Dabney Langhorne, railway entrepreneur & Nancy Witcher Keene; *e.* local day schools; *m.* Robert Gould Shaw 1897, divorced 1903; one son; second marriage, Waldorf Astor, 1906; one daughter, four sons; *r.* tennis, riding, golf; *a.* St James's Square, London and Cliveden, Bucks, Rest Harrow, near Sandwich, Kent; 35 Hill Street, Berkeley Square, London W1 (1945), 100 Eaton Square, London SW1 (1958)

A Christian Scientist from 1914, she had a keen sense of morality that informed her public work; her second husband was MP for Sutton, Plymouth, assisted him in election campaigns and constituency work; stood for her husband's Plymouth seat when he inherited the family title and went to the House of Lords; ironically, as an American and a Conservative, and much to the concern of the Women's Movement, Astor was the first woman MP in Britain to take her seat, 27 November 1919; 'She was a rebel and a Conservative and a feminist, a new kind of firebrand' (Astor, 1963); the only woman MP in the House of Commons and, as such, had a very difficult time from 1919 to 1921; MP for Plymouth until 1945; soon after entering the Commons, she circulated an offer of support for Women's Movement campaigns to a wide number of women's organizations; operated a policy of cross-party cooperation with other women MPs, suggested the idea of a women's party; in order to facilitate the political campaigning work of the Women's Movement, she organized a Conference of Women, 1921, which was the forerunner to the CCWO, 1922; as a staunch temperance supporter she introduced and successfully carried through her own Private Members' Bill to raise the age to 18 for the purchase of alcohol, 1923; appreciating the value of networking, she held regular receptions at her London home for women from all backgrounds, to share information and meet influential people; as a committed feminist, she worked on many women's issues inside and outside Parliament; supported Criminal Law Amendment Act, legislation for nursery schools, women police, franchise extension, international peace, divorce reform, abolition of child labour in unregulated trades, issues relating to mothers and children, welfare reform; canvassed support for Ellen Wilkinson's (see entry) amendments to the Pensions Bill and Wilkinson's Bill on Municipal Corporations Act on women police, 1925; introduced the Public Places (Order) Bill, 1926; supported Wilkinson's proposal to allow women entry into the Diplomatic Service, 1928; gave extensive support to the Women's Movement – for instance, she was a member or held office for 15 women's organizations during 1926 alone. The following are some brief examples of her work for women: attended the IWSA's Geneva Congress, 1920; spoke on child assault at a NUSEC/SPG meeting, 1923; was adviser and speaker for NUSEC; wrote a preface for their *Notes on Election Work*, 1922; was first President EAW in 1924; speaker at a NCW conference in Brighton in 1925; Chair WES Conference of Women, hosting a reception at her London home 1925; Vice President SPG 1925–8; speaker at many equal franchise rights demonstrations, 1926; President Maidenhead and Windsor WCA, 1927; Vice President Council Representation of Women in the League of Nations, 1928; Vice President WSIHVA, 1929; gave generous financial assistance over the years to many women's organizations, including the WSPU, and welfare causes; awarded CH, 1937; during WW2 she became Lady Mayoress of Plymouth, where she had a very close relationship with her constituents; her outspoken style, inability to suffer fools, and sometimes acerbic wit, increasingly alienated her from political colleagues and her husband dissuaded her from standing for re-election to Parliament, which caused a rift in their relationship and left her in a vacuum after devoting her life to politics, 1945; she went on speaking tours in the USA and Canada during the early 1950s; denounced McCarthyism during the 1950s; made a Freeman of Plymouth, 1959; as a woman with immense reserves of physical energy and a love of serving in public life, her retirement seems to have been an arid and restless end to a dynamic life; died at her daughter's home, Grimsthorpe Castle, Lincolnshire, having suffered a stroke.

p. A Problem for Women (maiden speech, 1920); *Are Temperance Reformers Cranks?* (1922); *My Two Countries* (1923).

s. Astor Papers, University of Reading; *ABC Weekly*, 27 August 1949; *Dictionary of National Biography*, 1961–70; Astor (1963); *The Times*, 4 May 1964; Sykes (1972); Collis (1966); Harrison (1987); Banks (1990).

AUERBACH, Helena, rural welfare; *m.* Julius? Auerbach, farmer; *a.* Piemede, Merstham, Surrey.

From a Jewish family; member LSWS; Treasurer NUWSS 1915–17; served on the Surrey Women's War Agricultural Committee, 1914–18; member NFWI

Committee, 1919; Honorary Treasurer NFWI, 1920–27; Vice Chairman NFWI, 1927–30; Vice President NUSEC 1927; gave a paper on *Feeding a Rural Family*, Women's Section, the International Commission of Agriculture in Prague, 1930.

s. Jenkins (1953).

AYRTON, Phoebe Sarah (Hertha) (née Marks), MIEE (28 April 1854–26 August 1923) mathematician, physicist, inventor, suffragist; *b.* Portsea, Plymouth; *do.* Levi Marks, clockmaker and jeweller & Alice Theresa Moss; *e.* private Dame school, Camden, London, Girton College, Cambridge; *m.* Prof. William Edmund Ayrton, 1885; one daughter, Barbara Ayrton Gould (see entry), one stepdaughter, Edie (known as Edith, see entry); *r.* novel-reading, sketching; *a.* 41 Norfolk Square, London W2 (1923).

Educated at her aunt Marion Hartog's school; began her career as a governess, followed by six years as a mathematics teacher, 1870–76; Otilie Blind, a lifelong friend, gave her the name of Hertha; Blind took Hertha to her first suffrage meeting and helped to enrol her in the Hampstead branch of the CSWS, 1872; later she became a Vice President NUWSS; protégée and friend of suffrage pioneer and founder of Girton, Cambridge, Barbara Bodichon, from 1873; gained a scholarship to Girton, 1876; gained third-class honours Mathematical tripos, 1880; during this period she discovered her ability in design and inventing; her first invention was a sphygmograph, which monitored the human pulse, also an instrument which acted as a line-divider, 1884; attended Finsbury Technical College, 1884; studied under W.E. Ayrton, Professor of Applied Physics, and subsequently married him, 1885; helped to complete her husband's experiments on the electric arc when he was away in America, 1893; became the leading expert in this field; first woman member of the Institution of Electrical Engineers, 1899; also research into the movement of water, discovered the cause of sand ripples on the shore, 1901; Ayrton's nomination for fellowship of the Royal Society was rejected, as the Council said it had no power to elect a woman, 1902; attended a suffrage congress in Hull, 1905; she went to a WSPU meeting with her daughter, at which her daughter became a member, summer 1906; joined the WSPU later in 1906; despite her brilliance in the field, she was not allowed to give lectures at the Royal Society until 1906; awarded the Royal Society's Hughes Medal, 1906; participated in the NUWSS 'Mud March' (so called because of the atrocious weather conditions, significant as being the law-abiding NUWSS's first public demonstration, with over 3000 women walking), 1907; took part in the militant suffrage demonstration, afterwards known as Black Friday, because of the ferocity of police violence against the women, 1910; provided fugitives from the 'Cat and Mouse Act' with a safe house in which to recover from force-feeding; joined the US in early 1914; afterwards she became Vice President of the US and donated £100 to its funds, a perennial financial supporter of the Women's Movement; both her daughters were involved in the suffrage movement, her stepdaughter, Edie, married Israel Zangwill, the suffrage supporter; invented the Ayrton fan, which was an anti-gas fan for use by hand in the trenches, 1915; over 100,000 were used in WW1, although she was extremely frustrated that the government would not put them into use sooner, thus saving more lives; also invented an improved searchlight; after WW1, worked on adapting the fan for ventilation in mines, sewers and warships; representative WIL; original member of the IFUW, 1919; involved in the formation of the NUSW, 1920; Vice President of SPG;

b: born; do: daughter of; e: education; m: married; r: recreation;
c: club; a: address; p: publications; s: sources

member Committee of International Relations, BFUW; Vice President BFUW; member LP; had a firm friendship with the French pioneer, Madame Curie, with whom she corresponded; her scientific achievements are remarkable, even more so when considered in the light of her early lack of sound education; died in North Lancing from blood poisoning.

p. 12 papers on the electric arc in *The Electrician* (1896); *The Electric Arc* (1902); papers given before the British Association (1895, 1897–8), the Institution of Electrical Engineers (1899), the International Electrical Congress (1900), the British Association (1904), La Société Française de Physique (1911), the Royal Society (1901, 1904, 1908, 1911, 1915, 1919).

s. Sharp (1926); *Who Was Who*, 1916–28; Banks (1985); Golemba (1992); *Dictionary of National Biography Missing Persons* (1993).

BACON, Alice Martha, CBE (1911–24 March 1993) teacher, Labour MP; *do.* Benjamin Bacon, miner; *e.* Normanton Girls' High School, Stockwell College, External London University; *a.* 3 Artillery Mansions, London, 53 Snydale Road, Normanton, Yorkshire.

From an activist family, her father was Secretary of the MF, joined the LP at 16 years of age; the youngest member of the LP's NEC, 1941–70; NUT officer; Chairman SJCIWO, 1946–7; teacher; successful LP candidate for Leeds North East, 1945–55; subsequently MP for Leeds South East, 1955–70; Bacon made her first parliamentary contribution during the National Insurance (Industrial Industries) Bill, 1945; member of the Ministry of Labour's Women's Consultative Committee, concerned with the resolution of women returning to civilian life; delegate to the Consultative Assembly of the Council of Europe, 1950–53; Opposition Minister for Home Affairs, 1959–64; voted to allow homosexuality between consenting adults, 1960; Chair of the LP, 1950; awarded the CBE, 1953; became Minister of State at the Home Office in 1964–7; Privy Councillor, 1966; Minister of State for Education and Science, 1967–70; created life peer, 1970.

s. Brookes (1967); Stenton and Lees, vol. 4 (1981).

BAKER, Hannah Jane (Jennie) (née Elcum) Dip. RSI, Dip. NHS (1864–1939) health lecturer; *b.* London; *do.* Hugh Elcum, solicitor; *e.* North London Collegiate School; *m.* John Baker, Steel Smelters' Union; *a.* 1 Grosvenor Villas, Junction Road, London N19 (1873), 88 Hertford Road, London N2 (1924).

Poor Law Guardian, Barnet; member Finchley Urban District Council; Executive Committee WLL, 1914–18; NCUMC representative at CCWO, 1921; Deputy Chairman NCUMC, 1925; Honorary Secretary NCUMC; Vice President Finchley Division LP; President Finchley Women's Section; member SJCIWO; member East Finchley WCG; served on Adult Education Committee Ministry of Reconstruction; Departmental Committee Old-Age Pensions; National Council Combating Venereal Disease; speaker on birth control and all labour issues.

s. List of Women Nominated for Service in Connection with the League of Nations (NUWT Archive, nd 1920–21?); *Labour Who's Who* (1927); Collette (1989); North London Collegiate School for Girls Archive.

BALFOUR, Lady Francis (née Campbell) LLD, DLitt (22 February 1858–25 February 1931) women's rights campaigner; *b.* Argyll Lodge, Kensington; *do.* George Douglas Campbell, Eighth Duke of Argyll, Postmaster General and Secretary of State for India & Lady Elizabeth Leveson Gower; *e.* at home; *m.* Colonel Balfour, architect, brother of A.J. Balfour, prime minister, 1879; three daughters, two sons; *a.* 32 Addison Road, London W14, 31 Bedford Gardens, London W8 (1927).

She came from a line of campaigning women, as her mother and grandmother (the Duchess of Sutherland, friend of Caroline Norton) were active in the anti-slavery movement; an enthusiastic promoter of the Scottish Church; briefly a member of the Primrose League before becoming an active supporter of the WLUA; member CCWS; member Executive Committee WLG; started work for LSWS 1889; Executive Committee LSWS, 1892; President LSWS, 1896; representative London Committee on Joint Committee NUWSS, 1898; worked for the SFWSS; Chairman of the first Provisional Committee of the Lyceum Club, c.1902; subsequently, Chairman Executive Committee and President Lyceum Club, serving for 15 years; member Commission on Matrimonial and Divorce Laws, 1910; Executive Committee NUWSS 1907–19; involved in the struggle for better conditions for women workers and greater opportunities for women, she urged women to use their new political power for change during 1918; indefatigable speaker, worked with Millicent Fawcett (see entry); gave a lecture on 'The Future of Women' Portsmouth WCA, 1919; awarded honorary degrees from the Universities of Durham and Edinburgh, 1919 and 1921; spoke on 'The Nations and the New Age', meeting for young people, 1922; member Expert Advisory Panel LSWS, 1923; President NCW, 1923; present at the initial meeting for the ODC, 1926; Executive Committee member ODC, from 1926; Vice President, Executive Committee NCW, 1927; proposed the vote of thanks to Ellen Wilkinson (see entry) at meeting of Kensington and Paddington SEC on Equal Franchise, 1927; Vice President of the Society of Women Journalists, 1928; member Travellers' Aid Society, 1929; active in the NCW until her death; buried in Whittingehame, East Lothian.

p. Memoir, Lady Victoria Campbell (1911); *The Life and Letters of Rev. James M. MacGregor of St Cuthbert's* (1912); *Memoir, Dr Elsie Inglis* (1918); *The Life of George, Fourth Earl of Aberdeen* (1922); *A Memoir of Lord Balfour of Burleigh* (1925); *Ne Obliviscaris*, 2 vols (1930).

s. Manchester Guardian, 10 June 1918; *Pall Mall Gazette*, 6 June 1918; *The Woman's Leader*, 6 March 1931; Banks (1985); *Dictionary of National Biography*, 1931–40.

BAMBER, Mary (Ma Bamber) (née Little) JP (1874–4 June 1938) trades union and Labour activist; *b.* Linlithgow; *do.* Andrew Little, lawyer, Liberal councillor & Agnes Glanders Thomson; *e.* private school, elementary school; *m.* Hugh (Harry) Bamber, bookbinder; two daughters, one being Elizabeth Margaret (Bessie Braddock, LP MP); *r.* gardening, music; *a.* Zante Street, Liverpool (1899), Smollett Street, Liverpool (1907), 25 Freehold Street, Fairfield, Liverpool (business) and Oakley, Wilmslow Road, Manchester (1927).

Bamber was from an affluent Edinburgh legal family who lost their money when her father took to drink and eventually abandoned his family, leaving her mother

　　b: born;　do: daughter of;　e: education;　m: married;　r: recreation;
　　　　　　　c: club;　a: address;　p: publications;　s: sources

penniless to raise her children; her riches-to-rags experience of seeing her mother having to clean the houses of people she had formerly socialized with in Edinburgh, being forced to move to Liverpool where they lived in desperate poverty, made Bamber a socialist; Bamber was described by her daughter, Bessie Braddock, as 'a great revolutionary'; first job was at a printer's; started to speak at street-corner meetings and joined the ILP; with other socialists she used to make and distribute soup to Liverpool's unemployed from the Clarion van, taking her daughters with her, winter 1906–07; member Ladies' Committee Walton Workhouse; became a paid official for Warehouse Workers' Union, working for the poorest-paid women, who became known as 'Ma Bamber's sack and bag women', from 1911; later Women's National Organizer for the WWU; also involved in teaching women to read; delegate for NUWGW, TUC 1918; one of the founding members of the CP, 1919; Labour Liverpool City Councillor for Everton, 1919–22; member 'Hands Off Russia Committee; attended the Second Congress of the Third International in Moscow, 1920; Joint Woman Organizer, with Ellen Wilkinson (see entry), NUDAW, 1922; left the CP in the early 1920s; national organizer NUDAW, from 1925; delegate TUC Women's Conference, 1925; delegate Women's Conference, seconded a resolution on the organization of women, 1926; member SJCIWO; delegate Labour Women's Conference, Huddersfield, fought against SJC from the floor, 1927; Executive Committee Liverpool Trades Council and LP; member Women's Committee Liverpool Employment Exchange; National Organizer for USDAW, from which she retired on 1 July 1933; Sylvia Pankhurst called her 'the finest fighting platform speaker in the country' (Crawford et al. 1983); a tireless worker for the poor, the unemployed and women's welfare, she wore herself out for the struggle; Bamber had a secular funeral, her coffin draped with a red flag, carried by members of the International Brigade, who sang socialist anthems at her graveside.

s. Labour Leader, 20 May 1920; Crawford et al. (1983); *The New Dawn*, 11 June 1938; *Labour Who's Who* (1927); Toole (1957); J. and B. Braddock (1963); *Labour Woman*, January 1971.

BARLOW, Hon. Lady Anna Maria Heywood (née Denman) (1873–?) moral welfare; *b.* Liverpool; *do.* Richard Denman & Helen McMicking; *e.* private; *m.* Sir John Emmott Barlow MP, 1895; two daughters, two sons; *c.* Lyceum, Anglo-German; *a.* Torkington Lodge, Hazelgrove, Stockport, Cheshire (1929), Bryn Eirias, Colwyn Bay, Denbighshire (1929), 150 Grosvenor House, Park Lane, London W1 (1934), Cloverley Hall, Whitchurch, Salop.

Assisted her husband with his work as MP for Frome for 26 years; President Lancashire and Cheshire Band of Hope Union for 22 years; member Free Trade Committee; PPC Independent Liberal, High Peak, Derbyshire, 1922; PPC Independent Liberal, Ilkestone, Derbyshire, 1924; speaker at WFL public meeting against the Criminal Law Amendment Bill and its withdrawal, 1918; speaker at Peacemakers' Pilgrimage Rally, Hyde Park, 1926.

s. Who's Who, 1929; *Women's Who's Who, 1934–5*.

BARRETT, Lady Florence Elizabeth (née Perry) CH, CBE, MD, MS, BSc (1867–7 August 1945) obstetric and gynaecological surgeon; *b.* Compton Greenfield, Gloucestershire; *do.* Benjamin Perry of Avonleigh, Stoke Bishop & Elizabeth; *e.* private tuition, University College Bristol, LSMW; *m.* Dr F. Ingor Willey, 1896, Sir

Barry WOMEN, A MODERN POLITICAL DICTIONARY

William Fletcher Barrett, FRS, 1916; *r.* riding, walking, reading; *c.* Cowdray; *a.* 31 Devonshire Place, London W1 (1914) and Hill House Cottage, Cookham Dean, Berkshire.

Matriculated 1893; gained first-class BSc degree 1895; qualified and registered as medical practitioner, 1900; assistant anaesthetist, 1900–01; lecturer and examiner LCC Infant Care, 1901–12; house surgeon, 1901–02; clinical pathologist and assistant pathologist, 1902–03; surgical and gynaecological registrar, X-ray Department, 1903–06; took the MS, 1904; MD, 1908; progressed from assistant anaesthetist to clinical gynaecological assistant and anaesthetist at RFH, 1908; honorary staff appointment at the RFH as assistant physician for Women's Diseases, 1908; before WW1, she was active in establishing voluntary centres for feeding expectant mothers and their children; senior consulting obstetric surgeon, Mothers' Hospital, Clapton; lecturer on midwifery, LSMW, 1913–21; Fellow Royal Society of Medicine; President MWF 1923; Dean and later President LSMW; consulting obstetric and gynaecological surgeon, RFH; honorary surgeon to the Marie Curie Hospital; Vice President of the Section of Obstetrics and Gynaecology at the BMA's Annual Meeting, Newcastle upon Tyne, 1921; member BMA Parliamentary Sub-Committee, 1921–7; President MWIA; President Sectional BMA meeting, Bath, 1925; medical representative Conference of Women Ministers and Missionaries, 1926; member Committee on the Causation of Puerperal Morbidity and Mortality, 1927–8; shared her second husband's interest in psychical research; served on a large number of committees concerning women's social problems; largely responsible for the creation of the obstetrics unit at the RFH; attended important congresses of medical women and maintained contact with medical women's interests, internationally.

p. Notes on the Smaller Fibromyomata, Royal Society of Medicine (1909); *'Menstruation and Menorrhagia'*, *Journal of Obstetrics and Gynaecology* (1909); *A Plea for the Feeding of Nursing Mothers as a Means of Preventing the Waste and Maiming of Child Life* (1912); *Diseases of Women, a Handbook for Nurses* (1912); *Conception Control and its effects on the individual and the nation* (1922); *Personality Survives Death: Messages from Sir William Barrett* (1937).

s. Who Was Who, vol. 4; *Who's Who*, 1929; *Women's Who's Who, 1934–5*; *The Times*, 9 August 1945; *British Medical Journal*, 18 August 1945; Bank and McDonald (1998).

BARRY, Florence Antoinita (4 May 1885–27 January 1965) Catholic suffragist, internationalist, sociologist; *b.* Birkenhead; *do.* Zacharie Balthazar Barry (Bahri), Catholic Persian businessman & Francis Jane Shroder, Austrian; *e.* Faithful Companions of Jesus Convent, Upton Hall, Birkenhead, English Convent in Bruges, School Social Sciences, University of Liverpool; *r.* travel; *c.* St Andrew's House; *a.* Hampstead, Golders Green.

Her childhood ambition was to become a priest; the barriers which prevented her from fulfilling her aspiration helped to foster her interest in the Women's Movement; she spoke French and the family always returned to Myrna in Turkey for family holidays, which gave her an awareness of Western assumptions and bias in arguments; this background provided the internationalist perspective to her work and life; studied philosophy; initially, she was a WSPU member, selling *Votes for Women* on the streets in Birkenhead, c.1911; she helped establish the CWSS in

22 b: born; do: daughter of; e: education; m: married; r: recreation; c: club; a: address; p: publications; s: sources

Merseyside and became its Honorary Secretary, c.1911; she worked on propaganda for the Catholic Congress in Norwich, where she met Gabrielle Jeffery, one of the CWSS's founders; Barry then went to London to assist the CWSS, 1912; subsequently, Barry moved to London, and when Jeffery became ill, Barry became CWSS/SJSPA Honorary Secretary for the next 50 years, 1913–62; she and Jeffery became lifelong companions, living together in Hampstead; Barry only retained a minimum of her private income for her own needs, using much of it to supplement the Society's limited funds and to help people in financial distress; during WW1 she worked on the equal moral standard campaigns; also had a great talent for publicizing the suffrage cause, for which she continued to campaign throughout the 1920s seeking cooperation with other feminists, in particular those in the AMSH; CWSS representative at CCWO, 1921; attended the initial meeting of the ODC, 1926; officially became Honorary Secretary SJSPA, 1928; regularly attended ILO conferences and was of international standing in the Catholic world; Executive Member ODC, 1927–33; after the equal suffrage success of 1928, she continued working on equality issues such as equal pay; established the French section of the SJSPA, 1931; established sections in five other continents, which led eventually to the founding of the SJIA, of which she was Honorary Secretary; British representative on the IWSA's Enfranchised Women's Committee; very aware of the need for equal treatment to be a principle and part of the working practices of new international groups such as the LN and, subsequently, of the UN; a key person in her work for providing evidence to the Slavery Committee and Mandates Commission of the LN, UN, Colonial and Commonwealth Office on practices against women in developing countries; Barry was a representative to the Vatican Council working for the ordination of women in the Catholic Church; awarded the 'gold rose' medal by the Pope; other dear friends included Alison Neilans (see entry), Nancy Stewart Parnell (see entry), Fedora Gadsby (WSPU); she and Jeffery were joined by Christine Spender in their Hampstead home, and in later years Barry shared a house with Spender in Golders Green; Barry not only maintained her devout faith by going to church each day, but actively practised her religion in the way she lived her life with compassion for others and dedication to the cause of women suffering discrimination and harm; died in Hammersmith and was interned in the family grave in Birkenhead.

s. *The Lady's Who's Who*, 1938–9; Papers SJIA, general correspondence 1911–62; Parnell (1965); *The Catholic Citizen*, 15 February 1965; *International Woman Suffrage News*, March 1965; *The Shield*, October 1965.

BARTON, Eleanor (Nellie) (née Stockton) JP (1872–9 March 1960) Co-operative and Labour Party activist and pacifist; *b.* Manchester; *e.* Elementary school; *m.* Alfred Barton (later alderman, active LP worker), insurance agent, 1894; one daughter, one son; *c.* ILP; *a.* 46 Stannington Road, Malin Bridge, Sheffield (1922).

Joined WCG's Brightside and Carbrook Co-operative Society, Sheffield, 1901; secretary Hillsborough branch for 17 years; gave evidence as a WCG representative to the Royal Commission on Divorce, 1910; member WCG Central Committee, 1912–14; National President WCG, 1914; member education committee Brightside and Carbrook Co-operative Society, 1914–25; also became a Director of the above, 1917–25; member 'Hands Off Russia' campaign; prime mover in the WCG's Peace Pledge card and promoter of the white peace poppy, it was her idea that women should wear both the white and the red poppy; toured America lecturing on maternity and child welfare with the Labour Party of America, 1919; employed as the Assistant Secretary WCG, 1921; General Secretary WCG 1925–37; Co-operative and Labour member Sheffield City Council, 1919–21; member Women's Housing Committee under Ministry of Reconstruction; member Committee of Inquiry into Drinking Amongst Women; stood as Prospective Parliamentary Candidate for Co-operative and Labour Party in King's Norton, Birmingham 1922, 1923, and Central Nottingham, 1929; WCG representative SJCIWO; Chair SJCIWO, 1934; presided over annual conference of Labour women, 1934; first woman Director of the Co-operative Newspaper Publishing Society; represented the WCG on the NPC executive, 1930–36; represented the WCG at the conference of War Resisters' International, Copenhagen, 1937; President South Yorkshire Federation of Co-operative Societies, 1947–8; left England to live with her daughter in 1949 and died in New Zealand.

p. The History and Progress of Poor Law Nursing (Law and Local Government Publication, c.1920s); *Through Trade to the Co-operative Commonwealth* (WCG, 1927).

s. Labour Who's Who (1927); *Dictionary of Labour Biography*, vol. 1.

BEAUMONT, Florence Margaret (1876–16 August 1929) women's rights campaigner; *b.* Wakefield; *a.* 17 Campbell House Road, London W8 (1927).

Her interests were in equal citizenship, local government and temperance; founder of the Wakefield Suffrage Society; treasurer of the Yorkshire Suffrage Federation for 12 years; served as a superintendent in the QMAAC, 1917–19; stood as Welfare candidate in the Kensington borough election; member of NUWSS; subsequently a member NUSEC; Honorary Librarian and speaker; member Committee on Social Insurance, 1926; attended the initial meeting of the ODC, 1926; one of the 11 NUSEC Executive Committee members who resigned over protective legislation, 1927; Executive Member ODC, 1927–9; Honorary Secretary Council Representation of Women in League of Nations, 1928; Honorary Secretary, ODC; Acting Honorary Treasurer, ODI.

s. The Times, 22 August 1929; *The Woman's Leader*, 23 August 1929.

BEILBY, Lady Emma Clark (née Newnam) (1858–12 January 1936) engineering profession campaigner; *do.* Rev. Samuel Newnam; *e.* Barnstaple, Devon, Edinburgh University; *m.* Sir George T. Beilby, industrial chemist, 1877; one daughter (see Winifred Soddy entry), one son; *a.* 29 Kidderpore Avenue, Hampstead, London NW3.

One of the original members of the Edinburgh Hospital and Dispensary for Women and Children; joined the WES, 1921; benefactor to the WES, saving it from extinction on several occasions; also a benefactor to other women's organizations involved with women's employment; member of advisory council of the Conference of Women, 1925; Vice President NUSEC, 1927–32; member ODC; she died at her home in Hampstead.

s. Women's Who's Who, 1934–5; *The Woman Engineer*, vol. iv/6 (March 1926), p. 82.

BENNETT, Louie (1870–November 1956); trade unionist and pacifist; *b.* Temple Hill, Dublin; *do.* Charles? Bennett, auctioneer and valuer & Susan Boulger; *e.* school in England, Alexandra College, Dublin; *a.* Dublin.

Came from a wealthy family; her earliest ambition was to be a writer, produced two novels; teacher in the west of Ireland for a brief time; spent some time in Bonn, Germany, attending lectures and taking singing lessons; became involved in the suffrage movement, helping to form the IWSF; the inaugural meeting was held in the Shelbourne Hotel, Dublin – Bennett shared the position of the first Honorary Secretary with Helen Chevenix, who became a lifelong friend and colleague, 1911; formed the IWRL, affiliated to the IWSF, 1911; during the great strike and lockout in Dublin, she went to a soup kitchen being run by Constance Markievicz (Sinn Feiner, first woman elected to the British Parliament) and Hanna Sheehy Skeffington (see entry), where she discovered the extent of women workers' poverty and the hardship of their working lives, triggering her involvement in the trade union movement, 1913; another influence was reading women writers, greatly influenced by the New Woman movement and by South African feminist, Olive Schreiner (*The Story of an African Farm*, 1883; *Woman & Labour*, 1911); worked with Skeffington and her husband, Francis, and with the pioneer Irish suffragist, Anna Haslam; Helena Molony, secretary of the Women's Trade Union and imprisoned as a member of the IRA, wrote to Bennett, driving her to become involved in organizing women and girl workers; Bennett agreed and, with Helen Chevenix, attended the Irish Trades Union and Labour Party Congress in Sligo, 1916; starting from scratch, first started organizing women in the printing trade, then women laundry workers, forming the IWWU, its General Secretary 1917–55; took over as joint editor of, and contributor to, the suffrage paper, *The Irish Citizen*; influenced by Francis Skeffington, became involved in pacifism and joined the WILPF; with Hanna Sheehy Skeffington (see entry), Charlotte Despard (see entry) and Maud Gonne MacBride (Irish Nationalist and founder of the IWPL), they tried to prevent the Irish Civil War by instigating negotiations; the Irish section of the WILPF formed 1915; represented Ireland on the International Executive Committee of WILPF; President of the Fifth WILPF Congress in Dublin, 1926; represented *The Irish Statesman* journal at the LN meeting, Geneva, 1928; first woman President Irish Trades Union Congress, 1932; spoke out against rise of Fascism; introduced the concept of establishing a National Economic Council for trade unions to be involved in economic planning; Chair TUC 1948; stood as Irish Labour candidate for Dublin County, General Election, 1944; member Dún Laoghaire BC; member Administrative Council, Irish LP; always concerned with effecting practical improvements such as housing conditions; involved in the Council of Action to address issues emerging from WW2, 1941; signatory to the Housewives' Petition (see IHA), suggested to Hilda Tweedy (see entry) the need for action on the basis of the petition and provided the IWWU hall for the IHA's inaugural meeting, 1942; defended the need to sustain an independent IWWU to protect the position of women in industry; worked against racism in the British Colonies; although she avoided strikes whenever possible, one of her great IWWU successes was to win two weeks' paid holiday, plus a pay increase and a limit on overtime, for women laundry workers, with a two-week strike in 1945; achieved many successes for IWWU members such as tea-breaks, health and safety provision, canteens; 'retired' as Secretary IWWU at the age of 85, but still active as an adviser; died a year later at

Killiney, Helen Chevenix wrote in *Pax et Libertas* (January–March 1957) that Bennett was 'the best-loved woman in Dublin' and that 'Peace and Freedom were her twin ideals.'

p. *The Proving of Priscilla* (1902); *A Prisoner of His Word* (1908); *Ireland and a People's Peace* (1918); numerous articles.

s. Fox (1958); Tweedy (1992); Luddy (1995a); Ryan (1996).

BENNETT, Dr Victoria Evelyn May, MB, BS (Lon), DPH (Cantab), Fellow SMOH (?–October 1955) women and children's health; *b.* Waterford, Ireland; *do.* Samuel Trevethan Bennett; *e.* Cardiff University, LSMW, University College London; *c.* BMA; *a.* 10 Mecklenburgh Street, London WC1 (1907), 52 Lower Sloane Street, London, SW1, 45 Adair House, Oakley Street, London SW3 (1934–5), 99 Oakley Street, London SW3 (1938).

Bennett qualified LSA, 1903; joined the BMA, 1903; MB and BS (Lon), 1904; appointed as an LCC Inspector under the provisions of the 1902 Midwives Act, 1904; studied Public Health and Sanity Law at UCL, gaining a Certificate from the School of Hygiene and a Diploma in Public Health, 1908; DPH Cambridge, 1908; School Medical Officer, Durham; Medical Superintendent, Victoria Caste and Gosha Hospital, Madras; member Medical Executive Council WSIHVA, 1918–19; Medical Officer to Kensington antenatal clinic; Lecturer and Examiner in public health, Battersea Polytechnic Training School for Health Visitors; Lecturer and Examiner NCMCW; Lecturer and Examiner to Maternity and Child Welfare Society; examiner to RSI; Medical Officer to Brixton Antenatal and Infant Clinics (1938); retired c.1955.

p. *Health in the Nursery*, 1930; *Health and Education in the Nursery* (with Susan Isaacs), 1931; *The Welfare of the Infant and Child*, 1932; numerous articles and papers connected with health and hygiene.

s. *Women's Who's Who, 1934–5; LWW*, 1938–9; UCL Records; BMA Archive.

BENTHAM, Dr Ethel, MD MP, LRCP, JP (5 January 1861–19 January 1931) child welfare and industrial women's health campaigner; *b.* London; *do.* William Bentham, insurance executive & Mary Ann Hammond; *e.* Alexandra School and College, Dublin, LSMW; *c.* PEN, National Labour, 1917; *r.* walking, music, gardening; *a.* 74 Lansdowne Road, London W11 (1909), 110 Beaufort Street, London SW3 (1927).

A descendent of the philosopher Jeremy Bentham, a committed Quaker, born in London but spent her first years in Dublin; organized a Sunday club for shop girls in Dublin; further medical study at the Rotunda Hospital, Dublin, postgraduate study in Brussels and Paris; gained a triple Scottish qualification, LRCP, LRCS (Edin) and LREPS (Glasg), 1894; attained the Brussels MD, 1895; joined the BMA, 1895; briefly, she was a clinical assistant at the New Hospital for Women in London; set up in general practice in Newcastle upon Tyne with Dr Ethel Williams (see entry), her friend with whom she had studied at the LSMW, c.1896–1909; joined the LP, 1902; first woman Labour candidate for Newcastle municipal election, 1907; returned to London in connection with her political work with the Fabian Society and the WLL, 1909; as a London GP, it was her suggestion to found the Baby Clinic and Hospital in North Kensington in memory of Margaret MacDonald and Mary Middleton, pioneer socialists who had both been dear friends of hers;

became the Senior Medical Officer at North Kensington and was still a consultant there at her death; a suffrage activist and member Executive Committee NUWSS, which she influenced to work more closely with the LP; Marion Phillips (see entry) and Mary Longman moved into Bentham's house and lived with her until she moved; member Executive Committee NUWSS, 1909; Medical Officer for Blackfriars Provident Dispensary for Women and Children, clinical assistant for the throat and ear departments from 1910; Executive Committee WLL, 1912–18; President WLL, 1913; prominent member FWG; involved in Maude Pember Reeves' study of working-class families in Lambeth, *Round About a Pound a Week* from 1909; member ILP; elected to Borough Council of North Kensington, 1913; served 13 years with LP group there; member SJCIWO, 1919; became a JP as soon as women were permitted to do so, being involved with the Juvenile and Lunacy Courts; member of the Society of Friends at Friends' House, Euston Road, from 1920; member BMA Parliamentary Sub-Committee, 1921; member Association of Registered Medical Women; member of the Panel Committee for the County of London at the start of the NHS Insurance Act; Chairman BMA Finance and General Purposes Committee; nominated as President for WSIHVA, 1922; LP delegate International Conference of Socialist Women, Hamburg, 1923; Vice Chairman SJCIWO, 1923; speaker at Peacemakers' Pilgrimage Rally, Hyde Park, 1926; member SJCIWO's Sub-Committee on Birth Control, 1925; she was the first female doctor and the first woman Friend to become an MP; member LP National Executive 1918–20, 1921–6, 1928–31; member LP Advisory Committees Public Health, Army and Navy Pensions and Foreign Policy; government nominee on Metropolitan Asylums Board; PPC for Islington East in 1922, 1923, 1924; by nursing the constituency, she raised her share of the vote from 3000 to 15,199 to win, 1929–31; her entry to the House of Commons was distinguished by her being the first woman doctor, the first woman Friend and the oldest woman, at 68, to enter the House of Commons, 1929; she was a member of the Select Committee on capital punishment; as an MP she introduced the unsuccessful Nationality of Married Women Bill, 1930; she died at her home in London from heart failure as a result of pleurisy, following influenza, and was interned at Jordan's new burial ground; representatives from the WFL, WCA, WCG, NCW; Picton-Turbervill wrote of her 'calm – almost a demure manner… a quiet strength and power of work that commanded the respect and admiration of all who knew her'.

s. List of Women Nominated for Service in Connection with the League of Nations (NUWT Archive, nd 1921–2?); *Labour Who's Who* (1927); *Daily News*, 8 June 1929; *The Times*, 20, 23 January 1931; *The Vote*, 23 January 1931; *British Medical Journal*, 24 January 1931; *The Woman's Leader*, 23 January 1931; *Who Was Who*, vol. 3; Bank and McDonald (1998); Banks (1990); Stenton and Lees, vol. 3 (1979).

BETHUNE-BAKER, Edith (née Furneaux Jordan) JP (c.1863?–1949) welfare campaigner; *b.* Birmingham; *do.* Furneaux Jordan, surgeon; *e.* Edgbaston High School for Girls, Mason College; *m.* Rev. Dr James Franklin Bethune-Baker, Liberal theologian, 1891; one son; *a.* 23 Cranmer Road, Cambridge (1927), Beudy Cil, Talsarnon, Merioneth (1938).

Studied at Mason College (subsequently the University of Birmingham) taking Zoology, Systematic Physiology, Physics, Chemistry, Latin and Composition 1881–8; member NUWSS; engaged in girls' welfare work; Poor Law Guardian and

JP, Cambridge; member NCW; Executive Committee AMSH, 1923; member SJCIWO; SJCIWO representative on the NCUMHC deputation to Home Secretary, 1923; member NUSEC, one of the 11 Executive Committee members who resigned over protective legislation, 1927; Executive Member ODC, 1928; member AMSH; SJCIWO representative on the National Council for Combating Venereal Disease; replied for the SJCIWO on Old Age Pensions Committee, drew up a minority report.

p. Equal Moral Standard.

s. Hutchinson (1934); *Dictionary of National Biography*, 1951–60; Edgbaston High School Archive; University of Birmingham Archive; BMA Archive.

BIDELEUX, Hilda, DipH, SI Cert (1871–1960) pioneer in health and social services; *e.* Clapham High School, Bedford College; *r.* gardening, reading; *a.* La Choza, Little Chalfont, Amersham, Buckinghamshire.

Diploma in Hygiene (distinction), Sanitary Inspector's Certificate; took the Froebel teachers' course and worked at her old school for a few years; Assistant Superintendent in the Women's Department, Battersea Polytechnic, 1894; appointed lecturer in Hygiene, Food and Dietetics plus Physiology, Battersea Polytechnic, 1904; pioneered the first health visitors', school nurses' and sanitary inspectors' training courses, 1907; such work guaranteed the polytechnic a prime place in this area at home and abroad; as a delegate to the International Congress on School Hygiene, Paris, studied infant and child welfare work and visited trades schools for girls, 1910; Associate WSIHVA, 1911; HM Inspector Domestic Science in Devon and Cornwall, 1913; inaugurator and first Head of the Department of Hygiene and Public Health, Battersea Polytechnic, 1915–27; had to resign her post at the Polytechnic due to ill health and the governors recorded that 'the creation and success of the Department has been almost entirely due to her own initiative and energy'; innovated coeducational classes for disabled ex-servicemen and female health visitor students to act as a mutual support system, exchanging traditional skills while studying for their Sanitary Inspectors' Examination Board examination, 1919–20; member Royal Society of Teachers; Vice President WPHOA; also devised training classes for sister tutors and preparatory courses for young women before they started at hospital training schools; Vice President WSIHVA, 1925–8; as an expert on employment and salaries she was recommended to the WSIHVA by Philippa Strachey (see entry); suffered throughout her life from neuritis, which she developed during WW1 and retired on doctor's advice in 1927; however, she continued to attend WSIHVA meetings until a road accident confined her to the ladies' club where she lived, 1956; a woman with a vivid personality who, despite making great demands on her students, was held in great regard by them.

s. Minutes of the Battersea Polytechnic Governing Board 1022 Meeting, 17 May 1927; extracts from an unreferenced history of the Polytechnic, University of Surrey Archive; *Hutchinson* (1934); *The Times*, 28 July 1960; *Women Health Officer*, vol. xxxiii/9 (September 1960).

BONDFIELD, Margaret Grace (pen-name Grace Dare) MP, CH, LLD (17 March 1873–16 June 1953) trade unionist and Labour politician; *b.* Chard, Somerset; *do.* William Bondfield, foreman lace maker and political radical & Ann Taylor; *e.* Chard

Elementary School; *r.* travelling; *c.* YWCA Central; *a.* Gower Street, London WC1 (1903), 28 Tavistock Square, London WC1 (1927).

Began her working life as a pupil teacher at her old school, 1886; apprentice shop assistant in a colonial outfitter's, Brighton, which gave her first-hand experience of employee exploitation, 1887; Mrs Martindale, Liberal advocate of women's rights, enabled her to continue her studies; having saved £5, she moved to London where her brother, Frank, was a printer and trade unionist, and obtained work as a shop assistant, 1894; joined the Ideal Club, met radicals such as Shaw and the Webbs; member Shoe Assistants Union, 1894; member Fabian Society, 1894; wrote articles for the *Shop Assistant* as Grace Dare, 1896; did two years' research on the conditions of shopworkers for WIC, 1896; member SDF then ILP; wrote an article in the *Shop Assistant* describing an ideal marriage where both partners went out to work and shared household chores, 1898; full-time Assistant Secretary NAUSAWC, 1889–1908; only woman delegate to the TUC Conference, 1899; became friends with Mary MacDonald (Socialist pioneer), Mary Macarthur (see entry) and Gertrude Tuckwell (see entry), they worked together in WTUL, NFWW and the Adult Suffrage Society; as a socialist she believed in adult suffrage not partial suffrage reform, although this was not the view of the WLL, of which she was Secretary and which she co-founded with Macarthur (with whom she lived) in 1906; forced to resign as Union Secretary through ill health induced by overwork, 1908; National Officer GMWU, 1908–38; freelance Labour and socialist lecturer, from 1908 to 1912; assisted with WIC's inquiry into married women's work, 1910; lecture tour USA, 1910; member Advisory Committee Health Insurance Bill to secure inclusion of maternity benefits and make them the property of the mother, Insurance Act, 1911; stood as ILP candidate at the LCC elections in Woolwich, first election at which women were eligible to stand, 1910–13; on MacDonald's death, became Organizing Secretary WLL, 1911; worked with Margaret Llewellyn Davies (WCG) on minimum wage legislation, infant mortality and child welfare, 1912–15; elected to ILP National Administration Council, 1913; her firm religious faith ensured her pacifism during WW1, spoke at a Trafalgar Square pacifist demonstration, 1914; joined UDC and the Woman's Peace Crusade; during the war worked for NFWW; member Central Committee on Women's Training and Employment, from 1915; during the war also member of TUC Advisory Committee to the Ministry of Munitions and the War Emergency Workers' National Committee; helped to found SJCIWO, 1916; delegate at International Labour and Socialist Conference, Berne, 1918; Chairman of Women's International Council of Socialist and Labour Organizations; first woman member Parliamentary Committee TUC, 1918; member of the Governing Body of Ruskin College, Oxford; member General Council TUC, 1918–24, 1926–9; attended first ILO Conference in Washington, 1919; joint LP and TUC delegation to Russia, met Lenin, 1920; Chief Woman Officer NUGMW and Chairman SJCIWO, 1921; adviser to delegation of the Third ILO Conference, Geneva, 1921; Vice President of BAWC; unsuccessfully contested Northampton, 1920 and 1922; Chairman Conference of Unemployed Women, 1922; British Vice President IFWW, 1923; elected MP Northampton, 1923; first woman Chair TUC, unable to take up position because of parliamentary work, member Labour Party Emergency Committee on Unemployment, 1923; Parliamentary Secretary Ministry of Labour, 1924; Honorary Vice President Blue Triangle Forward Movement, YWCA, 1924; member Overseas Settlement

Committee, from 1925; re-elected to TUC General Council, 1925; involved in decision to call a General Strike, 1926; unpopular with the Left when she signed the Blanesborough Committee report, which suggested a cut in benefits and contributions, 1926; spoke at the WES Conference, 1925; speaker at Peacemakers' Pilgrimage Rally, Hyde Park, 1926; speaker at the Equal Franchise Demonstration, Hyde Park, 1926; NUSEC sent workers and cars to assist her in the Wallsend election campaign, 1926; assisted NUSEC with aspects of their parliamentary campaigning and spoke on equal franchise at NUSEC's Annual Council, 1927; elected MP Wallsend, 1929; first woman Cabinet member as Minister of Labour; awarded Honorary LLD of Bristol, 1930; further criticized for accepting a bill to deprive some married women of unemployment benefit, 1931; defended Wallsend but never regained her parliamentary seat, 1931 and 1935; travelled to USA and Mexico to study labour conditions, 1938; Vice President National Council of Social Services; Chairman Women's Group on Public Welfare, 1939–45; went on a lecture tour of the USA and Canada for the British Information Services, 1941–3; appointed a CH, 1948; she maintained her deep religious faith; died in a nursing home, Sanderstead, Surrey.

p. A Life's Work (1929); pamphlets and articles – *Sex Equality versus Adult Suffrage* (1908); *Shop Workers and the Vote* (People's Federation, 1911); *War Against Poverty* (Standing Committee ILP, 1912?); *The National Care of Maternity* (WCG, 1914); *Sentenced to Life* (*Woman Worker*, 1 January 1916); *The Future of Women in Industry* (*Labour Year Book*, 1916); 'Women as Domestic Workers' in Marion Phillips, *Women in the Labour Party*, 1918; *Recollections of Working with Mary Macarthur* (*Woman Worker*, February 1921); *Women and Unemployment* (*Labour Magazine*, i/9 (January 1923); *Women's Trade Unions* (*The Woman's Year Book*, 1923); *Women Workers in Britain and Ireland* in R.W. Houghe (ed.), *British Labour Speak* (1924); *Women in Industry in Great Britain* (*American Federationist*, May 1927); *Public Opinion: Women in Industry* (*American Federationist*, July 1927); *Women within the Trade Unions* (*American Federationist*, November 1927); *Public Welfare in Our Towns* (Preface to NCSS Women's Group, 1943). For a complete list of her publications, see *Dictionary of Labour Biography*, vol. 2.

s. LWW (1927); *The Times*, 18 June 1953; Banks (1985); *Dictionary of Labour Biography*, vol. 2.

BONHAM-CARTER, Lady Helen Violet (née Asquith), Baroness Asquith of Yarnbury (15 April 1887–19 February 1969) Liberal activist; *do.* Herbert Henry Asquith, Liberal politician and Helen Kelsall Melland; *e.* Dresden and Paris; *m.* Maurice Bonham-Carter, 1915; four children; *a.* 21 Hyde Park Square, London W2 (1969).

President WLF, 1923–5, 1939–45; Vice President SPG, 1925; spoke at the Peacemakers' Pilgrimage Rally, Hyde Park, 19 July 1926; Vice President Marriage Law Reform League, 1928; worked with Eleanor Rathbone (see entry) on family allowances; member WPC, 1940s; unsuccessfully contested two elections for the Liberal Party in Wells in 1945 and Colne Valley, 1951; involved in the birth control movement; finally entered Parliament as Baroness Asquith, 1964.

s. Brookes (1967); *The Times*, 20 February 1969; *Who Was Who*, vol. 6.

　　　b: born;　do: daughter of;　e: education;　m: married;　r: recreation;
　　　　　　c: club;　a: address;　p: publications;　s: sources

BOSANQUET, Theodora, BSc, MBE (3 October 1880–1 June 1961) literary figure; *b.* Sandown, Isle of Wight; *do.* Frederick C.T. Bosanquet & Gertrude Mary Fox; *e.* Cheltenham Ladies' College, University College London; *c.* University Women's, Arts Theatre, PEN, English-Speaking Union; *a.* 38 Cheyne Walk, London (1929).

Her childhood and youth were spent in the Isle of Wight and later she lived in Lyme Regis; Secretary to Henry James, 1907–16; assistant in the '*Who's Who*' Section War Trade Intelligence Department, 1917–18; assistant to Secretary Ministry of Food, 1918–20; awarded the MBE, 1919; Executive Secretary IFUW 1920–35; close friend of Ellen Gleditsch (President IFUW, 1926–9); her close friendship with Lady Rhondda (see entry) began soon after WW1, they lived together from 1933; co-founder and editor *Time & Tide*; literary editor of *Time & Tide*, 1935–43; Director *Time & Tide*, 1943–58; executrix of Rhondda's will; encouraged and fostered many young writers; held an idealistic faith in international co-operation; had a deep Christian faith and was extremely interested in ESP and the paranormal, being a member of the Society for Psychical research; died in a London hospital.

p. Spectators (with Clara Smith, 1916); *Henry James at Work* (1924); *Harriet Martineau: An Essay in Comprehension* (1927); *Paul Valery*, (1933).

s. Hutchinson (1934); *Who's Who* (1929); *Women's Who's Who, 1934–5*; *The Times*, 3 June 1961; Eoff (1991).

BOUCICAULT, Nina (Mrs D. Innes-Smith) (27 February 1867–2 August 1950) actress; *b.* Marylebone, London; *do.* Dionysius Boucicault, playwright and actor & Agnes Kelly Robertson; *m.* Donald Innes-Smith; *a.* 6a Blomfield Road, Maida Vale, London W9 (1934).

Member of a distinguished theatrical family, made the first of her 15 Atlantic crossings with her father when she was 7; but made her first stage appearance in America at 15 with her father's company, as Eily O'Connor in *The Colleen Bawn*, 1885; this was followed by an Australian tour with her father; her first British appearance was in *The New Wing* at the Strand Theatre playing Flossie Trivett, 1892; made her name and became a star as the first actress to play the role of Peter in *Peter Pan*, 1904; member Executive Committee and Joint Honorary Secretary, AFL; replaced Adeline Bourne as Honorary Secretary AFL, 1913; shared a house with Adeline Bourne; although she retired when she was 60 in 1927, she returned to appear in *Frolic Wind*, 1935; her last stage appearance was in *Waste* in 1936; she died at Hamilton Road, Ealing.

s. Who's Who in the Theatre, 1922; *Daily Mail*, 5 August 1950; *Daily Telegraph*, 7 August 1950; *The Times*, 7 August 1950; Hartnoll (1988).

BOURNE, Adeline (8 January 1873–8 February 1965) actress; *b.* India; *e.* private schools in Eastbourne and Blackheath; *r.* dancing, skating, painting; *c.* Ladies' Army and Navy; *a.* 19 Overstrand Mansions, Battersea Park, London SW (1922), 6a Blomfield Road, London W9 (1934), Willow Cottage, Birds Lane, Thurston, Bury St Edmunds (1963).

Born in India and sent back to England for schooling, but was expelled from three schools and eventually had a governess; studied drama under Sarah Thorne, joining her company and making her stage debut in Chatham, 1898; played Shakespeare and many of Shaw's plays and also established the New Players Society;

at the start of the century often appeared in plays that were either avant-garde or feminist; worked and lived with Nina Boucicault (see entry); was one of the founders and Joint Secretary of the militant AFL; believed that apart from its work for women's rights, the AFL had also challenged the public's image of the profession by demonstrating that actresses could achieve solidarity and contribute to society; founded the British Women's Hospital, which raised £150,000 for the Star and Garter Home for disabled soldiers, 1915; served overseas as an officer in QMAAC, also an acting paymaster in the War Office during WW1; raised over £750,000 for many causes, such as the Elizabeth Garrett Anderson Hospital (£37,500), between 1915 and 1963; Vice President of AMSH's Josephine Butler Appeal Fund, 1928; after WW2, started a women's employment organization to help women return to civilian jobs, and later founded the Wayfarers' Trust to provide residential homes for elderly women; on her 90th birthday in 1963, she maintained that women still lacked equality in the professions and were still 'the hewers of wood and the drawers of water'.

s. *Lady's World*, October 1911; *Who's Who in the Theatre*, 1922; *Manchester Guardian*, 8 January 1963; *The Times*, 10 February 1965.

BOYLE, Constance Antonina (Nina) (21 December 1865–4 March 1943) writer, lecturer; *b.* Bexley, Kent; *do.* Capt. Robert Boyle, RA & Francis Sydney Sankey; *a.* 20 Talbot House, St Martin's Lane, London, WC2 (1934), 20 Oakley Street, Chelsea (1943).

Went to South Africa, worked as a journalist and established the Women's Enfranchisement League of Johannesburg; returned to England, 1911; joined the WFL, 1911; imprisoned three times for suffragette activities, holder of the WFL's Prison Badge; head of the WFL's Political and Militant Department, 1912; with Margaret Damer Dawson, helped form the Women Volunteer Police Corps, 1914; went to work with the Scottish Women's Hospitals in Macedonia and Serbia, 1916; awarded the Samaritan and Allied medals for this work; in the light of the postwar limited franchise reform, she campaigned for women to become MPs, bringing a test case by standing in the Keighley by-election, March 1918; although her nomination papers were excluded because of an error, the principle was established; founder and Vice President of WEC; member IAWSEC, but she was opposed to the organization's work for peace; went to the USSR to work on an SCF famine relief programme, 1921; member CCWO drafting committee meeting, 1922; member ODC; member Commission on Women Police, held at NUSEC HQ on training methods, 1926; the other great love of her life, apart from working for the Women's Movement, was the SCF, for which she worked during the 1920s and 1930s, working with SCF's founder, Eglantyne Jebb; she was Jebb's personal representative at the International Conference on Social Work in Paris, 1928; also during the 1920s and 1930s she campaigned on behalf of the NUWT and the WEC; wrote three influential articles entitled 'Slavery' for the *Women's Leader* which dealt with the oppression of women in Africa, India, Ceylon, Mauritius and China, and fuelled parliamentary campaigns (see Rathbone entry), 1929; member Anglo-Hellenic League; member Suffragette Fellowship; in later life she wrote novels; SCF honoured her with a dinner at the Lyceum Club – prominent among her friends and colleagues there were Emmeline Pethick-Lawrence (see entry), Ethel Snowden (see entry), Florence Underwood (see entry), with messages being sent by Maude Royden (see entry) and

Eleanor Rathbone (see entry), 1936; died in a London nursing home after a sudden illness, having been lamed by an accident some years earlier; her catchphrase was 'I am, as you know, a bred-in-the-bone, dyed-in-the wool feminist'; she was praised by the MP, F.W. Pethick-Lawrence for 'her dazzling wit, her splendid comradeship and the vigorous part she played in all activities which came her way' (Summer 1943).

p. Out of the Frying-Pan (1920); *What Became of Mr Desmond* (1922); *Nor All Thy Tears* (1923); *Anna's* (1925); *Moletey's Concession* (1926); *The Stranger Within the Gates* (1926); *The Rights of Mallaroche* (1927); *Treading on Eggs* (1929); *My Lady's Bath* (1930); *The Late Unlamented* (1931); *How Could They?* (1932); *Good Old Potts* (1934); pamphlets – *The Traffic in Women, Child Marriage, What is Slavery?, The People's Policy*; articles in *The Vote* and SCF publications.

s. Women's Who's Who, 1934–5; *The Lady's Who's Who*, 1938–9; *The World's Children*, spring, summer and autumn 1943; *Dictionary of National Biography Missing Persons* (1993).

BRERETON, Maud Adeline Cloudesley (née Ford) MJI (1871–16 April 1946) public health worker; *b.* London; *do.* Mathew Ford & Ellen Catherine MacDonald of Glencoe; *e.* Hockerill College, Bishop's Stortford, *m.* John Charles Horobin, 1897, two sons; Cloudesley Shovell Henry Brereton, 1904, two sons; *r.* needlecraft, travel, light literature; *c.* Efficiency, Soroptomist; *a.* 101 Eaton Place, SW1 (1934), 32 Victoria Street, Westminster, SW1 (1935), Brampton Hall, near Norwich (1946).

Senior Scholar, Bishop's and Archbishop's Exhibitioner, Divinity first; first headmistress St Andrew's Girls' Secondary School, Willesden, 1893; headmistress Baroness Burdett-Coutts School, Highgate, 1894; Principal, then Bursar, Homerton Training College, Cambridge; decorated by French government, 1907 (Officier d'Academie) for international services to public health; one of the founders, consultant of publications at, British Commercial Gas Association (later merged with British Gas Council) and editor *Gas Journal* from its foundation in 1912 to 1932; Fellow RSI; only woman Honorary Fellow Institution of Sanitary Engineers; member Royal Institute of Public Health; member Institute of Journalists; Chairman Association for Education in Industry and Commerce, 1923–4; member Advisory Council WES Conference of Women, 1925; Vice President SWJ, 1928; President of the Efficiency Club, 1931–2; died in Norfolk.

p. pamphlets – *Continuative Education under the Fisher Act: Points for Employers: A Brief Memorandum* (1920?); *Clean Kitchen Management* (1928); *Unemployed or Reserve?* (1930).

s. Women's Who's Who, 1934–5; *The Times*, 14 May 1946; *Who Was Who*, vol. 4.

BRIGHT, Edith Heywood (née Turner) (1861–23 January 1929) industrial women's rights worker; *b.* West Derby; *do.* Alfred Turner JP; *m.* Allan Heywood Bright, merchant and shipowner, leader Liverpool Liberal Party, MP, 1885; one daughter; *a.* 10 Mill Bank, West Derby (1893), Ashfield, Knotty Ash, Lancashire (1917), Barton Court, Colwall, Herefordshire (1929).

Born into a wealthy, conservative Liverpool family who moved to West Derby; spoke fluent German, Italian, French; in her early years, involved in philanthropic work with the Liverpool Ladies' Union; a popular public speaker although she was partially deaf and suffered with poor health, and it was these disabilities that prevented her from standing as a PPC; became a member of the Guild of the

Unrepresented at Southport, c.1887; joined the CSWS, 1893; founder member and first Honorary Secretary LWFS, 1894; member of a deputation of suffragists to the PM, Campbell-Bannerman, 1906; became active in 'progressive' movements in Liverpool before WW1; Honorary Secretary Liverpool Ladies' Union of Workers among Women and Girls; member Freedom of Labour Defence Council; Secretary Liverpool Women's Legislative and Local Government Committee; Co-Secretary Diocesan Mothers' Union; member Liberal Party; founder of the Liverpool branch of the UWW, later the NCW, of which she was the Honorary Secretary for many years and, later, President; member Executive Committee NUWSS; President NCW, 1912–13; attended Conference of Women, about the representation of women on LN, seconded a resolution for the League to appoint women to serve women's interests, 1919; Vice President and Executive Committee NCW, 1927; also interested in housing issues and was associated with several hospitals; served on NCW's Government Emigration and Immigration Committee; staunch church-woman; died after a long illness, requesting that there should be no mourning for her.

s. Tooley (1895); *The Times*, 23 January 1929; *The Women's Leader*, 1 February 1929; Helmond (1992).

BRITTAIN, Vera Mary MA (29 December 1893–29 March 1970) writer, journalist, and lecturer; *b.* Newcastle under Lyme; *do.* Thomas Arthur Brittain, paper manu-facturer & Edith Mary Bervon; *e.* St Monica's School, Kingswood, Somerville, Oxford; *m.* George Edward Gordon Catlin, academic, 1925; one daughter (Shirley Williams, politician), one son; *r.* walking, travel, reading; *c.* Arts Theatre, PEN, Royal Commonwealth Society; *a.* 19 Glebe Place, London SW3 (1934), 2 Cheyne Walk, London SW3 (1938), 4 Whitehall Court, London SW1.

Won an open exhibition to Somerville College, 1914; interrupted her education during WW1 to become a VAD, served in London, France and Malta, 1915–19; returned to Somerville, second-class degree in History, 1921; at Oxford met and became close friend of Yorkshire writer Winifred Holtby (see entry) with whom she subsequently lived; later, she had a 'semi-detached' marriage to enable her to continue her writing career; member LNU; active campaigner on feminist issues through her writing and lecturing; member SPG, 1923; frequently wrote for *Time & Tide*; wrote for *The Women's Leader*; active supporter of the birth control move-ment; spoke on 'Feminism at Geneva', autumn meeting SPG, 1928; Vice Chairman SPG's newly formed International Committee, 1928; member Executive Committee ODC, 1928–33; speech on 'Professions for Women' at a celebration for Ethel Smyth, 1930; member WAWF, 1934; frequent lecture tours of the USA and Canada, in the years 1934–59; lectured in Holland, Scandinavia, Germany, India and Pakistan; member Chelsea LP; joined PPU, 1936; member WCAWF; involved in the Milk Fund Appeal for Spanish children, 1937; Vice President SPG, 1938; Vice President WILPF; Vice President NPC; member WIL; criticized Allied blanket bombing 1939–45; director of Femina Books; honorary DLitt from Mills College, California, 1940; involved in a campaign for a parliamentary bill to end legal sex discrimination, 1943; Honorary Life President Society of Women Writers and Journalists; President MWA; member and campaigner for CND in the 1950s; died in London.

p. Verses of a VAD (1918); *The Dark Tide* (1923); *Not Without Honour* (1925); *Woman's Work in Modern England* (1928); *Halcyon or the Future of Monogamy* (1929);

     b: born;   do: daughter of;   e: education;   m: married;   r: recreation;   c: club;   a: address;   p: publications;   s: sources

Testament of Youth (1933); *Poems of the War and After* (1934); *Honorable Estate: A Novel of Transition* (1936); *Thrice a Stranger* (1938); *Testament of Friendship: The Story of Winifred Holtby* (1940); *War-Time Letters to Peace Lovers* (1940); *England's Hour* (1941); *Humiliation with Honour* (1943); *One of These Little Ones* (1943); *Seeds of Chaos: What Mass Bombing Really Means* (1944); *Account Rendered* (1945); *On Becoming a Writer* (1947); *Born 1925* (1948); *In the Steps of John Bunyan: An Excursion into Puritan England* (1950?); *Search After Sunrise* (1951); *The Story of St Martin's: An Epic of London* (1951); *Lady into Woman: A History of Women from Victoria to Elizabeth II* (1953); *Testament of Experience* (1957); *Selected Letters of Winifred Holtby and Vera Brittain* (1960); *The Women at Oxford* (1960); *Pethick-Lawrence: A Portrait* (1963); *The Rebel Passion: A Short History of Some Pioneer Peacemakers* (1964); *Envoy Extraordinary, A Study of Vijaya Lakshmi Pandit and Her Contribution to Modern India* (1965); 'Literary Testaments' (Katja Reissner Lecture, 1960) in *Essays by Diverse Hands*, vol. 34 (RSL, 1966); *Radclyffe Hall: A Case of Obscenity?* (1968); *Chronicle of Youth* (1981); *The Journalism of Vera Brittain and Winifred Holtby*, eds P. Berry and A. Bishop (1985); *Chronicle of Friendship: A Diary of the Thirties 1932–9* (1986).

s. *Women's Who's Who, 1934–5*; *The Lady's Who's Who*, 1938–9; *Dictionary of National Biography*, 1961–70; *Who Was Who*, 1961–70; Banks (1990); VB Papers, McMasters University, Hamilton, Ontario, and the Bodleian Library, Oxford.

BROCKLEHURST, Nellie (Mrs Brooman) CMB (1885–22 December 1963) health worker; *do.* Henry Brocklehurst & Kate; *e.* Portland Street High School, Manchester; *m.* William Brooman, 1945; *r.* theatre, travel, books, gardening, art; *a.* 47 Southend Lane, London SE6 (1938), Winchelsea, Hither Green, Kent (1934).

Dip SIE Board, London; Health Visitor Derbyshire County Council, 1912–16; elected Associate of the Women Public Health Officers' Association, 1917; health visitor, Poplar, London 1916–18; appointed with 11 other WPHO by the Ministry of Health to work as temporary Housing Sub-Inspectors to administer the Addison Housing Act, worked in the East Midlands region, 1919–21; WSI Executive Committee, 1918–19, 1921; TB Visitor, Lewisham, 1921–45; member WSIHVA; WSI representative Housing Deputation, 1923; WSI representative on NALGO, 1923; WSI representative on editorial board *Maternal and Child Welfare*, 1923; WSI representative at NUSEC Equal Franchise demonstration, 1923; Vice Chair WSI, 1925; representative WPHOA, TUC, Swansea, 1928; to circumvent the situation of her having to give up her career, she did not get married until her retirement, 1945; cremated at Charing, Kent.

s. *The Lady's Who's Who*, 1938–9; *Health Visitor*, xxxvii/2 (February 1964).

BURTON, Elaine Frances (Baroness Burton of Coventry) (2 March 1904–6 October 1991) MP; *b.* Scarborough, Yorkshire; *do.* Leslie Burton & Frances; *e.* Leeds Girls Modern School, City of Leeds Teacher Training College; *a.* 47 Molyneux Street, London, 18 Vincent Court, Seymour Place, London W1 (1991).

Distinguished herself as a sprinter, being the world girls sprint champion when she was only 16 in 1920; also represented Yorkshire at hockey and cricket, which she gave up on becoming an MP and took up skating instead; teacher in Leeds, 1924–35; moved to Wales and taught in Settlements, which was where she had experience of working among the unemployed and the poor; worked for the South

Wales Council of Social Service, 1935–7; organizer National Fitness Council, 1937–9; feminist; founder member of the BFBPW; during WW2, joined Richard Acland's Commonwealth Party, standing as PPC in Hartlepool by-election; then joined the LP and stood as a PPC for Hendon South, 1945; Retail Trade Executive, John Lewis Partnership, 1940–45; became Labour MP for Coventry South, 1950–59; spoke in the equal pay debate of 1952; first woman chairman of a sub-committee of the Select Committee of Estimates, worked on consumer protection matters that were implemented by the subsequent government; a member of the Council of Europe; voted against the Street Offences Bill because it did not deal with male offenders, 1958; lost her seat in Coventry to a Conservative, 1959; made a life peer, 1962; involved in more consumer issues when she was involved in the Weights and Measures Bill and the Hire Purchase Bill, 1962; chairman of the Domestic Coal Consumers Council, 1962–5; member Council for Industrial Design, 1963–8; one of the first members of the newly constituted Sports Council, 1965–71; member ITA, 1964–9; Chairman of the Council of Tribunals, 1967–73; left the LP to become one of the founder members of the SDP in 1980.

    p. A Year's Work in Dancing for the Elementary School (1930s); *What of the Women: A Study of Women in Wartime* (1941); *And Your Verdict?* (1942); *Domestic Work, Britain's Largest Industry* (1944); *What's She Worth? A Study of the Report on Equal Pay* (1947).

    s. Brookes (1967); *Guardian*, 10 October 1991; Stenton and Lees, vol. 4 (1981); *Who's Who* (1991).

BUTLER, Joyce Shore (1910–22 January 1992) MP; *do.* Arthur Wells; *e.* King Edward's High School, Birmingham; *m.* Victor Butler; one daughter, one son; *c.* University Women's; *a.* 8 Blenheim Close, London N21 (1992).

    Lectured in USA on foreign policy and local government; leader of the Labour group, Wood Green Borough Council 1947–64; member WCG; Leader of Wood Green Council, 1954–55; became Labour MP for the safe seat of Wood Green, 1955–74; Vice Chairman LP Housing and Local Government group, 1959–64; first Chairman of the new London borough of Haringey, 1964; interested in educational issues; PPS to Minister of Land and Natural Resources, 1965–7; along with Evelyn Emmet (see entry), she tackled the Financial Secretary to the Treasury concerning the discrimination involved in the tax laws for married women, asserting that married women should be taxed separately, 1960; introduced the first women's anti-discrimination PMB, 1967; member Wood Green Division of Haringey BC, 1974–9; retired 1979; Founder and first President Women's National Cancer Control Campaign; Chairman Hornsey Housing Trust, 1980–88; Vice Chair Wood Green Age Concern.

    s. Brookes (1967); Stenton and Lees, vol. 4 (1981); *Who's Who* (1992–3).

CADBURY, Dame Elizabeth (Elsie) Mary (née Taylor) OBE, DBE, Honorary MA Birmingham JP (24 June 1858–4 December 1951) social reformer; *b.* Peckham Rye, London; *do.* John Taylor & Mary Jane Cash; *e.* privately in England, boarding school Germany, North London Collegiate School; *m.* George Cadbury 1888; five children, five stepchildren; *r.* golf, music, motoring; *c.* Lyceum, Portman (1906), Ladies' Empire, Garden, English-Speaking Union (1934); *a.* Manor House, Northfield, Birmingham (1894–1951).

      b: born; do: daughter of; e: education; m: married; r: recreation;
            c: club; a: address; p: publications; s: sources

Her parents were both Quakers and engaged in philanthropic work, which set the tone for her life; passed the Senior Cambridge Examination in ten subjects, attended lectures at the London Institution and many courses at University of London; a fine musician, took singing lessons at the Guildhall School of Music and played the organ; after leaving school, involved in social work in London's East End, began teaching Sunday School in the Evangelical movement of the Friends, 1876; interested in education especially for women, worked at an adult school for women at a mission centre, where she gave talks on health and hygiene, organized a choir and orchestra; interested in practical ways to relieve sickness and poverty, to educate and improve housing and working conditions; read an Essay on Poverty to the Quaker Portfolio Society, 1883; she worked in a Protestant mission in one of the poorest areas of Paris, 1885; baptized into the Church of England, 1886; concerned about the provision of leisure facilities for women workers, became District Referee for city branches and first President Warwickshire YWCA, 1888; first President Midland Division YWCA, 1913–36; joined the NUWW, 1896; Honorary Treasurer NUWW, 1898–1907; President NUWW 1906 and 1907; founded and ran the Birmingham Union of Girls' Clubs, 1898–1927; President BUGC, 1898–1944; founded Bournville Girls' Athletic Club, 1899; Convenor of Peace and Arbitration Committee ICW, 1911–36; regularly attended ICW conferences abroad accompanied by her daughters, 1914–46; member of Education Committee, Chair, Sanitary Medical Service Sub-Committee, 1911–30; supported the NUWSS, went to suffrage meetings in Birmingham; a pacifist, she was on the platform with Millicent Fawcett (see entry), Louise Creighton (see entry) and Helena Swanwick (see entry) at NCW meeting at the outbreak of WW1, August 1914; first Convenor and Chair NCW Peace and International Relations Committee, October 1914; worked for Belgian and Serbian refugees during WW1; elected to NPC, 1916; Treasurer NPC, 1924–46; as a pacifist, her first concern was peace-building, member of women's deputation to Congress of Versailles Peace Treaty Conference to press for the inclusion of women in the talks, 1919; representative at the LN assemblies, Geneva; awarded OBE, 1919; elected as a Progressive Independent for Birmingham County Council, 1919–25; Vice President NUSEC, from 1919; Vice President Birmingham SECWCA, 1920; Chair Bournville Village Trust, 1922; Vice President WLF; unsuccessful Liberal PPC, King's Norton, 1923; mainly responsible for construction of flats for professional and businesswomen in Bournville, 1923; President National Council Evangelical Free Churches, 1925; one of the founders Free Church Women's Council; chaired the morning session WSIHVA Conference, 1927; Executive Committee and Vice President NCW, 1927; President NCW; Vice President, WSIHVA, 1929; Vice President City of Birmingham Gardens Association; President Midland Adult School Union, 1931; created DBE, 1934; member WCAWF; President NUEI, 1935; part of the British delegation to an ICW Conference in Dubrovnik, 1936; Chair Peace and Arbitration Committee NCW, led the British delegation at world conference, Calcutta, 1936; member Milk Fund Appeal for Spanish children, 1937; Vice President Women's Farm and Garden Union; member Home School Council; Chair Management Committee Bournville Schools; active supporter LNU and President Bournville, UNA; honours awarded – Order of Queen Elizabeth of Belgrade, Belgian Ordre de la Couronne, Serbian Red Cross, Order of St Sava of Yugoslavia, Officer of the Order of the Hospital of St John of Jerusalem; her lifelong habit of a daily cold bath may have contributed to her astonishing vigour and enthusiasm for public work, which never waned; died from a cerebral thrombosis in Birmingham.

p. articles on education, peace, housing, social questions.

s. Manchester Guardian, 5 December 1951; *New Chronicle*, 5 December 1951; Scott (1955); *Who Was Who*, vol. 5.

CAMPBELL, Dr Janet Mary, MD, MS (Lon), DBE, FRSP, CB, JP (5 March 1877–27 September 1954) pioneer in woman and child health care; *b.* Brighton; *do.* George Campbell, banker & Mary Letitia Rowe; *e.* Brighton High School, Moravian School, Neuwied, Germany, LSMW; *m.* Michael Heseltine, 1934; *c.* Victoria; *a.* Dene, Limpsfield, Surrey (1934), 50 Paultons Square, London SW3 (1954).

Began studying at the LSMW, 1896; graduated MB, BS, 1901; MD, 1904; MS, 1905; took a postgraduate course in obstetrics in Vienna; house surgeon and physician RFH, 1902; Senior Resident Medical Officer, Belgrave Hospital for Children, 1904; Assistant School Medical Officer, London County Council, 1905; became the Medical Officer Board of Education and fought for increased pay and status for women doctors in this post – physical training was one of her special interests in this post, 1908; member of the Women's Committee Liquor Control Board, 1915; initially a member of the MWF from its inception, later became Honorary Secretary, 1938, Vice President and President, 1917; member of the Medical Sub-Committee Health of Munition Workers' Committee; member of the Committee of Inquiry: War Cabinet Committee on Women in Industry, 1918; she wrote a 35-page brief as part of the above committee's report on women's health in industry; when the Ministry of Health was set up, became Senior Medical Officer for Maternity and Child Welfare, Ministry of Health, 1919–33; retained an advisory post at the Board of Education; appointed Chief Woman Medical Officer, Board of Education, 1919; waged a successful struggle to obtain suitable status and pay for women doctors in this post; establishing the school medical service was one of her ambitions; responsible for a team of physical training inspectors for primary and secondary schools throughout the country; at first she was Honorary Secretary, then Chairman of Dartford Physical Training College; supported WSIHVA's Diploma course, 1922; innovative report on maternal mortality published, 1924; spent some time working with Dr Jane Walker (see entry) in her Nayland sanatorium, 1924; awarded the DBE, 1924; her work between 1923 and 1932 contributed to the reduction of maternal and infant mortality; member of Executive Committee CWCS, 1926; spent six months in Australia working on the campaign against maternal and infant mortality, 1929; she also visited the USA for the Ministry of Health to report on welfare services and medical education in the maternal and child welfare services; member of various committees dealing with women in industry; member of Health Committee, LN, 1930–36; forced to retire due to her pending marriage, in line with civil service rules, 1933; after her retirement, active on a number of BMA committees and with the MWF; regarded as 'one of the most distinguished medical women of her time'; resumed the use of her maiden name, 1940; an invalid for the last seven years of life, suffering a painful illness with great patience.

p. Official Reports on the Arrangements for Teaching Obstetrics and Gynaecology in the Medical Schools (1923); *The Training of Midwives* (1923); *Maternal Mortality* (1924); *The Protection of Motherhood* (1927); *Infant Mortality* (1929); *Maternity Services* (1935); numerous official reports.

s. Women's Who's Who, 1934–5; *Dictionary of National Biography*, 1951–60; *The Times*, 29 September 1954; *Who Was Who*, 1951–60; *British Medical Journal*, 9 October 1954; *Journal of the Medical Women's Federation*, xxxvii/1 (January 1955).

CARLIN, Mary (13 August 1873–5 April 1939) trade union and Labour activist; *b.* Eastwood, Nottinghamshire; *do.* George Carlin, coalminer & Elizabeth Harrison; *m.* Fred Farnsworth; one daughter; *r.* tennis, swimming; *a.* Croydon, c/o Transport House, Smith Square, London SW1 (1934).

Started her career as one of the first women National Organizers for the Dock, Wharf, Riverside and General Workers' Union, later the TGWU, 1916 to late 1930s; during WW1 she was a member Women's Advisory Council, Ministry of Munitions; member Government Committee of Inquiry into WAAC scandals; involved in the organization of food; one of the organizers of the NMW demonstration, 29 July 1922; member of the LP National Executive for many years, from 1924; member SJCIWO; National Secretary TGWU Women's Guild; delegate at the TUC Women's Conference, 1925; Secretary of the CWG; speaker at Equal Franchise Demonstration, Hyde Park, 3 July 1928; LP PPC for the Abbey Division of Westminster, 1930; a pacifist; retired in the late 1930s.

s. Labour Who's Who (1927); *Hutchinson* (1934); *Daily Herald*, 6 April 1939.

CASTLE, Barbara Anne, Baroness of Blackburn (née Betts) (6 October 1911–) Labour politician; *b.* Chesterfield, Derbyshire; *do.* Frank Betts, editor Socialist paper; *e.* Bradford Grammar School, St Hugh's College, Oxford; *m.* Ted Castle, journalist, 1944.

Her first job was as a journalist; member St Pancras Borough Council and, later, deputy leader of the Labour Group, 1937; during WW2 she acted as a temporary civil servant in the Ministry of Food; housing correspondent of the *Daily Mirror*; Labour MP for Blackburn, 1945–79; PPS to the President of the Board of Trade, 1945–51; under the ten-minute rule, she successfully introduced the Criminal Law Amendment Bill, which amended a 1885 act to extend protection to prostitutes against 'misuse and abduction'; AMSH organized a celebratory lunch to recognize her achievement, 1950; won a place on the NEC, 1951–2; Chairman of the LP, 1958–9; Minister of Overseas Development, 1964–6; Minister of Transport, 1965–8; first Secretary of State and Secretary of State for Employment and Productivity, 1968–70; architect of the Equal Pay Act, 1970; together with Shirley Summerskill (see entry) and Joan Vickers (see entry), she opposed the government's attempt to replace Family Allowances paid to mothers with tax credits to be included in the father's pay, 1973; Secretary of State for Social Services, 1974–6; set up a Select Committee on the problem of battered wives, 1974; became an MEP, leader of the Labour Group, Vice Chairman of the International Socialist Group, 1979–86; life peer, 1990; has continued in public life as a vigorous campaigner for increased state pensions and a critic of New Labour; in the House of Commons, she was regarded by some as being a tough politician who operated 'on men's terms, attacking hard and expecting no quarter'; on the other hand it might have been that she would not tolerate the patronizing attitude in the Commons towards women MPs and consequently she behaved and expected to be treated as an equal by male MPs.

p. NHS Revisited (1976); *The Castle Diaries 1974–6* (1980); *The Castle Diaries 1964–70* (1984); *Sylvia and Christabel Pankhurst* (1987); *The Castle Diaries 1964–76* (1990); *Fighting All the Way* (1993); *We Can Afford the Welfare State* (1996).

s. Brookes (1967); *Penguin Biographical Dictionary of Women* (1998); *Who's Who*, 1999.

CAZALET-KEIR, Thelma (née Cazalet) CBE (1899–13 January 1989) Conservative MP and women's rights campaigner; *do.* William Cazalet & Maud Heron Maxwell; *e.* private; *m.* David Keir, journalist, 1939; *a.* 33 Belgrave Square, London SW1 (1938), Raspit Hill, Ivy Hatch, Sevenoaks, Kent.

Strongly influenced by her mother who was a feminist, many suffragettes visited their house; her mother was a friend and confidante of Emmeline Pankhurst (see entry) and took her to meet Pankhurst when Thelma was 16; when Thelma asked Pankhurst how she could start a political career, Pankhurst's advice was to start in local government; after WW1, Thelma then did some campaigning work with the one of the WSPU's chief organizers, Flora Drummond, with the right-wing WGE in Scotland; studied Fabianism at the LSE; first woman member Rural District Council, Malling, Kent, 1922–5; youngest member of the LCC for East Islington, 1925–31; became an Alderman, 1931; National Conservative MP for Islington East, 1931–45; the first woman MP to marry, 1938; PPS to the Parliamentary Secretary at the Board of Education, 1938–40; member CWP during WW2; Parliamentary Secretary Ministry of Education, 1945; during her parliamentary career, as a member of the Tory reform group, she was in charge of amendments to the 1944 Education Bill and succeeded in abolishing the marriage bar for women teachers and got within 35 votes of raising the school-leaving age to 16; worked for women to enter the diplomatic service, leading a WPC deputation, initiated by NCW, to request from Anthony Eden that the ban on women entering the Diplomatic and Consular Services be lifted, 1941; sat on a Government Select Committee that succeeded in gaining equal compensation for men and women for wartime injuries; involved in defending British women's right to retain their nationality when marrying foreigners; lost her parliamentary seat in 1945 and was unable to find a seat to contest; Chairman of the Status of Women Committee; Member of the Arts Council, 1940–49; member of the Women for Westminster group; Vice President of the Fawcett Society; President of the Fawcett Society, 1966–71; moved an amendment giving equal pay to women teachers to the Education Bill, 1944; Chairman of the Equal Pay Campaign Committee, working with her friend Irene Ward (see entry), 1947–56; CBE, 1952; organized the Milestone dinner, which celebrated the intro-duction of equal pay for equal work in the public services, 1955; Governor of the BBC, 1956–61; Chaired the Fawcett Society's celebration equal-pay-target dinner, with Barbara Castle (see entry) as guest of honour, 1970; she continued her support for the Fawcett, particularly for the library; appeared on the platform at the House of Commons for the Fawcett Society and 300 Group celebration of 70 years of women's suffrage, 1988; friend of Megan Lloyd George MP and intimate of the family; Kathleen Halpin (see entry) wrote that, 'I realized how much we owed to her wisdom and help in all our efforts and campaigns for the abolition of sex discrimi-nation and the general advance of the status of women', although she was described by Ellen Wilkinson (see entry) as an 'old-fashioned girl, likes soft fluffy clothes and nice simple theories that will put everything right straight away' (Brookes 1967).

p. I Knew Mrs Pankhurst (1945); *From the Wings: An Autobiography* (1967).

s. LWW, (1938); Brookes (1967); Stenton and Lees, vol. 3 (1979); *Guardian*, 19 August 1982, 18 January 1989; Banks (1990); Pugh (1992).

CHALLONER, Phyllis Crawhall, MA (1888–7 August 1966) women's rights activist; *do.* F.C.T. & E. Challoner; *e.* University of Oxford.

Read English at Oxford; Vice President SJSPA, succeeded Vera L. Mathews in 1939–66; Chairman of the British Section of the SJIA; dedicated her life to the work of the Alliance; close working relationship with Florence Barry (see entry); concentrated on international issues, with considerable contact with the International Sections and the UN; in this capacity she visited Geneva regularly and founded a section of the Alliance in South Africa; known for her combination of gentleness, charity and administrative excellence.

p. Towards Citizenship (with Vera Matthews, 1928).

s. The Times, 9 August 1966; *The Catholic Citizen*, September 1966.

CHANCE, Janet (née Whyte) (1885–1953) campaigner for sexual liberation and abortion law reformer; *b.* Edinburgh; *do.* Rev. Alexander Whyte & Jane Elizabeth Barbour; *m.* Clinton Chance, stockbroker; one daughter, Rachel Conrad; *a.* Kitelands, Micheldever, Winchester (1936).

Her father was a Presbyterian minister and Moderator of the Church of Scotland; she read a paper at the Sex Reform Conference, London, late 1920s; active supporter (in Hampshire) of WBCG, 1924; worked at the Walworth Women's Welfare Centre, a marriage and sex education centre which became a model for later advice centres, where she discovered a high incidence of attempted abortions using pills, drugs and alcohol among the working-class women clients; it was her experience at the Walworth Centre that fuelled her determination to campaign for legalization of abortion and became ALRA's first chairman, which was supported by and financed with money from her husband's business, 1936; ALRA representative on the Birkett Committee on abortion; wrote on women's need for a healthier and freer sex life; gave open-air speeches from a soapbox on street corners on the abortion issue; during WW2 she worked on behalf of PEN, caring for Czech refugee writers while running a chicken farm; she had suffered from depression throughout her life and committed suicide during one of these attacks: 'a determined, passionate… woman'.

p. The Cost of English Morals (1931); *Intellectual Crime* (1933); *The Romance of Reality* (1934); *The Case for the Reform of the Abortion Laws* (ALRA, 1936); *Back-Street Surgery* (with Maud Ryan and Margot Edgecombe, 1947).

s. ALRA Archive, Wellcome Institute, Box 29; Simms and Hindell (1971); Banks (1990).

CHESTERTON, Ada Elizabeth (née Jones) (pen-name Sheridan Jones, family nickname Keith) OBE (1870–20 January 1962) writer, pioneer social worker and philanthropist; *b.* London; *do.* Frederick John Jones & Ada Charlotte; *m.* Cecil Edward Chesterton, 1917; *r.* human intercourse, dancing; *c.* PEN, Critics' Circle; *a.* 3 Fleet Street, London E4 (1934), 82 Gower Street, London WC1 (1938), 16 Phillimore Place, London W8 (1962).

Despite a great interest in theatre and drama, she followed the profession of her father and brother, who were both journalists, and later married a journalist; started work in Fleet Street at 16 years of age and during her career contributed to London daily and weekly papers and magazines on social, economic, psychological and literary subjects; special correspondent in Poland for the *Daily Express*, 1919; Assistant Editor of *New Witness*, originally called, *Eye Witness*; during the course of her career travelled to Russia, China and Japan; posed as a destitute woman during 1925, living rough, and as a result of her research, wrote articles for the *Sunday Express*, 1926; also wrote a book, *In Darkest London*, which caused a huge controversy, and because of her experiences she subsequently became involved in setting up the Cecil Houses, which were public lodging houses for women and girls, where women could get a bath plus bed and breakfast for one shilling; awarded the OBE, 1938; by WW2 there were five such houses, which were also used for sheltering women and children whose own homes had been bombed; by the end of WW2 the Cecil Residential Club for Working Girls had been opened for women living on low wages who had no access to any leisure facilities; finally, established a home for women pensioners, the Cecil Residential Club in North Kensington catering for 72 elderly women, 1953; along with a diverse range of women in the Women's Movement, was a member of the Women's Public Housing organization; died in a Croydon nursing home.

p. The Man Who Was Thursday (with Ralph Neale, 1926); *In Darkest London* (1926); *St Theresa* (1927); *The Love Game* (with R. Neale, 1929); *Women of the Underworld* (1930); *My Russian Venture* (1931); *Young China & New Japan* (1933); *Sickle or Swastika?* (1935); *I Lived in a Slum* (1936); *This Thy Body, An Experience in Osteopathy* (1936); *What Price Youth* (1939); *The Chestertons* (1941); *Salute the Soviet* (1942).

s. Women's Who's Who, 1934–5; *The Lady's Who's Who*, 1938–9; *The Times*, 23 January 1962; *Who Was Who*, vol. 6.

CLARK, Dr Hilda MB, BS (Lon) (12 January 1881–24 February 1955) peace activist; *b.* Street, Somerset; *do.* William S. Clark & Helen Priestman Bright; *e.* Mount School, York, Birmingham University; *r.* riding; *c.* University of London; *a.* Mill Field, Street, Somerset (1920–21), 44 Upper Park Road, London NW3 (1923), 8 Mylne Street, Myddelton Square, London EC1.

Inherited her deep commitment as a Quaker and her campaigning spirit from her maternal grandfather, John Bright, the Radical Quaker and Liberal who agitated against the Corn Laws and worked to reform Parliament; also inspired by her aunt, Dr Annie E. Clark, to enter medicine, and lived with her while studying in Birmingham; committed member NUWSS (her elder sister, Alice, was on the Executive Committee); qualified as a doctor, 1908; house surgeon Birmingham Maternity Hospital, 1909–10; made a special study of tuberculosis; honorary medical officer Street Tuberculin Dispensary, 1910–11; became Tuberculosis Medical Officer, Portsmouth, 1912–13; member WIL; she had intended to start an urban practice in order to research causes of bad health among the working class, but the outbreak of WW1 prevented this; also interested in other aspects of preventive medicine such as infant welfare and maternity work; Medical Organizer and Secretary of the Friends' War Victims Relief Committee, France, organizing a maternity hospital for displaced and refugee women and other civilian needs, 1914–18; Head of the Friends' Relief Work Mission in Vienna, working for children, 1919–22; on her return, devoted herself to the promotion of peace, lived with Kathleen D'Olier Courtney for some time (see entry); Executive Committee

AMSH, 1923; Honorary Secretary WIL, 1925; worked in the League of Nations Union, spending much time in Geneva; Peacemakers' Pilgrimage speaker Hyde Park, 19 June 1926; worked with Greek refugees, 1923–30; in the Vienna crisis, was involved with refugees fleeing from Hitler, 1938.

p. The Street Tuberculin Dispensary (1911); *The Municipal Dispensary and Tuberculin Treatment* (with Dr A. Mearns Fraser, 1912); *The Dispensary Treatment of Pulmonary Tuberculosis* (1914).

s. List of Women Nominated for Service in Connection with the League of Nations (NUWT Archive, nd 1920–21?); *Journal of the Medical Women's Federation,* July 1955; *Women's Who's Who, 1934–5*; *Dictionary of Quaker Biography* (unpublished, Bank and McDonald 1998).

COATES, Alice Schofield JP (3 May 1881–19 June 1975) suffragette and LP activist; *b.* Prestwich, Lancs; *do.* Richard Schofield, cotton finisher & Mary Jane Westbrook; *e.* Nelson Street Board School, Manchester; *m.* Charles Coates, 1910; one son, two daughters, both given their mother's maiden name; *r.* walking, cycling, golf; *a.* various in Middlesbrough.

Gained a scholarship to Stockwell Teacher Training College, London, 1899; her teaching career was interrupted by joining the WSPU in Manchester; full-time WSPU agent, 1906; joined WFL, 1907, and became full-time organizer, 1908; imprisoned in Holloway Prison for failure to pay a fine for attempting to see Asquith in Downing Street, 1909; campaigned all over North East England; met her husband when he rescued her from a hostile crowd when she was campaigning in Guisborough, 1909; first Secretary Middlesbrough Maternity and Infant Welfare Committee, 1916–19; subsequently she and her husband opened a vegetarian restaurant in Middlesbrough with the WFL offices above; ILP supporter, but encouraged the Middlesbrough branch into the LP, 1918; first woman Labour councillor for Middlesbrough Ayresome ward, 1919–22 and Grove Hill, 1923–26; in this capacity she was on the Education Committee and was active in ensuring a pure milk supply, housing and sanitation improvements; magistrate 1921–56; Chairman West Middlesbrough CLP; President WFL, 1924; lost her council seat on her platform to raise the school leaving age to 15, 1926; started a private school on Montessori principles; chaired WFL conference on the election of women to Parliament, March 1928; political activism continued into the 1950s, when she worked for equal pay for equal work campaign.

s. Dictionary of Labour Biography, vol. 9.

COLLISSON, Marjorie Chave, BA, MA (1887–1982) lecturer/moral reformer; *b.* Texas; *e.* Tasmania, University of Sydney, Columbia Graduate School, New York, London School of Economics; *a.* 10 Thurlow Road, London NW3 (1938).

Daughter of a clergyman, born in America, came to London, emigrated to Tasmania and returned to London; academically gifted; first woman organizer and lecturer Academic Department, WEA, Sydney; Lecturer Columbia College for Men, New York; Board of Education, New York; Lecturer City Literary Institute, London; freelance lecturer, for example, to SPG on the 'Woman Citizen and Realism in Politics', 1927; as the Australian representative of the IAW, she became one of the founders and first General Secretary of the BCL; manager of overseas tour with Maude Royden (see entry), Australia and New Zealand, 1928; owner and manager of a small experimental cinema in London, 1930; involved with the JBL through meeting Alison Neilans (see entry); Secretary AMSH, 1950; mounted a vigorous campaign in the JBS against the proposed British Street Offences Bill, 1957–9; when this fight was lost (the Act gave the police the power to arrest women suspected of soliciting, while men went free), Collisson retired in 1960; still involved in supporting the Anti-Slavery Society, a member of the international committee of the IAF and a member of the IAW Board; her intellectual ability and powerful public speaking presence combined to make her a formidable contributor to the equal moral standard campaign.

    s. LWW, (1938); *Commonwealth Countries League Newsletter*, January/April 1983.

COLVILLE, Lady Helen Cynthia (née Crewe-Milnes) DCVO, FRCM, JP (20 May 1884–15 June 1968), women's health campaigner; *do.* First Marquess of Crewe & Sibyl Marcia Graham; *e.* at home, Royal College of Music, London; *m.* Hon. George Colville, 1908; three sons; *a.* 66 Eccleston Square, London SW1 (1938), 4 Mulberry Walk, London SW3 (1960s).

    Although she was a gifted musician, her father was a Liberal politician and this background influenced her to pursue an interest in social work and become a co-opted member of the Shoreditch BC Maternity and Child Welfare Committee; this involvement in voluntary work resulted in 1923 in the offer of standing for Parliament; simultaneously she was invited to become Woman of the Bedchamber to the Queen on a part-time basis, she chose the latter as it would give her more time to continue with her social work, and also used her extended connections to further this voluntary work, 1923–53; member of the Committee inquiring into the working of the Midwives Acts, 1928; under the Local Government Act of the LCC and BCs, subsidized all voluntary organizations dealing with child welfare and maternity, which included the three organizations Colville worked with in Shoreditch, consolidating her involvement with public social work, 1929; President TG; member WPHOA; JP for the County of London, from 1929; through her connection with Tuckell, she was asked to be Vice President of the WPHOA in 1929 and President, 1930–60; member of the Mary Macarthur Holiday Homes Committee, providing holidays for working women; worked on a committee on problems of maternal mortality resulting in the pamphlet, *Motherhood*, published in 1931; Chairman of the Great Marlborough Street Local Employment Committee from 1934.

    p. Social Progress and the Individual (1954); *Crowded Life: The Autobiography of Lady Cynthia Colville* (1963).

    s. LWW (1938); Colville (1963).

CORBETT, Marie (née Gray) (30 April 1859–28 March 1932) suffrage and local government worker; *b.* Kennington, London; *do.* George Gray; *m.* Charles Henry Corbett, barrister, Liberal MP, 1881; two daughters (Margery Corbett-Ashby, see entry, and Cicely), one son; *c.* International Women's Franchise; *a.* 75 Victoria Street, London SW1, Woodgate, Danehill, Sussex (1929).

    Member Uckfield (Sussex) Board of Guardians for 36 years; founder and secretary East Grinstead WSS; founder Ashdown Forest Boarding-Out Committee for Poor Law children; President Danehill and East Grinstead WLA; attended IWS conference with her two daughters in Berlin, 1904; with Margery, broke from the WLF to form the Liberal Women's Suffrage Group, 1907.

    s. Women's Who's Who, 1913; *The Woman's Leader*, May 1932; Banks (1990).

CORBETT-ASHBY, Margery Irene, honorary LLD, BA (Cantab. and Dublin) (19 April 1882–15 May 1981) international feminist campaigner; *do.* Charles Henry Corbett, landowner, MP & Marie Gray; *e.* at home by her parents, Newnham College, Cambridge; *m.* Arthur Brian Ashby, barrister, 1910; one son; *r.* walking, gardening; *c.* Pioneer, Forum, International Suffrage, University Women's; *a.* 22 Langside Ave, London SW15 (1913), 33 Upper Richmond Road, London SW15 (1924), Wickens, Horsted Keynes, Sussex (1936–81).

    This remarkably energetic and tenacious fighter for women's rights came from a politically active family; her father was a one-time Liberal MP, her mother a feminist and Poor Law Guardian (see above); at 18, she formed the YS organization with her sister; studied at Newnham, 1901–03, and took Classical tripos honours; BA Dublin; joined the suffrage movement at Cambridge; after gaining her degree went to teacher training college, Cambridge; attended the IWS Conference in Berlin with her mother and sister, 1904; Head of the Hull Municipal Vacation School, 1906–07; she and her mother left the WLF to form the Liberal Women's Suffrage group, 1907; Secretary NUWSS, 1908–09; delegate to the International Suffrage Congresses in Amsterdam and Stockholm, 1910; delegate to the ICW in Brussels; Executive Committee member NUWSS, 1910–12; political speaker since leaving College, travelled to the Near East, USA and Canada speaking on education and land questions from a Liberal standpoint; lectured on feminist issues in France, Germany, Holland, and could speak French and German; during WW1, engaged in some relief work; served on education, food control, infant welfare and Women's Institute committees; NUWSS representative, one of only three British delegates to the Allied Women's Conference during the Peace Conference, Versailles, 1919; went to Germany for the War Office to research and advise them on the problems being caused by occupying troops, 1919; Honorary Recording and League of Nations Secretary and interpreter at IWSA conference, 1920; Vice Chairman NUSEC; Honorary Secretary London Branch NCW; Executive Committee WLF; Executive Committee Home Counties Liberal Federation; Honorary Secretary IWSA; member Committee Wandsworth Welfare Centres; nine years as Poor Law Guardian, with two years as Chairman of the Board of Guardians; Vice Chairman Wandsworth Board of Guardians; President BCL; gave classes in public speaking for women, 1931; President NUGC, from 1931; President Sutton Coldfield WCA, 1931; contested eight elections as a Liberal PPC, first time for Ladywood, Birmingham, 1918, subsequently at general elections in 1922–24, 1929–35 and at two by-elections in 1937 and 1944; with Lady Aberdeen (see entry), President IWSA, 1923–46; member AMSH; member WFL; President BCL; Vice President Council for Representation of Women in the League of Nations, 1928; with Eva Hubback (see entry), she was one of the founders of the NUTG; President NUTG, 1929–35; representative NUSEC on the Women's Peers Committee, 1929; Vice President FES; as a result of pressure from women's groups, she was appointed substitute delegate to the Disarmament Conference, but she later resigned because of the government's lack of will to support practical resolutions, 1932–5; leading member WCAWF; involved in the Milk Fund Appeal for Spanish children, 1937; worked on behalf of women

in Palestine and India; President IFUW; Vice President WSIHVA, 1940; Editor of
the *International Women's News*, 1952–61; made a DBE, 1967; at the age of 91 she
went on a demonstration at the Women in Media rally, 1973; continued to attend
the IWSA congresses until 1976; she died at her Sussex home.

p. articles in suffrage papers and journals.

s. List of Women Nominated for Service in Connection with the League of Nations
(NUWT Archive, nd 1920–21?); *Women's Who's Who, 1913*; Gates (1924); *Who's
Who*, 1929; *The Lady's Who's Who*, 1938–9; *Dictionary of National Biography*,
1981–5; Alberti (1989); Banks (1990).

COURTNEY, Janet Elizabeth (née Hogarth) (pen-name 'One of the New Poor') JP,
OBE (1865–?); writer; *b.* Barton-on-Humber; *do.* Rev. George Hogarth; *e.* Ladies
College, Grantham, Lady Margaret Hall, Oxford; *m.* William Leonard Courtney,
journalist and author; *a.* Woodside, Seer Green, near Beaconsfield (1938).

Particularly interested in writing biographies, and she published work
concerning women and their organizations; JP County of London Children's
Court; life member Cambridge UN Trust; editor of the *Fortnightly Review*
1894–1928; acting editor 1928–9.

p. Freethinkers of the Nineteenth Century (1920); *Recollected in Tranquillity* (1926);
The Making an Editor: W.L. Courtney 1828–50 (1930); *Oxford Portrait Gallery*
(1931); *Countrywomen in Council: The English and Scottish WIs, with Chapters on the
Movement in the Dominions and on the Townswomen's Guilds* (1933); *The Adventurous
Thirties: A Chapter in the Women's Movement* (1933); *The Women of My Time* (1934);
Simple Annals (under pen-name, 1936); regular contributor to *The Times, Telegraph,
Fortnightly Review*.

s. Women's Who's Who, 1934–5; LWW (1938).

COURTNEY, Kathleen D'Olier, DBE (11 March 1878–7 December 1974) suffrage
worker and international relations advocate; *b.* Gillingham, Kent; *do.* Major David
Charles Courtney, RE & Alice Margaret Mann; *e.* Anglo-French College,
Kensington, boarding school, Malvern, Dresden, Germany, Lady Margaret Hall,
Oxford; *r.* travelling, walking; *c.* University Women's; *a.* 51 Morpeth Mansions,
London SW1 (1921), 44 Upper Park Road, London NW3 (from 1922), 3 Elm Tree
Court, Elm Tree Road, London NW8.

Took Modern Languages degree, French and German; independent income
enabled her to dedicate herself to campaigning; Treasurer OWSS; experience of
social work at a Lambeth LMH girls' club settlement and in Dublin; Secretary
Manchester Society for Women's Suffrage, 1908–11; Honorary Secretary NUWSS,
1911–15; involved in relief work in Europe during and after WW1; resigned from
NUWSS, attended the Hague conference and was involved in establishing WILPF,
1915; Secretary National Council for Adult Suffrage, 1916; relief work among
Serbians during WW1; postwar relief work with Society of Friends in Austria,
Poland and Greece; Chair original Family Endowment Committee, 1917; worked
with Eleanor Rathbone (see entry) to get Family Endowment adopted by the
NUSEC; Chair Executive Committee NUSEC, 1919; WIL representative on
Organizing Committee of Conference of Women seeking representation at LN,
1919; shared a house with Dr Hilda Clark in the 1920s (see entry); Chair WILPF,
1923; chaired NUSEC meeting/conference on miners' strike with speakers,

Eleanor Rathbone (see entry) and Maude Royden (see entry), November 1926; NUSEC delegate at IAWSEC Congress, Paris 1926; Executive Committee, 1927; Honorary Secretary BAWC, 1928; member Executive Committee NCEC, 1931; involved in the WIL Disarmament Campaign, 1931–2; Executive Committee LNU, 1928 and Vice Chair, 1939; Honorary Secretary Women's Peace Crusade; worked for the Ministry of Information during WW2, travelling to the USA to lobby for an international security organization; an observer at the San Francisco UN Conference, 1945; she spoke to convince the USA of the importance of the UN; Deputy Chair UNA, 1945; Chair Executive and joint President, UNA, 1949–51; Vice President Disarmament Committee of Women's Organizations; active in the UNA in her nineties; awarded DBE, 1952; UN peace medal, 1972; she died in London.

p. Extracts from a Diary During the War (1927).

s. List of Women Nominated for the League of Nations (NUWT Archive, nd 1920–21?); *Hutchinson* (1934); *Women's Who's Who, 1934–5*; *Guardian*, 11 March 1968; *Who Was Who*, vol. 7; *The Times*, 10 December 1974; Banks (1990); *Dictionary of National Biography Missing Persons*, 1993.

COUSINS, Margaret (née Gillespie) BMus (7 November 1878–1954) suffragist; *b* Boyle, County Roscommon; *e.* Victoria High School, Derry, Royal Irish Academy of Music, Dublin; *m.* James H. Cousins, accountant and poet, 1903; *a.* Strand Road, Sandymount (1907), Liverpool (1913–14), various places in India (from 1915).

Wrote of herself that she was 'born a natural equalitarian' (Cousins, 1950); gained a BMus, 1902; after her marriage, became a vegetarian, while speaking at a conference on vegetarianism in Manchester; also attended a NCW conference, her first encounter with the Women's Movement, 1906; inspired and excited by the NCW encounter, on her return to Dublin arranged to meet the founder of the IWSLGA, Anna Haslam; organized her first suffrage meeting in her house, 1907; when next in London met WSPU leaders, Emmeline and Christabel Pankhurst (see entry), Emmeline Pethick-Lawrence (see entry), Charlotte Despard (see entry), 1907; co-founder of the militant IWFL, with Hanna and Frank Sheehy Skeffington (see entry), Cousins as Treasurer, 11 November 1908; worked as a volunteer for three summer months with the WSPU to get experience to transfer to the Irish campaign, 1909; organized Emmeline Pethick-Lawrence's IWFL speaking events at Cork and Derry, October 1910; spent a month in Holloway Prison, 1910; when women were excluded from the Home Rule Bill, participated in the window-smashing campaign at Dublin Castle, spending one month in prison in Mountjoy, Dublin and then in Tullamore Prison, 1912–13; with the Sheehy Skeffingtons, helped to establish the suffrage paper, the *Irish Citizen*, 1912; having dedicated so much of their income to the suffrage movement, the Cousins were in financial difficulties, and they left for Liverpool en route to emigrating to India to pursue their interest in Eastern religion and other aspects of South Asian life, 1913; in Liverpool, again worked for the WSPU and with Charlotte Despard in the WFL; became involved in the Church of the New Ideal, which initially only allowed women to preach, and preached at some services, 1914; arrived in Madras, 1915; involved with the WIA as Honorary Secretary of the local branch of which Annie Besant, the birth control pioneer, was President, 1916; drafted the first request for votes for Indian women, 1917; part of the women's education movement, became headmistress of a girls' school in Mangalore; worked on campaigns to mobilize Indian women to use their vote after getting the vote in 1921; involved in the Indian liberation movement, meeting Gandhi; assisted with a campaign for women political candidates in southern India, 1937; first woman magistrate in India.

p. The Awakening of Asian Womanhood (1922); *The Music of the Orient and Occident* (1935); *Indian Womanhood Today* (1941).

s. Cousins and Cousins (1950); Luddy (1995a).

CREIGHTON, Louise Hume (née von Glehn) JP (7 July 1850–15 April 1936) writer, education and social worker; *b.* Sydenham; *do.* Robert von Glehn, merchant & Agnes Duncan; *e.* privately, at home by governesses; *m.* Mandell Creighton, Bishop of London, 1872; four daughters, three sons; *a.* Hampton Court Palace, Kingston (1901–27), 5 South Park Road, Oxford (1927–36).

When 18 she joined a Self-Help Essay Society; travelled with her parents to Germany and Italy, which gave her an interest in painting; entered the London University Higher Examination for Women, 1869; the continuation of her private studies was encouraged by her mother and there was a stimulating home atmosphere of intellectual debate; after her marriage, she spent many years moving around the country, but became involved in social and education work in each new location; as a don's wife in Oxford, one of the first three women to attend a lecture at Merton College; with Mrs Humphrey Ward, Mrs T.H. Green and Mrs Max Muller, organized a system of lectures to women, which became the Oxford Association for the Education of Women, 1872–5; during her time at Oxford she and her husband attended a meeting addressed by the pioneer suffragist, Lydia Becker, and both signed her petition for women's suffrage; moved to Northumberland, 1875; helped to start and run the MU in Cambridge (1884) and Worcester (1886); although she believed that women were equal to men, became part of the movement against women's suffrage because of her loathing of political parties and her belief that women could do more for women outside the system, c.1889; founded a women's settlement in Fulham, Bishop Creighton House, 1907, and was Chair of its council until 1934; only woman member Joint Committee of Insurance Commissioners, 1912; believing she had been mistaken, she announced her change of allegiance to become a supporter of women's suffrage, at the NUWW conference, 1912; member Royal Commission on University Education in London; member Middlesex School Board; member Church Assembly and Missionary Council; three terms as President NUWW (NCW); Vice President NCW, 1918; supporter of the LSWS's Women's Service Bureau, 1918–22; convenor of Consultative, Peace and Arbitration and Women Patrols NCW sectional committees, from 1918; member of Expert Advisory Panel LSWS, 1923; Vice President of CEBSCA, 1925; Vice Chairman NCW, 1927; Vice Chairman Central Conference of Women's Church Work and President Women's Diocesan Association; died in Oxford.

p. The Black Prince (1876); *England A Continental Power: From the Conquest to Magna Carta 1066–1216* (1876); *Sir Walter Raleigh* (1877); *The Life of John Churchill, Duke of Marlborough* (1879); *A First History of England* (1881); *Stories from English History* (1882); *The Government of England* (1884); *A Social History of England* (1887); *Life of Mandell Creighton, Bishop of London; Life of Thomas Hodgkin; First History of France; Heroes of European History; The Economics of the Household; Missions; The Social Disease and How to Fight It; Life and Letters of*

     b: born;   do: daughter of;   e: education;   m: married;   r: recreation;
c: club;   a: address;   p: publications;   s: sources

Thomas Hodgkin (all 1917); *Life of G. A. Selwyn, DD, Bishop of New Zealand and Lichfield; Tales of Old France* (1924); edited – *The Church and the Nation; Thoughts on Education, Historical Essays and Reviews (Dr Creighton); The Letters of Oswin Creighton* (1920); and a number of her husband's works: *Memoir of a Victorian Woman: Reflections of Louise Creighton, 1850–1936* (1994).

s. The Times, 16 April, 18 April, 23 June 1936; Bank and McDonald (1998); Creighton (1994).

CREWE, Margaret Etrenne Hannah, Marchioness of (née Lady Peggy Primrose) CI (1 January 1881–13 March 1967) campaigner for employment and public office access; *do.* Fifth Earl of Rosebery, Archibald Philip Primrose, Liberal Prime Minister & Hannah de Rothschild; *e.* private; *m.* Marquess of Crewe, 1899; one daughter, one son; *a.* Crewe House, Curzon Street, W1, West Horsley Place, near Leatherhead, Surrey (1934), 50 Charles Street, London W1 (1967).

Liberal; Chair Central Committee Women's Training and Employment, 1914; President Mary Macarthur Holiday Home for Working Women, arising from her friendship with Macarthur (see entry), whom she met on the CWTE; one of the first seven women magistrates, 1919; Chair of the Advisory Committee to the Lord Chancellor on further such appointments; awarded the LH by General de Gaulle because of her service to the Free French in WW2, 1947; died in London.

s. Women's Who's Who, 1934–5; The Times, 14 March, 15 March 1967; *Daily Telegraph*, 14 March 1967.

CROSBY, Edith Elizabeth, LLA (22 November 1878–14 November 1939) suffragette and teacher; *b.* Stratford, London; *do.* Thomas Crosby, bookmaker & Ann Sherrick; *a.* Abbey Lane, Stratford, Essex (birth), Burgh Hill, Surrey (1939).

Founder member of the NUWT, a member Central Council and Chairman of the Council's Education Committee; responsible for devising much of the NUWT's policy and influencing the production of publications; Editor of *The Woman Teacher* for two years; associated with the NUWT West Ham Branch from its start; represented the NUWT on the Education Advisory Committee LNU; President NUWT, 1925: member Advisory Council and patron to WES's Conference of Women, 1925; member of the ODC; died after a long illness at the home of Mrs Dawson Follett (also a teacher and NUWT member; sister of Agnes Dawson, (see entry) in Surrey and was cremated in Streatham; her colleague, Ethel Froud (see entry), wrote of her 'unbroken service to education and the woman's cause' (1939).

p. Why I Left the NUT (Crosby et al.); *Keeping Fit: A Health Book for Senior Girls* (1936).

s. Phipps (1928; *The Woman Teacher*, 1 December 1939; Kean (1990).

CROWDY-THORNHILL, Rachel Eleanor, DBE, RRC, LLD (March 1884–10 October 1964) pioneer international diplomacy; *do.* James Crowdy & Isabelle Fuidge; *e.* Hyde Park New College, Guy's Hospital; *m.* Colonel Cuthbert J.M. Thornhill, 1939; *r.* travel, winter sports, small boat sailing; *c.* Albemarle, VAD Ladies', Service Women's, ESU, Efficiency; *a.* 100 Beaufort Street, London SW3 (1929), 16 rue Plantamour, Geneva (1929), 14 Grosvenor Crescent Mews, London SW1 (1934), Sheppards, Outwood, Surrey (1964), 35 Duchess of Bedford House, Campden Hill, London W8 (1964).

Trained as a children's nurse; worked at Guy's Hospital, 1908; obtained an Apothecaries Hall Certificate, 1910; ran a slum dispensary for two years prior to WW1; after having joined the Red Cross, met Katharine Furse (Director of the WRNS during WW1) in 1911, with whom she went abroad with the Red Cross; lecturer and demonstrator, National Health Society, 1912–14; Principal Commandant to VAD's France and Belgium, 1914–19; mentioned in dispatches and received the Royal Red Cross, second and first class, 1916 and 1917; made DBE, 1919; Chief of the Humanitarian Section on Social Questions and Opium Traffic at the League of Nations, she was the only woman Head of Department, her section controlled the traffic in opium and women and worked for the welfare of children globally, 1919–31; part of the International Typhus Commission to Poland, 1920–21; Secretary to the Commission on the Trade in Women and Children, 1922; gave a talk to the SPG, 'The Work of the Social Section of the League of Nations', 1927; delegate to Conference on Pacific Affairs, Honolulu, 1930; her League work was honoured with a celebration dinner in London attended by 600, including leading feminists Charlotte Despard (see entry), Nancy Astor (see entry), Maude Royden (see entry) and Margery Corbett-Ashby (see entry), June 1931; delegate to Conference on Pacific Relations, Shanghai, 1931; attended International Red Cross Conference, Tokyo, 1934; sat on the Royal Commission on the Private Manufacture of Armaments, 1935–6; member Parliamentary Commission to the Spanish War with Eleanor Rathbone (see entry), Ellen Wilkinson (see entry), Duchess of Atholl, 1937; Regions Adviser to the Ministry of Information, reporting on conditions in bombed cities, 1939–45.

p. The Report of the Special Body of Experts on Traffic in Women and Children (1927).

s. Who's Who, 1929; *Manchester Guardian*, 26 June 1931; *The Times*, 19 October 1964; *International Women's News*, March 1965.

CULLIS, Winifred Clara, MA (Cantab), DSc (Lon), LLD (Hon.), CBE (2 June 1875–13 November 1956) Professor of Physiology, equalitarian feminist; *b.* Tuffley, Gloucester; *do.* Frederick John Cullis, surveyor and civil engineer & Louisa Corbett; *e.* King Edward VI High School for Girls, Birmingham, Newnham College, Cambridge; *r.* golf, reading, cross-stitch; *c.* Lyceum, University Women, Overseas, Efficiency; *a.* 8 St Martin's Place, London WC2 (1929), Vincent House, Pembridge Square, London W2.

Prof. Sidgwick scholarship to Cambridge, 1896; took the Natural Science tripos parts I and II, 1899 and 1900; demonstrator in physiology at LSMW, 1901; became Head of Department, 1908; during WW1 went to Canada as Acting Professor of Physiology at the University of Toronto; first holder Sophia Jex-Blake Professor of Physiology, University of London, 1926–41; undertook physiology research in the laboratories of the Royal College of Physicians and Surgeons; member Executive Committee SPG, 1921–2; Vice President SPG, 1925; Director of *Time & Tide*; lecture to SPG, 'Industrial Psychology Applied to the Home', 1927; Vice President WSIHVA, 1929; co-founder of BFUW and IFUW; President BFUW, 1925–9 and IFUW, 1929–32; President ATDS, 1925–6?; member WES Advisory Council, Conference of Women, 1925; CBE, 1929; member ODC; member of the Joint Broadcasting Committee, 1939 (see Hilda Matheson, entry); Emeritus Professor of Physiology, University of London, 1941; Head of the Women's Section British Information Services, USA, 1941–3; sent by the government to the Far East (1940), and Middle East (1944–5) to provide information on the activities of British women in the war; during the 1950s, member of the Central Council for Broadcast Adult Education, a member of the Council for the National Institute of Industrial Psychology, Chair of the Education Committee ESU, member of the Education Board BFI, member British Social Hygiene Council, on the Board of Studies of the University of London and member of the Royal Society of Medicine; among her friends in the movement were Nancy Astor (see entry) and Margaret Haig Thomas (Lady Rhondda) (see entry).

p. The Body and Its Health (with M. Bond, 1935); *Your Body and the Way it Works* (1949); numerous papers, and articles in medical and scientific journals.

s. The Gateway for Women at Work, vol. ii/10 (February 1930); *Dictionary of National Biography*, 1951–60; *University Women's Review*, vol. xvii (1957), p. 278; *Journal MWF*, xxxix (1957); *Who Was Who*, vol. 5.

DANE, Clemence (real name Winifred Ashton) (stage-name, Diana Cortis) FRSL, CBE (21 February 1888–28 March 1965) playwright and novelist; *b.* Blackheath, London; *do.* Arthur Charles Ashton, commission merchant & Florence Bentley; *e.* England, Germany, Switzerland, Slade School of Art, London; *a.* 12 Tavistock Street, Covent Garden, London WC2 (1933), Hunthay, near Axminster, Devon (1933), Lower Holywych, Cowden, near Edenbridge, Kent (1937), 20 Tavistock Street, Covent Garden, London WC2 (1940), Pendean, near Midhurst, Sussex (1958), 1 Draycott Place, London SW3 (1959).

Brought up in the country, attending rural schools; at 16 taught French in Geneva for a year, c.1904; studied art for three years in London and Dresden; began a career as an actress, 1908; regarded her years on tour before the war as one of the happiest times of her life, however, health problems during WW1 caused her to give up acting; taught in a girls school, during which time she discovered her talent for writing; chose her writer's name after St Clement Dane Church in London; 'played a prominent part in the agitation for the emancipation of women'; wrote a play, *A Bill of Divorcement*, 1921, in protest at the inequality of the divorce laws as revealed by the Royal Commission on Divorce; wrote for *Time & Tide* and was a member Executive Committee SPG 1921–2; Vice President SPG, 1925; Charlotte Despard (see entry) conducted a protest meeting against Dane's imprisonment for non-payment of taxes outside Holloway Prison; regarded as a very good broadcaster, 'the woman commentator' they had been searching for, worked for the BBC as a literary critic broadcasting reviews of contemporary novels, giving talks, conducting interviews, adapting her plays for broadcasting, writing poems and as a scriptwriter, from 1931 to early 1960s; during WW2, contributed broadcasts and scripts, which she regarded as her war work and returned to acting, taking Sybil Thorndike's part with the Old Vic, touring for CEMA in the play *Jacob's Ladder*, in such places as Risley, Preston, Halifax and Hull to bring entertainment to, among others, munitions workers, July to December 1942; the experience inspired her to write about the lives of the women as, like the rest of the company, she was sharing hostels with them (*Touring in Wartime with CEMA*); two of her plays were made into films, *A Bill of Divorcement* (1932) and *Murder* (1930); President SWJ, 1935–6 and 1944; critic for the Book Society, 1933; made a CBE, 1953; suffered from poor health throughout her life; increasingly from the mid-1940s she suffered from severe arthritis, suffering a heart attack in 1958; the severity of these attacks often meant she was unable to write, even when assisted by her secretary, Olwen Bowen; she worked at a frenetic pace as evidenced by her prodigious output.

p. Regiment of Women (1917); *First the Blade* (1918); *Legend* (1919); *A Bill of Divorcement* (1921); *Will Shakespeare* (1921); *Shivering Shacks or the Hiding Place* (1923); *The Way Things Happen* (1923); *Wandering Stars* together with *The Lover* (1924); *Naboth's Vineyard* (1925); *Granite* (1926); *The Woman's Side* (1926); *Mariners* (1927); *Mr Fox* (1927); *A Traveller Returns* (1927); *The Dearly Beloved of Benjamin Cobb* (1927); *The Babylons* (1928); *Adam's Opera* (with Richard Addinsell, 1928); *Enter Sir John* (with Helen Simpson, 1929); *The King Waits* (1929); *Author Unknown* (with H. Simpson, 1930); *Printer's Devil* (with H. Simpson, 1930); *Tradition and Hugh Walpole* (with Hugh Walpole, 1930); *Broome Stages* (1931); *Omnibus Collection: Recapture* (1932); *Re-enter Sir John* (with H. Simpson, 1932); *Wild Decembers* (1932); *Broome Stages* (1933); *Moonlight in Silver* (1934); *Fate Cries Out* (1935); *Come of Age* (with R. Addinsell, 1938); *The Moon is Feminine* (1938); *The Arrogant History of White Ben* (1939); *Friedrich Hebbel's Herod and Mariamne* (1939); *Cousin Muriel* (1940); *England's Darling* (1940); *Trafalgar Day 1940* (1940); *The Saviours, 7 Plays* (1942); *The Lion and the Unicorn* (1943); *He Brings Us Great News* (1944); *Call Home the Heart* (1947); *Three One-Act Plays* (1949); *The Flower Girls* (1954); *Eighty in the Shade* (1959); *The Godson* (1964); *London Has a Garden* (1964).

s. The Lady's Who's Who, 1938–9; *Guardian*, 29 March 1965; *The Times*, 29 March 1965; *Who Was Who*, vol. 6; *Dictionary of National Biography*, 1961–70; Bank and McDonald (1998); 1861, 047–8; CD Talks and Scriptwriter Files, BBC Written Archives Centre.

DAVIDSON, Lady Frances Joan (née Dickinson) (Baroness Northchurch) OBE (29 May 1894–25 November 1985) MP; *do.* Lord Dickinson MP; *e.* private; *m.* Viscount Davidson MP, 1919; 2 daughters, 2 sons; *a.* 3 Barton Street, London SW1 (1929), 16 Great College Street, London SW1 (1934), Norcott Court, Berkhampstead, 16 Lord North Street, London SW1 (1985).

Her father was an MP and supported the women's suffrage struggle; OBE, 1920; inherited her husband's seat on his entering the House of Lords, became Conservative MP for Hemel Hempstead, 1937–59; member CWP during WW2; elected to the Executive of the 1922 Committee (backbenchers), 1947; supported the Deserted Wives Bill, 1951; signatory to a letter to *The Times* signed by women MPs directed to the Conservative and Unionist Associations asking them to select more women candidates to fight better parliamentary seats, 1952; DBE, 1953; Davidson participated in the debate on equal pay in the public services, 1952; introduced a private member's bill on the Protection of Animals (Anaesthetics) Bill, 1954; started a new career as Baroness Northchurch of Chiswick in the House of Lords, joining her husband in the Lords, January 1964.

s. Women's Who's Who, 1934–5; *LWW* (1938); Brookes (1967); Stenton and Lees, vol. 4 (1981).

DAVIES, Margaret Llewelyn (Caroline) (1861–1944) Co-operative Party activist; *b.* London; *do.* Rev. John Llewelyn Davies & Mary Crompton; *e.* Queen's College for Women, London, Girton College, College, Cambridge; *a.* Marylebone, London W1 (1861–89), Kirkby Lonsdale, Cumbria (1889–1908), Well Walk, Hampstead, London NW3 (1908–44).

Her father's sister was the educationist and women's rights pioneer, Emily Davies; Rev. Davies supported women's suffrage and women entering the medical profession; in place of 'Caroline', she adopted the family name, Llewelyn, which had been given to all her brothers but not to her; became a voluntary social worker in Marylebone, where her father worked at Christ Church; her father was a trade union and Co-operative Movement supporter, she joined the Marylebone Co-operative Society, 1886; Secretary of the WCG Marylebone branch, 1887; member WCG National Executive, 1888; WCG Honorary Secretary 1889–1922; when the family moved to Kirkby Lonsdale, she met Lilian Harris (see entry), who became a lifelong friend and colleague; Davies turned the WCG away from domestic concerns and toward social and political issues; campaigning for the suffrage, from 1893; worked with the WTUA and the WIC, supporting women workers in their attempts to improve their working conditions; from 1900 she concentrated the WCG's force on welfare reforms for mothers and children, part of the campaign being the publication of *Maternity, Letters from Working* Women in 1915; working for equal divorce laws, gave evidence as the WCG representative to the RC on Divorce Law, 1910; moved to Hampstead with Harris and her father on his retirement, 1908; involved in establishing the IWCG, 1921; supporter of the Russian Revolution, first chairman Society for Cultural Relations with the USSR, spent much of the 1920s engaged in work for Russia; both Davies and Harris retired from the WCG in 1922; still involved in the movement, first woman chairman Co-operative Congress, 1922; pacifist campaigning work in the 1920s; friendship with the writer, Virginia Woolf.

p. The Women's Co-operative Guild (1904); *Maternity, Letters from Working Women* (ed. 1915); 'The Claims of Mothers and Children' *in Women and the Labour Party* (ed. Marion Phillips, 1918); *Life as We Have Known It* (ed. 1931); many articles and pamphlets, (Co-operative Press).

s. Banks (1985).

DAVIES, Mary E. (Mrs Lewis) (1882?–1967) sanitary inspector and welfare worker; *m.* Rev. Elvet Lewis, 1930; *a.* Penarth, South Wales (1930?), Riverlea, Llandyssul (1934).

Member WSIHVA, 1917; Sanitary Inspector, Glamorgan; member Cardiff and East Wales Centre; pioneer of girls' clubs in Wales; representative YWCA deputation to Home Secretary on Family and Welfare Bill, 1924; representative EAW, 1925–8; representative NUSEC, 1926; TUC delegate, 1926; attended TU conference about the plight of the miners, 1926; Honorary Secretary WSI, 1925–7; delegate on deputation to Minister of Health to demand the registration of women Public Health Officers, 1927; Chair WSI, 1928; Chair Finance Sub-Committee, 1928; Chair Salaries Sub-Committee, 1928; county organizer Cardigan NFWI.

s. Woman Health Officer, iv/9; *Health Visitor*, xli/6 (June 1968), p. 286.

DAWSON, Agnes JP (1875–1953) teacher, activist; *b.* Peckham, London; *do.* Isaac Dawson, journeyman carpenter & Sarah; *e.* Elementary School, Saffron Walden Training College; *r.* gardening, motoring *c.* National Labour; *a.* 5 Borland Road, London SE15, The Hut, Newport, Essex (1934).

A pupil-teacher, working in schools in Camberwell; NUWSS member; took part in the census boycott of 1911; Head Crawford Street Infants and Junior Mixed School, 1917–25; founder member NUWT; Vice President NFWT, 1918;

President NUWT, 1919–20; Vice President SPG, 1925; elected to LCC, 1925–37; Chairman of the NUWT Legal and Tenure Committee, 1925; LCC member North Camberwell, 1925 and 1928; on her election to the LCC she gave up her teaching job to devote herself to her numerous political activities, 1925; speaker Equal Franchise Demonstration, Hyde Park, July 1928; LCC Labour member Camberwell North, 1931; Deputy Chair LCC, 1931–2; Chair LCC General Purposes Committee and member Special Services Sub-Committee, 1934–7; senior LP whip, LCC, 1929–31; Chairman Rose Lamartine Yates Clinic Committee (named after a leading WSPU activist); member London LP; she was a vociferous campaigner for the removal of the marriage bar and equal pay; Chair of Legal and Tenure Committee, LCC, 1934; she lived for 27 years with another teacher, Miss Munns, who died in 1952.

p. Nursery Classes; Nursery Schools; Why I Left the NUT (Dawson et al.).

s. History of the NUWT (1928); *Women's Who's Who, 1934–5*; *The Lady's Who's Who*, 1938–9; *The Woman Teacher*, June 1953; Kean (1990); Oram (1996).

DAWSON, Mrs Boyd, sanitary inspector; *a.* 16 Denbigh Place, London SW1.

Qualified sanitary inspector; French speaker; involved in juvenile employment work; Secretary WIC for two years; involved in an investigation in connection with women's employment relating to industrial fatigue and the effects of industry on motherhood; member London and South-Eastern Employment Council Ministry of Labour and Chair Women's Standing Committee, until these Councils were dissolved, 1919; General Secretary NWCA; representative NWCA on Organizing Committee Conference of Women to seek representation on the LN, 1919.

p. The Quality of Maternity in Relation to Industrial Occupation.

s. List of Women Nominated for Service in Connection with the League of Nations (NUWT Archive, nd 1920–21?).

DEAKIN, Evelyn (?–13 October 1942) teacher; *a.* 9 Alexander Drive, Liverpool.

An active member Birkenhead and Wirral Women's Suffrage Society and its Branch Secretary, 1912; worked at Canterbury Road School, then at Church Road School, from 1930; Conservative women's activist; member NUSEC; Executive Committee NUSEC, 1927–8; NUWT local secretary; President NUWT 1939–40.

s. The Woman Teacher, 27 November 1942.

DESPARD, Charlotte (née French) (15 June 1844–10 November 1939) women's rights and socialist activist; *b.* Ripple Vale, Kent; *do.* Capt. William French, retired naval officer & Margaret Eccles; *e.* privately, finishing school; *m.* Maximilian Carden Despard, Anglo-Irish businessman, 1870; *c.* International Suffrage; *a.* 2 Currie Street, Nine Elms, London SW8 (1913), Roebuck House, near Dublin (1923).

After her marriage, she began to write novels, ten in all, three of which remained unpublished; her political career began on her husband's death, which left her a wealthy widow, 1890; first became a Poor Law Guardian at Kingston-on-Thames; started one of the first child welfare clinics and ran a working men's club in Nine Elms, Battersea; guardian for the Vauxhall board, Lambeth Poor Law Union, 1894–1903; activist in the Labour movement and emerging Labour Party, member ILP; Joint Secretary WSPU; imprisoned twice in Holloway Prison, 1907;

led a split in the WSPU caused by the Pankhursts' undemocratic methods, and formed the Women's Freedom League, becoming its President from 1907; during WW1 she fought on four fronts, she 'kept the suffrage flag flying', worked for the welfare rights of women and children in the East End, led campaigns for an equal moral standard against the government's attempts to control working-class women, and championed the pacifist cause (a great embarrassment to her brother, who was Field Marshal Sir John French); member Women's Peace Council; stood as a LP PPC for Battersea, general election, 1918; alderman Battersea BC, 1920; moved to Ireland to support the Irish cause, gave a great deal of both her time and her money to Sinn Fein, 1921; still maintained a significant presence in Women's Movement campaigns in Britain, especially in the extension of the suffrage, equal moral standard and pacifist work; in Ireland she supported the republican cause and was regarded as a subversive (again, embarrassing her brother who was now Lord Lieutenant of Ireland); lived with Maud Gonne, actress and Sinn Fein activist, from 1923; President WPDL during the Irish civil war; the WFL held a birthday party for her annually and she attended all major demonstrations for the suffrage campaign in the 1920s and was present for the final success, 1928; visited Russia as she was increasingly attracted by Communism, 1930; moved to the north of Ireland, involved in anti-Fascist demonstrations, 1934; a legend of the Women's Movement, an ascetic, vegetarian and advocate of simple dress; died of multiple injuries in a fall at her home at Whitehead, County Antrim, buried in Glasnevin cemetery, Dublin, with Maud Gonne MacBride giving the oration and Hanna Sheehy Skeffington (see entry) laying the WFL wreath on her grave.

p. Chaste as Ice, Pure as Snow (1874); *Wandering Fires* (three volumes, 1874); *A Modern Iago* (1879); *A Voice from the Dim Millions* (1884); *Jonas Sylvester* (1886); *The Rajah's Heir* (three volumes, 1890); *An Old Inmate, Her Story as Told by Herself* (1895); *Outlawed: A Novel on the Woman Suffrage Question* (with Mabel Collins, 1908); pamphlets – *Economic Aspects of Women's Suffrage* (1908); *Women in the Nation* (1908); *Women's Franchise and Industry* (1908); *Woman in the New Era* (1909); *Theosophy and the Women's Movement* (1913).

s. The Times, 11 November 1939; Banks (1985); Mulvihill (1989); Tweedy (1992); *Dictionary of National Biography Missing Persons*, 1993; see also Linklater (1980).

DOUIE, Vera Ruth Gordon (1894–1979) *b.* Lahore, India; *e.* Godolphin School, Salisbury, University of Oxford; *a.* 4 Charrington Street, London NW1 (1954), Oxford (1967).

Her father was an Indian civil servant; attended the Honours School of English at Oxford before degrees were open to women; Library Assistant at the War Office Library, 1916–21; Indexer of the *Medical History of War*, London, 1921; Librarian of the LNSWS's WSL, 1926–67; it was Douie's hard work, imaginative use of available resources to enlarge the collection, and knowledge of the Women's Movement that developed the WSL into the magnificent Fawcett Library that exists today; in herself she was a resource for the Women's Movement, an activist particularly in the AMSH; her research on the discrimination operating against women's employment was especially useful for post-WW2 campaigns; in London she lived a modest, almost basic existence, and in retirement moved to Oxford, where she died.

p. The Lesser Half (1943); *Women their Professional Status, A World Survey* (1946); *Daughters of Britain* (1949); entries in the *Chambers Encyclopaedia* and the *Lexikon der Frau*, Zurich.

s. Bank and McDonald (1998); Doughan and Gordon (2000).

DURRIE MULFORD, Rosetta Elizabeth (née Gardiner) public health worker; *b.* India?; *do.* T.W. & G. Gardiner; *e.* various schools in Punjab, Leighton House College Upper Norwood, Freeburg; *m.* W.J.A. Durrie Mulford, Assistant Secretary RSI; one daughter; *r.* reading, swimming; *a.* 7 Offington Drive, Worthing, Sussex.

Sanitary inspector and health visitor; certificates from the College of Preceptors and the Royal Sanitary Institute; one of the first health visitors in Birmingham and West Ham; worked for many years at Balham Day Nursery and Infant Welfare Centre; life member Child Study Society and Life Association, RSI; member WSIHVA; her chief interests were in public health work among women, peace, freedom; representative NCW on Public Health and Insurance Committee, 1923; involved in a campaign concerning sanitary arrangements for women at railway stations, 1923; attended NCW Conference, 1924; member NCW Public Health Committee, 1927.

s. Women's Who's Who, 1934–5.

ELIOTT-LYNN, Sophie Catherine Theresa Mary, ARCSc, FRGS (a.k.a. Lady Heath/Mrs Williams) (née Peirce-Evans) (10 November 1897–1939) aviator; *b.* Limerick, Ireland; *do.* John Peirce-Evans; *e.* Dublin University; *m.* Major W. Eliott-Lynn, 1918?, Sir James Heath, 1927, G.A.R. Williams, airman; *r.* tennis, motoring, archery; *c.* United Arts; *a.* c/o Kildonan Aerodrome, Finglas, County Dublin (1936).

Studied agriculture and intended to gain a diploma and take up farming in the colonies; took her degree at the Royal College of Science for Ireland; lectured on Agriculture at Aberdeen University; at the outbreak of WW1, enrolled for service, drove mechanical vehicles and became a dispatch rider for the RFC; an outstanding athlete, claimed the women's record for the high jump; one of the founders of the WAAA, 1922; liaised with women's societies to protect the interests of women and girls with regard to the establishment of the National Playing Fields Association; Vice President and Secretary WAAA and the Ladies' Athenaeum, 1922; member WES; 'discovered' flying when she was 22, had the private wealth to buy her own planes, went on to take her 'A' flying licence and become one of the first members of the London Aeroplane Club, 1925; attained her 'B' flying licence, being the first woman to gain such a licence since the war, 1926; encouraged aviation as a career for women by lecturing on the subject; made an attempt on the light-aeroplane height record and equalled the achievement of Lady Bailey of 17,283 feet, 1927; one of the speakers at the Equal Franchise Demonstration in Hyde Park, after a ceremonial flight over the procession, 1928; first woman to pilot a plane from Cape Town to London, 1928; assisted in the foundation of the Irish Aero Club, later becoming its Vice President, 1928; first 'English' woman to take up flying professionally, becoming a commercial pilot for KLM, acting as co-pilot on flights between Amsterdam, Paris and Croydon, 1929; another first was as the President of the Women's Aeronautical Federation; gave exhibitions of stunt flying, being the first woman aviator to 'loop the loop'; when in the USA for a flying and lecturing tour, had a serious flying accident in Cleveland, Ohio, and was unconscious for three days, 1929; test pilot and demonstrator for Cirrus Engines Inc, USA; Assistant Manager Ina National Airways, Dublin, 1933; President of the National Irish Junior Aviation Club, 1933; known by the NUSEC as 'a sturdy feminist' (*The Woman's Leader*, 6 September 1929); by 1936 she had amassed 2750 flying hours in 76 different types of aeroplane and glider; died prematurely from serious injuries she incurred in a fall from a London tram.

    p. Athletics for Women and Girls: How to be an Athlete and Why (1925); *Woman and Flying* (as Lady Heath, with Stella Wolfe Murray, 1929); articles on aviation for *The Woman Engineer*.

    s. Daily Telegraph, 10 May 1939; *The Times*, 10 May 1939; Boase (1979); Bank and McDonald (1998).

ELLIOTT, Dorothy Mary (Mrs J.D. Jones) BA, JP (1897–25 November 1980) trade unionist; *b.* Maidenhead; *e.* County Girls' School, Maidenhead, University College, Reading, London School of Economics.

    Both parents were teachers, her father Head of a Church of England Boys' School; won a scholarship to the University of Reading, where she was taught English by Prof. Edith Morley, a pioneer academic, and took an honours degree in Modern Languages; suffrage supporter; during WW1, when Elliott was unsure of how to support the war effort, Morley advised her to do munitions work; she went to work at Kynoch's in Aston, Birmingham and it was this experience that set her on her trade union career, 1916; stayed at the Women's University Settlement in Southwark while attending classes at the LSE taught by Prof. Tawney; she was introduced to the trade unionist Mary Macarthur (see entry) and was sent as an organizer for the NFWW to Woolwich Arsenal from 1918; organizer for the NUGMW, from 1921; worked as an organizer in Lancashire, 1924; in the absence of Margaret Bondfield (see entry) she became the NUGMW's Chief Woman organizer 1924–5 and again 1929–31; represented the union on a number of Trade Boards; Chairman of the National Labour Women's Conference, 1931; member SJCIWO; spoke at a WES meeting to encourage the need for closer cooperation between women professional and factory workers in order to improve their joint conditions of work, 1937; worked with the WEA and was a speaker at LP Women's Sections and the CWG; member of the Council and Executive Committee of Hillcroft Women's College; during WW2 she was a TUC representative member CWP; member Ministry of Labour's WCC, from 1941; awarded OBE, 1942; believed in married women's right to work; campaigned for equal pay; member of the TUC committee on double day-shift working and of the committee on the admission of women to the senior foreign service, 1945; member of the WCC on the resettlement of women in civilian life, 1945; granted leave of absence by the union to accept the Ministry of Labour's invitation to become Chairman of the Board of Directors of the NIH, 1946; attended ILO meetings in regard to domestic workers' conditions; visited Hamburg to meet with women trade unionists, 1947; retired from the NIH in 1957–8 and from all her commitments in 1961; she was deeply respected within her union.

    p. Women in Search of Justice (unpublished autobiography, TUC).

    s. LWW (1927); *GMW Journal*, December 1980; Summerskill (1989); Graves (1994); TUC Biographical Card Index.

EMMET, Hon. Evelyn Violet Elizabeth, Baroness Amberley (18 March 1899–10 October 1980) MP; *b.* Cairo; *do.* First Baron Rennell of Rodd & Lilias Guthrie; *e.* abroad, St Margaret's School, Bushey, Lady Margaret Hall, Oxford; *m.* T.A. Emmet, RN, 1923; two daughters, two sons; *a.* 3 Grosvenor Cottages, Eaton Terrace, London, Amberley Castle, Amberley, Sussex.

Member LCC, 1923–34; appointed JP, 1936; member West Sussex CC 1946–67; joint chairman of a committee established by R.A. Butler to investigate women's issues in preparation for the next general election, which reported on matters relating to the family and the housewife, 1949; Chairman Women's National Advisory Committee of the Conservative Party, 1952–4; first woman to be a full member of the British delegation to the UN, 1953; became an alderman, 1954; Chairman of the National Union of Conservative and Unionist Associations, 1955; entered Parliament as MP for safe seat of East Grinstead, 1955–64; voted for the abolition of the death penalty, 1956; together with Joyce Butler (see entry), as a representative of all women MPs, they put the case for the separate taxation of married women to the Financial Secretary to the Treasury (a married woman's earnings were added to that of her husband and he paid the tax for both), 1960; voted in favour of decriminalizing homosexual acts between consenting adults, 1960; vigorously supported Britain's entry into the Common Market, 1961; first woman to be elected as a Vice Chairman of the Conservative back bench Foreign Affairs Committee, 1963; member of the Joint Committee of the Peerage Bill, 1963; Emmet explained the wider significance of the Peerage Bill in that, at last, it enabled the UK to become a signatory to the United Nations Covenant on the Political Rights of Women, which had been adopted in 1952 when Emmet had been a delegate to the UN; awarded a life peerage, 1964; Chairman of Lord Chancellor's Legal Aid Advisory Committee, 1968–77; Dept.-Lieutenant for West Sussex, 1977.

s. Brookes (1967); Phillips (1980); Stenton and Lees, vol. 4 (1981); *Who Was Who*, vol. 7; Pugh (1992).

EMMOTT, Lady Mary Gertrude (Mrs Alfred Emmott, Baroness Emmott of Oldham) (née Lees) OBE, JP (1866–16 November 1954) welfare campaigner; *b.* Oldham; *do.* John William Lees, master cotton spinner & Elizabeth; *e.* Queen's College, London; *m.* Rt. Hon. Lord Alfred Emmott, Liberal MP, 1887; two daughters; *c.* Ladies' Empire; *a.* 30 Ennismore Gardens, London SW7 (1934).

With her husband as mayor, she was the Mayoress of Oldham, 1891–2; one of the original committee members of the Oldham branch and a lifelong supporter of the NSPCC, from 1891; the prime mover in initiating an NCW branch in Oldham, the first meeting took place at her home in 1897; as the first woman member, she was elected to the Oldham Board of Guardians, 1898; Vice Chairman WNLF; strong supporter suffrage movement; member Executive LSWS; member of the Executive Committee, President of the London Branch, Chairman NCW Parliamentary and Legislation Committee, from 1909 to the 1930s; represented the Women's Industrial Council on the Council of the National Association for Women's Lodging Homes, 1910; during WW1 she worked on behalf of Belgian refugees and was given Queen Elizabeth's Belgian medal; Executive Committee LNSWS; Chairman Women's Sub-Committee Advisory Council, Ministry of Reconstruction, 1918; member of the Housing Advisory Council, Ministry of Health; member of the Metropolitan War Savings Association; Chairman LSWS special General Meeting, May 1918; became a member of the WNLF executive, 1919; member of the Advisory Council to the Local Government Board on housing, 1919; one of the first women JPs; Governor of the Hulme Grammar School for Girls; National Liberal PPC Oldham, 1922; NCW representative at the AMSH Conference on Criminal Law Amendment Bill, 1922; Executive Committee LNSWS, 1923; member WES Advisory Council for the Conference of Women, 1925; acting Vice President NCW, 1927; President NCW, 1928–9; member, from its inauguration, of the BBC Appeals Advisory Committee choosing charities to make a Sunday-night appeal on BBC Radio; as President of the NCW she represented the interests of women's organizations on the Committee, 1927–38; President United Women's Homes Association, 1930s; President Oldham Women's Liberal Association, 1930s; member Women and Children Protection Society; member Garden Cities and Town Planning Association; member Royal Commission on Gambling and Lotteries, 1932–3; particularly interested in the welfare of young girls, supporting the London Council Welfare Women and Girls; President Fawcett Society, 1954; continued her relationship with the Oldham WCA throughout her life; she remained politically active, attending meetings until the penultimate year of her life; Marjory Lees, an Oldham feminist and friend, wrote of Emmott that she had 'great charm... ready sympathy... great public spirit and was also a wise counsellor' (*Oldham Evening Chronicle*, 23 November 1954); her estate totalled £7514.

   s. Census 1861, 3021, Folio 5; *List of Women Nominated for Service in Connection with the League of Nations* (NUWT Archive, nd 1920–21?); Glick (1925); Central Appeals Advisory Committee Minutes, 1927–39, BBC Written Archives Centre; *Aberdeen Press and Journal*, 3 June 1931; Hutchinson (1934); *The Lady's Who's Who*, 1938–39; *Oldham Evening Chronicle*, 2 May 1942; *The Times*, 26 November 1954; *Oldham Evening Chronicle*, 19 November, 23 November 1954, 3 March 1955; Bank and McDonald (1998); Oldham MBC Archives, D-Lee 134, items 8, 38.

EUSTACE, Violet (1875–?) artist; *b.* Wolseley Hall, Staffordshire; *do.* Admiral J.B. Eustace & Lady Katherine Eustace; *e.* Slade School of Art; *r.* travelling, reading; *c.* New Century, University Women's; *a.* Montague House, Wokingham, Berkshire (1913), 25 Bedford Gardens, London W8 (1919), c/o Rowley Gallery, Church Street, Kensington, London W8 (1934).

   Studied at the Slade 1901–02, 1903–04, 1918–19, gaining a Certificate in Drawing; Honorary Secretary NUWSS Wokingham branch; Vice Chair Ascot WSS and Press Secretary, Reading; Honorary Secretary NUWSS 1916–17; Secretary WIAC, 1922–4; member Society of Women Artists; exhibited at the Goupil Galleries, RBA, NEAC.

   p. Women Citizens' Association Handbook.
   s. Who's Who in Art, 1934; UCL Records.

EVANS, Dorothy, MA (1893–?) barrister and trade unionist; *b.* Stockport; *e.* Stockport National School, Stockport High School, Manchester University; *c.* PLC, Langbourn; *a.* 116 Belgrave Road, London SW1 (1927).

   Graduated with a second-class BA degree in History, 1915; gained her MA, 1916; Secretary AWKS, 1918–31; delegate and speaker at TUC, 1923; delegate at TUC participating in the insurance debate, 1924; delegate TUC Women's Conference, 1925; first LP woman to be called to the Bar, 1925; delegate Women's

Conference, spoke in support of the 'Resolution and Organization of Women', 1926; spoke at a meeting for LP PPC Mary Carlin (see entry), 1930; contested South Paddington seat for LP, 1929–30.

s. Daily Herald, 17 November 1925; *Labour Who's Who* (1927); University of Manchester Archives.

EVANS, Dorothy Elizabeth, MA (6 May 1889–28 August 1944) pioneer suffragette and socialist activist; *b.* London; *e.* North London Collegiate School, Dartford College, Chelsea Training College; unmarried, partner Albert Emil Davies, LCC councillor; one daughter, Lyndal; *r.* gardening; *a.* Redcap, Farnborough, Kent.

One of the outstanding women of the movement, regarded as a woman of genius, courage and kindness; matriculated in 1907; trained as a gymnastics teacher; joined WSPU, July 1907; left her teaching post to become a full-time WSPU Organizer and, when trained, was sent to organize Birmingham and Midland Counties, 1909; first arrested for attempting to confront a Cabinet Minister at a public meeting, 1909; first imprisoned for failing to pay dog tax as part of the 'No Taxation Without Representation' campaign and went to Winson Green jail, 1910; imprisoned a further nine times, she endured a great deal of physical suffering from repeated hunger strikes and brutal force-feeding; took part in the great West End window-smashing raid, 1912; liaised between London and Paris when Christabel Pankhurst was in hiding in Paris; in Ireland she was arrested for being in possession of explosives and conspiracy, 1913; kept on remand in various prisons in Ireland until 1914, when released under an amnesty; during WW1 she took a post as a gymnastics and mathematics teacher at Shrewsbury County School; the barbarity of the war made her a pacifist and she made speeches in the street for the pacifist cause, when she was attacked by the crowds; refused to register for a ration card and went hungry on many occasions; after the war she attempted to attend the Peace Conference, later going to the USA on a peace campaign, travelling on the Pax Special train; became a WIL organizer when she returned; post war WFL organizer; took part in WFL Nottingham campaign, during the LP conference, where she enrolled over 50 new WFL members, 1918; demanded the withdrawal of the CLA Bill, WFL meeting, 1918; supporter of legal rights for unmarried mothers; did not believe in marriage, believed in a woman's right to have children in or out of wedlock, having her own child as an unmarried mother; part of a deputation to the House of Lords, led by Women's Industrial League, demanding retraining for women; represented AWCS at CCWO, 1921; member of Drafting Committee CCWO, 1922; worked in her holidays in Geneva for Equal Rights Treaty at LN; Secretary WILPF, 1923; initiated the SPG sub-committee on housewives' issues, which became the MWA; contributed a memorandum to the 16th Assembly LN on all legal discriminations against women in Britain and the Dominions, which was incorporated into the World Report on the Status of Women; member Equal Pay Demonstration Committee, 1943; National Organizer WPPA for the WFW movement, 1944; author of the Equal Citizenship (Blanket) Bill, calling for the revision of over 30 English laws detrimental to women's equality, 1944; international speaker; attended the LN Geneva Assembly annually; worked and spoke for the US National Woman's Party; taken ill, operated on and died within two days in Glasgow; her enormous circle of devoted friends was shocked at her sudden death and many assessed that she had worn herself out in the service of justice and equality, the greatest loss to the cause for many years; a tribute was written and compiled by her long-standing friend, Monica Whately (see entry).

p. Land Nationalisation, the Key to Social Reform (with A.E. Davies, 1921); *Women and the Civil Service* (1934); *Equal Citizenship (Blanket) Bill* (WPPA, 1944); *June Dawn: A Comedy in Three Acts* (with J. Ware, 1949).

s. Women's Who's Who, 1913; *Hutchinson* (1934); *Daily Herald*, 29 August 1944; *Daily Telegraph*, 29 August 1944; *Manchester Guardian*, 6 September 1944; Whately (1945); NLCS Archive; Crawford (1999).

EVE, Lady Trustram (Fanny Jean Turing) (1864–1 February 1934) social reformer; *b.* Edwinstone, Notts?; *do.* Rev. John R. Turing; *m.* Sir Herbert Trustram Eve, rating and valuation expert, 1893; one daughter, three sons; *a.* 42 Bramham Gardens, London SW5 (1929).

During WW1, Chairman of the London and Middlesex Women's Land Army; Chairman Women's Agricultural Federation, 1918–19; a staunch Conservative, as Chairman Conservative Women's Reform Association, 1917–28; Chairman Mid-Beds Unionist Association, 1919–25; a prominent local government councillor, member LCC for North Hackney, 1919 and 1922; member of the Education Committee, 1919–31; President women's branch North Hackney Unionist Association, 1919–25; Chairman South Kensington WUA, 1923–9; represented South Kensington on the LCC 1925–31; became a magistrate, 1928; Vice Chairman Higher Education Committee, 1925; first woman to be appointed chairman of any council Committees; Chairman Local Government Committee, 1925–9; Chairman managing committee Bow Road Open-Air School, 1920–34; Honorary Treasurer NCW, 1921–31; spoke on housing of destitute women at NCW Conference, 1922; Chairman Kensington branch Infant Welfare, 1924–34; Vice President Council for Representation of Women in League of Nations, 1928; appointed Honorary Treasurer ICW, 1930; President NCW, 1933; active churchwoman, member London Diocesan Board of Education, 1921–34 and member National Assembly, 1925–30.

s. Daily Telegraph, 2 February 1934; *The Times*, 2 February 1934.

FAIRFIELD, Dr Josephine Letitia Denny, MD (Edin), DPH (Lon), ChB, CBE (10 March 1885–1 February 1978) barrister and doctor; *b.* Melbourne, Australia; *do.* Charles Fairfield, journalist & Isabella Campbell Mackenzie; *e.* Richmond High School, Edinburgh University, University College London; *c.* Emerson, Adelphi, Arts Theatre; *a.* Fairlie-hope, Chatham Close, Hampstead Garden Suburb, London NW11 (1913), 1 Raymond Buildings, Grays Inn, London WC1 (1934), 60 Beaufort Mansions, Beaufort Street, London SW3 (1978).

Sister of writer Rebecca West; attended Edinburgh Medical College for Women on a Carnegie Scholarship, winner of the Bathgate Memorial Prize Royal College Surgeons, Edinburgh, 1904; qualified, 1907; house surgeon Children's Hospital, 1909; assistant pathologist, Royal Asylum, Edinburgh, 1910; MD, 1911; DPH London, 1912; won several medals; Vice Chairman Executive Committee CLWS; Honorary Secretary Fabian Women's Group Suffrage Committee; Senior Medical Officer for the LCC, 1911–48; member of the Executive of the Fabian Society, since 1913; member FWG; joined the army and became Area Medical Controller QMAAC, 1917; transferred to RAF Medical Service in charge of the WRAF, 1918;

Chairman LCM; Lecturer to the RSI's National Council for Combating Venereal Disease; member Executive RSI; Lecturer to the National Association for the Care of the Mentally Defective; became a barrister, Middle Temple, 1919; Editor of *School Hygiene*; nominated for President WSIHVA, 1922; received into the Catholic Church, 1923; initially, her Catholic faith meant that she opposed all forms of birth control, however toward the end of her career she was supporting the campaign to get birth control accepted by the Catholic Church; member RSM; Fellow RSI; President LAMW, 1931–2; President London branch MWCF, 1930–32; senior woman doctor with the army during WW2, Lieutenant Colonel RAMC 1940–42; Assistant Director General War Office, first person to hold this post; it was due to her that the medical services for women in the army ran as smoothly as they did; she retired from this to return to the LCC, 1942; left the LCC, 1948; President Medico-Legal Society, 1957 and 1958; Papal Medal, 1966; an authority on witchcraft; although regarded as being dogmatic and difficult by some colleagues, she suffered a long, difficult illness with great courage.

p. Witchcraft in England (1925); *The Trial of Peter Barnes and Others* (1953); *Epilepsy* (1954); *The Trial of John Henry Straffan* (1954).

s. Women's Who's Who, 1913; List of Women Nominated for Service in Connection with the League of Nations (NUWT Archive, nd 1920–21?); *Hutchinson* (1934); *Who Was Who*, vol. 7; *British Medical Journal*, 11 February 1978; Bank and McDonald (1998); Glendenning (1998).

FAWCETT, Millicent Garrett, LLD (Honorary), GBE, JP (11 June 1847–5 August 1929) leader constitutional suffrage movement; *b.* Aldeburgh, Suffolk; *do.* Newson Garrett, merchant and shipowner & Louisa Dunnell; *e.* private girls' school, Blackheath; *m.* Rt. Hon. Henry Fawcett, Postmaster General, 1867; one daughter, Philippa (see entry); *r.* walking, needlework, music; *c.* Albemarle, University of London; *a.* 2 Gower Street, London WC1 (1929).

Inspired by her elder sister, Elizabeth Garrett Anderson, pioneering doctor and her friend, Emily Davies, the pioneering educationalist; she was educated at a Miss Browning's school in Blackheath for only three years, her education being supplemented by the intellectual and political debate of her home; acted as secretary to her blind husband, who was a Cambridge professor and Liberal MP, mixing with political colleagues such as John Stuart Mill; joined the first women's suffrage group, the London Suffrage Committee, in 1867; campaigned for the Married Women's Property Act; involved in the establishment of Newnham College; participated in work with the Vigilance Association, from 1885; joined the Liberal Unionists, 1887–1903; active in Ireland, making speeches opposing Home Rule, 1887–95; elected President NUWSS, 1897–1919; travelled to South Africa, to lead a women's commission to investigate Boer War concentration camps, 1901; received an honorary LLD from St Andrew's University, 1905; elected first Vice President IWSA, 1913; encouraged participation of Women's Movement in relief work of WW1 in order to prove their competence for the vote and to promote women's interests; member delegate of women to the Peace Congress, Paris, 1919; member parliamentary committee to open the legal profession to women; sustained her campaigning throughout the 1920s; made DBE, 1925; her tenacity and hard work for the cause were legion; died in London having lived long enough to see her lifetime's ambition for equal suffrage achieved.

b: born; do: daughter of; e: education; m: married; r: recreation;
c: club; a: address; p: publications; s: sources

p. Political Economy for Beginners (1870); *Essays and Lectures on Social and Political Subjects* (with Henry Fawcett, 1872); *Janet Doncaster* (1875); *Tales in Political Economy* (1875); *Some Eminent Women of Our Time* (1889); *Life of Queen Victoria* (1895); *Home and Politics* (1898); *Life of Sir William Molesworth* (1901); *Five Famous French Women* (1906); *Women's Suffrage* (1912); *Women's Victory and After* (1919); *What I Remember* (1924); *Easter in Palestine* (1926); *Josephine Butler: Her Work and Principles and Meaning for the Twentieth Century* (with E.M. Turner, 1928); numerous articles in political and suffrage journals and papers, starting with 'The Lectures for Women in Cambridge' in *Macmillan's Magazine* (1868).

s. Dictionary of National Biography, 1922–30; *Who's Who*, 1929; Strachey (1931); Crawford et al. (1983); Banks (1985); *Penguin Biographical Dictionary of Women* (1998).

FAWCETT, Philippa Garrett (1868–10 June 1948) suffragist and educationalist; *do.* Henry Fawcett, Postmaster General & Millicent Garrett Fawcett, women's suffrage leader (see entry); *e.* Newnham College, Cambridge; *a.* 2 Gower Street, London WC1 (1929), 50 Lyttelton Court, Finchley, London N2 (1948).

On graduation she was the only woman mathematician ever to be classed above Senior Wrangler by 400 marks in the Mathematics tripos, 1890; however, she could not be awarded her degree until the year of her death; accompanied her mother on the Government Ladies' Commission to the Transvaal, South Africa, to inspect conditions in the concentration camps after the Boer War, 1901; she returned to the Transvaal as Private Secretary to the Director of Education, to work on establishing public elementary education, 1902; first woman to be employed as a civil servant by the LCC as Principal Assistant in the Higher Education Branch of the Education Officers' Department, 1905; engaged on the development of secondary education; Assistant Education Officer, 1920; became, temporarily, the Principal of Avery Hill Training College, when its principal was taken ill; with her excellent administrative ability she reorganized the college and ensured its survival, 1907–08; retired, 1934; Shorney regards her as 'perhaps the greatest woman to serve the cause of education in London this century'; a training college was named after her by the LCC in 1949.

p. Memorandum on the Position of English Women in Relation to That of English Men (1935).

s. Strachey (1931); *The Times*, 12 June 1948; *Daily Telegraph*, 12 June 1948; *The Times*, 16 June 1948; *The Catholic Citizen*, 15 September 1948; Shorney (1989).

FRAMPTON, Rosina M.; trade unionist; *m.* James W. Pearson, 1928.

Leading Railway Clerks' Association activist; she joined the RCA, 1915; attended her first RCA conference, 1917; delegate Women's Conference, spoke on organization of women, 1926; delegate from South London branch to RCA Women's Conference, moving a resolution that women members be allocated a seat on the Executive Committee, 1926; at the above conference, she was appointed as member to the National Women's Organizing Committee to initiate propaganda campaigns for increasing women's participation in the Union; retired in order to marry, 1928.

s. Railway Service Journal, January 1927, July 1928; Wallace (1996).

FRANKLIN, Hon. Mrs Ernest (Netta) (née Hon. Henrietta Montagu), CBE (9 April 1866–7 January 1964) education and religious reformer; *b.* London; *do.* First Lord Swaythling, Samuel Montagu & Ellen Cohen; *e.* private, Doreck College, King's College for Ladies; *m.* Ernest Louis Franklin, 1885; two daughters, four sons; *r.* reading, nature study, gardening; *c.* Pioneer, Lyceum, ESU; *a.* 9 Pembridge Gardens, London W2 (1885), 50 Porchester Terrace, London W2 (1898), Glenalla House, Rathmullen, Donegal, Ireland (1913), 88 Carlton Hill, London NW8 (1953).

From an orthodox Jewish family; as a child she insisted on learning algebra and Latin like her brothers; passed the Senior Cambridge and the College of Preceptors examinations; attended classes at King's under Miss Lily Faithful; her father endorsed his support of women's suffrage to the Liberal Council, 1885; her belief was that women should '*cesser d'être poupées*' (stop being like puppets); Honorary Organizing Secretary PNEU since 1890; Chairman of the Pioneer Club's Debates Committee; the Porchester Terrace house became known as 'The Henrietta Arms' as she welcomed refugees, political groups and others to stay and meet there – the Indian woman poet Sarojini Naidu and Paul Robeson were two famous guests; she was involved with her sister, Lily, in the instigation of Liberal Judaism in England, from 1902; a feminist who employed women wherever possible, she was Chairman of the NUWSS; her PNEU work led her to give lectures on the training of citizens; early member of the NCW; member Executive Committee NCW, from 1909; NCW delegate to the conference of the ICW, 1909; when she had to have her leg amputated, she insisted that the operation be carried out by a woman doctor, Louise Aldrich Blake, assisted by two other women, 1909; Convenor of International Sectional Committee, NCW; representative for NCW on International Commission for Education; Vice President, then first Jewish President NCW, 1927; NCW delegate at ICW meetings; Vice President NUSEC, 1927; Board of Management Liberal Jewish Synagogue; Chairman NCEC; member executive NUGC and NCEC, 1931; member WIL; member Women's Advisory Council, LNU; very involved with assisting German refugees from 1933 onwards; lecturer on educational and social issues; made a CBE, 1950; founder member of the Liberal Jewish Synagogue and member of its Advisory Committee; lectured on educational and social issues throughout Europe, South Africa, Canada and America; worked for the PNEU; founded the PNEU schools for girls, Overstone in Northampton and a preparatory boys' school, Desmoor; Chairman NCEC; Vice Chairman South London Hospital; close friends included Elizabeth Cadbury (see entry), Lady Aberdeen (see entry), Millicent Fawcett (see entry), Maude Royden (see entry) and Lady Francis Balfour (see entry); her biographer has written that 'Netta was born to direct and explore… a tornado of energy and high endeavour'; died at home.

p. pamphlets and articles on education issues for magazines and newspapers, including *The Parents' Review.*

s. List of Women Nominated for Service in Connection with the League of Nations (NUWT Archive, nd 1920–21?); *LWW* (1938–9); *Who Was Who*, vol. 4, 6; Gibbon (1960); Bank and McDonald (1998).

FRASER, Helen, political activist and suffrage worker; *e.* Glasgow; *c.* Forum; *a.* 191 Cromwell Road, London SW5 (1922?), 6 Kensington Park Gardens, London W11 (1927).

A specialist in women's legal position, particularly interested in national and international finance; a well-known suffragist before WW1 and continued to lecture on women's sweated labour and the vote during WW1; member NUWSS; Commissioner National War Savings Committee during WW1; part of the British War Mission to USA and Canada, 1917–18; on the ESU Committee; member of the Council for the Representation of Women in the LN; member of the British Institute of International Affairs; member Executive Committee NUSEC; lecture tours to US and Canada, 1920 and 1923; PPC as a Coalition Liberal, for Govan Glasgow, 1922, as a Liberal, Hamilton Lanark, 1923, and as a Liberal, Kelvingrove by-election, 1924; member AMSH, 1923; resigned from the Liberal Party and joined the Unionist Party, 1925; elected as a member of Kensington Borough Council, 1925; LNSWS representative to BCL Conference, speaking on 'The Educated Woman', 1926; NUSEC delegate IAWSEC Paris Congress, 1926; present at the initial meeting of the ODC, 1926; British representative on the Industrial Committee, IWSA; member Professional and Business Women's Hospital league; awarded 'special thanks for all her speaking' in the NUSEC Annual Report, 1926; one of the 11 members of NUSEC who resigned from the Executive Committee over the issue of protective legislation, 1927; member NUSEC sub-committee on Trade and Commerce; Executive Committee member ODC, 1927–30; British representative at the first international Conference of Business and Professional Women, Geneva, 1930.

p. *Women and War Work* (1918).

s. *Grimsby Daily Telegraph*, 14 May 1914; *List of Women Nominated for Service in Connection with the League of Nations* (NUWT Archive, nd 1920–21?); Gates (1924); Bank and McDonald (1998).

FRIEL, Dr Sophia Seekings, MD, BS, DPH (3 December 1873–17 July 1954) maternity and child welfare campaigner; b. Gloucester; do. Joseph John Seekings, engineer & Mary; e. Girls' Endowed School, Girls' Church High, Gloucester Municipal Schools, LSMW; m. Alfred Richard Friel, MD; c. ESU; a. 15 Woodside Ave, London N6 (1934), Sidmouth, Devon (1940).

Came from a Quaker family; when qualified she worked for the development of a state medical service and to this end pioneered projects with Tottenham Council as School Medical Officer and Assistant Medical Officer of Health, 1908; put forward the idea for a school for mothers, 1911; she and Jessy Kent-Parsons (see entry) rented a house in an area with the highest infant mortality rate and opened the school, 1912; one of the first Maternity and Child Welfare Inspectors, Local Government Board; Honorary Secretary National Baby Welfare Council; member RSI; member FMW; Vice President WSIHVA, 1918–19; Vice President and Trustee WSIHVA over 30 years; Trustee of WSI, 1923; member Health and Cleanliness Council; HCC delegate to WSIHVA Conference, 1928; member Association Women Panel Practitioners, 1934; all her public appointments terminated on her marriage.

p. *The Baby* (1918).

s. LSMW application form, 1900, RFH Archive; 'Tottenham Maternity and Child Welfare Work', Mrs J. Kent-Parsons' papers, Archives of HVA, Wellcome Institute, SA/HVA/G.2/1; *Journal of the Medical Women's Federation*, October 1954.

b: born;   do: daughter of;   e: education;   m: married;   r: recreation;   **65**
c: club;   a: address;   p: publications;   s: sources

FROUD, Ethel Elizabeth (11 April 1880–21 May 1941) teacher and women's rights activist; *b.* Loose, Maidstone; *do.* George Christopher Froud, butcher & Frances Danells; *a.* The Willows, Loose, Kent (birth).

WSPU activist 1907–14; instrumental in forming the West Ham Women Teachers' Association within the NUT branch, 1912; the West Ham women then joined the NFWT and Froud became Honorary Secretary and Treasurer of the NFWT, 1913–17; as the work of the union developed it reqired a full-time official and Froud gave up her teaching job to become the first General Secretary NUWT from 1917; one of a lobby group to the President of the Board of Trade on equal pay, 1920; gave evidence to the Departmental Committee on the training of teachers, 1924; stood unsuccessfully as a Labour candidate in the London Borough elections, 1925; organizer of a joint deputation to the prime minister on equal political rights, 1927; member Equal Rights General Election Campaign, 1929; led the deputation to Ramsay MacDonald with Margery Corbett-Ashby (see entry), 1929; member Executive Committee ODC, from 1927; died in Brighton; 'a brilliant platform speaker, an incisive writer on feminist subjects… the greatest asset the Union has ever possessed' (Phipps).

s. Phipps (1928); Kean (1990); Oram (1996).

GLASIER, Katherine Bruce BA (née St John Conway) 'Fighting Kate' (25 September 1867–14 June 1950) socialist activist; *do.* Rev. Samuel Conway, Congregational preacher and Amy Curling; *e.* High School for Girls, Hackney Down, Newnham College, Cambridge; *m.* John Bruce Glasier, editor *Labour Leader*, ILP National Council/Chair and writer, 1895; one girl, two boys; *a.* Glen Cottage, Earby by Colne, Lancashire (1927).

Educated at home by her mother up to the age of 10; BA Hons Classics, 1889; Senior Classics Mistress, Redland High School, Bristol; friend of the Pankhursts; after witnessing a demonstration of low-paid women workers she became a socialist, 1890; member Bristol Socialist Society, c.1893; not finding revolutionary socialism to her taste she joined the Fabian Society; changed jobs to work in a Board School in a working-class district of Bristol; left this post to become a Fabian lecturer; contributor to the *Workingman's Times*; attended TUC Congress, 1892; speaker for the ILP and SDF, 1893; only woman organizer ILP Arrangements Committee, 1893; only woman co-founder and member ILP NAC, 1893; member committee of six to summon first ILP Conference, Bradford, 1983; spellbinding lecturer and public speaker; assisted husband to edit *Labour Leader*, 1904–09; as 'Iona', edited the women's column of the *Labour Leader*, 1906–09; founder member WLL; member Executive Committee WLL, 1907–18; in line with her Socialism she believed in adult suffrage, although she wrote a pamphlet (unpublished), '*Why Working Women Want the Vote*'; contributed to the *League Leaflet* and to *The Labour Woman*, after 1913; supported nursery school movement, miners' pit head baths, old-age homes, school means, SCF; Editor *Labour Leader*, 1916–21; nursing her husband, his death and overwork caused a nervous breakdown, 1921; became a Quaker and member of the Theosophical Society; delegate Labour Women's Conference moved a resolution against imperialism, 1927; National ILP propagandist, 1927; according to Ellen Wilkinson, Glasier was known as 'dear saint of the Women's Movement'; involved in rebuilding the LP after the 1931 election defeat, supported the LP when the ILP split from the Party, 1932; with Lucy Middleton, became a 'goodwill ambassador' for the LP on extensive speaking tours, 1935; columnist for *Northern Voice*; limited her travelling because of age and caring for her sister, late 1930s and 1940s.

p. Husband and Brother: A Few Chapters in a Woman's Life of Today (1894); *Aimee Furniss, Scholar* (1896); *Tales from the Derbyshire Hills* (1907); *Marget: A Twentieth-Century Novel* (serialized in *The Weekly Times* and *Echo* 21 September 1902–1 March 1903); *The Glen Book* (1948); pamphlets – *Socialism and the Home* (1908); *Enid Stacey, a Commemorative Souvenir*; *The Road to Socialism*; *Baths at the Pithead and the Works* (1912); *National Old-Age Homes* (1914); *The Price of War* (1916); *Socialism for Beginners* (1929); *Socialism for Children* (nd); *The Cry of the Children* (nd); *Eglantyne Jebb and the World's Children* (nd); *Margaret MacMillan and Her Life Work* (nd); *National Homes for Disabled Soldiers and Sailors and the Ages* (nd); *The Religion of Socialism: Two Aspects* (with Bruce Glasier, nd).

s. The Glasier Papers, Sydney Jones Library, University of Liverpool; *Labour Who's Who* (1924 and 1927); Thompson (1971); Collette (1989); Banks (1990).

GODWIN, Beatrice Anne, DBE (6 July 1897–11 January 1992) trade unionist; *b.* Farncombe, Surrey; *e.* British School, Godalming; *a.* Worcester Park, Surrey (1963).

Left school at 15 to work as a counting house-clerk in a West End store, working long hours for poor wages; at this time she became a suffragette; worked as a civilian clerk for the Army Pay Office, from 1916; involved in a deputation to get increased wages for the women workers where all they received was an aggressive rebuff; this incident prompted her union activism; after the war, when women over 18 won the right to vote, Godwin was a leading figure in the YS's vigorous attempts for franchise extension; a Fabian; she joined the AWKS, 1920; became an organizer for AWKS, 1928; activist in the NJCWWO from 1931; became AGS AWKS, 1941; elected member TUC GC, 1949–68; devised the ILO's Convention 100 concerning equal pay for work of equal value, 1951 (not ratified by Britain until 1971); when the AWKS merged with the NUC to become CAWU (later APEX), she remained as AGS; OBE, 1952; Chairman TUC WAC from 1952; became General Secretary of a mixed union in 1956–62; concerned with improving the educational opportunities for women clerical staff as part of her overall interest in extending educational opportunities to all sectors of society; President TUC, 1961–2; DBE, 1962; retired from the TUC GC in 1963; during retirement she became member of the editorial board of the Labour paper, *Socialist Commentary*; founder member of the SDP because she believed militant were taking over the LP; member of the CACE and signatory to the Crowther Report; worked for the Mary Macarthur (see entry) educational trust to provide opportunities for working women; BBC Governor, 1962–8; full-time member of the Industrial Court, 1963–9; lived with her sister during retirement; she was regarded as passionate and humorous with a 'sunny' personality, but formidable in negotiations.

s. Daily Telegraph, 12 January 1992; *Independent*, 13 January 1992; *The Times*, 13 January 1992; *Guardian*, 20 January 1992.

GOODERED, Gladys (née Rogers) AA, CMB, SIEB; public health officer; *do.* Walter T. Rogers, FRSL & Elizabeth Mary Hall; *e.* private; *m.* Kaimakam Goodered Bey; two sons; *r.* tennis, theatre; *a.* 58 Pathfield Road, London SW16 (1934).

Secretary Marylebone Skilled Employment Committee, 1910–12; one of the first women Pension Officers, 1917–23; Pastime Supervisor and House Visitor, MSB, 1924–33; life member WPHOA; Certificate of the College of Teachers of Blind; member LSWS Employment of Married Women Committee, 1923, 1925–8; NCW Housing Committee, 1928; Honorary Secretary NCW Cooperation Sub-Committee, 1928.

s. Women's Who's Who, 1934–5.

GORDON, Ishbel Maria Gordon, Marchioness of Aberdeen and Temair (née Marjoribanks) GBE, LLD, JP (14 March 1857–18 April 1939) women's rights campaigner and philanthropist; *b.* London; *do.* Sir Dudley Coutts Marjoribanks, later first Lord Tweedmouth & Isabella Hogg; *e.* private; *m.* John Campbell Gordon, Marquess of Aberdeen and Temair, Liberal politician, 1877; two daughters, three sons; *r.* Skye terriers and Persian cats; *c.* Lyceum, Ladies' Empire, English-Speaking Union, Aberdeen Town and County; *a.* 58 Grosvenor Street, London W1 (1906), House of Cromar, Tarland, Aberdeenshire (1920–21), 9 Ely Place, Dublin (1929), Camphill House, Milltimker, Aberdeenshire (1934), Gordon House, Rubislaw Den North, Aberdeen (1939).

Educated by governesses and later attended some classes in London; her family background consisted of intermarriage with Irish and French families; a sense of social responsibility together with religious faith was instilled in her by her mother; in addition to her work for women, she shared other philanthropic educational projects with her husband, such as the Onward and Upward Association, an educational and recreational project on their Scottish estate; their home was known for its generous hospitality; President of the Canning Town Women's Settlement, 1890; freedom of the City of Limerick conferred in 1894; President ICW, 1893–9, 1904–20, 1922–36; Vice President ICW 1899–1904; President of the Lyceum Club; Chairman Scottish Committee for Women's Training and Employment; while her husband was Governor General of Canada, she became the founder and President NCW of Canada, 1893–8; founder and first President Victorian Order of Nurses in Canada, 1898; became involved in work with Irish women during her husband's term as Lord Lieutenant, 1906–15; founded and became President Women's National Health Association of Ireland, which carried out pioneering work for mother and child welfare, 1907; President Irish Industries Association, Civic Institute of Ireland; in conjunction with the Conference of Women Suffragists, she organized a deputation to the LN Commission of Peace Conference, 1919; this deputation obtained the promise of a clause opening the League's offices to women; one of the first women to become a JP, 1919; President WLF in England, the SWLF and WIC; chaired the Education and Propaganda session at the first International Child Welfare Congress, Geneva, 1925; given the freedom of the City of Edinburgh, 1928; awarded an LLD from Queen's University, Canada and Aberdeen, 1929; awarded GBE, 1931; recognition of the scale of her contribution to the organization was made at the Jubilee celebrations of the ICW in Edinburgh, 1938; died in Aberdeen and was buried in the cemetery at Haddo House.

p. Ireland's Crusade Against Tuberculosis (3 vols, 1908); *Through Canada with a Kodak* (with Lord Aberdeen); *We Twa* (1925); *More Cracks with We Twa* (1929); *The Musings of a Scottish Granny* (1936); edited Transactions of the ICW (1899–1909, 1914, 1920, 1925, 1930).

b: born; do: daughter of; e: education; m: married; r: recreation; c: club; a: address; p: publications; s: sources

s. The Roll of Honour for Women (1906); *List of Women Nominated for Service in Connection with the League of Nations* (NUWT Archive, nd 1920–21?); *Who's Who*, 1929; *Women's Who's Who, 1934–5*; *The Lady's Who's Who*, 1938–9; *Dictionary of National Biography*, 1931–40; *Who Was Who*, vol. 3; Crawford et al. (1983).

GOULD, Barbara Bodichon Ayrton, JP (1886–c14 October 1950) politician and social reformer; *do*. Prof. W.E. Ayrton, FRS & Hertha Ayrton MIEE, engineer and inventor (stepsister to Edith Ayrton (see entry), married to Israel Zangwill); *e*. Notting Hill High, and UCL; *m*. Gerald Gould, writer and journalist, 1910; one son; *a*. 1 Hamilton Terrace, St John's Wood, London NW8 (1934), 54 St Mary's Mansions, London W2, 76 Belsize Park Gardens, London NW3 (1938).

On leaving school, joined the LP; along with her mother, she became a WSPU member, 1906; rode at the head of a suffragette procession dressed as Joan of Arc; WSPU Organizer, 1912–14; suffered imprisonment; as a result of her leading part in the militancy campaign, she fled to France to avoid recapture, 1913; one of the founders and Honorary Organizing Secretary US, 1914–18; Honorary Secretary Women's Advisory Council; worked at WILPF's HQ during WW1; leading member 1917 Club; Honorary Secretary WIL, 1918–19; organized WILPF's collection of rubber teats for Germany, 1918; executive member Fight the Famine Fund; member ILP, Fabian Society; joined the NFWW at the end of the war; Executive Committee NPC; publicity manager *Daily Herald*, 1919–21; LCC School Manager three County Schools in South London, 1921–4; member SPG; voluntary worker NUGMW, 1922–32?; Organizing Secretary National Council Lunacy Reform, 1921–3; Labour PPC North Lambeth, 1922, Northwich, 1924, 1929, 1931, Hulme Division Manchester, 1935, Norwood Division Lambeth, 1935; Vice President SPG, c.1921–2; member Executive Committee NUSEC, 1926; helped organize national transport for the TUC during the General Strike, 1926; subsequently ran the Relief Committee for Miners' Wives and Children during the miners' lockout, 1926; could not stand for re-election because of pressure of work, 1927; sat on the Royal Commission on Civil Service, 1929–31; member Executive Committee LP 1926–7, 1929–50; Chairman LP Executive Committee, 1939–40; member SJCIWO; Chair SJCIWO, 1932–3; representative NUGMW on main committee Court of Referees and Board of Assessors of Borough Labour Exchange; acting Chief Woman Officer, LP, 1932; member LP Distressed Area Commission, 1936–7; Vice Chairman LP, 1938; led a LP delegation to Republican Spain, 1938; Chair LP, 1939–40; finally became Labour MP, Hendon North, 1945–50; after losing her seat, announced that due to ill health she would not contest it again; Honorary Secretary Parliamentary Committee MPs and Suffragists; member Arts Council; Vice Chairman British Council, 1948; JP for St Marylebone; Chair Workers' Film Association; regarded as one of the most outstanding women leaders in the LP.

p. numerous press articles on social, political and economic issues.

s. The Lady's Who's Who, 1938–9; *Daily Herald*, 16 October 1950; *Daily Telegraph*, 16 October 1950; *Manchester Guardian*, 16 October 1950; *The Times*, 16 October 1950; Stenton and Lees, vol. 4 (1981); Banks (1990).

GRIFF, Cleone de Heveningham B., AMIAE; *c.* Efficiency, Lyceum; *r.* breeding bulldogs, fencing; *a.* Wildwood, Hill Village, Four Oaks, Warwickshire (1921).

Certificate from LBE and LC&G in Motor Engineering; during WW1 she was a Government Aircraft Inspector with Messrs Vickers; member Birmingham Metallurgical Society, c.1918; member WES; first woman AMIAE, 1920; first woman to have the RAC Mechanical Proficiency Certificate; worked for a large firm of engineers in the Midlands on materials, 1920; elected to Iron and Steel Institute and Cast Iron Research Association, 1921; Director and majority shareholder of the Stainless Steel and Non-Corrosive Metal Company, Birmingham, a pioneer manufacturer in high-quality stainless steel and chrome metals and goods, founded in 1923; WES representative on EAW Council; Chair WES, 1923; read a paper on the commercial use and working of stainless steel to the Conference of Engineering Societies, Wembley, 1924; chaired the Engineering, Chemical and Research Session at the International Conference of Women, 1925; gave four talks on different aspects of 'Engineering as a Career for Women' on *Woman's Hour* for BBC Radio Birmingham, starting in December 1925; member of Birmingham Metallurgical Society; she was a qualified pilot and started a column, 'Aviation Notes' in *The Woman Engineer* from 1927; the first woman technical contributor to the motor press.

p. 'The Working of Stainless Steel', *Foundry Trade Journal* (25 September 1924).

s. Journal of the Iron and Steel Institute, civ/2 (1921); *JISI* (1911–1921), index, (1924), ii.

GWYNNE-VAUGHAN, Prof. Dame Helen Charlotte Isabella DSc, DBE, GBE, Hon LLD, FLS (née Fraser) (21 January 1879–26 August 1967) academic; *b.* Westminster, London; *do.* Capt. Hon. Arthur H.D. Fraser, Scots Guards & Lucy Jane Fergusson; *e.* privately by governesses, Thurloe Square School, Kensington, Cheltenham Ladies' College, King's College University of London; *m.* Prof. D.T. Gwynne-Vaughan, palaeobotanist, 1911; *r.* reading; *c.* University of London, Ex-Service Women's; *a.* 93 Bedford Court Mansions, London WC1 (1929), Sussexdown, Storrington, West Sussex (1964).

Left school and had her society 'coming-out' in 1896; had to fight her family in order to continue her studies; became involved in Working Girls' Clubs in Camberwell and Peckham, 1898 onwards; studied for the Oxford Entrance examination at the Ladies' Department, King's College, London, 1899; continued with her studies in Zoology and Botany at King's College proper; Carter Medallist, King's College, 1902; BSc Hons Botany, 1904; Temporary Assistant, Department Botany, British Museum, 1903–05; Demonstrator in Botany, Royal Holloway College, 1905; Assistant Lecturer, 1906–07; DSc (Lon), 1907; women's suffrage supporter, speaking on women's suffrage; active canvasser for women's rights within the Academy, especially vigilant on the issue of equal pay; Lecturer in Botany, University College, Nottingham, 1907–09; Honorary Secretary Infant Welfare Centre, Nottingham, 1908–09; Head of Department Botany, Birkbeck College, University of London, 1909–17; Examiner in Botany, University of Aberdeen, 1912–16; member Council West Islington Infant Welfare; Chief Controller QMAAC, British armies in France, 1917–18; Commandant WRAF, 1918–19; CBE awarded, 1918; DBE, 1919; resumed her post at Birkbeck, 1920; member Home Office Committee Employment of Women in the Police, 1920 and 1924; Trail

Medal of Linnaean Society for research on protoplasm, 1920; Professor of Botany, Birkbeck, 1921; asked to stand for the LCC, North Camberwell, by the Women's Section of the London Municipal Society, but was not elected, 1922; Unionist PPC Camberwell North West, 1922–3; member Board of Trade Committee on Lace, Embroidery and Silk Industries, 1923; member Committee Food Prices, 1924; member Board of Trade Committee Lace and Embroidery to safeguard the trade, 1925, and of the Worsted Committee, 1926; President British Mycological Society, 1928; President Section K (Botany), British Association, 1928; speaker Equal Franchise Demonstration, Hyde Park, 1928; awarded GBE, 1929; member University of London Senate, 1929–34; Chief Controller ATS, 1939–41; returned to Birkbeck, 1941–4; Emeritus Professor of Botany, Birkbeck College, 1944; during retirement she maintained her service links with work as the Honorary County Secretary of the London branch of the SSAFA; gave up her work at SSAFA, 1962; moved to the RAF Convalescent home, 1964; died in her sleep.

p. Fungi (1922); *Structure and Development of the Fungi* (with B. Barnes, 1927); *Service with the Army* (1942); *The Junior Leader* (1943); numerous papers on cytology and mycology in *Annals of Botany* and other periodicals.

s. Who's Who, 1929; *The Times*, 30 August 1967; *Who Was Who*, 1961–70; Izzard (1969).

HADOW, Grace Eleanor, MA Oxon. (9 December 1875–19 January 1940) academic; *b.* South Cerney, Gloucester; *do.* Rev. William Elliott Hadow & Mary Lang Cornish; *e.* at home, Brownshill Court, Stroud, Truro High School, Somerville, Oxford; *r.* climbing, travel, gardening, walking; *c.* University Women's; *a.* St Ermin's Hotel, London SW1 (1920–21), 1 Jowett Walk, Oxford (1934), 7 Fyfield Road, Oxford (1936), Musgrave House, 1 South Parks Road, Oxford (1937).

Her family's poverty meant that she was initially taught by her mother at home; at 12 she went to Cirencester once a week for French, German, music and drawing lessons, with mathematics from a teacher in South Cerney; gained a scholarship to board at Brownshill Court, near Stroud, where she was a boarder from 13 to 15; at 16 she entered Truro High School, 1891–4; subsequently she travelled to Germany, boarding with a family where she took lessons, 1895–6; took up a junior teaching post at Cheltenham Ladies' College, 1899; attended lectures for her teacher training given by an Oxford don and was encouraged to sit the Women's First, English School, Oxford, 1899; passed the Cambridge Higher Local, 1900; attended Somerville, taking first-class honours School English Language and Literature, 1903; formed friendships with Mrs H.A.L. Fisher and Helen Darbishire, 1901–03; President OUWSS; took her degree, qualifying for her MA retrospectively, 1922; Reader in English, Bryn Mawr, US, 1903–04; English tutor, Somerville, 1904–06; resident English tutor, Lady Margaret Hall, 1906–11; she became a visiting lecturer two days a week only in order to care for her invalid mother, 1911–17; Honorary Secretary NUWSS Cirencester branch, 1912; Honorary Secretary CUWFA, Cirencester branch; involved in local war work with Belgian refugees, Cirencester, 1914; elected member Gloucestershire Chamber of Agriculture, 1916; President and chief speaker at the establishment of Cirencester Women's Institute, 1916; served in the Ministry of Munitions and Agriculture, Director of a sub-section of the Welfare Department for Women Munitions Workers, 1917–19; expert in rural reconstruction and village social work, which eminently suited her to her role in the NFWI; transferred to Ministry of Labour after the Armistice; Vice Chair NFWI, 1918; Secretary of Barnett House, Oxford, an information centre on economic and social questions for adult education, 1919–29; representative at CCWO, 1921; member of Drafting Committee Meeting CCWO, 1922; appointed to serve on the Rural Industries Bureau, 1923–36; served on the Hadow Committee inquiry into the place of adult education in broadcasting, 1927; involved with BBC Radio in several capacities, contributing scripts, from 1928 to 1933; gave a talk on the 21st Anniversary of the NFWI, July 1937; President Women's Employment Federation, 1934; Principal, Society of Oxford Home Students, later St Anne's, 1929–40; while at Oxford Home Students, was a member of Hebdomadal Council, Councillor Barnett House, Extra-Mural delegacy, member General Advisory Council BBC, representing Social Services, 1934–40; Adult Education Committee Board of Education, Executive Member NCSS and NFWI; an original member of the Hadow Committee on educational broadcasting; an NFWI representative member of the executive of the Central Council for Broadcasting for Adult Education; member Oxford County Education Committee; member Executive Committee National Council for Social Service; woman delegate to the second conference on the British Commonwealth Relations, Australia, 1938; President NFWI 1939–40; regarded as among one of the best women speakers in the country and as a great Principal at Oxford; died from pneumonia.

p. ed. *The Oxford Treasury of English Literature* (with W. Hadow, 1906); ed. *Essays on Addison* (1907); ed. *Selections from Dryden* (1908); ed. *Browning's Men and Women* (1911); ed. *Ideals of Living* (1911); translated *Litzmann's Life of Clara Schumann* (1913); *Chaucer and His Times* (1914); ed. *Sir Walter Raleigh, Selections from His Histoire of the World, His Letters, etc.* (1917).

s. Courtney (1934); *The Times*, 22 January 1940; Deneke (1946); *Women's Who's Who, 1934–5.*

HALPIN, Kathleen Mary (19 November 1903–4 January 1999) feminist and public servant; *e.* Sydenham Girls' High School.

Left school in 1922; lived in France for a year after leaving school; took a secretarial course and worked as an editorial assistant latterly at *The Architect's Journal*, where she developed an interest in social housing, which led to her involvement in the formation of the Soroptimist Housing Trust in Wandsworth; Honorary Secretary of the Junior Council of the LNSWS, 1926; campaigned for educational, employment and political equality throughout her lifetime of activity in the Women's Movement; Chair of the FS and a trustee and Friend of the Fawcett Library; she worked as private secretary to Sir John Simon, Foreign Secretary in the early 1930s; Organizing Secretary WGC in the 1930s; a party to the origination of the WVS in 1938; became WVS Chief Administrator (Regions), 1939–73; received an OBE for this work; after WW2, seconded to the Ministry of Health as an adviser to the UN Relief and Rehabilitation Association for refugees and gained a CBE for her achievement in 1953; member WST and Chair of the FS, 1967–71; continued to support the FS up to her death; involved in many women's rights campaigns throughout her long life, including equal pay and childcare; after being part of the struggle for the extension of the vote, Halpin maintained that one of her most thrilling experiences was being able to cast her vote for the first time at the age of 25 in 1929.

s. Independent, 16 January 1999; *Guardian*, 19 January 1999; *The Times*, 4 February 1999; Doughan and Gordon (2000); *Towards Equality* (Fawcett Society, spring 1999).

HAMILTON, Mary Agnes (née Adamson) (pen-name 'Iconoclast') CBE (8 July 1882–10 February 1966) writer, LP activist, economist; *b.* Withington, Manchester; *do.* Robert Adamson, Professor of Logic & Margaret Duncan; *e.* Girls' High School, Aberdeen, Glasgow Girls' High, Newnham, Cambridge; *m.* Charles J. Hamilton, academic, 1905; *r.* walking, sketching, listening to music; *c.* National Labour, Forum, 1917, PLC; *a.* York Buildings, London WC2 (1924), 62 Beaufort Mansions, London SW3 (1966).

Her father was a suffrage supporter, her mother had been a Botany teacher; read Classics, then passed Economics, first class, as part II of the History tripos; Assistant to Professor of History, University College South Wales, Cardiff, 1904; gave up her job on marriage, but the marriage subsequently failed; involved in the suffrage movement; economic necessity assisted with the development of her writing career; she took a job on *The Economist* 1913–16; worked in Lloyd George's Land Commission, 1913; joined the ILP, 1914; member UDC, 1914; engaged in opposition to the war and resigned from *The Economist*, 1916; then worked on *Common Sense*, 1916–20; also on *War & Peace*; joined the 1917 Club; Executive Committee member ILP Information Committee from 1919; member of the UDC Executive from 1920; wrote for the *Review of Reviews*, 1920–21; PPC Chatham, 1923; as PPC for Blackburn, she polled the highest number of votes of any woman candidate, 1924; member of the ILP Information Department, started in 1923; spoke to Faversham Women's Section LP on 'Women's Part in Politics', 1924; wrote for *Time & Tide*; Assistant Editor of *New Leader*; worked on the Balfour Committee on Industry and Trade, 1924–9; elected as LP MP for Blackburn, 1929; member Royal Commission on Civil Service, 1929–31; British delegate to the LN assemblies, 1929 and 1930; PPS to Attlee, 1930–31; front-bench spokesman for a few weeks on budget issues for the Opposition, 1931; worked on the LN Refugee Committee and Committee for Intellectual Co-operation; on the Executive Committee PLP, 1931; joined New Fabian Research Bureau, 1931; she spent a large part of the 1930s spent in lecturing and broadcasting; Governor BBC, 1933–7; co-opted alderman, Labour-controlled LCC, 1937–40; during WW2, worked in the Ministries of Information and Reconstruction; head of the American Section of the Foreign Office, 1946–52; made a CBE, 1949; retired, 1952; the 'dearest friend' of her last ten years was Ray Strachey (see entry), wrote a chapter for Strachey's *Our Freedom and Its Results*, 1936; Hamilton was described as the 'Godmother' of Strachey's last book, as she drew on Hamilton's 'trained skill' for the book.

p. prolific output on Greek and Roman history, novels, translations, political and trade union articles, journal papers, only a selection of which is given here; children's – *Abraham Lincoln; Junior History of Rome* (1910); *Greek Legends* (1912); *Antic Rome* (1922); novels – *Less than the Dust Dead; Yes; Yesterday* (all 1916); *Full Circle* (1918); *Her Last Fortnight* (1920); *Follow My Leader* (1922); *Special Providence; Murder in the House of Commons* (both 1931); *Life Sentence* (1935); biographies and politics – *J. Ramsay MacDonald; Margaret Bondfield* (both 1924); *Mary Macarthur* (1925); *Beatrice and Sidney Webb* (1933); *John Stuart Mill* (1933); 'Changes in Social Life' in *Our Freedom and Its Results*, ed. Ray Strachey (1936); *Newnham: An*

Informal Biography (1936); *Arthur Henderson* (1938); *Women at Work: A Brief Introduction to Trade Unionism for Women* (1941); autobiography – *Remembering My Good Friends* (1944); *Up-Hill All the Way* (1953).

s. her private papers were destroyed after her death; *Labour Who's Who* (1924); *Remembering My Good Friends* (1944); *Dictionary of Labour Biography*, vol. 5; *Who Was Who*, 1961–70; Banks (1990).

HANCOCK, Florence May OBE, CBE, DBE (25 February 1893–14 April 1974) trade unionist; *b.* Chippenham; *do.* Jacob Hancock, weaver & Mary Harding; *e.* Elementary School; *m.* Jack Donovan, dockers' leader, 1964; *a.* 20 Berkeley Street, Gloucester (1927).

She came from a family of fourteen, father was a political radical and politics were discussed in the home; leaving school at 12, she washed dishes in a café and later worked in a condensed milk factory; at 17, her mother died and she looked after the family; when her father later died, she kept herself and three other siblings on her wage of less than ten shillings a week; she supported the suffragette movement and attended a WU meeting to unionize the Nestlé factory she worked in, 1913; became a member of the strike committee at the factory and subsequently, when the union was established, Dues Collector and Branch Secretary; joined the ILP, 1917; Women's Organizer, District Officer for Wiltshire, WU, from 1917; Chairman and Secretary of the ILP Gloucester branch, early 1920s; Women's Officer, Bristol TGWU, 1929–42; worked with Ellen Wilkinson (see entry) and Anne Loughlin (see entry) to establish a Women's Advisory Committee in the TUC and was a member of it; TGWU delegate in the annual conferences of the UCWW, she campaigned for shorter hours, overtime and holiday pay, as well as increased status; member WCC, 1941; National Woman Officer, TGWU, 1942; member of the TUC General Council, 1935–58; TUC nominee of the ILO, visiting many countries in this capacity; worked in the Anglo-French TUC; particularly concerned with the issues relating to women and young girls in the regions, working for an improvement in the distribution of work throughout Britain; campaigned against legislation that would enable women and young people to work excessive overtime, 1937; interested in the establishment of a national maternity service; involved in increasing wages for women in the laundry, confectionery and tobacco industries; Chairman of the Women's Advisory Committee, 1941–4; appointed National Woman Officer of the TGWU, 1942; during WW2 she worked in the NCNS, the Red Cross and St John War Organization, the Ministry of Labour's Consultative Committee and the TUC Advisory Committee of the Ministry of Food; worked for equal pay for women in ammunition factories, urging them to join trade unions and worked against 12-hour shifts for women, 1941; with Violet Markham, a member of numerous government boards, she issued a report for the Minister of Labour for domestic workers to be brought into the unemployment insurance scheme and to be offered training in the postwar years; worked on the drafting of the ILO convention in Geneva for equal pay for work of equal value, although she sided with the male belief in the delay of equal pay in the face of national need in postwar Britain; joint author of a report on domestic employment, resulting in the NIH; speaker at a conference on the report of the RC on equal pay, February 1947; Chairman of the TUC General Council, 1947–8; urged employers to provide nurseries to enable more women to enter industry; Chairman TUC Women's Advisory Committee, 1948–52;

succeeded in getting domestic workers included in ILO maternity benefit provision, 1952; Director of the *Daily Herald*; President of Hillcroft Women's College; OBE, 1942, CBE in 1947, and the DBE, 1951; she died in Bristol.

s. LWW (1927); *Dictionary of Labour Biography*, vol. 9; *TUC* (1955); TUC Report, 1974; *The Times*, 16 April 1974; Summerfield (1987).

HARDIE, Agnes Agnew (Mrs George Downie Hardie) (née Pettigrew) (c.1874–24 March 1951) political campaigner and MP; *b.* Glasgow; *do.* John Pettigrew; *m.* George Downie B.C. Hardie MP, 1909; *a.* 44 Hillside Court, London NW3.

Began her working life as a shop assistant; she was a pioneer as the first woman organizer of the NUSA, campaigning for the reform of shop assistants' conditions, working with the trade unionist Mary Macarthur (see entry); Women's Organizer of the LP, 1918–23; married Keir Hardie's brother; elected in a by-election to her husband's former seat after his death, became Labour MP for Glasgow, Springburn, 1937–45; member CWP during WW2; regarded by the Labour movement as a much-needed representative for the working-class housewife; spoke in the significant manpower debate in which women's participation in wartime employment was one of the aspects of women's employment that was discussed, and as an avowed pacifist she expressed her opposition to women's conscription, March 1941; followed this in a later debate by declaring that '…war is not a woman's job', December 1941; sat on the Select Committee investigating the issue of equal compensation for civilian war injuries, 1942–3; also member of a consultative committee established by the Minister of Health; decided not to stand again in the general election of 1945; a kind woman who worked passionately against social injustice while keeping a very low personal profile, which has resulted in little being known about her parliamentary career.

s. LWW (1927); *Who's Who* (1929); *Daily Sketch*, 14 October 1938; *The Times*, 4 April 1951; Brookes (1967); Stenton and Lees, vol. 3 (1979); Pugh (1992); *Who Was Who*, vol. 5.

HARRADEN, Beatrice, BA (24 January 1864–5 May 1936) novelist; *b.* St John's Wood Park, London; *do.* Samuel & Rosalie Harraden; *e.* Dresden, Cheltenham College, Queen's and Bedford Colleges, University London; *r.* travelling, music; *c.* Lyceum, Halcyon; *a.* 5 Cannon Place, London NW3 (1899), 10 Netherhall Gardens, London NW3 (1913).

Started writing at an early age, had an international bestselling novel *Ships that Pass in the Night*, 1893; member WSPU; Vice President WWSL and London Graduates' SS, did not favour militancy; wrote on suffrage issues in the suffrage and public press, as well as numerous novels; served on the Lyceum Club's first provisional committee for Great Britain and Northern Ireland, representing the interests of literature, journalism and music; friend of the suffrage actress/writer, Elizabeth Robins; worked on relief work during WW1; organized, stocked and ran a library at the Endell Street Hospital with Dr Flora Murray (see entry) and Dr Louisa Garrett Anderson (see entry), 1915–19; after the Armistice worked with the Save the Children Fund and in Poland on relief work; Vice President SPG, 1925; travelled in the USA; awarded a civil list pension in recognition of her literary work, 1930.

p. Things Will Take a Turn (1891); *Ships that Pass in the Night* (1893); *In Varying Moods* (1894); *Hilda Strafford* (1897); *Untold Tales of the Past* (1897–1927); *The*

Fowler (1899); *Katherine Frensham* (1903); *The Scholar's Daughter* (1906); *Interplay* (1908); *The Grinding Thread* (1916); *Where Your Treasure Is* (1918); *Out of the Wreck I Rise* (1920); *Patuffa* (1923); Preface for *Women as Army Surgeons* (by Flora Murray, 1920); *Spring Shall Plant* (1920); *Thirteen All Told* (1921); *Youth Calling* (1924); *Rachel* (1926); *Search Will Find it Out* (1928); 'Discipline or Deceit' in *The Woman's View* (Women's True Temperance Committee, July 1929).

s. *Women's Who's Who, 1913*; *Manchester Guardian*, 7 May 1936; *The Times*, 7 May 1936; *Who Was Who*, 1929–40.

HARRIS, Lilian (1866?–12 January 1950) Co-operative activist; *do.* Alfred Harris, banker; *a.* Kirkby Lonsdale (1850), Well Walk, London NW3 (1908), Dorking, Surrey.

From a wealthy family who moved from Bradford to Kirkby Lonsdale in 1850; Lilian met Margaret Davies, the leader of the WCG, when she came to live in Kirkby Lonsdale and began to work with her; Treasurer WCG, 1893; Assistant Secretary WCG, 1901; member of Women's Advisory Committee, Ministry of Reconstruction, 1918–19; member WCG, 1919: member SJCIWO, 1919; retired from the WCG, 1921; presented with the Freedom of the Guild, 1922; lifelong friend of Margaret Davies, and after retirement they lived together in homes in London and Surrey.

s. *Dictionary of Labour Biography*, vol. 1; Banks (1985).

HARRISON-BELL, Florence Nightingale (née Harrison) (1865–October 1948) teacher, socialist activist; *b.* Newcastle upon Tyne; *do.* Dr. Thomas Harrison; *e.* Elementary School, Armstrong College, Newcastle University Extension Courses in English, History, Economics; *m.* Joseph Nicholas Bell MP, General Secretary National Amalgamated Union Labour, 1896; *r.* walking, reading, motorcycling; *c.* AWKS; *a.* 90 Friern Park, London N12 (1922), 60 Lady Somerset Road, London NW5 (1927).

Continuation School and adult teaching experience; lecturer for Co-operative Movement; General Secretary NAUL; ILP member from its establishment, 1893–1919; first ILP Federal Secretary; first Secretary Newcastle Labour Representation Committee, 1900; Secretary NESWS; first socialist candidate Newcastle Board of Guardians, 1893; member Newcastle and Northumberland Insurance Committees; director Newcastle Co-operative Society, 1902–06?; Branch Secretary Newcastle WLL, 1910; Executive Committee WLL, 1913; Secretary Central London Branch Teachers' Labour League; member Royal Commission on National Health Insurance; member Overseas Settlement Committee, from 1918; elected to National Executive LP, 1918–25; LP representative SJCIWO, 1919; Vice President SJCIWO; delegate WCG Annual Congress, 1921; Treasurer IFWW from 1921; delegate IFWW Congress, Vienna, 1923; member LP Emergency Committee on Unemployment, 1923; chair SJCIWO and member SJCIWO's Sub-Committee on Birth Control, 1923; representative for the SJC on the Overseas Committee; delegate from SJC on WCG deputation on housing to Minister of Health, 1923; member committee representing British Empire Exhibition employees, 1924; representative LP Executive, 1924; Vice President Teachers' Labour League, 1926; member NUT; speaker for WSI.

p. occasional magazine contributions.

s. LWW, 1927; *Women's Who's Who, 1934–5*; *Labour Woman*, October 1948; *List of Women Nominated for Service in Connection with the League of Nations* (NUWT Archive, nd 1920–21?); Collette (1989).

HART, Judith Constance Mary (née Ridehalgh) (1924–) politician; *do.* H. Ridehalgh, Linotype operator; *e.* Elementary School, Clitheroe Royal Grammar School, LSE; *m.* Anthony Hart, 1946; two sons.

Influenced by her background, both parents being committed to the Progressive Baptist Church, her mother was a lay preacher, also by the extent of the unemployment in Lancashire during the 1930s when she was growing up; Chairman of the Cambridge University Labour Club when LSE was evacuated to Cambridge during the Blitz; Lecturer and Research Worker in Sociology, 1945–9 and 1955–7; LP requested that she contest the municipal seat of Parkstone, Dorset; contested Bournemouth West for the LP in 1951; to the left of the Party, member of the Victory for Socialism group; worked in local government; unsuccessful Labour PPC for Aberdeen South, 1955; Labour MP for Lanark, 1959–87; concerned about the nuclear issue, speaking on the issue from various aspects in the Commons and attending the WILPF conference, where she maintained that Britain should leave NATO, 1959; became a Privy Councillor, 1959; together with Joan Vickers (see entry), she successfully opposed the Employment of Women Bill (designed to limit women's employment after childbirth) at the committee stage, 1963; Under-Secretary of State, Scottish Office, 1964–6; Vice Chairman of the Movement for Colonial Freedom; Minister of State, Commonwealth Relations Office, 1966–7; Minister of Social Security, 1967–8; Paymaster General, 1968–9; member NEC LP, from 1969; Minister of Overseas Development, 1969–70 and 1974–5; Minister for Overseas Development (FCO), 1974; also 1977–9; Opposition Spokesman for Overseas Development 1970–74 and from 1979.

p. articles on Scottish affairs for *Tribune*.

s. Brookes (1967); Phillips (1980); Stenton and Lees, vol. 4 (1981).

HARTLEY, Christiana, CBE, JP (1872–14 December 1948) public servant and philanthropist; *b.* Colne, Lancashire.; *do.* Sir William Pickles Hartley, jam manufacturer & Martha O'Connor Horsfield; *e.* at home with governesses and private schools; *a.* 2 Lord Street, Southport (1904), 11 Oxford Road, Birkdale (1920), Horsfield Cottage, 4 Lord Street, Southport (1933).

Her family were members of the Primitive Methodists and her father's whole life was run in accordance with his religious principles – he had a strong sense of social justice, paying his women workers a higher rate and building a model village for his workers, who were also entitled to profit-sharing; Christiana followed these principles and started her social and religious work in Southport, 1907; Poor Law Guardian, Ormskirk Board of Guardians, for 18 years; Liberal member of Southport Town Council, 1920–32; there was 'trepidation' among the male elders of the town when she was elected as the first woman Mayor of Southport, being addressed as 'Mr Mayor', 1921–2; during her office she handed over her mayoral salary of £500, matched by a further £500 from her father, to one of the Labour councillors, to assist Southport's poor; her specific intervention in work for young people gave her the accolade of the 'Children's Mayor' and she chaired the Town

Council meetings with 'masculine vigour and directness'; Freeman of Southport; maternity worker, member Maternity and Child Welfare Sub-Committee; speaker NCW Annual Conference debate on Housing of Destitute Women, 1922; appointed a Southport Borough Magistrate, 1923; also a County Magistrate for the Formby Police sub-division; spent seven nights in common lodging houses and spoke of her experiences; made a Freeman of Colne, 1927; continued her father's tradition of philanthropy when she made donations to Southport Trades Council and LP, for the unemployed; gave Southport a maternity hospital, 1932; built the Christiana Hartley Maternity Hospital in Colne, 1935; a nurses' home was endowed by her in Southport, 1940; received the Freedom of Southport, 1940; endowed two scholarships for women at Liverpool University and two at Girton College, Cambridge one being for a war orphan; Freeman of Colne, Lancashire; awarded an honorary MA from the University of Liverpool in recognition of her philanthropic work, 1943; CBE, 1943; governor of the King George V School and the High School for Girls; she was actively involved with the Church Street Methodist Church, Colne; Chairman and a Director of her father's flourishing jam and marmalade business, W.P. Hartley, Aintree and London; died from bronchial pneumonia; her public life was characterized by 'clear and concise speech, patience and courage ...a love of humanity... and was not afraid to speak her mind' (1922).

s. Southport Guardian, 23 November 1922; *The Lady's Who's Who*, 1938–9; *Manchester Guardian*, 15 December 1948; *Southport Visitor*, 16 December 1948; *The Times*, 16 December 1948; Jeremy (1984).

HASLETT, Caroline Harriett, DBE, JP, CIEE, MRI (17 August 1895–4 January 1957) engineering and electricity pioneer; *b.* Worth, Sussex; *do.* Robert Haslett, railway signal fitter, pioneer of the Co-operative Movement & Caroline Sarah Holmes, NFWI and WCG; *e.* Haywards Heath High School, Commercial College; *r.* gardening, golf, motoring, cinema; *c.* Forum, Lyceum, WASA, Soroptomist; *a.* 20 Regent Street, London SW1 (1934), 25 Foubert's Place, London W1 (1957).

Joined WSPU, 1913; began work as a junior clerk, Cochran Boiler Company, London, 1914; trained at the Cochran works, Annan, Scotland during WWI; manager London office, Cochran Boiler Company, 1918; left Cochran's to become first Secretary WES, 1919; edited *The Woman Engineer*; co-Director with Rachel Parsons (see entry) and Georgiana Shelley Rolls (see entry) of Atalanta, an engineering workshop for women, founded June 1920; representative WES, WCC, 1921; Executive Committee SPG, 1921–2; member Industrial Welfare Society, 1923–55; founded EAW, 1924; interested in 'scientific management in the home' by transferring time-and-motion studies from the factory to the home and in harnessing the benefits of electrical power to emancipate women from household drudgery to enable them to gain economic rights outside the home; Director, EAW, 1924–56; organizer of WES Conference of Women, 1925; Editor *The Electrical Age*, 1926–56; Honorary Secretary BUC; Chair IWSG; sole woman delegate World Power Conference, Berlin, 1930; made CBE for her services to women, 1931; first woman CIEE, 1932; Chairman British Federation Business and Professional Women, 1932; member Central Committee Women's Training and Employment, 1932; member ILO Advisory Committee on Women's Work, 1934; member of the British delegation to the World Power Conferences before WW2; Vice President International Federation Business and Professional Women, 1936; member Women's

b: born;   do: daughter of;   e: education;   m: married;   r: recreation;
c: club;   a: address;   p: publications;   s: sources

Consultative Committee, Ministry of Labour, from 1941; on a government mission to the USA both before and after Pearl Harbour, she was able to see aircraft production in the USA and Canada, 1941; Vice President, member of council, RSA, 1941–55; member Advisory Council of the Appointments Department, MOL; member National Industrial Alliance; first woman to be appointed Chair to a government working party, Chairman Board of Trade's Hosiery Industry Working Party, 1945–6; only woman member British Institute of Management, 1946–54; member Crawley New Town Development Corporation, 1947–55; only woman member British Electricity Authority, 1947–56; made a DBE for her work at the Board of Trade and Ministry of Labour, 1947; Chair Council Scientific Management in the Home; President IFBPW, 1950–56; appointed JP for the County of London, 1950; Vice President, 1948, and first woman Chair British Electricity Development Association, 1953; governor for LSE, Bedford College for Women (1947), Queen Elizabeth College (1953); President Hillcroft College for Women (1951); nephritis and a series of thromboses forced her to retire in 1954; died of a coronary thrombosis at her sister's (Rosalind Messenger) home in Bungay, Suffolk.

p. The Electrical Handbook for Women (ed. 1934); 'Caroline Haslett', Oxford (1938); *Teach Yourself Household Electricity* (in collaboration with E.E. Edwards, 1939); *Munitions Girl, A Handbook for the Women of the Industrial Army* (1942); *Problems Have No Sex* (1949); numerous journal articles and conference papers.

s. her papers are held at the National Archives for Electrical Science and Technology, IEE, London; *Hutchinson* (1934); *The Woman Engineer*, viii/4, (Spring 1957); Messenger (1967); Banks (1990).

HAYDEN, Mary Teresa, MA (1862–1942) academic; *b.* Dublin; *do.* Dr Thomas Hayden, physician & Marianne Ryan; *e.* Sacred Heart Convent, Alexandra College, Dublin; *a.* 47 Windsor Road, Dublin (1923), 26 Cambridge Road, Dublin (1942).

Graduate of RUI, BA, 1885; won a Modern Literature scholarship of the RUI, 1886; gained her MA, 1887; Junior Fellowship in English and History, RUI, 1896–1900; Advising Examiner in History for the Intermediate Education Board of Ireland, 1907 and 1912; Professor of Modern Irish History, University College Dublin, 1911–38; only woman member of the Senate of the National University of Ireland, 1909–24; member Executive Committee of the Gaelic League; member of the IWSLGA; chaired a mass suffrage meeting of all women's organizations in Dublin as a means of uniting women of all faiths, classes and political allegiances in their demand for women's inclusion in the Home Rule Bill, 1912; President NCW of Ireland; involved in establishing the ICWSA, 1915; awarded honorary DLitt, 1935.

p. A Short History of the Irish People from the Earliest Times to 1920 (with G. Moonan, 1921); historical and literary articles in *The Fortnightly*, *New Ireland*, *Dublin*, *Irish Educational*.

s. Women's Who's Who, 1941–50; Bank and McDonald (1998); Luddy (1995a); Ryan (1996).

HEAD, Mildred (13 June 1911–) public servant; *b.* Sudbury, Suffolk; *do.* Philip Strudwick Head, furniture and drapery businessman & Katie Head; *e.* Sudbury Girls' Secondary School, Chelsea College of Physical Education; *a.* Red House, Meadow Lane, Sudbury, Suffolk.

Began her professional life as a teacher, lecturer in PE, 1933–50; considered that her career in public service was characterized by being the 'token woman' in male-dominated institutions; first such post being a Commissioner of Inland Revenue, 1959–86; became senior partner in her father's extensive furniture business; President of the NFBPWC, 1966–9; campaigner for equal pay in the national campaign, 1968; Mayor of Sudbury, 1970–71; awarded OBE, 1971; member Retail Consortium, 1971–83; first woman President National Chamber of Trade, 1977–79; member of the Price Commission; President IFBPW, 1977–80; member Auld Committee of Inquiry into Shop Hours, 1984–5.

s. *Financial Times*, 11 October 1968; *The Times*, 4 May 1977; *Who's Who*, 1991.

HEWITT, Annie Gertrude, LLA (14 October 1880–11 December 1953); *b.* Southcoates, Hull; *do.* Leonard Hewitt, merchant's clerk & Sarah Jane Carlin; *e.* early education Hull, Homerton College, Cambridge.

First teaching appointment was for Plashet Lane School, East Ham for ten years; an active member WSPU; during WW1 she founded and ran an NFWT branch in East Ham, in order to improve the status of women teachers 1914; Head Mistress Shrewsbury Road Girls' School, until 1915; took an active part, nationally and locally in the newly founded NUWT; Head Teacher Brampton School, 1915–39; member Central Council NUWT until her retirement; President NUWT, 1921; Honorary Treasurer NUWT; NUWT representative at CCWO, 1921; NUWT representative at Conference on Women, 1921; attended Conference of Women's Organizations and seconded Ray Strachey's (see entry) NUSEC motion on 'Flying Squads', 1921; Vice Chairman Legal and Tenure Committee; Honorary Pensions Secretary, 1934–6; retired and went to live with her friend Miss Ferguson at St Leonard's, 1939; underwent a serious operation in 1947; developed, and died from, a heart condition; described by a colleague as having immense intellectual abilities and being greatly loved.

s. *The Woman Teacher*, 27 March 1936, January 1953; Kean (1990).

HIGGS, Mary (née Kingsland) OBE (2 February 1854–19 March 1937) social worker; *b.* Devizes, Wiltshire; *do.* Rev. William Kingsland; *e.* private, College for Women, Hitchin and Girton; *m.* Rev. Thomas Kilpin Higgs, 1879; three daughters, one son; *a.* Hanley, Staffordshire (1879), moved to Oldham (1893), The Bent House Social Centre, 180 West Street, Oldham (1893?–1934).

Won an exhibition to college; first woman to take the Natural Science tripos, gaining second-class honours, 1874; Assistant Lecturer in Natural Science, Girton, 1875–6; teacher at Bradford Girls' Grammar and Saltaire School, Shipley; had to give up her teaching career when she married; went to live in Oldham with her husband in 1891; member Oldham Branch NUWSS, 1913; her major interest was housing for homeless women, which she researched by going to live on the street and finding out at first hand what was available for working-class women; after her husband's death, 1907, moved into Bent Cottage and turned Bent House into a women's lodging house and a centre for the Guild of Help; her work encouraged the founding of the National Association for Women's Lodging Houses and she was its northern secretary; established a School for Mothers at Bent House and clinics, which gave rise to welfare centres and a Council of Social Welfare; organized a workroom for women, which spawned the Queen Mary's Workrooms for Women,

b: born; do: daughter of; e: education; m: married; r: recreation;
c: club; a: address; p: publications; s: sources

1914–18; advocate of wartime pensions for the poor and of the endowment of mothers; speaker at NCW Conference on Housing of Destitute Women, 1922; elder of the Society of Friends; awarded an OBE for her social work, 1937; died after several years of ill health, at her daughter's, in Greenwich, London.

p. pamphlets – *Five Days and Nights as a Tramp Among Tramps*; *The Tramp Ward* (1904); *A Night in a Salvation Army Shelter*; books – *How to Deal with the Unemployed* (1904); *The Master, The Vision of a Disciple* (1905); *Three Nights in Women's Lodging-Houses* (1905); *Glimpses into the Abyss* (1906); *Where Shall She Live? The Homelessness of the Woman Worker*; *The New Creation*; *The Evolution of the Child Mind* (all 1910); *How to Start a Women's Lodging Home* (1912); *The Housing of the Woman Worker* (1915); *My Brother the Tramp* (1924); *Mother Wareing* (1920–25?); *Casuals and Their Casual Treatment* (1928); *Where Shall He Live?* (1931); *The Way to the Joyous Life* (1937).

s. Manchester Guardian, 20 March 1927; *The Times*, 22 March 1937; *Manchester Guardian*, 5 April 1937; *Women in Council*, 26 (spring 1966); Girton College Archive.

HILL, Eveline (née Ridyard) (16 April 1898–22 September 1973) MP; *do.* Richard Ridyard & Mary; *e.* Manchester Education Committee Schools; *m.* John Stanley Hill, 1922; two daughters, one son; *a.* Grand Hotel, Southampton Row, London, 115 Styal Road, Gatley, Cheadle, Cheshire.

When she left school she went into her parents' catering business; on her father's death she became joint director with her brother; member of Manchester City Council, 1936–66; WVS Organizer in Manchester, 1943–50; made a JP for Manchester, 1945; successful Conservative candidate for Manchester Wythenshawe, 1950–64; introduced the Deserted Wives Bill, which would prevent women from being evicted from the family home after their husbands had left them and, although she had support from many women MPs, the Bill failed to get sufficient votes, 1951; signatory to a letter to *The Times* requesting that Conservative and Unionist Associations select more women candidates, 1952; alderman, 1957–66; lost her seat in the 1964 election.

s. Brookes (1967); Stenton and Lees, vol. 4 (1981); *Who Was Who* vol. 7.

HOBBS, Mrs, industrial welfare.

Member RWG, 1919; member SJCIWO, 1919; representative for SJC on NCUMHC, 1922; member SJCIWO sub-committee on birth control, 1923; SJCIWO representative on Council for Overseas Settlement of British Women, 1923; SJCIWO representative on Women's Section of Garden Cities Association, 1923; SJCIWO representative on WCG Deputation to Ministry of Health on Housing.

s. SJCIWO Papers, TUC Collection.

HODGE, Esther (17 January 1908–30 December 1994) teacher; *e.* Bedford High School, St Hilda's College, Oxford, University of Manchester.

Read History, then took her PhD at Manchester; taught at Cheltenham Ladies' College, 1933–8; then at Chislehurst and Sidcup Country Grammar Schools, 1940–46; travelled to Australia and taught at a college in Melbourne, 1957; she was an IFUW observer at the Pan-Pacific and SE Asia Women's Association in 1959 on her way home; an active feminist in the SPG, WILPF and the Fawcett Society; Editor of the feminist paper, *Speaking of Women* (later *Women Speaking*) from 1965; continued to teach part time at the East Ham Grammar School for Girls, whilst doing her editorial work; last President of the ODI; President of the MOW; briefly edited MOW's paper, *Chrysalis*; discussed her sexuality in her autobiography, giving her self-definition of herself as a lesbian; the Rev. Margaret Mabbs was her companion.

p. pamphlet – *A Woman's International Quarterly Over 30 Years: Are the Arguments to be Feminine or Feminist?* (1984); *A Woman-Oriented Woman* (1989).

s. Hodge (1989); *Guardian*, 18 February 1995; *Feminist Archive Newsletter*, February 1998; the Archive holds her papers.

HOLMES, Verena Winifred, BSc, MIMechE, AMIMarE, AMILocoE (23 June 1889–20 February 1964) engineering pioneer and inventor; *b.* Ashford, Kent; *do.* Edmund Gore Alexander Holmes, Chief Inspector Elementary Schools, England and Florence Mary Syme; *e.* Oxford High School, Newcastle High School, Armstrong College, Newcastle, Kings College, London, Lincoln Technical School, Shoreditch Technical Institute, Loughborough Engineering College; *a.* 127? 137 (*Hutchinson* 1934) Highbury New Park, London N5 (1938).

As a child she was fascinated by the mechanics of objects and how they could be improved; became a VAD, 1914; captured by the Germans when she was part of the Elsie Inglis Unit in Serbia; wartime service gave her early experience while repairing ambulance engines; pursued a long and arduous engineering education via an apprenticeship and attendance at a Mechanical Engineering course, starting with an evening class and progressing to a daytime course at Lincoln, 1917–20; attended Loughborough, culminating in a London University External degree in Engineering, 1922; during the war, worked on making wooden propellers, then centre lathe turner with an apprenticeship at Ruston and Hornsby in Lincoln, and became Superintendent of Women Workers, 1917–18; founder member WES, 1919 (her sister, Lily Isobel, was also a WES member); postwar, when all other women in the firm were dismissed, remained as a junior draughtsman, 1919–20; design, construction and testing of experimental valve gear, 1921–2; member NUSEC; working on designs for various clients, machine tools, salvage apparatus, dividing engine, 1922–4; elected Associate Member of Institute of Mechanical Engineers and Institute of Marine Engineers, 1924; the postwar slump, plus her gender, made employment difficult to find, so went to USA; Second Assistant to Chief Engineer, New London Ship and Engine Company and other work, USA, 1924–5; returned to England, 1925; worked on designs for surgical and medical apparatus, paint-spraying machinery and petrol engines; one invention, in partnership, was an artificial pneumothorax apparatus for TB treatment, originally bearing the name of Holmes and Wingfield, 1925–8; member NUSEC Sub-Committee Trade and Commerce, 1926; present at the initial meeting of the ODC, 1926; Executive Committee ODC, 1927–30; draughtsman, North British Locomotive Company, Glasgow, 1928–30; elected President WES, 1930 and 1931; worked on another invention, the poppet valve gear for locomotives; also torpedo rotary gyro valves and further Admiralty designs at Research Engineers, 1932–9; working with Caroline Haslett, she devised a munitions training course for women, 1939; became HQ Technical Officer, Ministry of Labour, 1940–44; created the Women's Technical

Service Register to improve wartime and postwar opportunities for qualified women; first woman admitted as Member of Institute of Mechanical Engineers, 1944; got her pilot's licence; her idea for 'sandwich courses', which she had been trying to promote prewar, was now taken on by the Ministry; she produced her own invention, the Safeguard Guillotine, at her own all-woman company, Holmes and Leather, which she established 1946; member Education Advisory Committee of the Air Ministry, 1948; Honorary Secretary WES, 1957; she died in the Haslemere Nursing Home.

p. many conference and journal papers, including *Mechanical Injection of Fuel as Applied to Diesel Engines*; *Reversing the System of Large Marine Oil Engines* (both 1923); *Heavy Oil Engines* (1924); *New Infinitely Variable Poppet Valve Gear* (1931); *Engineering Training for Women.*

s. private papers at the Fawcett; *The Woman Engineer*, ix/12 (spring 1964).

HOLTBY, Winifred (1898–29 September 1935) journalist, writer; *b.* Rudston, Yorkshire; *do.* David Holtby, wealthy farmer & Alice Winn, county councillor; *e.* Queen Margaret's School, Scarborough, Somerville College, Oxford; *a.* 19 Glebe Place, London SW3 (1934).

Became a probationer in a London nursing home to release an experienced nurse for foreign service, 1916; went to Somerville, 1917; left Somerville to enter the war effort as a hostel forewoman in QMAAC, 1918; returned to Somerville, 1919; after graduating in Modern History, offered a job as History tutor at St Hugh's but wanted to be more proactive in society; started lecturing to supplement her small private income until her journalism was established, subsequently enjoyed the required research, 1921–31; had an intense relationship with Vera Brittain (see entry) whom she met at Oxford; they began sharing a flat, 1922; speaker for the SPG and the LNU, 1922; LCC Manager for schools, Bethnal Green, 1922; contributing to *Time & Tide*, 1924; wartime experiences led her to join the LNU to lecture on international peace and related issues; attended LN Assembly, Geneva, every year as a writer, speaker, organizer, 1923–30; she and Brittain undertook an investigation on the political conditions of European depressed areas after visiting Geneva, 1924; Executive Committee SPG, 1925; frequent speaker at SPG events; under great pressure in all areas of her work as her commitments increased and she kept taking on more; determined on a programme of self-education on international affairs by visiting key continents; to this end she toured South Africa, visiting schools, lecturing, made broadcasts, established an LNU branch at Ladysmith, 1926; a significant figure in creating a trade union for black transport workers in Johannesburg, which she supported for the remainder of her life, from 1926; became a director of *Time & Tide*, 1926; supported the NUWT and wrote a column for their paper, *The Schoolmistress*; wrote prolifically on equality issues and characterized herself as an Old Feminist; member ODC; became extremely ill and had to drop her multiple obligations by the end of 1931; then spent some time in Yorkshire, recuperating; returned to London, 1932; attended most Parliamentary Joint Select Commttees on Closer Union in South Africa, 1932; belonged to a Committee on forced labour in Africa and advised the ILO, Geneva, on these issues; edited *Time & Tide* in Lady Rhondda's absence, 1933; became the first woman political leader writer of the *News Chronicle*, 1933; with a strong hatred of oppression and a commitment to equality she gave considerable time and money to many organizations as a member of the Friends' Service Council, the ODC, the NUWT, the WIL, SF, NCEC, NAWCS, WNLF, the ODI for the Economic Emancipation of the Woman Worker, the African Committee, the London Group of African Affairs, SCF; became engaged shortly before her death and died in London from a kidney disease, which she had fought bravely for many years; buried at All Saints' Church, Rudston; the women representatives at her funeral indicate the level of her involvement in the Women's Movement, as well as the world of literature – Vera Brittain, Margaret Haig Thomas (Lady Rhondda, see entry), Mrs Franklin (see entry), Theodora Bosanquet (see entry); Chrystal Macmillan (see entry), Caroline Haslett (see entry), Prof. Winifred Cullis (see entry), Florence Underwood (see entry), Monica Whately (see entry), M. Chave Collisson (see entry), Mary Phillips and Miss Macleod (SF), Elizabeth Abbott (see entry), plus the writers Storm Jameson, Phyllis Bentley, E.M. Delafield, Evelyn Sharp and Rebecca West.

p. Anderby Wold (1923); *The Crowded Street* (1924); *The Land of Green Ginger* (1927); *Eutychus or The Future of the Pulpit* (1928); *A New Voters' Guide to Party Programmes* (1929); *Poor Caroline* (1931); *Virginia Woolf* (1932); *The Astonishing Island* (1933); *Mandoa! Mandoa!* (1933); *Women in a Changing Civilization* (1934); *Truth is Not Sober and Other Stories* (1934); *The Frozen Earth and Other Poems* (1935); *South Riding* (1936); *Letters to a Friend* (1937); *Pavements at Anderby* (1937); *Take Back Your Freedom* (1939); *The Position of Women.*

s. Holtby Papers, Hull University Library and Humberside Public Library; *The Times*, 30 September 1935; *Daily Telegraph*, 30 September 1935; *Morning Post*, October 1935; *Yorkshire Herald*, October 1935; White (1938); Banks, (1990); *Dictionary of National Biography Missing Persons* (1993).

HOOD, Eleanor Dagleas (née Smith), JP (1865–?) Labour activist; *b.* Newcastle on Tyne; *do.* William Smith; *e.* Elementary School; *m.* John Hood; *r.* reading; *c.* PLC; *a.* St Gorran, Cecil Road, Enfield, Middlesex (1927).

President WCG 1918–19; member of deputation to support Equal Citizen Council in Paris re Peace Treaty, 1919; SJCIWO representative on a deputation to the Milk Department of Ministry of Food, 1919; Vice President SJCIWO 1923–6; SJC Sub-Committee on Birth Control, 1923; gave evidence on behalf of SJC to the Parliamentary Joint Committee on Guardianship of Infants Bill, 1923; member Edmonton BG; member Middlesex National Insurance Committee; Chair SJC, 1927.

s. Labour Who's Who (1927).

HORSBRUGH, Florence Gertrude MBE, CBE (1889–6 December 1969) politician; *do.* Henry Moncrieff Horsbrugh; *e.* St Hilda's, Folkestone; *a.* 11 Bedford Terrace, Edinburgh (1938), Lansdowne House, Edinburgh, 21 Marsham Street, London, 18 East Camus Place, Edinburgh.

A background in voluntary work for which she was given an MBE for her work in WW1; later continued this work in the British Legion; she sometimes represented the Scottish Unionist Central Office; Conservative MP for Dundee, 1931–45; delegate, LN Assembly 1933–5; Parliamentary Secretary at the Ministry of Health, 1939–45, where she was involved in arrangements for evacuation, billeting, health in air-raid shelters and many other arrangements relating to the war; had a reputation as an excellent public speaker and was a regular contributor in the Commons; first woman selected to reply to the Royal Address, 1936; another ground-breaking event for her was being the first MP to be interviewed on television at Alexandra Palace; successfully introduced a PMB, the Methylated Spirits (Sale by Retail) Bill, 1937; further legislative success with another PMB, the Adoption of Children (Regulation) Bill in 1938; awarded the CBE, 1939; contributed to the woman power debate of March 1941; made a Privy Councillor in the New Year's Honours of 1945; member of the delegation to San Francisco concerning the UN's creation in March 1945; Parliamentary Secretary Ministry of Food, 1945; lost her seat in the Labour landslide victory of 1945; did not want to return to the Commons, but under pressure she agreed to stand in a Labour stronghold, that of Midlothian and Peebles, in the 1950 election; the sudden death of the Conservative candidate for Manchester Moss Side meant that Horsbrugh was coerced into becoming a last-minute substitute, becoming Conservative member for Manchester Moss Side, 1950–59; Minister of Education but without a seat in the Cabinet for the first three years, 1951; delegate to the UNA, 1951; resigned her Education post in October 1954; made a life peer, Baroness Horsbrugh of Horsbrugh, 1959; first woman member of a RC giving Royal Assent to bills, 1961.

s. LWW (1938); Brookes (1967); Stenton and Lees, vol. 4 (1981); Pugh (1992).

HOSTER, Constance (née Kalisch) FISA, FIL, FIPS (8 July 1864–1 June 1939) women's employment; *do.* Dr Marcus Moritz Kalisch, Talmudic scholar & Clara Stern; *e.* at home by father, private schools; *m.* Albert Hoster, 1889; *r.* music; *c.* Ladies' Carlton, Pioneer, Forum, Overseas, Cowdray, Music and Musicians; *a.* 1 Linden Gardens, Flat 5, Bayswater, London W2 (1929), Flat 4, 7 Sheffield Terrace, London W8 (1939).

Proud of her Jewish heritage and was an original member of the UJW and a longstanding Council member; engaged in providing training for secretarial, commercial and political posts, together with the promotion of foreign languages, and established the Typewriting, Shorthand and Translation Offices and Secretarial Training College for Educated Girls and Women with over 30,000 students in her lifetime; claimed to have found work for over 15,000 qualified women; founder of the Educated Women Workers' Loan Training Fund, later amalgamated with the Society for Promoting the Training of Women; founder of the Educated Women's War Emergency Training Fund; awarded a free scholarship to her college for a Jewish girl through the UJW in the early 1930s; member NUSEC; President City of London SEC; Vice President SWJ; Vice President UJW from 1927; Vice President Anglo-American Women's Crusade; member LSWS Advisory Council on Industry, Commerce, the Professions, Politics, Publicity and Training from 1918; member City of London Women's Branch Conservative and Unionist Society, member Council for the Representation of Women in the LNU; Vice President City Branch, LNU; member BHA; member CCWO; member Court of Referees, Ministry of Labour; member ICW; life governor RFH and London Jewish Hospital; chaired Commerce and Salesmanship Session at the Conference of Women, 1925; Chair SPG meeting, 1927; speaker at the Conference of UJW when she and Nettie Adler (see entry) spoke on the necessity for the UJW to extend their work 'in the whole world' rather than restricting themselves to the Jewish community, to enable them to be more effective in assisting Jewish girls by working with other organizations, 1927; Vice President SWJ, 1928; member NUTG;

member German Jewish Aid Committee, assisting and advising German Jewish refugees, from 1933.

p. newspaper and journal articles on women's work, and contributor to *Encyclopaedia Brittanica*; *Style & Title* (with Ellen Countess of Desart, 1924).

s. *Who's Who*, 1929; *Women's Who's Who, 1934*; *The Times*, 3 June 1939; London School of Jewish Studies; Archive UJW University of Southampton, MS129/AJ73/21.

HOW-MARTYN, Edith (née How), MScEcon, BSc, ARCSc, (4 August 1875–3 February 1954) suffrage and birth control worker; *b.* Cheltenham?; *do.* John How, tea dealer; *e.* The Hall, Cheltenham, Grosvenor College, Bath, North London Collegiate School for Girls, Royal College of Science, LSE, University College, Aberystwyth; *m.* Herbert Martyn, 1899; *r.* travel, walking, reading; *a.* 33 Cambray Place, Cheltenham (1891), 38 Hogarth Hill, London NW11 (1913).

Member WFS and LGUWS; Mathematics Lecturer at Westfield College, University of London; Honorary Secretary WSPU 1906–07; active in protests, arrested and imprisoned, 1906; one of the founders WFL, 1907; Honorary Secretary WFL 1907–11; an advocate of birth control, she joined the Malthusian League, 1910; Honorary Head Political and Militant Department, WFL, 1911–12; stood as an Independent candidate for Hendon in the first election contested by women, 1918; first woman member of Middlesex County Council, 1919–22; Vice President and founder of WEC; founded the Birth Control Information Centre to give working-class women access to information, 1929; as Honorary Director Birth Control International Information Centre, attended the India Women's Conference before touring India, 1935; visited Jamaica to lecture and work with the Women's Movement on birth control, 1939; founded the Suffragette Fellowship and was its President until her death, 1926–54; emigrated to Australia and was active in feminist circles in Australia also up to her death, 1939–54.

p. *The Birth Control Movement in England* (1930); *Reports on Birth Control Tours in India and Round the World*; *The Need for Women Members of Parliament* (1921) and other pamphlets.

s. Her diaries and papers, 1926–40, British Library, Oriental and India Office Collects, NRA 25125; India Office Library MSS EurD 1182; *Women's Who's Who, 1913*; *The Lady's Who's Who*, 1938–9; *Daily Gleaner*, 22 March 1939; Banks (1990); North London Collegiate School Archive.

HOWSE, Edith Helen JP (19 December 1883–1955) trade unionist; *b.* Chorlton-upon-Medlock, Lancaster; *do.* Howard Edgar Howse, hosier's assistant & Helen Joss; *a.* 43 Cromwell Road, London SW7 (1924).

Active in the UPOW for over 30 years, special interest in low pay; joined the GPO as a 'telephone learner' in Manchester, 1900; union involvement began in her local branch; became a union official, 1909; first full-time women's organizer Postal and Telegraph Clerks' Association, 1916–19; became the Woman's Organizer and Assistant Secretary (Telephones/Telecommunications Section) of the newly amalgamated UPW, 1920–37; delegate to IFWW Congress, Vienna, 1923; SJC delegate to WCG Annual Congress, 1923; delegate to the TUC Women's Conference, 1925; delegate Women's Conference, spoke on women's organizations, 1926; on retirement, still active in struggle for postal workers' improved pay, representing them before an arbitration tribunal in 1938; went on to become a councillor in Wembley, then an alderman and, finally, mayor.

s. Labour Who's Who (1927); *Daily Herald*, 28 June 1938; *The Post*, 9 July 1955.

HUBBACK, Eva Marian, MA (née Spielman) (13 April 1886–15 July 1949) educationist and social reformer; *b*. London; *do*. Sir Meyer Adam Spielman, Inspector of Home Office Schools & Gertrude Emily Raphael; *e*. St Felix School, Southwold, Newnham College, Cambridge; *m*. Francis William Hubback, corn merchant, 1911; two daughters, one son; *r*. walking; *a*. 19 Wellgarth Road, London NW11 (1934).

Her father devoted many years to child welfare and her mother was one of the founders of the UJW; sent to finishing school in Paris, 1905; had a wide circle of friends in academic and political spheres, one of her circle at Cambridge being Amber Reeves (see Amber Blanco White entry); joined the Fabian Society while at university; graduated, first class in Economic tripos, part II, 1908; she became an LCC Care Committee organizer, Whitechapel, 1909–11; Poor Law Guardian, Paddington, 1910; joined the WSPU, but did not approve of many of their methods and gradually became an inactive member, 1910; temporary Economics Lecturer Newnham College, Cambridge, 1916–17; began work in the Information Bureau, NUWSS, 1918; succeeded Ray Strachey (see entry) as the paid NUSEC Parliamentary Secretary, responsible for drafting and promoting franchise and other legislation relating to women and children, 1920; in this role edited *The Woman's Leader*; worked on drafting and campaigning for the Matrimonial Causes Act, 1923, the Guardianship of Infants Act, 1925, the Widows, Orphans and Old Age Contributory Pensions Act, 1925, the Summary Jurisdiction (Separation and Maintenance) Act, 1925; combined her NUSEC work with lecturing for London University tutorial classes, Oxford University extra-mural courses and teaching Economics at Streatham Hill School for Girls; birth-control supporter, worked in the FES, with Eleanor Rathbone (see entry), 1924; member BHA, 1925; member of the LNU Council; NUSEC delegate to IAWSEC Paris Congress, 1926; as NUSEC Pariamentary Secretary and General Secretary, she edited *The Woman's Leader*; active in the promotion of women citizenship education, giving frequent lectures, such as to Church Stretton SEC summer school and at a large Edinburgh school event with the Edinburgh and Glasgow SEC and Glasgow WCA, 1926; became Principal of Morley College for Working Men and Women, 1927; instituted the Morley College Annual Dinner as a means of gaining publicity for the college – Ellen Wilkinson (see entry) was one of the chief guests at the first dinner, 1928; instigated the transformation of local WCAs into Townswomen's Guilds, 1930; member executive NUGC, 1931; President NCEC, 1931; Labour candidate for Hendon BC, 1932; President NCEC; Vice Chairman Children's Minimum Council; one of the founders and promoters of the Association for Education in Citizenship, 1934; member Milk Fund Appeal for Spanish children, 1937; involved with peace work during the 1930s; became JP, London, 1939; elected as LCC Labour member for North Kensington, 1946; Chair Primary and Secondary Schools Sub-Committee; first woman sent by the British Council to lecture in Persia, 1947; Chairman FES, 1948; consulted by the Ministry of Education on its pamphlet, *Citizens Growing Up*, 1949; campaigned on legislation for abused children, which resulted in the Children's Act, 1948; further lobbying for the establishment of a government child welfare service; died from an internal haemorrhage in hospital

in London; Eleanor Rathbone said that Hubback had a 'talent for combining perti-
naceous attack with friendly and reasonable cooperation'.

p. Training for Citizenship (with Sir Ernest Simon, 1935); *Education for
Citizenship in Secondary Schools* (1936); *Bibliography of Social Studies: A List of
Books for Schools and Adults* (with W.H. Hadow, 1936); *Education for Citizenship in
Elementary Schools* (1939); *The Neglected Child and His Family*; *Discussion Groups for
Citizens and Suggestions for Reading* (1941); *The Making of Citizens: Practical
Suggestions for Informal Methods* (1942); *The Report on Population*; *The Population of
Britain* (1947); *The Family Allowances Movement 1924–47* (with Eleanor Rathbone);
Citizenship in the Training of Teachers (1948); 'The Family Allowances Movement
1924–48' in *Family Allowances, A New Edition of The Disinherited Family* (1949);
pamphlets – *The Case for Equal Franchise* (with Elizabeth Macadam 1926); *The
Political Year, July 1922–August 1923* (1923); *Equal Franchise 1918–28* (1928);
Population Facts and Policies (1944); *How to Lead Discussion Groups* (194?); *Any
Grumbling?* (1948); plus numerous articles in educational and political journals.

s. The Times, 14 January 1936; *The Lady's Who's Who*, 1938–9; Hopkinson
(1954); Banks (1985); *Dictionary of National Biography Missing Persons* (1993).

HUFFINLEY, Beryl (née Sharpe) (22 August 1926–) trade unionist; *do.* Wilfred &
Ivy Sharpe; *m.* Ronald B. Huffinley, 1948; *a.* Cornerways, South View, Menston,
Ilkley, West Yorkshire.

Active throughout her career organizing women in the trade union movement;
equal pay campaigner; member of the NWAC of the CP; Secretary Leeds Trades
Council, 1966; stood as a CP candidate in local municipal elections, 1962–7; member
Association of Supervisory and Clerical Workers, TGWU; Chairman Regional
Committee TGWU No9 Region, 1972; member Yorkshire and Humberside TUC
Regional Council, 1974; Chairman Leeds and York District Committee TGWU,
1974; member Regional Economic Planning Council (Yorkshire and Humberside),
1975–9; member Press Council, 1978–84; Executive Committee Labour Action for
Peace; Chair Luban Action for Peace; President NCW; Vice President British Peace
Assembly.

s. Morning Star, 30 December 1967; *Who's Who*, 1999.

HUGHES, Margaret M., trade unionist.

A tenacious fighter for women's equality in union organization; member of the
RCA, began working on the railways during WW1; wrote in *Lines for Ladies* in the
Journal from 1919; RCA delegate (Gorton Branch) TUC Women's Conference,
Leicester, 1925; RCA delegate 1926 TUC Women's Conference, spoke in support
of the resolution on organization of women, 1926; instrumental in persuading the
Executive Committee to increase women's participation in the union by moving a
resolution (Manchester No6 branch) on the appointment of a National Woman
Organizer for the RCA at the Conference of RCA Women, London, 1927; became
a member of the newly constituted RCA National Women's Organizing Committee,
1927; RCA delegate to the National Conference Labour Women, 1929; RCA delegate to the SJCIWO, 1930.

s. Railway Service Journal, February 1919, May 1925, January 1927; Wallace
(1996).

INNES, Kathleen Elizabeth, BA (née Royds) (?–1967) peace worker, writer; *e.* Jersey Ladies' College, High School, Andover, Highfield, Hendon; *m.* George Alexander Innes, 1921; *r.* foreign travel, walking, swimming; *a.* 29 High Oaks Road, Welwyn Garden City, Hertfordshire (1934); Portway, St Mary Bourne, Andover, Hampshire (1938).

From a Quaker family; took a degree in Modern Languages, Cambridge Teachers' Diploma, Chancellor of London University Diploma Literature, first prize; during WW1 she left her teaching post to work with refugees in Serbia, helping them to safety in Corsica; organized collection of rubber teats for Germany in 1918; awarded Order of St Sava; 'driven by war into politics', she joined the WILPF; Chairman of WILPF; Honorary Secretary WIL; member LNU; appointed as referent for LN affairs, 1926; member of BAWC; Chair WIL; Secretary of the Peace Committee, Society of Friends; Honorary Secretary Unity History Schools; member All Peoples' Association; member Royal Institute of International Affairs; third International Chair WILPF, 1937; due to the WW2 bombing of the League's London office, it was moved to Innes' home in Hampshire; voted Vice President, 1946.

p. Lives of Coleridge and E.B. Browning; Story of the League of Nations Told for Young People (1925); *How the League of Nations Works* (1926); *The League and the World's Workers* (1927); *The Reign of Law: A Short and Simple Introduction to the Permanent Court of International Justice* (1929); *Story of Nansen and the League; The Prevention of War* (1932); *The Bible as Literature* (1930); *Life in a Hampshire Village* (1944); *St Mary Bourne Records: Notes on Events, 1896–1946* (1947); *Hampshire Pilgrimages* (1948); *Sunday School Lessons on Peace for Special Sundays* (nd); *The Health Work of the League of Nations* (nd).

s. Women's Who's Who, 1934–5; The Lady's Who's Who, 1938–39; *Pax et Libertas*, xxxii/2 (April-June 1967).

JEWSON, Dorothea (Dorothy), BA, JP (17 August 1884–29 February 1964) Labour MP; *b.* Thorpe Hamlet, Norwich; *do.* Alderman George Jewson JP MP, coal and timber merchant & Mary Jane Jarrold; *e.* Norwich High School, Cheltenham Ladies' College, Girton College, Cambridge, Trinity College, Dublin, Cambridge Training College; *m.* R. Tanner Smith, 1936, then Rev. Campbell Stephen ILP MP, 1945; c.1917; *a.* 14a Knollys House, Compton Street, London WC1 (1924), 58 Bracondale, Norwich (1927), Riverdene, Lower Hellesdon, Norwich (1929), Wensum, Lower Hellesdon, Norwich (1934), 5 Aberdour Road, Ilford, Essex.

Came from a Liberal Party family; attended Girton College, 1904–07; took Classics tripos, 1907; received an *ad eundem* BA degree from Trinity College, Dublin, 1907; gained a Teacher's Certificate from Cambridge Training College, 1908; joined Fabian Society while she was at Girton; Assistant Mistress in a school, West Heath, Ham Common, Richmond, 1908–11; returned to Norwich, where she taught in a local school for some years; during this time she and her brother worked on a report into the payment of out-relief to the poor by the local Guardians, their report resulted in a considerable increase in relief, 1912; stood as a Poor Law Guardian; became a militant suffragette; became a prominent member of the ILP; a pacifist and at the outbreak of WW1; took charge of a toy-making workroom for girls under 17 established by Norwich Distress Committee to relieve unemployment, 1914; invited by Mary Macarthur (see entry) to be Chief of the Organizing Department,

NFWW, 1915–21; after the NFWW merger with the NUGW, became head of the Women's Section, 1921–2; worked closely with Margaret Bondfield (see entry); Stella Browne, prominent advocate of birth control, converted Jewson to the idea, 1923; working with Dora Russell, an LP campaigner for birth control, who was Secretary, Jewson became President WBCG, 1924; faced great opposition to her birth control work both inside and out of the Labour movement; elected Labour MP for Norwich, 1923–4; her feminist attitude was evident in her short parliamentary career, as her maiden speech was on the franchise extension; she was particularly critical of the waste of time in parliamentary politics and openly criticized the press for its preoccupation with women MPs' dress habits; her special interests were unemployment, housing, maternity and child welfare; she spoke in the House of Commons on the Guardianship of Infants Bill, April 1924; unsuccessful Labour PPC 1924, 1929, 1931, for Norwich; member British delegation to international conference on Labour and socialist women in Marseille, 1925; after leaving Parliament, she was on the House of Lords Committee dealing with legal aid for the poor, 1925; member Executive Committee NUSEC, 1926; at the LP Conference she seconded a resolution for welfare centres to provide advice on birth control, 1926; one of two ILP delegates on the SJCIWO; served on many ILP Committees, member NWAC, she edited its *Monthly Bulletin* for the women's groups; on the ILP National Administrative Council as representative for the East Division, 1925–35; supported children's allowances, and as an ILP delegate moved the referendum back on children's allowances in the Executive Report at the ILP Conferences, 1928 and 1929; also moved a resolution on the subject at the Labour Conference, 1929; Norwich was an ILP stronghold and she remained with the ILP after it had disaffiliated from the LP, 1932; member Norwich City Council 1927–36; as a pacifist, she had joined the Society of Friends and had worked in opposition to both world wars; died in Norwich.

p. The Destitute of Norwich and How They Live: A Report into the Administration of Out-Relief (1912); 'The Labour Party Conference and Birth Control' in *New Generation*, November 1925; *Socialists and the Family: A Plea for Family Endowment* (1926).

s. Northcroft (1922?); *Labour Who's Who* (1924); *Girton College Register*, vol. 1, 1869–1946; *Dictionary of Labour Biography*, vol. 4; Banks (1985); Stenton and Lees, vol. 3 (1979).

KENT-PARSONS, Jessy Eugenie (née Usher) (Mrs K.P.) MBE (1882?–26 February 1966) mother and child health campaigner; *b.* Birmingham; *do.* John Usher, coach painter; *e.* Royal Academy of Music; *m.* Edward Kent-Parsons, commission agent, 1900; one daughter; *a.* 63 Coventry Road, Small Heath, Birmingham (1900), 245 Wightman Road, Hornsey, London N4 (1908), 34 Grange Park Avenue, Winchmore Hill, London N21 (1935), Rosemullion, Cliff Road, Torquay (1966).

As a promising contralto who began her training at the RCM when she was 17, she intended to pursue a career in music, and made some appearances before her marriage and subsequently with her husband at recitals, but upon the death of her husband in 1908, as a young widow with a small daughter, she turned to social work; Certificate SI Board, Certificate Central Midwives' Board, Ministry of Health Visitor's Diploma; qualified as woman sanitary inspector, 1911; concerned with issues relating to women and children; joined the WPHOA, 1912; working with Dr

Sophia Seekings (Friel), she established the first School for Mothers in St Anne's Ward because of the high infant mortality rate, 1912; joined the voluntary committee of the first creche to be opened in Tottenham, 1913; this school laid the foundation of the Maternity and Child Welfare Department of the BC of which she became superintendent, 1915–45; organized one of the first antenatal clinics in the country, 1917; member BMA Committee on Infant Mortality, 1921; worked for higher salaries for health visitors; Executive Committee WSIHVA 1918–19; Vice Chair WSIHVA 1919; WSI's representative on NCW until 1922; representative NCUMC, 1926–8; Chair Midwifery Training Sub-Committee, 1928; member NCMCW, NAPIM, NBWC, SJCIWO, NCW, WAHC, PTC; served as representative on NALGO committees; took part in the Association's educational tours abroad, her work being recognized by the Public Health Section of the LN; received MBE, 1935; representative Association at TUC, 1943; she retired after 34 years' service with Tottenham Borough Council and the tribute was to her 'valuable services... and her unrelenting and determined spirit' in her work throughout WW2, 1945; in retirement she went to live with her friend, Miss Blanchard, in Torquay and, despite her failing sight, she represented the Association on the National Association of Maternity and Child Welfare Centres and on the SJCWWO; died peacefully in her sleep in a Torquay nursing home and her obituary noted her 'zeal..., abundant vitality and great sense of humour'.

s. Woman Health Officer, xviii/5 (1945); *Health Visitor*, xxxix/4 (April 1966); see her papers SA/HVA Box 82, Wellcome Institute.

KITSON-CLARK, Georgina (Ina) (née Bidder) LLD (1864–?) mother and child welfare worker; *b.* London; *do.* George Parker Bidder QC & Marion Greenwood; *e.* home and Slade School of Art; *m.* Lt. Col. Edwin Kitson-Clark, engineer, 1897; one daughter, two sons; *r.* painting, writing; *c.* Ridley Art, International Art; *a.* Ravensbury Park, Mitcham, Surrey (1892), Meanwoodside, Leeds (1920–21).

Studied at the Slade, 1892–3; first President Leeds' Babies Welcome Association, 1909; President Meanwood Nursing Association and the Yorkshire Home for Mothers and Babies; member National Infant Welfare Association from its inception; long-standing member NCW and Executive Committee member; Honorary Secretary Yorkshire Ladies' Council of Education, from 1910; member Juvenile Advisory Committee and Women's War Employment Committee, Leeds; President Meanwood Women's Institute.

p. plays – *Alesia*; *The Interpreters*; *The Children's Christ*; *The Wise Men*; *Outside the Gate*; *Wharfedale Witches*; *The Family Ghosts*.

s. List of Women Nominated for Service in Connection with the League of Nations (NUWT Archive, nd 1920–1?); *The Lady's Who's Who*, 1938–9; UCL Records.

KNIGHT, Elizabeth MB, DPH (August 1869–31 October 1933) medical practitioner and women's rights activist; *b.* Northfleet; *e.* Kensington High School, Newnham College, Cambridge, LSMW; *c.* International Women's Franchise, Lyceum; *a.* 7 Gainsborough Gardens, London NW3 (1913).

A Quaker; she studied Classics at Newnham, 1888–91; graduated MB, 1904; joined the BMA, 1907; became a member WFL, to which she dedicated a great deal of her time and income, 1907; WFL Honorary Treasurer, 1913–33; imprisoned 1908; prosecuted numerous times and imprisoned twice for non-payment of taxes;

one of the first women doctors in the country, doing her medical training with Louisa Garrett Anderson (see entry); Clinical Assistant, Evelina Hospital, Waterloo; subsequently worked at the Waterloo Hospital for Children and Women, and Mount Vernon Hospital; committed to the implementation of an equal moral standard and was one of the main protagonists of the opposition campaign to Regulation 40a of DORA, 1914–18; President WFL, 1923; close friend of Florence Underwood, Secretary WFL; involved throughout the 1920s in the suffrage extension movement; WFL member, Advisory Committee WES Conference of Women, 1925; knocked down by a car in Brighton and, unaware of her internal injuries, she died two weeks later and was buried in the Society of Friends' graveyard.

p. Social and Sanitary Conditions of Prison Life (1908).

s. Women's Who's Who, 1913; Daily Telegraph, 1 November 1933; *Manchester Guardian*, 1 November 1933; *British Medical Journal*, 11 November 1933; Banks (1990); Newnham College Archives.

LANE-CLAYPON, Dr Janet Elizabeth (Lady Forber) BSc, MD, MB, DSc (3 February 1877–17 July 1967) pioneer cancer researcher, women and children's health activist; *b.* Boston, Lincolnshire; *do.* William Ward Lane-Claypon, magistrate & Edith Stow; *e.* at home, University College London, LSMW; *m.* Sir Edward Rodolph Forber, 1929; *a.* 71 Carlisle Mansions, London SW1, Bishopstone Manor West, Seaford, Sussex (1953).

Brilliant first-class honours Physiology and gold-medal-winning student, 1902; awarded a BMA research scholarship, 1902–03; took DSc, 1905; MB, BS, 1907; MD, 1910; spoke French and German; research scholar, Lister Institute, travelled to Germany and Sweden to study infant mortality in relation to infant feeding, breast versus milk substitutes, 1909–11; lecturer in physiology and hygiene, Battersea Polytechnic, 1910–12 and at King's College for Women, 1912–23; Assistant Medical Inspector, London Government Board, 1912–16; Dean of the Household and Social Science Department, King's College for Women, 1916–23; as a result of long-term research in the field of infant feeding, commissioned by the Medical Research Committee to write a book, 1916; member of Women's Sub-Committee of Advisory Council of Ministry of Reconstruction, 1918; Vice President WSIHVA, 1918–19; President WSIHVA, 1920; appointed a magistrate, 1920; Investigation Officer to Ministry of Health Cancer Committee, 1923–30; physician, RFH; surgeon, Belgrave Hospital for Children; published distinguished research on breast cancer, 1926; her research interests also included midwifery practice, child welfare, cervical and other forms of cancer.

p. total 32 publications, sole or co-authored – *Poor-Law Babies in London and Berlin* (1910); *Milk and Its Hygienic Relations* (1916); *The Child Welfare Movement* (1920); *Hygiene of Women and Children* (1921); *Cancer of the Breast and Its Surgical Treatment: A Review of the Literature* (1924); *A Further Report on Cancer of the Breast with Special Reference to Its Associated Antecedents* (1926); *Report on the Late Results of Operation for Cancer of the Breast* (1928).

s. The Lady's Who's Who, 1938–9; *British Medical Journal*, 29 July 1967; Bank and McDonald (1998); unpublished notes, Warren Winkelstein, University of California at Berkeley, 1995.

LAWRENCE, Arabella Susan, BA (12 August 1871–25 October 1947) trade union organizer and Labour politician; *b.* London; *do.* Nathaniel Tertius Lawrence, solicitor & Laura Bacon, daughter of a judge and sister of two others; *e.* privately at home, Francis Holland School, Baker Street, University College London, Newnham College, Cambridge; *r.* travel; *c.* Fabian; *a.* 16a John Street, London WC2 (1924), 28 Bramham Gardens, London SW5, 41 Grosvenor Road, London SW1 (1934), Buscot Park, Berkshire.

Took the Mathematical tripos at Cambridge after winning a Mathematics prize at University College London; independently wealthy; began work in public life as a school manager, elected as a 'moderate' Conservative member London School Board, 1900–04; church schools were her first interest; co-opted member, Vice Chairman LCC Education Committee, 1904; first woman elected to LCC for West Marylebone, represented the Municipal Reform Party, 1910; became concerned about low wages and poor working conditions in schools, particularly those of women cleaners employed by the LCC as casuals; her attempts to improve their treatment brought her into contact with Mary Macarthur (see entry), to whom she became devoted and whose influence changed Lawrence's life; as her Municipal Reform Party colleagues were unconcerned with the plight of working women, Lawrence resigned from the LCC in disgust at the women's treatment; joined the Fabian Society, 1911; member FWG; joined the LP, 1912; elected under a Labour ticket as LCC member for Poplar, 1913–27; joined the WTUL; became an organizer for NFWW, 1911–20; Secretary Working Women's Legal Advice Bureau; joined the ILP, 1913; member Executive Committee FS, 1913–45; in WW1, concerned with the protection of working women during the upheavals on the home front and represented the Fabian Society on the War Emergency Workers' National Committee, the Central Committee on Women's Employment and the Ministry of Re-construction Committee on Relations between Employers and Employees; member Special Arbitration Tribunal on women's wages, 1916–19; member SJCIWO; alderman, Poplar BC, 1919–24; worked on the administration of the Poor Law – with other Poplar Guardians they refused to set a Poor Law rate because people's extreme poverty meant they were unable to pay, which resulted in the councillors being imprisoned; during her six weeks in Holloway Prison, she worked on a pamphlet on local taxation, 1921; fought a by-election in Camberwell, 1920; unsuccessfully contested North East Ham, 1922; represented the Women's Section NUGW on five Trade Boards, 1923; LP delegate to the International Conference of Socialist Women, Hamburg, 1923; first London woman MP to be returned to the House of Commons, representing Labour for North East Ham, 1923; appointed PPS to the President of the Board of Education, 1924; first woman in the new parliament to make her maiden speech, on the omission of education from the King's Speech and the cuts imposed by the Board of Education on feeding needy children; first woman MP to visit the Soviet Union, 1924; defeated in the next election, 1924; Deputy Chairman LCC, 1925–6; always a generous contributor to numerous causes – for instance, she gave £5000 to the Miners' Federation Strike Fund, 1926; re-elected as MP for North East Ham, 1926–31; Vice Chairman SJCIWO, 1927; NUSEC supported her during her parliamentary campaigns by sending workers and cars; Vice President of NUSEC, 1927; NUSEC's Annual Report stated that she had 'spoken powerfully on women's interests' during 1927–8; her dynamic parliamentary performance during the Second Reading of the Local

Government Bill gained her great acclaim, 1928; Parliamentary Secretary to the Minister of Health, 1929–31; appointed Ellen Wilkinson (see entry) as her PPS, 1929; elected Chairman LP, 1930; second woman to obtain a place in a Labour Ministry; delegate to the LN Assembly, Geneva, 1930; unsuccessfully contested Stockton-on-Tees, 1935; during WW2, carried out research work for the LP; left the LP NEC in 1941; gave her time to voluntary work for the blind, learning Braille in order to be able to translate political works for the blind; a close friend of the Webbs, having a flat in their house at one time; suffered from ill health during WW2, which caused her gradually to recede from public life; died at her home in London; held in high regard and with great affection by the people of the East End.

p. Women in the Engineering Trades (with Barbara Drake, 1917); *Labour Women on International Legislation* (with Gertrude Tuckwell and Marion Phillips, 1919); *A Letter to a Woman Munition Worker* (Fabian Letter no 5, 1942). See her entry in the *Dictionary of Labour Biography* for a complete list of publications.

s. List of Women Nominated for Service in Connection with the League of Nations (NUWT Archive, nd 1920–21?); Northcroft (1922?); *Labour Who's Who* (1924) *The Lady's Who's Who,* 1938–9; *Dictionary of Labour Biography*, vol. 3; *Dictionary of National Biography*, 1941–50; *The Times*, 25 October 1947; *Manchester Guardian*, 25 October 1947; Banks (1990)

L'ESTRANGE MALONE, Leah (née Kay, formerly Klingenstein) MA, JP (1886–4 September 1951); social welfare; *b.* London; *do.* Arthur Kay (Klingenstein), City merchant & Regina; *e.* Paddington and Maida Vale High Schools, Somerville, Oxford; *m.* Lt. Col. Cecil L'Estrange Malone, Labour MP, 1921; one daughter; *r.* walking, mountaineering, swimming, reading, theatre, travel, ballet, opera; c.1917, PLC, Fabian, University Women's, Forum, Service Women's; *a.* 15 Sutherland Avenue, London W9 (1904), 36 Buckingham Gate, London SW1, 6 Phene Street, London SW3 (1927), 82 Overstrand Mansions, London SW11 (1938).

Took an honours degree in Modern History, 1907; Inspector, Ministry of Health, National Health Insurance Department, 1912–16; Private Secretary to Lord Henry Cavendish Bentinck MP, 1917–21; MA, 1920; Executive Committee Member LP WBCG, 1924; worked with Dora Russell on persuading the LP to adopt birth control for working women as a party policy; elected LCC Labour member West Fulham, 1934–7; became an alderman LCC, 1937–51; Vice Chairman and Chairman Public Assistance Committee, 1934–44; Executive Committee FWG; Executive Committee SJCIWO; Vice Chair Education Committee, 1944–6; Honorary Secretary Labour Parliamentary Association; member of the Board of Trade Committee on Re-Sale Price Maintenance, 1947–9; Chair Welfare Committee, 1949–51; member Welwyn Garden City and Hatfield Development Corporation; Almoner of Christ's Hospital; juvenile court magistrate; governor of Sadler's Wells; Vice Chair of the Old Vic; died on holiday in Italy.

p. The Great Infanta – Isabel, Sovereign of the Netherlands (1910); numerous articles in periodicals.

s. Labour Who's Who (1927); *The Lady's Who's Who,* 1938–9; *Daily Telegraph*, 11 September 1951; *The Times*, 11 September 1951; *Manchester Guardian*, 12 September 1951; Russell (1977); Somerville College Register, Somerville Archive.

LE SUEUR, Violet Mary Winifred (née Marks) MA (12 June 1888–1954) campaigner for improvement of status of women workers; *b.* Liverpool; *do.* William Woodfine Marks; *e.* Bedford High School, Bedford College for Women, University of London; *m.* Arthur Dennis Carrington Le Sueur, forestry consultant; *r.* philology, bridge, motoring; *c.* Forum, Hertford, Mayfair; *a.* 25a The Embankment, Bedford (1909), Beech Hill, Farnham Common, Farnham Royal, Bucks (1927), 35 Lyttleton Court, London N2, 345 Latymer Court, London W6 (1938).

Attended Bedford College, 1909–15; studied French, taking a BA Hons, Teachers Diploma, 1913; MA in 1915; Head Women's Inspection Department Aircraft Manufacturing Company and temporary civil servant Ministry of Shipping, 1915; temporary higher-grade civil servant, Ministry of Shipping, 1916–17; interested in careers for girls, served on the Care Committees of Islington schools; Rotherfield Street and Shepperton Road (Islington) Care Committees, 1924–6: member NUSEC; member NUSEC Sub-Committee Trade and Commerce, 1926; member NUSEC Committee on Social Insurance, 1926; member Executive Council NUSEC, 1926–7; one of the founders and Executive Committee member ODC, 1927–32; special thanks were given to her in the NUSEC Annual Report for her work, 1927; Honorary Secretary ODI, 1929; member Executive Committee WNLF, 1930–31; became the half-time paid Secretary ODC, from 1932; reported as having given a 'brilliant speech' on the marriage bar, NUWT Eastbourne Conference, 1938; retired from public life, 1938; a semi-invalid during her retirement; Emmeline Pethick-Lawrence (see entry) said that Winifred was 'possessed of practical legal knowledge', which she used to great advantage in her work with the ODC.

p. The Use of Lead Paint by Women (1929); *Dangerous Trades and the Protection of the Woman Worker*; *The History of the Night-Work Convention* (1931); *Why We Want Economic Equality* (1935); *Should Women have the Right to Work at Night?*; *Women and the Right to Work in Mines.*

s. Hutchinson (1934); *The Lady's Who's Who*, 1938–9; *The Woman Teacher*, February 1955; The Bedford Centre for the History of Women.

LEWIN, Dr Octavia Margaret Sophia, MB, BS (Lon) (2 February 1869–27 December 1955) physician; *b.* Widford, Ware, Herts; *do.* Spencer Robert Lewin, solicitor & Jessie Augusta Cantwell; *e.* Francis Holland School, Queen's College, Harley Street, Girton College, Cambridge, LSMW, Rotunda Hospital Dublin; *a.* 25 Wimpole Street, London W1 (1891–1934), 8 Manchester Square, London W1.

Arnott Scholar, Queen's College; Goldsmith Scholarship to Girton, Natural Science tripos class III, attended 1888–91; studied medicine at LSMW and the RFH; graduated MB, BS, 1896; resident Medical Officer at Chorlton Union Infirmary; MD, Chicago, 1903; Rotunda Hospital, Dublin, 1905; Registrar London Homeopathic Hospital; Assistant Physician there, 1906–36; assistant anaesthetist at RFH; her specialism was in oto-rhinology; a leading member, lecturer and Honorary Treasurer, WFL; School Manager, LCC; Assistant Surgeon, English Military Hospital Dieppe, 1914–15; Médécin Chef, French Military Hospital Charenton, 1915–16; Aural Surgeon, Women's Hospital Corps, Endell Street Military Hospital, 1917–18; Rural Surgeon to the WAAC, 1918–19; consulting rhinologist to the Almeric Paget Corps; Medical Adviser to the Westminster Health Society; Clinical Assistant to the Central London Throat and Ear Hospital;

Governor Bedford College, University of London; member Convocation University of London; Honorary Rhinologist Society of Women Journalists; lecturer on civic responsibility; member FMW; member Medical Graduates' Society; member British Homeopathic Society; active in the BFUW; member IFUW; member RI; Rhinologist to the LCC and to the Roll of Honour Hospital; Vice President WSI, 1926–8; lectured on her specialism to NFWI, WCA, NCW; member Council SWJ, 1936–7; elected member of the Faculty of Homoeopathy, 1945.

p. Breathing and Human Welfare; *Sneezing*; *The Breathing Alphabet*; numerous articles on personal hygiene, nasal hygiene, education and training of children in personal hygiene.

s. Women's Who's Who, 1934–5; *Who Was Who*, vol. 5; *Girton College Register*, vol. 1, 1869–1946; *British Medical Journal*, 14 January 1956.

LOUGHLIN, Anne (28 June 1894–14 July 1979) trade unionist; *b.* Leeds; *do.* Thomas Loughlin, boot and shoe operative; *b.* Leeds; *e.* Elementary School, Leeds; *a.* Union Chambers, 20 Park Place, Leeds (1927).

Her mother died when she was 12, looked after the family and when her father died four years later she also became financially responsible for them; working in the clothing trade, she joined the union and soon became a shop steward; full-time organizer TGWTU, 1915–48; conducted the famous Hebden Bridge clothing workers' strike of 6000 workers when she was only 22, 1916; during WW1 she was sent to Bristol to lead women workers in a strike concerning parity for war bonuses; the last woman to receive the WTUL's gold badge for her services to Leeds clothing workers, 1919; appointed National Organizer of the TGWTU, from 1920; member WTAT; member Trade Boards Great Britain and Ireland; member and Chairman SJCIWO, 1935; member TUC women's delegation to Russia, 1925; member LP; member TUC Women's Committee; elected member TUC GC, 1929–53; awarded OBE, 1935; member of the CWP during WW2; second woman Chairman of the GC of the TUC; first woman to be President of the Annual Congress, 1943; Chairman of the National Conference of Labour Women, 1943; one of the members of the panel of the Royal Commission on Equal Pay, together with Lucy Nettlefold (see entry) and Dr Janet Vaughan, who wrote a *Memorandum of Dissent* to the Commission's Report in the name of women's equality, 1944–6; served on other RCs and government committees covering holiday pay, safety at work and industrial insurance; first working–class woman to be awarded the DBE, in recognition of her war services, 1943; first woman to take over as General Secretary of a mixed union, the TGWTU, 1948–53; President General Council of the TUC, 1943; advised the government on the industrial welfare issues relating to the employment of women during WW2; ill health, due to years of overwork, forced her to retire, in 1953; the Anne Loughlin Room was dedicated to her at NUTGW HQ to commemorate her work for women's rights and the trade union movement, 1975; 'she deservedly won an international reputation as a resolute champion of the cause of the workers, particularly women, throughout industry' (Chevins 1975).

s. LWW, (1927); Brittain (1953); TUC, 1955; *Industrial Newsletter for Women*, April 1956; *Who Was Who*, vol. 7; Chevins (1975); TUC Report 1979; Summerfield (1987).

　　　b: born;　do: daughter of;　e: education;　m: married;　r: recreation;
　　　c: club;　a: address;　p: publications;　s: sources

LOWE, Eveline Mary (née Farren) JP, LLD (1870–30 May 1956) teacher and Labour activist; *b*. Bermondsey, London; *do*. Rev. J. Farren; *m*. Dr George C. Lowe; *c*. Labour; *a*. 15a Thorburn Square, London SE1 (1927).

Lived and worked in Bermondsey for a great part of her life; one of the earliest members of the WLL and at her death the last surviving League Chairman; Vice Principal of Homerton Training College; one of the founder members of the Bermondsey ILP and of the West Bermondsey Divisional LP, of which she was the Treasurer from 1919; President of the West Bermondsey Women's Section; member of the London LP Executive, which she represented on the London Women's Advisory Committee from 1918; active in local government, especially as a teacher on the education committee as LCC member for Bermondsey from 1922 onwards; Chairman of the London Education Committee, 1934; Chairman of the Establishments Committee, 1937; first woman Chairman of the LCC, 1939; a woman of 'immense gifts and abilities, of great charm, serenity and wisdom' (1956).

s. LWW, 1927; *Women's Who's Who, 1934–5*; *The Labour Woman*, March 1939, July 1956.

MACADAM, Elizabeth, MA (1872?–1948) social worker; *b*. Edinburgh?; *e*. Strathroy Collegiate Institute, Canada, Dresden; *r*. travel; *c*. Women's University; *a*. 50 Romney Street, London SW1 (1919), later integrated with number 52 (early 1930s), 5 Tufton Court, near Smith Square, London SW1 (1940); Nile Gross Grove, Edinburgh (1948).

Little is known about her early life; there appear to have been various family scandals forcing her to leave Scotland for London to take up social work; worked at the Women's University Settlement, Southwark; Warden Victoria Women's Settlement, Everton, Liverpool, where she met Eleanor Rathbone (see entry), life-long friend and companion, 1903–11; active in the LWSS, especially in the election campaign, 1910; Chair of the Women's Improvement Group, a sub-committee of the Liverpool Council Voluntary Association; became involved in the development of social studies as a academic discipline; as a Lecturer in Social Work in Liverpool, she was so effective that students queued to attend her lectures; became Director of Social Studies, in association with Liverpool University, 1911–19; NUWSS Executive Committee; during WW1 her involvment in industrial welfare work for the government obliged her to move to London; Eleanor Rathbone also needed a base in London and bought the house that she and Macadam were to share from 1919, with Macadam taking responsibility for all their domestic arrangements; member Women's Advisory Committee to Liquor Control Board, 1915–16; member Advisory Committee appointed by Ministry of Reconstruction on Health and kindred services, 1918–19; member Executive Committee Domestic Workers' Insurance Society; member Executive Committee NCW, Liverpool; member Liverpool WIC; member Lancashire Diocesan Advisory Board for Training Rescue Workers; member Liverpool Executive Committee for Training Women Police; Chair Committee Presbyterian Synod for Training Women Workers; Honorary Secretary Joint University Council for Social Studies; member Liverpool Insurance Committee; member Juvenile Advisory Committee, Ministry of Labour; manager Day Industrial Schools, Liverpool; involved with Special Schools for Defective Children; NUSEC Honorary Secretary, 1919, 1921, 1923, 1927; particularly involved in her NUSEC role with promoting training for women to tackle the post-WW1 high unemployment rates, for example speaking at the UJW's AGM on training for unemployed women, 1921; member of NUSEC Deputation to Home Secretary on Municipal Corporations Amendment Bill, 1925; member of NUSEC Press and Publishing Committee; member Society Insurance Committee, NUSEC, 1926; member Women Police Committee, held at NUSEC HQ, concerned with training programme, 1926; member of FE Committee, member Executive Committee, 1927; lectured on social issues, such as on social reconstruction at Morley College, 1928; representative NUSEC on deputy to Ramsey MacDonald on family allowances, 1929; Joint Editor *The Woman's Leader*, 1923; member of Board of Directors of *The Woman's Leader*, 1927; principal speaker at a summer school arranged by the Church Stretton SEC, under NUSEC, 1926; went on speaking tour to Yorkshire, 1926; Honorary Secretary, Joint University Council for Social Studies; co-opted member representative women's organizations on Council LNU; member Royal Institute of International Affairs; assisted and accompanied Rathbone in much of her work and travels relating to women's rights during the 1930s; member Executive Committee NCEC, 1931; worked for the relief of homeless people in London during WW2; after Rathbone's death in 1946, Macadam returned to Edinburgh, where she died only two years later, leaving an estate of £22,008; Macadam displayed an extreme reluctance to have personal details about herself known; Margaret Simey describes her as a sensible, outspoken, determined and eminently practical woman (March 1999).

p. The Universities and the Training of the Social Worker (1914); *The Equipment of the Social Worker* (1925); *The Case for Equal Franchise* (with Eva Hubback, 1921–6?); *The New Philanthropy: A Study of the Relations between the Statutory and Voluntary Social Services* (1934); *The Social Servant in the Making* (1945).

s. List of Women Nominated for Service in Connection with the League of Nations (NUWT Archive, nd 1920–21?); *Hutchinson* (1934); *The Lady's Who's Who*, 1938–9; Stocks (1949); *Liverpool Daily Post*, 31 January 1949; conversation with Margaret Simey, a writer on social work and a local Liverpool activist who knew Macadam, March 1999.

MACARTHUR, Mary Reid (Mrs Mary Anderson) (13 August 1880–21 January 1921) trade unionist pioneer; *b.* Glasgow; *do.* Glasgow draper; *e.* Girls' High School, Glasgow; *m.* William S. Anderson, trade unionist, 1911; *a.* Ayr (1880–1903), Gower Street, London WC1 (1903) .

On leaving school spent a year in Germany learning German and French, 1896; on her return, wrote occasional articles while working as a book-keeper in her father's drapery business; became involved in trade unionism as a result of hearing NAUSAWC's founder and President, John Turner, at a Glasgow meeting which, ironically, she went to cover for a Conservative newspaper; despite her 'privileged' position, she joined the Union in 1901, became Secretary of the Ayr branch; President of the Scottish National District, 1902; also became involved with the ILP; met Margaret Bondfield (see entry) at the Scottish annual conference; Macarthur's union work caused conflict with her Conservative father, subsequently went to live with Bondfield in Bloomsbury's Gower Street, 1903; working with Bondfield and Gertrude Tuckwell (see entry) made General Secretary of the WTUL, dedicated her short life to tackling the oppression of women and child workers in the sweated industries and as homeworkers, particularly famous for her successful strikes and work with Cradley Heath chainmakers, Nottingham lace-makers; with Tuckwell she was a significant initiator of the Anti-Sweating League, 1906; established the NFWW, 1906; started the paper, *Woman Worker*, 1907; delegate to ICW in Berlin and US, 1904 and 1908; member National Council ILP, 1909–1912; involved in the campaign for establishing minimum wages via the Trade Boards Act, 1909; during WW1 worked unceasingly on behalf of women munitions workers who were being ruthlessly exploited by Government and employers (see Law:97:13) with the growth of the WTUL mirroring Macarthur's success in unionizing the women's labour force; worked with Bondfield, Susan Lawrence (see entry), Marion Phillips (see entry) as a member of the Executive Committee of the Workers' War Emergency Committee which held a National Conference on War Service for Women with resolutions on equal pay and votes for women, 1915; spoke on the importance of equal pay for work of equal value at the TUC Conference, 1916; also a member of the CCWTE during the war; one of the principal speakers at a London suffrage meeting, 1917; after WW1 working to ensure female ex-munitions workers received fair treatment, as part of which she marched on an NFWW demonstration with 6,000 women down Whitehall in protest at the Government's broken pledges, 1918; Macarthur and her husband were official LP candidates in the post-War General Election of 1918, Macarthur being PPC for Stourbridge constituency where she had worked with the women chainmakers; Macarthur was expected to win, however, despite being known in the constituency by her maiden name, the Returning Officer insisted on her married name being put on the ballot paper, as many women workers were poorly educated and only able to recognize Macarthur's maiden name, she believed that this cost her the election; heartbroken by her husband's death in the great influenza epidemic of 1919; attended ILO conference in Washington, 1919; Chairman of the LP Women's Conference, 1920; Vice President Birmingham Society for Equal Citizenship and Women's Citizen's Association, 1920; her early death from cancer was a great blow to the cause of women's employment and equality as her achievements to date had been immense, a woman of great energy, magnetism, with an expressive ability in writing and speaking, a fitting epitaph from herself, 'Knowledge and organization mean the opening of the cage door' (*The Woman Worker*, June 1908).

    s. Boston (1980); Crawford et al. (1983); Law (1997); Uglow (1999).

McDONALD, Edith, trade unionist.

    Secretary to the AWKS Employment Department, 1921; contributed to the preparation of a report to the NEC on the working of the Unemployment Insurance Act; under her good management, the Union's reserve funds increased, enabling the Union to provide women members with support when their state benefit applications were refused, 1921; delegate to IFWW's congress in Vienna, 1923; Assistant Secretary IFWW; became International Secretary of IFWW, 1923.

    s. The Woman Clerk, ii/5 (August 1921).

MACMILLAN, Chrystal, BSc, MA (13 June 1872–21 September 1937) lawyer and women's rights activist; *b.* Edinburgh; *do.* John Macmillan & Jessie Chrystal Finlayson; *e.* first school in Edinburgh, St Leonard's School, St Andrew's, Edinburgh University, Berlin University; *r.* gardening, talking, walking; *c.* Ladies' Caledonian, Edinburgh, Lyceum, International Franchise; *a.* 71c Harcourt Terrace, London SW10 (1920–21), 4 Pump Court, Temple, London EC4 (1927).

Refused an open scholarship to Girton College, Cambridge, 1891; graduated Edinburgh with first-class honours degree Mathematics and Natural Philosophy, 1896; MA in Mental and Moral Philosophy, Berlin, 1900; Honorary Secretary and Treasurer of the Committee of Women Graduates of the Scottish Universities (Parliamentary Franchise), 1906–08; involved in the WGSU's fight to establish their right to the vote as members of the University General Council in the law case *Nairne v. the Universities*, presenting the appeal herself to the House of Lords, 1908; member Scottish and North-Eastern Federations, Vice President Edinburgh Society, member Executive Committee NUWSS, Honorary Secretary SUWSU, member Executive Committee NUWW, 1913; Secretary IWSA, 1913–20; some work before the war for the Scottish Education Department on school inspections; organized dispatch of first food sent to Belgian refugees, 1914; Secretary of the Hague International Women's Peace Congress, 1915; after the Congress, she travelled to neutral countries in an attempt to halt the conflict of WW1, and on to the USA, working in peace groups to prevent America's intervention in the war; Secretary to Peace Congress in Zurich and delegate from it to Paris Peace Conference, 1919; member of the Board of Officers of the IWSA and the WILPF; acted as Secretary at two Congresses of the IWSA and at two congresses of the International Committee of Women for Permanent Peace; attended the Geneva Congress, 1920; member Executive Committee AMSH; member of the Committee of Enquiry into Sexual Morality, 1920; IWSA representative at the Conference of Women, 1921; witness before the War Cabinet's Committee on Women's Work, the Select Committee on the Guardianship of Children and the Select Committee on the Nationality of Married Women, 1922; member Departmental Committee on Street Offences; Committee on Powers of Ministers and Delegated Legislation; Royal Commission on Unemployment Insurance; trained as a barrister in the Middle Temple and became one of the first women called to the Bar, 1923; contributed her legal expertise on the position of women to NUSEC and other women's organizations; leading member and one of the founders, of the ODC (the introductory meeting was held in her home in May 1926), for which she worked exceptionally hard, the introductory meeting of the ODC being held at her home in May 1926–37; Chairman NUSEC's Married Women's Committee 1926; committed to the campaign for British women to retain their nationality when marrying aliens; NUSEC delegate to IAWSEC Paris Congress, 1926; one of the 11 NUSEC Executive Committee members who resigned because of the change of policy from pure equalitarianism at the AGM, 1927; founder member and President of the ODI, 1929; represented Edinburgh Society for Equal Citizenship on a deputation to Ramsay MacDonald, speaking on the Nationality of Married Women and separate taxation for married persons, 1929; Chairman of the Women's International Demonstration on the Nationality of Married Women at the Hague and led the deputation from it to the Bureau and Commission on Nationality of the Hague Codification Conference, 1930; member of the Committee on the Nationality of Women Representatives of International Women's Organizations instituted by the LN, 1931–3; stood as an Independent for Edinburgh North in the General Election, 1935; Chairman of the Nationality of Married Woman Pass the Bill Committee; member of the ILO Committee on Women's Work; ill for much of the early months of 1937, having to have her leg amputated in April and dying in September.

p. pamphlets/other – *The Struggle for Political Liberty* (1909); *Frauenstimmrecht in der Praxis* (1913); *Woman Suffrage in Practice* (1913 and 1923); *Facts versus Fancies on Woman Suffrage* (1914); *And Shall I Have a Parliamentary Vote?* (1918); *The Nationality of Married Women* (1931 and 1938); *The Legal Position of Women* (currently in 14th edition), *Encyclopaedia Britannica*; books – *Disabilities of the Married Woman* (1922).

s. *Women's Who's Who, 1913*; *List of Women Nominated for Service in Connection with the League of Nations* (NUWT Archive, nd 1920–21?); Banks (1990); *Who Was Who*, 1929–40; St Leonard's School Archive.

MAGUIRE, E. Christine (Molly) trade unionist; *b.* London; *do.* Army coach; *e.* school in Belfast, St Paul's Girls School; *a.* 116 Belgrave Road, London SW1 (1927).

Although born in London she was half Irish; while working at the Dublin Shell Factory, the wages and conditions were so poor that she began to organize the women to claim improvements, 1916; as a result of her work in Dublin she came into contact with the WWF and worked for them for some months organizing women in Dublin, Cork and Waterford; worked at the Ministry of Pensions, involved in the fight for improved wages and conditions and organizing the Temporary Women Clerks in the Civil Service; Honorary Organizer AWKS, 1918–21; President AWKS, from 1921; member National Whitley Council; Assistant Secretary CSCA, 1923–9; delegate to the Labour Women's Conference, Ellen Wilkinson (see entry) remarked that Maguire 'spoke brilliantly – pale, spiritual face and Quartier Latin air'; delegate TUC Women's Conference, 1925; SJCIWO representative on Advisory Council and read a paper, WES Conference of Women, 1925; resigned from the CSCA allegedly because of a quarrel with W.J. Brown, although a CSCA diarist claimed she was difficult to work with because she 'could not accept the discipline of co-operative effort within an organization', 1929 (interestingly, she was replaced by a Miss Sweet, 'fresh from college... untrammelled and unhampered by previous prejudices or preconceived ideas', *Red Tape* May 1930); at the CSCA Annual Conference, a resolution was passed to award Maguire three months' extra payment as the three months' pay she had been awarded on her resignation was regarded as 'niggardly', 1930; stood for Stoke Town Council; regarded with affection and great respect by her ex-colleagues at the CSCA because of her hard work for the members and her selflessness – refused to accept any superannuation and had lived on £3 a week of her salary, giving the rest of it away to people she thought needed it more; her CSCA colleagues discovered that, since leaving her post, she had found it difficult to obtain work and was living in the slums of Stoke in dire poverty, yet despite her own economic situation she was still working to help the poor of the area, so at the Annual Conference they voted a gift of £100 to the Christine Maguire Fund, 1936; she sent a 'farewell message of affectionate regard' to her previous colleagues at the CSCA, along with the news that she was entering a French convent as a novitiate, 1938.

s. *Red Tape*, May 1923, May 1930, June 1930, June 1936, July 1938; *Labour Who's Who* (1927).

MANICOM, Kate Zilpah (11 March 1893–27 October 1937) trade unionist; *b.* St Pancras, London; *e.* Southfields Girls School; *do.* Arthur Henry Manicom, baker journeyman & Louisa Childs; *r.* cookery; *c.* Trade Union, Fabian Society; *a.* 49 Chandos Street, London WC2 (1924), 6 Achilles Road, London W6 (1934).

Joined the Women's Movement and fought vigorously for the franchise, 1911; helped ELFS with their relief days to collect money for milk for babies and mothers; speaker at ELFS meetings; LP secretary, 1914; member WU; appointed WU organizer, travelling all over the country to recruit women members, 1917; 'heroine' of the Pearl Assurance workers' strike, c.1920; vociferous WU speaker on the franchise extension for women under 30 at the LP's National Conference of Women, 1920; Women's Officer, TGWU; member TUC Women's Advisory Committee; member and speaker WCG; member Court of Referees; member Public Assistance Committee; member SJCIWO; delegate to Working Women's International, 1921; delegate to ILO, Geneva; IFWW delegate to convey peace resolution to Disarmament Conference, Washington, 1922; served on the Catering Trades Council, 1923; delegate TUC, spoke on Union Insurance debate, 1924; worked as a Post Office Clerk, from 1924; delegate WSI Conference, 1928; served on the WTU Advisory Committee (TUC); worked on the Manor House Hospital Women's Committee, Golder's Green; member WCS, TGWU.

s. Daily Express, 22 March 1920; *Labour Who's Who* (1924); *Hutchinson* (1934); *The Record*, December 1937.

MANN, Jean (née Stewart) (1889–21 March 1964) MP; *do.* William Stewart; *e.* Kinning Park, Bellahouston Academy, Glasgow; *m.* William Lawrence Mann; two daughters, three sons; *a.* Redcliff, 18 Albert Road, Gowrock, Renfrewshire.

Suffrage supporter and member of SF; an accountant; Mann worked for the LP for many years before entering Parliament; member Glasgow City Council; Vice President Scottish Housing and Planning Council; Honorary Secretary of the Town and Country Planning Association of Scotland's Advisory Council; member of the first Rents Tribunal in Scotland; Chairman of the magistrates' Committee in Glasgow; unsuccessful PPC for Renfrewshire West, 1931 and 1935; Labour MP for Coatbridge and Airdrie, Scotland, 1945–59; working-class, had five children and grandchildren, her husband had been unemployed for many years in the interwar depression, and these experiences and her interest in housing, food prices and consumer issues led to her being known as 'the housewife's MP'; argued the need for a Housewives Union to pressurize Parliament into redressing injustices that related to the majority of women at that time – issues such as consumer protection, widows' pensions, the cost of living, problems of children and young people, difficulties of married women and the double shift – which she complained were neglected by Parliament and the trade unions because 'women are not worth considering in a man's world' (1967: 237); member of the MWA, worked with Helen Nutting (see entry) on the campaign to get every woman a part of her husband's income; involved in preventing the attempted removal of Emmeline Pankhurst's (see entry) statue from the Commons' grounds; supporter of Swiss women's attempts to secure the franchise for many years, only woman in three British delegates to Switzerland, 1949, 1952 and 1955; member LP NEC, 1953–8; editor *Scottish Town & County Councillor*; Mann resigned from the NEC after a row with Harold Wilson over the appointment of a woman organizer for the LP, 1957; in her autobiography, she attacked the women's organizations, saying that 'They lack tenacity, unity and courage'; criticized the constitution of the LP in which the Women's Sections had no real power or representation on the NEC and condemned the continued existence of this (gender) 'apartheid in the Sixties' (1962: 245); described as 'a witty and popular speaker' (Brookes 1967).

p. Replanning Scotland (1942); *Woman in Parliament* (1962).

s. Mann (1962); Brookes (1967); *Who Was Who*, vol. 6; Stenton and Lees, vol. 4 (1981).

MANNING, Elizabeth (Leah) (née Perrett) JP (1886–15 September 1977) teacher, MP; *b.* Droitwich; *do.* Charles William Perrett & Harriet Margaret Tappin; *e.* Misses Thorn's Select Academy for Young Ladies, Elementary, St John's School, Bridgewater, Homerton Teachers' Training College, Cambridge; *m.* William Henry Manning, 1915; *a.* Solar Physics Observatory, Cambridge (1915), Willow Cottage, Hatfield, Hertfordshire, Broad Oak, Bishop's Stortford.

Parents went to live in Canada when she was young; brought up by her Methodist grandparents in the East End of London; matriculated a year too early to attend college, taught in a boys' school in the Oldfield Road, where she joined the Fabian Nursery and the ILP; the death of her grandfather prompted a move to Hampshire; she formed a group, the Socialist League, at Homerton; member Cambridge University Fabian Society; first teaching appointment in New Street, Cambridge; soon after leaving college, she became Secretary of the Cambridge Branch of the ILP and a delegate to the Trades Council; member Cambridge branch of the NCW, worked with Clara Rackham (see entry) in Cambridge; took a pacifist stand during WW1 and became a VAD; after the 1918 election went to Germany working with the Quakers in the FOR; President Cambridge Trades Council and LP, 1921–2; Secretary Cambridgeshire and Huntingdonshire Labour WAC, 1919–22; President TLL, 1924–5; President East Anglian Federation Class Teachers, 1920–22; member NEC of TLL, 1923–6; member NEC of NUT; member WFL; involved with trade union work during the 1920s; worked in the Cambridge General Strike Committee with Rackham, 1926; continued with her teaching and supported by Margaret Bondfield (see entry) and Susan Lawrence (see entry), she organized the female college bedders, jam factory and other women workers; helped to run the first family planning clinic in Cambridge; one of the first group of women JPs; became the Head of the Open Air School in Cambridge, 1929–31; first woman to become a Chairman of a trade union when she was elected to the position in the NUT in 1929; contested Islington East for the LP standing against Thelma Cazalet (see entry), 1931; member LP NEC 1931–2; supporter of family allowances; served on the Select Committee investigating the conditions and hours of shop assistants; President NUT, 1930–31; wrote about the Fascist developments in Spain after her visit in 1934; member WCAWF, raised money and collected clothes for the International Brigade in Spain; unsuccessful PPC for Sunderland, 1935; became Assistant Education Officer NUT until 1942; parliamentary supporter of the EPCC; returned to Parliament as Labour MP for Epping, 1945–50; spoke strongly for peace in a debate in the Commons and voted against an increase in the length of national service, 1948; in contact with Ellen Wikinson (see entry) as both were lecturers for the NCLC; lost her seat in 1950; apart from a short spell in industry, she returned to teaching, 1950–70; worked with Lucy Middleton, Labour MP, in the Peace Movement; unsuccessful PPC at Epping in 1951 and 55; involved with the FPA and the first clinic in Harlow, and campaigned for contraception for the unmarried; in her capacity as a teacher and NUT activist, part of the struggle against American horror comics and their effect on children; DBE, 1966; died in an NUT retirement home.

p. What I Saw in Spain (1935); *A Life for Education: An Autobiography* (1970); articles in *The Schoolmaster* (1947).

s. LWW, (1927); *Women's Who's Who, 1934–5*; Brookes (1967); Manning (1970); Stenton and Lees, vol. 4 (1981); Banks (1990); Pugh (1992).

MARTINDALE, Hilda, CBE (June 1875–18 April 1952) Inspector of Factories; *b.* London; *do.* William Martindale & Louisa Spicer; *e.* Brighton and Hove High School for Girls, Royal Holloway College, Bedford College for Women, Regent's Park; *r.* travel, needlework; *c.* University Women's; *a.* Westminster flat (1901), 12 Ashley Gardens, London SW1 (1938), 44 Coleherne Court, London SW5 (1952).

On the death of her father, her mother took the family to live in Germany (briefly in Switzerland), where Hilda attended kindergarten and learned German, 1877–80; her mother was a suffrage campaigner and believed in equality of education and Hilda has recorded how her mother was a great source of strength and inspiration; the family returned to live in Lewes, 1880; they moved to Brighton to enable the girls to attend a girls' public day school, 1885; left college, 1895; Hilda studied hygiene and sanitation at the RSI, becoming an Associate of the Institute; studied hygiene and public health at Bedford College, obtaining the Hygiene Certificate, entered college, 1897; worked for Dr Barnardo's for eight months finding foster homes, 1899; she and her sister Louisa (see entry) accompanied their mother on her round-the-world trip, during which she investigated the care of orphan children in over 100 institutions and organizations, 1900–01; appointed HM Inspector of Factories, working in London, 1901; appointed as Inspector for the Potteries, 1904; sent to Ireland, where she was involved in campaigning to address issues relating to industrial problems of women and girls, 1905–12; Senior Lady Inspector for the Midlands, 1912; official Adviser to the Midlands' Division WEC during WW1; member of the Committee of Central Control Board to inquire into women's drinking, Birmingham, 1915; Deputy Principal Lady Inspector, London, 1918; in addition to being Deputy Principal, later made Senior Lady for the South Eastern Division, 1918; OBE, 1918; Treasurer and then Chairman, CWCS; Superintending Inspector of Factories for the Southern Division, 1921; Honorary Treasurer CWCS, 1920–24; thereafter, Executive Committee member CWCS; member Departmental Committee on Factory Inspection, 1928; member CWCS's Committee for the Retirement Appeal for Adelaide Anderson (see entry), 1928; Deputy Chief Inspector of Factories, 1925–33; British representative to a conference of Industrial Safety Museums, 1929; British representative at the ILO Conferences, Geneva 1931, 1932, 1934, 1937; member of the Committee appointed by the Secretary of State for Foreign Affairs to review the admission of women into the Diplomatic and Consular Services, 1934; Director of Women Establishments, HM Treasury, 1933–7; Technical Adviser to the British Governmental Delegates to the 15th, 16th 18th and 23rd sessions of the ILO Conference, Geneva; member of the Industrial Health Board, 1933–7; awarded CBE, 1935; member of the Institute of International Affairs; Governor of Bedford College for Women; Deputy Chairman

Council of Dr Barnardo's Homes; popular with her colleagues and when she retired she was honoured, uniquely, with a retirement party at Lancaster House attended by 600 people, 1937; gave the Fawcett Lecture at Bedford College for Women, 1939; served on advisory councils relating to women and men's specialist employment – Outside Welfare for Industrial Workers, Appellate Tribunal for Women Conscientious Objectors, committees for child evacuation during WW2; Manager of two boys' approved schools, postwar; member of the Council of the Froebel Institute; first woman to serve on the Council of Dr Barnardo's; she died at her London home.

p. Women Servants of the State, 1870–1938 (1938); *From One Generation to Another: A Book of Memoirs, 1839–1944* (1944); *Some Victorian Portraits and Others* (1948).

s. Who Was Who, 1951–60; *The Lady's Who's Who*, 1938–39; Martindale (1944); *The Times*, 19 April 1952; Banks (1990).

MARTINDALE, Louisa CBE, MD, BS, FRCOG, JP (1872–5 February 1966) surgeon; *b.* London; *do.* William Martindale & Louisa Spicer; *e.* Brighton and Hove High School for Girls, Royal Holloway College, Egham, London School of Medicine for Women; *r.* travel; *c.* Lyceum; *a.* 10 Marlborough Place, Brighton (1913), Weymouth Street, London W1 (1921), 25 Manchester Square, London W1 (1938), Little Rystwood, Forest Row, Sussex (1938), Harley Street, London (1945), 14 Avenue Lodge, Avenue Road, London NW8 (1966).

Her father died when she was very young and her mother was a woman of great vision (see Hilda Martindale entry) and it was the opening of the medical profession to women that gave her mother the greatest pleasure; clinical assistant at the RFH, Hampstead; after her initial training she took further training in Vienna; she graduated MB, BS, 1899; assisted Dr Mary Murdoch, a GP in Hull, for a brief period; member of the Brighton and Hove Committee, NUWSS; member LGUWS; member Royal Holloway College Suffrage Society; during the world trip with her mother and sister Hilda (see entry), she visited hospitals and medical institutions, 1900–01; House Surgeon at the Victoria Hospital for Children, Hull, 1901; in practice with Mary Murdoch in Hull for five years; further postgraduate study in Berlin, taking her MD, 1906; deciding to practise in Brighton, the first woman to do so, she became MO to Brighton High School and Roedean School; she joined the staff of a small dispensary for women and children in Brighton, which had been established by her mother and Dr Helen Boyle, 1907; further postgraduate study in Freiburg, 1913; over the years she was involved in extending this venture to become the New Sussex Hospital for Women and Children, formally opened in 1921; at the Brighton BMA Annual Conference, she was appointed as Honorary Secretary of Obstetrics and Gynaecology, 1913; after studying radiotherapy in Freiburg she returned to become the first woman (she worked with Mr F.L. Provis) to employ deep X-ray therapy in the treatment of breast cancer and fibroid uterus cases, 1913; also engaged in the isssue of venereal disease and prostitution at this time, writing *Under the Surface*, which caused great controversy in the House of Commons; during WW1 she remained at her work in Brighton, taking her holidays in France working at the Scottish Women's Hospital in Royaumont; she moved to Hove, 1919; visited America to study surgery in New York and other major cities, 1919; during this trip at a conference of medical women in New York, the MWIA was formed, of which she later became President, 1919; moved to London to take up a consulting practice in the treatment of breast and uterine cancer, 1921; installed higher-voltage apparatus for X-ray treatment for cancer in her home, 1922; member Obstetric Gynaecological Section of the BMA, 1923; Honorary Secretary, subsequently Treasurer, MWIA, 1924–9; elected as one of the seven members of the Cancer Research Committee of the London Association of the MWF, 1925; Executive Member ODC, 1928; President London Association of the MWF; over the ensuing eight years she worked with colleagues to extend the facilities for this work, eventually opening the Marie Curie Hospital in Hampstead, of which she became Honorary Consulting Surgeon, 1929; continued to travel to Brighton to work there and was appointed Honorary Consulting Surgeon, New Sussex Hospital, Brighton; President MWF, 1931; CBE, 1931; elected FRCOG, 1933; first woman JP, Brighton; co-opted on to the Council of the RCOG, 1935; during her work as MWF President, she ensured access for women to the new British Postgraduate Medical School from which they had been excluded, and became the first woman to be elected to the governing body; retired as surgeon from the New Sussex Hospital, 1937; member AMSH; continued on the Board of Management until the hospital was taken into public ownership under the NHS legislation, 1948; during WW2 she worked from her country home, travelling to London and Brighton to operate; after the war she returned to London to practise in Harley Street; eventually retired, 1947; FRSM; regarded as a highly skilled surgeon, but her love of entertaining and her desire to encourage and help young women entering the profession were also significant parts of her life; her courage and independence were demonstrated by the fact that, despite blindness in later life, she remained in her home assisted by a network of string arranged around the walls of her flat, which enabled her to find her way about.

p. Under the Surface (1909); *The Woman Doctor and her Future* (1922); *Treatment of Cancer of the Breast*; *The Artificial Menopause*; *The Prevention of Venereal Disease* (1945); *Venereal Disease, Its Influence on the Health of the Nation, Its Cure and Prevention* (1948); *A Woman Surgeon* (1951); papers to medical journals.

s. Women's Who's Who, 1913; *The Lady's Who's Who*, 1938–9; Martindale (1944); *Who Was Who*, 1961–70; *British Medical Journal*, 26 February 1966.

MASON, Bertha (between 1853–4 and 1861 -8 July 1939) social welfare activist; *b.* Ashton-under-Lyne; *do.* Hugh Mason, mill owner, Liberal MP & Betsey Buckley; *e.* privately; *r.* music, architecture; *c.* Albemarle; *a.* Brownlos House, Hindhead, Surrey, 6 Hans Place, London SW1 (1934).

Her father was an enlightened, if paternalistic, employer who built good housing and provided educational and recreational facilities for his workers; as an MP he spoke for the Women's Suffrage Association; Bertha's education was conducted on classical lines and she became an advanced Greek and Latin scholar; first woman Poor Law Guardian, Ashton, 1892–1904; introduced reforms in workhouse management, to improve children's lives; worker for the National British Women's Total Abstinence Union; member of the Executive of the British Committee for the Manchester Society for the Abolition of the State Regulation of Vice, 1897–1905; member Executive of the British Committee of the International Abolitionist Federation, 1897–1915; a colleague of Millicent Fawcett (see entry), joined the suffrage movement in 1890; Chair North of England Suffrage Society; Treasurer

NUWSS, 1902–10; moved to London, 1904; published a history of the movement, 1912; involved in British medical and overseas service, 1914–18; received several decorations from the French for her war work; member Executive Committee AMSH, 1915–31; Vice President NCW; Chair WLGS, 1924; Honorary Parliamentary Secretary NCW, 1927; Treasurer BWTAU; member British Society Hygiene and Public Morality Council; Council LNU; Honorary Secretary War Pensions Committee; died from double pneumonia.

p. The Story of the Women's Suffrage Movement (1912); articles and pamphlets on local government.

s. Hutchinson (1934); The Shield vii/2 (October 1939); Bank and McDonald (1998); Jeremy (1985), vol. 4.

MATHESON, Hilda OBE (1888–30 October 1940) broadcasting innovator; *b.* Scotland?; *do.* Rev. Donald Matheson; *e.* St Felix's School, Southwold, Oxford University; *a.* Rocks Farm, Withyham, Sussex.

Appointed librarian at the Ashmolean Museum, Oxford during the first six months of WW1; gave up her job during WW1 to become a VAD, then involved with intelligence work in Rome with the British Mission, serving under the Special Intelligence Directorate of the War Office; Parliamentary Secretary to Lady Astor (see entry), 1920–26; Acting Honorary Secretary CCWO Drafting Committee, 1922; joined the BBC, attached to the Department of Education, 1926; served on the Hadow Committee, which inquired into the place of adult education in broadcasting, 1927; appointed as the first BBC Director of Talks, 1927–32; used her intelligence, vision and considerable intellectual and artistic contacts to produce eclectic programming and was considered to have developed greater freedom of opinion on BBC Radio as a result; her department consisted of Women's, General and News sections; the talks in the Women's Programme often tackled controversial issues such as married women's right to work by ex-suffrage activists such as Ellen Wilkinson (see entry); according to Parker, 'she was very popular with women in the Corporation, seen as giving a lead and showing what women could achieve'; conflict between Lord Reith and Matheson soon grew – he felt that her speakers and their topics were too left-wing and she felt that Reith was a cultural ignoramus, and the result was a reorganization of the Talks Department, which 'differed fundamentally from the proposal I put up myself' [Hilda Matheson] and which, effectively, demoted Matheson to Director of General Talks, in February 1931; left the BBC, February 1932; according to the *New Statesman*, 'her departure was a disastrous turning point', 1932; in addition to her directness and political affiliations, her lesbianism must have affronted Reith, especially her liaison with Vita Sackville-West, whom she met during a poetry broadcast, 1928; after leaving the BBC she became Vita and Harold Nicolson's secretary; also a close friend of Dame Ethel Smythe, the composer and ex-suffragette, also a confessed lesbian; took over from Lord Hailey, undertaking the African Survey for the Royal Institute of International Affairs; OBE, 1939; one of the originators and Broadcasting Director of a private project, the Joint Broadcasting Commission, which supplied British programmes about England to foreign stations in order to promote international understanding, Harold Nicolson and Prof. Winifred Cullis (see entry) were on the Commission, 1939; however, due to wartime regulations relating to 'aliens' in Britain, many of her foreign staff were interned and she campaigned successfully for their release from the internment camps; she died as a result of a thyroid operation; Vita wrote in her obituary that 'She is gone, because she would not spare herself'.

s. Star, 1 November 1940; *The Times*, 1 November 1940; *New Statesman & Nation*, 6 November 1940; *Spectator*, 22 November 1940; Bank and McDonald (1998); BBC Written Archive Talks Department Files, JBC Files.

MATHEWS, Mabel Lucy, AIEE; electrical engineering; *a*. Cleredon, Brockwell Park Gardens, Herne Hill, London SE24, Consolidated Pneumatic Tool Company, Egyptian House, 170 Piccadilly, London W1 (1921).

Graduate member IEE, 1923; gave a paper on women's interest in domestic uses of electricity at the inaugural meeting of EAW, 1924; member EAW Council with an interest in electrical engineering; Vice President EAW; member Advisory Council, WES Conference of Women, 1925; member Council WES; Associate Member IEE, 1929; her last IEE member registration was in 1939.

s. WES Archive.

MATHEWS, Dame Vera Laughton (née Laughton) (a.k.a. Tug-boat Annie) MBE (1888–1959) women's services and women's rights activist; *do*. Prof. Sir John Laughton, historian & Miss Alberti; *e*. St Andrew's Convent, Streatham, Belgium, Kings College, London; *m*. Gordon D. Mathews, 1924; one daughter, two sons; *r*. swimming, rowing, walking; *a*. 11 Stanton Road, Wimbledon (1927), 57 Carlton Hill, London NW8 (1938).

Designated herself a feminist, joining the suffrage movement when she was 20; sub-editor of the *Suffragette*; gave up her job as sub-editor of the *Ladies' Field* in order to enter the WRNS in December 1917 and served for the remainder of WW1; Division Commander of the Girl Guides; represented the SJSPA when she gave evidence to a Select Committee of the House of Lords on the bill raising the legal age of marriage, 1929; represented the SJSPA in the British delegation to the International Congress of the IWSA in Berlin, where she proposed the resolution in favour of raising the legal age of marriage for boys and girls to 16, 1929; spoke in French in support of women's suffrage for French women at the IWSA in Marseille, 1932; Chairman of the SJSPA, 1932; member of the Executive Committee, AMSH, 1933–9; British representative on the IAF; appeared before the committee reviewing the admission of women to the Diplomatic and Consular Services on behalf of the SJSPA, 1934; speaker on a deputation to the Lord Chancellor for a Bill to make married women liable for their own debts, 1935; Chairman of the Nationality of Married Women Committee at the triennial Congress of the IWSA in Istanbul, 1935; spoke on behalf of the SJSPA to the Colonial Office against the forced marriage of African women; represented the SJSPA at the LN Assembly dealing with the status of women, also attending the various joint conferences of the International Women's organizations, 1935; gave evidence to a Parliamentary Committee inquiring into the economic aspect of the Women's Services, 1939; SJSPA gave her a congratulatory dinner on her appointment as Director of WRNS and her relinquishing the Chairman's post, 1939; Director of the WRNS and the only head of a women's service to serve for the duration of WW2, 1939–46; worked with Elizabeth Abbott (see entry) in AMSH and was a friend of Helen Archdale (see entry); considered that 'suffragettes were among the most noble, selfless and single-minded human beings it has been my privilege to meet'.

p. Towards Citizenship: A Handbook of Women's Emancipation (with Phyllis C. Challoner, 1928); *Blue Tapestry: The History of the WRNS* (1948)
s. Mathews (1948).

MAYO, Winifred Alice (née Monck Mason) (c.1870–1967) actress; *b.* India; *do.* Thomas Monck Mason, writer and theatrical impresario & Alice; *e.* privately in England and France; *r.* reading, history, theatre; *c.* Lyceum, IWF, *a.* 93 Oakley St, London SW3 (1913), 1 Selwood Place, Onslow Gardens, London SW7 (1934), Fir Tree Cottage, Hythe, Southampton (1952).

Spent some years in the theatre as an actress/director and was the founder of The Play Actors; her first recorded appearance was as Elizabeth Bennett in *The Bennetts* at The Court Theatre, which she co-directed, 1901; appeared with many other suffrage activist actresses, for example, in *Hannele* at the Scala with Cicely Hamilton and Inez Bensusan, 1908; member and worker in the WSPU; founder of the AFL with Adeline Bourne (see entry), with whom she also appeared in suffrage plays; served on the Executive Committee AFL; arrested and imprisoned on numerous occasions; Organizing Secretary SPG, 1921–6; Honorary Treasurer AFL, 1926; attended the initial meeting of the ODC, 1926; her last recorded stage appearance was in 1928; Honorary Secretary Equal Rights International, 1930–34; Honorary Treasurer SF, 1952.

s. Women's Who's Who, 1913; Hutchinson (1934); *Women's Who's Who, 1934–5*; Wearing (1981, 1982, 1984); Crawford (1999).

MOIR, Lady Margaret Bruce (née Pennycook) OBE (1864–1942) employment access campaigner; *do.* John Pennycook of Ravelstone & Dalmeny, Midlothian; *m.* Sir Earnest William Moir, civil engineer, 1887; two sons; *a.* Whitehanger, Fernhurst, Marley Common, near Haslemere, Sussex, 41 Cadogan Square, London SW1 (1934).

Referred to herself as 'an engineer by marriage', as she travelled with her husband on his engineering projects and became involved in inspecting and learning about these structures over the years (including the Forth Bridge); because of the pressure on women workers caused by the shell shortage during WW1, she organized the Weekend Relief Work scheme at munitions factories, where substitute workers enabled the regular women workers to have time off to rest; Moir participated as a relief lathe operator for 18 months; Honorary Treasurer and Honorary Secretary Women's Advisory Committee National War Savings Committee, organizing the sale of war savings certificates and bonds in large London stores and Victoria Station; awarded an OBE; co-founder and assisted with continued funding WES, 1919; realized the potential for applying the new technical innovations to the domestic sphere and became a Council member EAW, representing the WEA and later President of the EAW; Executive Committee SPG, 1921–2; organized a simplified engineering course for women at several polytechnics; supported and promoted the work of women pioneers – for instance, she held receptions at her home for Amy Johnson and Lady Bailey for them to give lectures on their return from their Australian and African flights; President WEA, 1934; established Certificate and Diploma examinations of the EAW; supported the Over 30 Housing Association and sponsored an all-electric flat in the block of flats erected for single women living alone; she also supported youth movements for girls.

s. Hutchinson (1934); *The Times*, 16 October, 19 October 1942.

MOORE-GUGGISBERG, Lady Lilian Decima (née Moore) (stage-name Decima Moore) CBE (11 December 1871–18 February 1964) actress; *b.* Brighton; *do.* Edward Henry Moore & Emily Strachan; *e.* Boswell House College, Brighton, Blackheath Conservatoire of Music; *m.* Brig. Gen. Sir Gordon Guggisberg, Governor Gold Coast and British Guiana, 1905; *r.* golfing, riding, driving; *c.* IWF, Royal Overseas, Lady's Army and Navy; *a.* 15 Buckingham Gate Gardens, Buckingham Gate, London SW1 (1906), 132 Clarence Gate, London NW1 (1913), Ludwick, Woodhall Spa, Lincolnshire (1935).

Left school, 1887; went to the Conservatoire, where she was the winner of the Victoria Scholarship for Singing and passed the Trinity College Cambridge Examination in Theory of Music with honours; made her stage debut at the Savoy, 1889; one of the original members AFL, 1908; when she was on tour, she used to leave the theatre between performances to give suffrage speeches; founder of the Women's Emergency Corps, 1914; attached to the French Army, 1915; nursed at a hospital in Amiens; founder of several leave clubs in France, 1915–18; made a CBE, 1918; Director Forum Club; Chair Overseas Section, Forum Club; exhibition commissioner and Chair British Empire Exhibition, Wembley, 1923, 1924, 1925; Vice Chair AFL, 1926; member Welcome Committee Royal Overseas League, for which she worked during WW2 as well as re-establishing the British Leave Club in Paris, also served on the Allies Welcome Committee.

p. We Two in West Africa (with her husband, 1909); *A Black Mark*; various articles.

s. Women's Who's Who, 1934–5; *The Lady's Who's Who*, 1938–9; *The Times*, 20 February 1964, 27 February 1964; Holledge (1981); Bank and McDonald (1998).

MURRAY, Dr Flora MD, DPH, CBE (1869–28 July 1923) woman activist and physician; *e.* University of Durham, LSMW; *r.* gardening; *a.* Penn, Buckinghamshire (1923).

Graduated with her MB, BS from Durham, 1903; took her MD, Durham, 1905; Cambridge DPH, 1906; member LSWS and the WSPU; treated suffragettes when they came out of prison; worked at the Royal Infirmary, Newcastle upon Tyne, particularly interested in child health and was one of a group of women who started the Hospital for Children in the Harrow Road, London, 1912; formed the Women's Hospital Corps with Dr Louisa Garrett Anderson (see entry) when war broke out, the first of the women's wartime voluntary units, 1914; Head of the Endell Street Military Hospital, where she was the first woman to be paid on the scale of a Lieutenant Colonel, 1914–19; Assistant Physician, Crichton Royal Institute, Dumfries; Clinical Assistant Belgrave Hospital for Children; anaesthetist at the Chelsea Hospital for Women; Vice President of SPG, 1921–2; Murray was buried in Penn and the last post was sounded at her graveside; left her entire estate of £3335 to Garrett Anderson to dispose of as she saw fit.

p. Women as Army Surgeons: Being the History of the Women's Hospital Corps in Paris, Wimereux and Endell Street, September 1914–October 1919 (1920); 'Ethyl Chloride as an Anaesthetic for Infants' in *The Lancet* (1905).

s. British Medical Journal, 4 August 1905; *The Times*, 30 July 1923; *The Vote*, 10 August 1923.

MURRELL, Dr Christine Mary, MD, BSc (18 October 1874–18 October 1933) women and children's health practitioner; *b.* Wimbledon; *do.* Charles Murrell & Alice Rayne; *e.* Clapham High School for Girls, LSMW; *a.* 86 Porchester Terrace, Hyde Park, London W2 (1914), 21 North Gate, Regents Park, London NW1 (1933), 9 Clifford Street, London W1 (1934).

Graduated MB, BS, 1899; gained her MD in Psychology and Mental Diseases, 1905; House Physician and Medical Registrar at the RFH; Clinical Assistant Northumberland County Asylum, Morpeth; Honorary Physician Paddington Creche and Marylebone Nursing Home; had a practice in Marylebone specializing in infants, 1907–25; specialist in neurology and women's mental health and disease; served as Medical Officer for the Metropolitan Special Constabulary, F Division, and Chairman WEC, during WW1; active on many BMA committees from 1917; President WEC; member SJSPA; member WEC; member Executive Committee SPG, 1921; first woman to be elected to the BMA Council, 1924–33; speaker at a NUSEC Conference on Restrictive Legislation, 1926; President MWF, 1926–8; President Metropolitan Counties Branch, 1928; Honorary Treasurer MWF, 1931–3; she was a generous donor to the MWF: one gift of £1000 was to form the John Rayne's Fund (in memory of her grandfather) to assist medical women in practice; Chairman of the Ladies' Centenary Celebration Committee, BMA, 1932; member of the Council of the Medical Defence Union; again she was the first woman to serve as the representative of the MWF on the conjoint committee of Epsom College, 1933; first woman practitioner elected as a representative of the practitioners of England and Wales to the GMC, 1933; Murrell worked for the interests of women doctors and patients liasing between women's medical organizations and the BMA to end the restrictions on women; friend and colleague of Lady Barrett (see entry) and Letitia Fairfield (see entry), but was particularly the 'beloved friend and colleague' of Dr Honor Bone, to whom she was 'devoted to the end'; the Christine Murrell Memorial Fund was established to equip a new infant welfare centre on the site where she had started her practice in Marylebone.

p. Womanhood and Health (1923).

s. Daily Telegraph, 20 October 1933; *The Times*, 23 October 1933; *British Medical Journal*, 28 October 1933.

NEILANS, Alison Roberta Noble (1884–17 July 1942) equal moral standard campaigner; *do.* Robert Neilans & Alison Ferguson Noble; *e.* private and Langley House, Dulwich; *r.* reading, gardening, mountain-walking; *a.* 19 Tothill Street, London SW1 (1920–21), 25 Asmuns Place, Hampstead Garden Suburb, London NW11 (1927), Livingstone House, Broadway, London SW1 (1934).

Worked in office administration in a business environment for five years; joined the suffrage movement and became the Financial Secretary and subsequently an Election and Propaganda Organizer for the WFL, during which time she was imprisoned three times, 1907–12; disciple of Josephine Butler; General Secretary AMSH, 1917–41; organizer, speaker and writer on social and legal aspects of sex-morality questions; Editor, *The Shield*; Executive Committee NCW; Secretary to the Committee of Inquiry into Sexual Morality; gave evidence to the Commission of Investigation re Clause 3 of the Criminal Law Amendment Bill and the Sexual Offences Bill, 1920; representative at Conference of Women, 1921; NUSEC delegate to IAWSEC Paris Congress, 1926; Executive Committee ICW; chaired two international committees dealing with the Traffic in Women and Moral Welfare work; Scottish speaking tour for NUSEC, 1926; member IAWSEC; attended the initial meeting of the ODC, 1926; Executive Committee ODC, from 1927; member NUSEC and ERGACC deputation to Ramsay MacDonald, spoke against legislation on 'common prostitutes', 1929; British representative Equal Moral Standard Commission, SEC, 1931; member WPC, 1940; described herself politically as a Radical, Individualist and Free Trader; stricken with paralysis in 1941 and died from the effects of a gradual paralytic disease, nursed by her lifelong friend from suffrage days, with whom she lived, Madge Turner (see entry); Neilans was steadfastly committed to the cause of sexual reform and its attendant issues and had travelled the world as an international speaker and campaigner.

p. *Ballot Box Protest*; *Are Moral Standards Necessary? An Address* (1935); 'Changes in Sex Morality' in Strachey (ed.) *Our Freedom and Its Results* (1936).

s. *List of Women Nominated for Service in Connection with the League of Nations* (NUWT Archive, nd 1920–21?); *The Lady's Who's Who*, 1938–9; *The Shield*, xi/2 (November 1948); *Who Was Who*, vol. 4.

NETTLEFOLD, Lucy Frances (Nancy) LLB, MA, OBE (15 June 1891–28 March 1966) industrialist; *b.* Notting Hill, London; *do.* Oswald Nettlefold, metal screw manufacturer & Emily Josephine Buckingham; *e.* private school, University of London, Newnham College Cambridge; *r.* bridge, fast motoring; *c.* Women's Provisional; *a.* 3 Raymond Buildings, Grays Inn, London WC1 (1923), 38 Clarence Gate Gardens, London NW1 (1938).

Nancy's mother was frustrated in her ambitions to become a doctor and supported her eldest daughter in her professional career; when still at school Nancy met suffragettes at the house of two of her teachers, Alice Jeffries and Miss Brown; when Nancy and her sister, Joyce, were still teenagers they held street meetings in the suffrage cause, their mother being prepared to stand bail if they were arrested; Nettlefold often refused to attend the balls during her coming-out season and found being presented at court an 'annoyance'; she wanted to be a lawyer and took an LLB at the University of London before going up to Cambridge to read Law, 1910; Olive Schreiner's – *Women & Labour* influenced her thinking greatly, 1911; sport was her great love until an accident while bob-sleighing left her with a permanent disability that troubled her all her life; achieved Class 1 in parts 1 and 2 of the Law tripos, attending Newnham 1910–12 and 1913–14, the year's interruption being due to her accident; although qualified as a solicitor, women were still unable to practise; in order to challenge this discrimination, Nettlefold together with Marjorie Bebb and two other women took the Law Society to court to force them to include women in their definition of a 'person' in the admission rules; they lost their case, took it to the High Court and lost again, 1913; became an articled clerk with Rider, Heaton & Co, Lincoln's Inn, London, working on cases that brought her into contact with women in the East End, 1914–16; travelled to South Africa to see her dear Cambridge friend, Mary Macintosh, and on her return she entered into war work as a temporary civil servant as Departmental Assistant Secretary (the highest civil service post open to a woman) in the Ministry of Food, 1916–19; at the termination of her war work she travelled to South Africa to visit Macintosh, who had been forced to remain there to look after her younger siblings because of her mother's ill health; while the Sex Discrimination (Removal) Act of 1919 enabled Nancy to take up her long-sought career in the law, her father's declining health obliged her to enter the family business of Nettlefold and Sons, 1920; member representative Consultation Committee, 1921; member Drafting Committee for CCWO meeting, 1922; her family responsibilities acquitted, Macintosh returned to Britain to live with Nettlefold in a relationship that was to last for 36 years; on her father's death, Nettlefold became Joint Managing Director of Nettlefold and Sons with her brother, 1924; she was appointed by the Minister of Education to a committee to inquire into 'the art of salesmanship, 1928; gave a paper at a WES Conference on 'The Place of the Wholesaler in the School of Distribution'; Honorary Treasurer of the BFUW, President of the London Association, member of the budget sub-committee of the International Federation, being interested in equal pay and equal opportunities for women, access to the professions and higher civil service posts, as well as more prestigious posts in industry; Director of Crosby Hall, the BFUW residence, 1925–42, then 1948–52; on the Managing Committee of the Elizabeth Garrett Anderson Hospital, 1931–60 (apart from during WW2), and Vice Chairman 1946–49; Governor and Council member Bedford College for Women, London 1932–60; attended the first meeting of BUC; elected as Conservative member to the St Marylebone Metropolitan BC, 1945–56; during WW2, appointed to the Royal Commission on Equal Pay, with a considerable input to the report published in 1945; co-opted Governor of Royal Holloway College and the Finance Committee, 1946; sold the business to Guest, Keen & Nettlefold, retiring from the firm, 1948; Conservative candidate LCC division of St Marylebone, leading member Welfare Committee, with special interest in homes for the elderly and work for the disabled, 1949–60; member of the LCC Education Committee, vigorously opposing the introduction of comprehensive education, 1949–51; Macintosh, her lifelong companion, died of pneumonia in 1959; OBE, 1960; retired and feeling desolate at the loss of Macintosh, needing the comfort of family, she went to live with her sister in South Africa (her sister was the first woman mayor of Cape Town); as far as her health permitted, with Pastor Niemoller's words as her maxim,* she became involved in women's groups and in opposing apartheid, whose racism she abhorred; died in Cape Town.

* 'First they came for the Jews
and I did not speak out –
because I was not a Jew.
Then they came for the communists
and I did not speak out –
because I was not a communist.
Then they came for the trade
unionists and I did not speak out –
because I was not a trade unionist.
Then they came for me –
and there was no-one left
to speak out for me.'

s. *The Lady's Who's Who*, 1938–9; *Daily Telegraph*, 30 March 1966; *The Times*, 30 March, 12 April 1966; Tredgold (1968); Newnham College Archives.

NEVINSON, Margaret Wynne (née Jones) LLA, JP (1857–8 June 1932) public speaker and writer; *b.* Leicester; *do.* Rev. Timothy Jones, Vicar of St Margaret's, Leicester; *e.* day schools Oxford, convent school Paris, Cologne, St Andrew's University; *m.* Henry Wood Nevinson, journalist, 1884; one daughter, one son; *r.* cycling, swimming, walking, music, travel, gardening; *c.* IWF, PEN; *a.* 4 Downside Crescent, Hampstead, London NW3 (1913–29).

Taught Latin and Greek by her father at the age of 7; took an LLA; began her career as a governess, then travelled to Germany as an au pair; she became a Classics teacher at the South Hampstead Girls' High School, 1880–84; collected signatures for a petition in support of the Married Women's Property Act, 1882; taught English evening classes in Whitechapel at Canon Barnett's Toynbee Hall; one of the first members of the Local Committee of the Hampstead NUWSS, 1905; member Committee of the Women's Franchise Declaration, 1906; joined the WSPU deputation to Parliament protesting at the omission of a suffrage bill in the King's Speech, 1907; a tax resister; one of the original members WFL; member CLWS; early member and Honorary Treasurer WWSL; extensive writing on suffrage issues; worked for the London School Board as a school manager for 25 years in the East End and Hampstead; Poor Law Guardian, Hampstead, 1904–22; pioneer of massage, joined the Almerie Paget Military Massage Corps, working in a hospital, 1914–16; signatory on a letter to the Undersecretary of State for War, concerning the repeal of Section 40D of the DORA, 1918; lecture tour on the need for women justices, along the South Coast, for WFL, 1919; appointed JP for Hampstead, being the first woman to sit on the criminal bench in the County of London, 1920; committed speaker on the LN; went to USA to study the probation system, 1921; one of the first three women appointed to sit on the Lord Chancellor's London County Justices Advisory Committee, 1921–30; elected to the Council of Society of Women Journalists, 1927–8; Vice President of the Women's Peace Crusade, 1928; died at her Hampstead home.

p. 'Workhouse Characters' in *Westminster Gazette*; 'Juvenal on Latter Day Problems' in *The Fortnightly Review* (1907); *In the Workhouse* (play, 1911); *Fragments of Life* (short stories, 1922); *Life's Fitful Fever* (autobiography, 1926); suffrage pamphlets – *Five Years' Struggle for Freedom: A History of the Suffrage Movement from 1908–12* (1912); *Ancient Suffragettes*; *The Spoilt Child of the Law* (1913); *The Legal Wrongs of Married Women* (1923); contributor to the *Fortnightly Review*, *National Review*, *English Review* and various newspapers and periodicals.

s. Women's Who's Who, 1913; *The Vote*, 30 July 1920; *Life's Fitful Fever* (1926); *Who's Who*, 1929; *Manchester Guardian*, 9 June 1932; *The Times*, 9 June 1932; *Daily Telegraph*, 9 June 1932; Banks (1985).

NORMANTON, Helena Florence KC (1883–14 October 1957) barrister, legal reformer for women's rights; *b.* Kensington, London; *do.* William Alexander Normanton, pianoforte manufacturer; *e.* Varndean Secondary School, Brighton, Edge Hill Training College, Liverpool, Dijon University; *m.* Gavin Bowman Watson Clark, 1921; *r.* doing absolutely nothing; swimming, cookery, visiting picture galleries; *c.* ESU; *a.* 41 Botanic Road, Liverpool, 22 Mecklenburgh Square, London WC1, 11 Coram Street, London WC1 (1922), 3 Dr Johnson's Buildings, Temple, London EC4 (1931), 25 Aldersmead Road, Beckenham, Kent (1934).

Attended Edge Hill, 1903–05; gained first-class honours Modern History, 1912; French Language, Literature and History diplomas; Scottish Secretary Teachers'

Diploma and English Board of Education Teachers' Diploma; her first teaching post seems to have been at Anfield Road Girls' School, Liverpool, followed by posts in London in Tottenham and Central Acton; Senior History Mistress, Glasgow High School for Girls, 1913–15; Lecturer to postgraduate History students, Glasgow University; first General Secretary NWCA, 1918–19; Editor, *India*, 1919–22; her application to the Middle Temple to become a student was refused in February, 1918; became the first woman to take advantage of the opening of the legal profession to women in the Sex Disqualification (Removal) Act, 1919, admitted to Middle Temple, 24 December 1919; University Extension Leturer at the University of London, lecturing on social, political, feminist and historical issues; became the second woman to be called to the Bar of the Middle Temple, 17 November 1922; first woman barrister briefed at the High Court of Justice, 1922; first woman barrister Central Criminal Court, 1924; first woman barrister London Sessions, 1926; pioneer worker for equal pay; appointed 'Legal Adviser' to the WUO, 1924; had a somewhat tempestuous career due to her fierce feminism, determination to challenge the status quo and outspokenness; gained public notoriety when she insisted on retaining her maiden name, secured a passport in that name and subsequently went to the USA to argue for that right in the American courts, being the first Englishwoman to conduct a court case in USA, Washington, 1925; elected member New York Women's Bar Association; Honorary Secretary Magna Carta Committee; member Honorary Standing Council, WES; wrote on legal discrimination against women, several articles in the 1920s on the adverse legal position of women in marriage and the need for reform of the marriage laws; member Executive Committee NCEC, 1931; appointed as Hon. Standing Counsel to the Married Persons Income Tax Reform Group for the separate assessment of married persons' tax, 1932; first woman to be elected to the General Council of the Bar (Harriet Cross had previously been co-opted), 1945–7; Associate Grand Dame for Europe of the International Society of Women Lawyers; originally a member for the Society for the Abolition of Capital Punishment, but her experiences at the Bar defending and prosecuting murderers caused a change of mind; Chairman international legislative sub-committee International Federation of Business and Professional Women; one of the first two women to take silk in England, appointed a KC in 1949; retired from legal practice, 1950; President MWA, drew up a memorandum of evidence for the Royal Commission on Marriage and Divorce, a document that was severely criticized by others in the Association as being 'anti-man' in tone, therefore resigned her Presidency in the same year, 1952; formed the CMW and submitted an amended document to the Royal Commission; President of this new body, 1952–4; died in a Sydenham nursing home.

p. The Work for Women MPs (1921); *India in England*; *Sex Differentiation in Salary* (1914); *Everyday Law for Women* (1932); *Magna Charta and Woman*; *The Work for Women Members of Parliament*; *Oliver Quendon's First Case* (1927); *The Trial of Norman Thorne* (1929); *The Trial of Alfred Arthur Rouse* (1931); contributor to the 13th edition of the *Encyclopaedia Britannica*; articles for many periodicals, newspapers in Britain, USA, Canada and India.

s. Who's Who, 1929; *The Lady's Who's Who*, 1938–9; *Manchester Guardian*, 16 October 1957; *The Times*, 16 October 1957; *Women's Bulletin*, 31 October 1957; Honourable Society of the Middle Temple Archive; Edge Hill College Archive.

NUTTING, Lady Helen (née Ogilvy) (1890–December 1973) women's rights campaigner; *do.* Sixth Earl of Airlie & Mabell, Lady Airlie; *m.* Clement B.O. Mitford-Freeman, 1909; Henry C. Brocklehurst, 1918; Harold B. Nutting, 1933; one son; *a.* 50 Carlisle Mansions, London (1973).

Perhaps it was her frequently married state that inspired her to campaign for equal status for married women; worked for the NBTF: member MWA from 1945; Deputy Chairman MWA, 1947; Vice President MWA, 1951; founder member of the breakaway CMW, 1952; worked with Jean Mann (see entry) collecting evidence for the campaign for women to have access to a proportion of their husband's income; Chairman CMW, 1953–69; during the latter years of the Council, it was Lady Nutting who sustained its existence; a friend wrote at her death that Lady Helen had been 'brave and brisk and beautiful'.

s. Lady Helen Nutting Papers, Fawcett Library; *The Times*, 8 December 1973.

OGILVIE GORDON, Maria Matilda (née Ogilvie) DBE, Honorary LLD (Edin. and Sydney), DSc, PhD, FLS, JP (30 April 1864–24 June 1939) geologist; *b.* Monymusk, Aberdeenshire; *do.* Rev. Dr Alexander Ogilvie, educationist & Maria-Matilda Nicoll; *e.* Ladies' College, Edinburgh, Royal Academy London, University College London; *m.* Dr John Gordon, 1895; two daughters, one son; *r.* music; *c.* Forum; *a.* 17 Goldhurst Terrace, London NW6 (1889), The White Lodge, 34 Abbey Road, London NW8 (1920–21), 155 Denmark Hill, London SE5 (1934), 174 Chase Side, London N14 (1934), 32 Hanover Gate Mansions, London NW1 (1939).

Her father was part of an educationally brilliant family and was an educational innovator, introducing the study of science and technology into the schools in which he taught and became headmaster, also establishing extension classes for men and women; Maria first studied piano, 1882; returned to Edinburgh to study, Dux medallist and travelling scholar; gained BSc at London University – studying at UCL – Zoology, Comparative Anatomy, Botany, Geology 1889–90; gold medallist in Zoology and Comparative Anatomy, 1889–90; studied Geology and Palaeontology at Munich University, 1890–95; DSc, 1893; the first woman to gain a PhD in Natural Sciences with the highest honours, London and Munich, 1900; first woman to conduct research in geology, largely in Munich and the Alps; apart from the WW1 years, went on field trips every year until two years before her death; attended first ICW meeting, 1899; first Vice President of the ICW; Honorary Secretary ICW, 1904–09; propaganda work concerning Juvenile Employment Committees and Choice of Employment Act, 1910; member Juvenile Organizations Committee, Board of Education; member ICW Sub-Committee Public Health, convenor of its Child Welfare and Education Committees; Vice President ICW, 1909–38; member Advisory Committee under Health Insurance Acts, 1912–18; Honorary Life President NWCA; President NCW, 1916–20; Honorary Parliamentary Secretary NCW; President NUWW, 1918; Chairman Committee for London Baby Week Exhibition, 1918; President Scottish Association of Health Insurance Committees, 1918–19; NCW representative on Organizing Committee for Conference of Women, to decide on the representation of women at the LN, 1919; Chairman Mothercraft and Child Welfare Exhibitions Committee, 1919–21; proposed the formation of the Women Citizens' Associations and became President, 1919–21, 1926–8, 1932–4; NWCA representative at the Conference of Women,

b: born; do: daughter of; e: education; m: married; r: recreation;
c: club; a: address; p: publications; s: sources

1921; on the BMAC to investigate infant mortality, 1921; member NCW Maternity and Child Welfare Committee, 1922; Vice President and Executive Committee NCW, 1927; President of the CRWLN, 1928; fellow of the Linnaean Society of London; Honorary President Associated Women's Friendly Society; Fellow Geological Society of London; Honorary Fellow Geological Society of Vienna; Honorary Member Science Department, Trento, Italy; Honorary Doctor Innsbruck University; awarded a Lyell medal and grant from the Lyell Geological Fund, 1932; expert on the geology of the Dolomites, with original research on structure in the region; awarded the DBE for her work for women and children, 1935; honorary doctorates from Edinburgh and Sydney, 1935 and 1938; died at her home in London; Elizabeth Cadbury (see entry) gave an address at her memorial service and the number of representatives present from the women's organizations with whom she had worked gave testimony to the extent of her contribution.

p. The Wengen and Cassian Strata in South Tyrol (1893); *Coral in the Dolomites* (1894); *Microscopic and Systematic Study of Madreporarian Types of Corals* (1895–6); *Die Korallen der Stramberger Schichten, A Monograph of an Upper Jurassic Fauna* (1896–97); *The Torsian Structure of the Dolomites* (1898–9); *Die obere cassianer Zone an der Falzarego Strasse* (1900); *History of Geology and Palaeontology* (1900); *The Geological Structure of Monzoni and Fassa* (1902–03); *Overthrust Structure in the Langkofl* (1907); *Handbook of Employments* (1908); *The Thrust Masses in the Western District of the Dolomites* (1910); *Das Grodner, Fassa und Enneberg Gebiet in den Sudtiroler Dolomiten* (1927); *Geologisches Wanderbuch in den Westlichen Dolomiten* (1928); *Geology of Pieve, St Cassian, and Cortina* (1929); *Geology of Cortina d'Ampezzo and Cadore* (1934); *Handbook of Employment for Boys and Girls*; *National Schemes of Education*; *Juvenile Deliquency*.

s. Aberdeen Journal, Notes and Queries (1912); *CSM*, 23 July 1923; *List of Women Nominated for Service in Connection with the League of Nations* (NUWT Archive, nd 1920–21?); *Who Was Who*, 1929–40; *The Times*, 26 June, 30 June 1939; *International Genealogical Index*; UCL Records; Archives of Robert Gordon's College, Aberdeen.

O'KELL, Lizzie Marguerite (16 February 1868–28 February 1960) women's public health pioneer; *b.* London; *do.* John O'Kell, medical student & Eliza Annand; *e.* Queen's College, Harley Street.

Attended only selected lectures at Queen's College, 1886–87; although she gained a scholarship she was unable to take it up due to her father's death, which meant she had to take a clerical post to support her mother and herself, 1887; hearing that women were now eligible to be sanitary inspectors, she studied the necessary subjects whilst continuing her clerical job until she was able to take the RSI examination, which she duly passed; started work in Paddington, investigating infant mortality, inspecting workhouses, restaurants and toilets; first woman sanitary inspector in Marylebone, 1898; one of the eight founding members and Executive Committee members of the London Women's Sanitary Inspectors' Association, who held their first recorded meeting April 1902; this subsequently became the WSIA; member WSIHVA, 1902–37; Executive Committee WSIHVA, 1918–19; representative on NUWW, 1918–19; representative on NCW; representative on NALGO; read a paper to RSI Conference, Hull, 1923; during her retirement she was involved in voluntary work, including Evacuation Officer at Abbots Langley during WW2; Enid Eve, also a sanitary inspector, was her great friend from 1917 until her death; died in hospital.

s. WSIHVA Archive, Wellcome Institute; *Woman Health Officer*, xxxiii/5 (April 1960); Queen's College Archive.

PALMER, Beatrix Maud, Countess of Selborne (née Cecil) JP (April 1858–27 April 1950) Conservative activist; *do.* Third Marquis of Salisbury, Lord Robert Cecil, Conservative Prime Minister & Georgina Caroline (Charlotte) Alderson; *e.* private; *m.* William Waldegrave Palmer, Second Earl of Selborne, 1883; one daughter, three sons; *a.* Blackmoore, Liss, Hampshire, 14 Buckingham Palace Gardens, London SW1 (1929).

An enthusiastic campaigner for women's suffrage, always interested in causes that addressed issues of oppression and suffering; President CUWFA; NCW representative Conference of Women for LN representation, 1919; President WHPMA, 1923; President Conservative Women's Reform Association; Vice President NCW, 1927: Executive Committee BAWC, 1928; member Council Queen's Institute District Nursing; an unconventional woman, disinterested in the trappings of her social position, whose sense of humour undermined other people's pretensions with regard to her rank.

p. several pamphlets.

s. The Lady's Who's Who, 1938–9; *The Times*, 6 May 1950.

PANKHURST, Emmeline (née Goulden) (14 July 1858–14 June 1928) suffrage pioneer; *b.* Manchester; *do.* Robert Goulden, calico printer & Sophia Jane Crane; *e.* Manchester, École Normale, Paris; *m.* Dr Richard Marsden Pankhurst, barrister, social reformer, 1879; three daughters, one son.

Her father was a supporter of the anti-slavery movement and the Anti-Corn Law League, and at 13 years old she was taken to her first suffrage meeting by her mother; member committee working on the Married Women's Property Act; member Manchester Women's Suffrage Committee; joined the Fabian Society and Holborn Women's Liberal Association, 1886; helped to found the WFL, 1889; had been a Liberal but joined the ILP, 1892; elected Board of Guardians, 1893–8; on her husband's death she worked as Registrar, Chorlton-on-Medlock, 1898; disenchanted by the lack of action on women's suffrage by the LP, she formed what was to become the most famous women's organization, whose members were subsequently known as suffragettes, the WSPU in Manchester; her three daughters – Sylvia, Christabel and Adele – were all involved, 1903; left the LP, 1907; led the WSPU's mounting campaign of militancy to secure the vote on military lines, and imprisoned on numerous occasions, 1905–14; lecture tour on the Women's Movement of USA and Canada, October 1909; at the outbreak of WW1, she suspended the WSPU and engaged in national propaganda recruitment tours supporting the war effort, also travelling to America for this purpose; visited Russia, 1917; Pankhurst lived in Canada, working as a lecturer in social hygiene for the National Council for Combating Venereal Diseases, 1919–26; then lived in Bermuda, and subsequently, the south of France, 1923–5; returned to Britain and joined the Conservative Party, 1925; an Equal Political Rights dinner and reception at Hyde Park Hotel to welcome her back to Britain was organized by SPG, 1926; marched in the NUSEC's 'old gang' group on the Equal Franchise demonstration of July 1926; member Women's

Advisory Committee and Executive Committee National Union of Conservative and Unionist Associations, 1927–8; PPC Conservative Party, Whitechapel and St George's, 1928; died in a West End nursing home and was buried at Brompton Cemetery; despite her autocratic management of the WSPU and what some women viewed as her betrayal of the Movement in WW1, she was hailed as the most courageous and significant heroine of the struggle for women's votes.

p. My Own Story (1914).

s. Women's Who's Who, 1913; Daily Telegraph, 15 June 1928; *The Times*, 15 June, 16 June, 19 June 1928; Banks (1985).

PARNELL, Nancy Stewart BA (14 May 1901–75) internationalist campaigner; *b.* London; *do.* Madeleine Damer Parnell; *e.* Notre Dame High School, Mount Pleasant, Liverpool, University of Liverpool; *r.* theatre, cinema; *a.* 91 Bedford Street, Liverpool (1919), St Gabriel's Hall, Victoria Park, Manchester 14 (1934), 8 Upper Belgrave Street, London SW1.

Great-niece of the Irish statesman; entered university, 1919; held a three-year Bibby Scholarship and a maintenance grant from the City of Liverpool for her first year; Honorary Secretary Liverpool University LNU branch; spoke at the Albert Hall on behalf of the CWSS in support of votes for women under 30, 1919; Secretary of the Students' Union, 1921–2; her BA dissertation was entitled *Irish Novelists of the Early Nineteenth Century: A Rapid Survey*; member Central Council NUWT; Warden St Gabriel's Hall, Manchester University; member of SJSPA; spoke on EPRDC, deputy to Baldwin as a representative of young voteless women, 1927; speaker at the Equal Franchise Demonstration, March 1928; worked in the Anti-Slavery Movement; taught for the WEA and the LNU; speaker on women's issues, peace, Liberal policy; member Central Council NUWT; member WIL; member LNU; member SJSPA; PPC Willesden East, 1935; President NUWT, 1936; became Assistant Organizer London Region Federation LNU, 1936; retired as London Regional Officer for the UNA because of ill health, 1960; excellent public speaker and did a great deal to build up the London LNU region to a success: 'everyone who knew Nancy loved her' (1975–6).

p. pamphlets – *Education for Peace; A Venture in Faith.*

s. Women's Who's Who, 1934–5; Hutchinson (1934); *The Woman Teacher*, 10 January, 15 May, 25 September 1936; UNA London Regional Council Annual Report, 1959–60, 1975–76; University of Liverpool Archive.

PARSONS, Lady Katherine (née Bethell) (1859–16 October 1933) employment access campaigner; *b.* Hull?; *do.* William Frogatt Bethell, Rise Park, Yorkshire; *m.* Hon. Sir Charles Algernon Parsons, distinguished engineering inventor and engineering magnate, 1883; one daughter (see entry), one son; *a.* Elvaston Hall, Ryton on Tyne, Durham (1884), Holeyn Hall, Wylam on Tyne (1894), 6 Windsor Terrace, Newcastle upon Tyne, Ray Estate, Kirkwhelpington, Northumberland, 1 Upper Brook Street, London W1 (1931).

In the early years of their marriage she accompanied her husband on many of his professional duties as he developed his Newcastle engineering works; an activist in the promotion of the Conservative Party's northeast women's group; first woman to speak to the North East Coast Institution of Engineers and Shipbuilders on women's participation in shipbuilding and engineering during WW1, 1919;

involved in creating engineering opportunities for women as a career; leader of the six women with whom she founded the WES in the post-WW1 period; President of the WES, 1919–26; helped her daughter, Rachel (see entry) to set up an engineering company with seven other young women, 1920; WES representative on the EAW Council; Chair of the Women's Committee of the Labour Co-Partnership Association, 1923; spoke on engineering at WES Conference, 1925; resigned as WES President because of a dispute with Caroline Haslett (see entry) over a lecture at the EAW Conference, 1925; held the introductory meeting of the EAW in her house, although she was not very enthusiastic about the aims of the Association, which she may have considered to be too traditional; known as 'a crusading pioneer' and 'a stalwart champion of women'; died at her home in Northumberland.

p. 'Engineering for Women', *Home and Politics* (July 1921).

s. Appleyard (1933); Messenger (1967); Jeremy (1985) vol. 4.

PARSONS, Rachel Mary (25 January 1885–2 July 1956) engineer; *b.* Ryton on Tyne; *do.* Hon. Sir Charles Algernon Parsons, engineer & Katherine Bethell (see entry); *e.* Roedean Girls' School, Newnham College, Cambridge; *r.* hunting, travel, golf; *c.* Ladies' Carlton; *a.* 5 Grosvenor Square, London W1, Ray Estate, Kirkwhelpington, Northumberland (1934), Belgrave Square, London SW1, Branches Park, Newmarket (1947), Landsdowne House, Falmouth Avenue, Newmarket (1954).

As a small child, she spent time with her father in his workshop while he made her mechanical toys complete with small engines – he always 'delighted' in his daughter's company; first woman to take the Mechanical Sciences tripos at Cambridge; during WW1, when her only brother was serving in France (he was killed at the end of the war), she took his place, working for her father as a Director in Heaton Works, her father's turbine and engineering plant at Newcastle upon Tyne; her mother helped her and a group of seven other women to found a women's engineering workshop in London, Atalanta, 1920; first President of the WES; member of the LCC, 1922–5; an unsuccessful Conservative PPC for Ince, Lancashire, 1923; Associate Member of the Institute of Naval Architects, one of the few women members; member of the Royal Institute for International Affairs; member Royal Institution; on her father's death, she inherited £840,000, 1931; during the 1930s she became one of London's well-known hostesses and developed an interest in horse breeding, moving to Newmarket after WW2 to breed horses; at the time of her death she owned about 20 horses; sold her Northumberland estate to the Ministry of Agriculture for £50,000 in 1950; liked fast cars and became known as an eccentric and a recluse, dying from head injuries inflicted with an iron bar after an attack by a 26-year-old stableman; the Countess of Rosse judged that Rachel had inherited her father's 'brilliant technical brain and volcanic temperament', also thought that Rachel had been frustrated in her high professional ambitions and, had she lived later – when professional women were more readily accepted – the second part of her life would not have been so disastrous, as she was plagued by sycophants, becoming lonely and frustrated.

s. Appleyard (1933); *Hutchinson* (1934); *Daily Telegraph*, 3 July 1956; *The Times*, 3 July, 18 July 1956; Jeremy (1985) vol. 4.

PARTRIDGE, Margaret Mary BSc, AMIEE (8 April 1891–27 October 1967) electrical engineer; *b.* Barton, Devon; *do.* John Bernard James Partridge, yeoman & Eleanor Parkhouse Joyce; *e.* Bedford High School, Bedford College, London.

Honours degree in mathematics, 1914; mathematics and art mistress, Yorkshire High School, 1914–15; pupil of heating and ventilating engineer, London, 1915–17; head tester of portable and static petrol-electric generators, motors and searchlight equipment, 1917–20; Chief Engineer, Klaxons, 1920–21; campaigned for access for women to electrical engineering, lecturing work; one of the earliest members WES; member EAW Council; spoke at WES Conference on 'The Domestic Application of Electricity', 1925; returned to Devon to open her own business, M. Partridge & Company, Exeter, 1921–32; with the help of the WES, employed girls direct from school as apprentices for an engineering career; appointed to Western Centre Council of Institute of Electrical Engineers, 1926; using water power or building and equipping required power stations, she laid on the electricity for Bungay, South Molton, Bampton (Devon) and Cheriton Fitzpaine by 1927; Director Exe Valley Electricity Company 1927; became associate member IEE, 1929; the establishment of high tension ring mains connecting towns and villages brought an end to such small companies as hers; actually contributed to the development of this system in the area as she worked with the consulting engineer and the scheme for the South-West was drawn up in her office; worked as a freelance engineer, 1932–9; founded and was the first secretary of the Exeter Munitions, 1939–41; one of Verena Holmes' (see entry) team of Labour Supply Inspectors with responsibility for researching the supply and working conditions of women in engineering factories, SW Regional Woman Technical Officer, Ministry of Labour, 1941–5; worked with Caroline Haslett (see entry) on the *Electrical Handbook for Women*; equipped and started a hotel, 1945–6; retired, 1946; during her retirement she did voluntary work for local community groups including being President of the local WI, where she trained WI members to carry out the electrical wiring for the new village hall.

p. Electricity (1925); *The Electrical Handbook for Women* (with C. Haslett, 1936–45).

s. The Woman Engineer, vii/20 (Spring 1956), x/8 (Winter 1967).

PETHICK-LAWRENCE, Lady Emmeline (née Pethick) (21 October 1867–11 March 1954) lecturer, writer, suffrage organizer; *b.* Weston-super-Mare; *do.* Henry Pethick, businessman & Miss Collen; *e.* boarding school, Devizes, France and Germany; *m.* Frederick William Lawrence, 1901; *r.* travel, gardening; *c.* Kibbo Kift; *a.* 11 Old Square, Lincoln's Inn, London WC2 (1917), Gomshall, Surrey (1921).

Worked for five years as a sister at the West London Mission and was the leader of a club for working girls, 1891; with Mary Neal she founded the Esperance Working Girls' Club, 1895; was involved with one of the first schemes to provide working women with holidays at the Green Lady Hostel at Littlehampton, 1898; founded the Maison Esperance, a co-operative dressmaking business, which implemented advanced ideas relating to conditions of work with an eight hour day, a minimum wage and annual holidays, 1897; vigorously opposed the South African War; worked at Percy Alden's Mansfield House settlement, Canning Town, where she met her husband; travelled to South Africa, met and became a good friend of Olive Schreiner, the feminist writer, 1905; previously involved in the suffrage movement but joined and became the Treasurer of the WSPU, 1906; she and her husband gave in excess of £6000 to the WSPU, with her husband she co-founded and co-edited *Votes for Women*, 1907; imprisoned five times and force-fed as a hunger-striker on several occasions; left the WSPU, at the request of Mrs Pankhurst, 1912; joined the

WFL; they joined the US and giving their paper, *Votes for Women*, to the US in order to keep the suffrage flag flying during WW1, 1914; joined the WEC committee, working with Belgian refugees, 1914; went to New York, instigating a new US suffrage campaign, as a pacifist she also spoke on the necessity for a negotiated world peace, October 1914; one of the organizers and one of the three British delegates (with Kathleen Courtney, see entry, and Chrystal Macmillan, see entry) of the women's international peace conference at the Hague, 1915; worked at WILPF HQ, Geneva during WW1; member ILP; Labour PPC Rusholme, 1918; Vice President Society for Constructive Birth Control and Racial Progress; involved in the campaign to lift the hunger blockade against Germany, 1919; attended the Second International Congress, Zurich, 1919; travelled from Zurich to Salzburg and Vienna, in an attempt to promote reconciliation; collected evidence and sworn statements to the violence perpetrated by the 'Black and Tans' against Irish women and children, writing an article for the *Daily News*, 27 April 1921; present at SPG's mass meeting, Queen's Hall, March 1922; Vice President WIL; member Theosophical Society; Vice President SPG; spoke at an international demonstration for peace at the German Reichstag, 1924; speaker at Peacemakers' Pilgrimage Rally, Hyde Park, 1926; President WFL, 1926–35?; spoke at WFL Equal Franchise meeting at Caxton Hall, January 1926; speaker at Equal Franchise demonstration, Hyde Park, 1928; spoke at the victory celebrations in Hotel Cecil on work still to be done by feminist societies, October 1928; Vice President CBC, 1929; WFL representative on NUSEC/ERGECC deputation to Ramsay MacDonald, spoke on the rights of women peers, April 1929; Treasurer ODC, 1931–2; Vice President Montessori Society; member Executive Committee ODC, 1933–6; delegate to IAW in Constantinople, 1935; attempted to establish a number of women's newspapers which failed due to wartime paper rationing, *Women's National Newspaper*, 1938, *Women's Daily Newspaper*, 1938, *Woman's Newspaper*, 1939; Vice President SPG, late 1930s; also worked to get the position of women addressed by the LN; a devoted couple, she and her husband dedicated their time and their fortune to redressing discrimination and in the pursuit of justice and peace; died at her home in Surrey.

p. numerous articles and periodicals in the feminist press; pamphlet – *Economic Emancipation Next* (1929); autobiography – *My Part in a Changing World* (1938).

s. *The Reformers' Year Book* (LP, 1908); *Women's Who's Who, 1913*; Pethick-Lawrence (1938); *The Times*, 12 March 1954; Banks (1985); Doughan and Sanchez (1984); Harrison (1987); *Dictionary of National Biography Missing Persons* (1993).

PHILLIPS, Juanita Maxwell (née Comber) JP (?–c.1950s) local government and social worker; *do.* Thomas Denison Comber; *m.* Thomas Phillips; *r.* theatre; *c.* Forum Club; *a.* Sudbury Lawn, Honiton, Devon, Awliscombe House, near Honiton.

Worked in the War Office for four-and-a-half years during WW1; JP, Devon, 1922; as first woman Mayor in the West Country, she held office in Honiton for a record eleven times 1920–24, 1925–6, 1936–9, 1945–6; regarded herself as an adopted 'Honitonian', worked hard for the town and was well-liked, particularlry concerned for children's welfare, her wealth ensured that she could spend money on local children, still remembered today by older Honiton residents; Chairman Devon FWI, President of the Honiton Branch, 1923; member NCW Committee on Social Insurance, 1926; member of NUSEC and one of the 11 resigning Executive Committee, over protective legislation, 1927; Executive Committee ODC, 1927;

County Councillor, Devon 1931; had a well-equipped theatre built in the grounds of her home to provide a permanent site for theatre in Devon, 1933; member Executive Committee NCUMC; Executive Committee NCW; presented with the freedom of the Borough of Honiton, 1937; President of the Honiton Infant Welfare Centre, 1938; during WW2 she was Food Executive Officer, involved in evacuation work and entertaining the troops before becoming Mayor again; she was regarded as 'a born leader and organizer' (1939).

s. *Women's Who's Who, 1934–5*; *Devonshire Gazette*, 13 November 1936; *Express & Echo*, 20 December 1937; *Western Times*, 17 February 1938; *Western Morning News*, 19 September 1939; *Western Times*, 15 November 1940.

PHILLIPS, Marion DSc (29 October 1881–23 January 1932) LP Chief Woman Officer; *b.* Melbourne, Australia; *do.* Philip David Phillips, lawyer, & Rose Asher; *e.* Presbyterian Ladies College, Ormond College, Melbourne University, LSE London University; *c.* National Labour; *a.* 74 Lansdowne Road, London W11 (1910?), 61 Lansdowne Road, London W11, 14 New Street Square, London EC4 (1918–19?).

BA History and Philosophy, 1903; research scholarship in Economics, LSE, 1904; although she was from a staunch Jewish family, her religion does not seem to have had a significant influence in her life; undertook research into the working of the Poor Laws, initially under Beatrice and Sidney Webb, 1906–09; joined the FS and ILP, 1907; member NUWSS; met Ethel Bentham through the LP (see entry) and moved into her house; member WLL, 1908; Executive Committee WLL, concerned with franchise and children's issues, 1909; started North Kensington Branch WLL, 1910; Secretary NUWSS, 1910; Organizing Secretary WTUL, 1911; lecturer in Public Administration, LSE, 1911–12; temporary Secretary WLL, 1911; elected Labour councillor London Borough of Kensington, 1912; appointed General Secretary WLL, 1912; Editor *League Leaflet* which became *Labour Woman* in 1913, 1912–32; during WW1 she was a member of the War Emergency Workers' National Committee, Queen's Work for Women Fund Committee, Consumers' Council Ministry of Food, Women's Advisory Committee of Ministry of Reconstruction, Consumers' Council, Ministry of Food, Standing Committee on Investigation of Costs under the Profiteering Act, Board of Trade, Army and Navy Pensions Committee, Civil War Workers Committee, Adult Education Committee; founding member and Secretary of the SJCIWO, 1916; member Reconstruction Committee, 1917; postwar she was concerned with female unemployment and housing; SJC representative Organizing Committee Conference of Women to seek representation on the LN, 1919; Vice Chair Women's Section Town Planners' and Garden Cities' Association, 1920; Social Science lecturer, LSE, 1918–20; as Chief Woman Officer LP, 1918–32, committed to industrial conditions for working women and improving the domestic conditions of working-class wives and children; involved with women's international network, International Secretary IFWW, to 1923; attended International Conference of Socialist Women, Hamburg as Secretary to the British delegation, 1923; member Advisory Council, WES Conference of Women, 1925; worked with the non-party Women's Movement on franchise extension and other issues, but faced fierce antagonism with regard to protective legislation debate; set up an impressive support system for the women and children of the mining communities involved in the miners' lock-out, 1926; Labour

MP Sunderland, 1929–31; died of stomach cancer Empire Nursing Home, Westminster; a dedicated LP woman, her early death was deeply felt by Labour women whose tributes to her work were profuse.

p. A Colonial Autocracy (1907); *The Working Woman's House* (with Mrs Sanderson Furniss, 1919); *Labour Women on International Legislation* (with Gertrude Tuckwell and Susan Lawrence, 1919); *The Young Industrial Worker: A Study of his Educational Needs* (1922); *English Women in Life and Letters* (with William Shirley Tomkinson, 1926); *Women and the Miners' Lock-Out* (1927); pamphlets – *How to Raise Money for Public Services without Increasing the Burdens of Poverty* (1909?); *The Green-Sprig Party: A Story for Young People* (1913); *Organization of Women within the Labour Party: A Handbook for Officers and Members of Women's Sections* (1921); *Women and Children in the Textile Industry* (1922); *Women's Work in the Labour Party: Notes for Speakers' and Workers' Classes* (1923); *Socialism and Women* (1931); other pamphlets co-authored, contributions to journals and periodicals, Royal Commissions and as editor, a significant amount of copy for *Labour Woman*.

s. List of Women Nominated for Service in Connection with the League of Nations (NUWT Archive, nd 1920–21); *Dictionary of Labour Biography*, vol. 5; *Dictionary of National Biography Missing Persons* (1993).

PHILIPSON, Mabel Hilton (née Russell) (1 January 1887–9 January 1951) actress and MP; *do.* Albert Russell; *m.* Stanley Rhodes, 1911, Hilton Phillipson, 1917; one daughter, two sons; *r.* reading, golf, riding, music; *a.* 19 St Edmund's Terrace, London NW8 (1934), 22 Berkeley Square London W1, Broom Hill, Esher, Surrey (1924), Claremont Farm, Esher, Surrey (1926), Limberhost, Ditchling, Sussex (1951).

Her parents were opposed to her becoming an actress, however, she made her stage debut as Fifi in the original production of the *Merry Widow*, 1907; her second husband was Liberal MP for Berwick, which had been a Liberal safe seat for 36 years, however, due to irregularities during his election perpetrated by his agent, he was disqualified from standing for Parliament for seven years, Mrs Philipson was then persuaded to stand for election as a substitute for her husband until he was able to stand again, however she only agreed to stand as a Conservative PPC, despite its Liberal history, she was elected in a by-election with a majority of 6142, 1923; member of a Joint Select Committee to consider provisions for the Guardianship of Infants Bill, 1923; the only woman on a parliamentary delegation to Italy, meeting with the Pope and Mussolini, 1924; specialized in the Commons in housing, agriculture, infant welfare and women's issues; sat on the Agriculture, Kitchens, Education (Institution Children) Bill Committees; first woman to become a member of the Air Committee; member Advisory Council, WES Conference of Women, 1925; Vice President of EAW, 1927; she sponsored the Nursing Homes (Registration) Act through Parliament as a PMB, 1927; reputedly participated in the Equal Franchise Demonstration, under the WEC banner, 1928; declined to stand in the next election as her husband was no longer interested in returning to Parliament and as that had been her motive for retaining the seat she stood down to spend more time with her children, 1928; she returned to her stage career, 1929; her last stage appearance was in 1933.

s. Gates (1924); *Hutchinson* (1934); *Who Was Who*, vol. 5; *The Times*, 10 January 1951; (1979), vol. 3; Brookes (1967).

b: born; do: daughter of; e: education; m: married; r: recreation; c: club; a: address; p: publications; s: sources

PHIPPS, Emily Frost BA (1865–1943); *b.* Devonport; *e.* Elementary School, Devonport, Homerton College, Cambridge; *r.* reading, music; *a.* 41 Chislehurst Avenue, Brondesbury, London NW6 (1934), 26 Arundel Road, Eastbourne (1938).

Certificated teacher, taught in Devonport; Headmistress Swansea Municipal Secondary School for Girls, 1894–1925; became a suffragette after seeing the violent treatment of women activists at a Lloyd George meeting in Swansea and joined the Swansea Branch WFL, 1908; participated in the census evasion, 1911; became one of the first women to be elected to the NUT Executive, 1914–16; President NUWT, 1914–18; stood as an Independent PPC for Chelsea, proposed and funded by the NFWT, polled sufficient votes to keep her deposit; first editor *The Woman Teacher*, 1919–30; Independent PPC Chelsea, sponsored by the NFWT, general election, 1918; Joint Trustee NUWT, 1918–38; retrained as a barrister, called to the bar, 1925; NUWT legal advisor; on becoming a barrister she left her job as a teacher, becoming an honorary full-time officer for the NUWT, as Secretary of the Legal and Tenure Committee and in the office of Standing Counsel, 1925; spoke Italian, German and French, gave private lessons and donated the money to the NUWT; member ODC; NUWT representative on NUSEC/ERGECC deputation to Ramsay Macdonald, spoke on equal pay, 1929; suffered from heart disease which severely restricted her work, early 1930s to 1943; lived for over 40 years with another teacher, Clare Neal, who was also an NUWT President, in a very close relationship; after Neal's death she lived with Adelaide Jones, also a teacher, and they retired to Eastbourne together.

p. Why I Left the NUT (Phipps et al.); *Equal Pay for Equal Work*; *Equality of Opportunity*; *History of the NUWT* (1928).

s. Phipps (1928); *The Woman Teacher*, 18 June 1943; Kean (1990); Oram (1996).

PICTON-TURBERVILL, Edith, OBE (13 June 1872–31 August 1960) social reformer and writer; *b.* Ewenny Priory, Bridgend; *do.* Colonel J. Picton-Turbervill & Eleanor Temple; *e.* school in Bruges, privately in Wales, Royal School, Bath; *r.* long cross-country walks with a silent companion; *c.* Lyceum; *a.* York Road, Brighton (1870s), 14 Gayfere Street, London SW1 (1927), 4 Duke St, Manchester Square, London W1 (1934), 62 Berkeley Court, Baker Street, London W1 (1938), Governor's House, Barkingside, Essex (1933), Ewenny Priory, Bridgend, Glamorgan (1933), Woodend, Sandy Lane Road, Charlton King's, Cheltenham (1960).

From a Conservative family who claimed ancient descent, their name had previously been Warlow and the name of Picton-Turbervill was assumed in 1891; brought up by an aunt as her parents were in India; her mother was a fervent Evangelical; the family moved to Bruges after her father's retirement, 1883; they went to live in Laleston, Vale of Glamorgan, 1884; became an Evangelical Christian, 1895; began her public work by evangelizing among the dock and railway workers, Barry, Glamorgan; spent a year at a training school for missionaries in London, during this time she did welfare work in Shoreditch; went as a missionary to Southern India with the YWCA, she was the Secretary for the student movement, 1900–08; National Vice President YWCA, 1914–20; appointed the warden of a munition hostel in Woolwich to which a hospital was attached, 1916; warden of a Government Housing Colony for 3000 women munition workers, with a staff of 200, 1917; visited the USA to speak on the organization of British welfare work,

1918; member WFL, NCW, IWSA; prominent advocate of women's ordination, close friend of Maude Royden (see entry); member Bishop of London's Centre for Pastoral and Evangelistic work; previously a Conservative, she joined the LP, 1918; member NUSEC; preached at the Anglican Church, Geneva as part of the IWSA Congress, 1920; Governor of Dr Barnardo's Village Home, Barkingside, 1920; member Council LNU; attended Conference of Women, suggested a new society – the Women's Reform Society, 1921; morning Chair Conference of Women's Organizations, 1921; National Vice President YWCA, 1922–8; Labour PPC North Islington, 1922; Chair Drafting Committee CCWO, 1922; nominated for President WSIHVA, 1922; Acting Principal World's YWCA, 1922; Vice President LCM, 1923; Labour PPC Stroud, 1924; adopted by the LP as PPC for Wrekin, 1924; gained popularity in her constituency through her work for the miners in the General Strike, 1926; Executive Committee NUSEC and Society Insurance Committee, 1927; NUSEC delegate IAWSEC Paris Congress, 1926; speaker at Peacemakers' Pilgrimage Rally, Hyde Park, 1926; attended Conference of Women Ministers and Missionaries, 1926; elected Labour MP for Wrekin, 1929–31; member Ecclesiastical Commission in Parliament, 1929–31; member Executive Committee NCEC, 1931; member parliamentary Committee for the Protection of Coloured Women, 1929; under 10-Minute Rule, successfully introduced the Sentence of Death (Expectant Mothers) Bill to abolish the death sentence on pregnant women, 1931; went on a fact-finding mission to Kenya, 1933; leader of the British delegation to the International Congress of Women Citizens, Istanbul, 1935, and Copenhagen, 1939; Government Commissioner to Hong Kong and Malaya to research into the practice of mui tsai (child brides), 1936; wrote the Minority Report on mui tsai published by the Colonial Office, 1937; this report was accepted by the government, 1939; attached to the Ministry of Information, 1941–3.

p. Women and the Church; Christ and Woman's Power; Musings of a Laywoman; Christ and International Life (with Lady Oxford and others, 1921); *Myself When Young* (1938); *Life is Good – An Autobiography* (1939); *In the Land of My Fathers* (1946); *Should Women Be Priests and Ministers?* (1953); *The Story of Algar Temple and the Indian Mutiny* (with Algar Temple, c.1958).

s. Labour Who's Who (1927); *Manchester Guardian*, 4 January 1933; *Women's Who's Who, 1934–5; The Lady's Who's Who* (1938–9); Brookes (1967); *Dictionary of National Biography*, vol. 5; *Who Was Who* (1951–60); Stenton and Lees, vol. 3 (1979); Bank and McDonald (1998).

POWER, Jennie Wyse (née ō Toole) (1858–5 January 1941) politician; *b.* Baltinglass, County Wicklow; *do.* Eamonn ō Toole & Mary Norton; *m.* John Wyse Power, journalist; one daughter, one son; *a.* 15 Eailsfort Terrace, Dublin (1941).

In elected public positions as Poor Law Guardian, governor of a mental hospital, Councillor of Dublin's Corporation, Chairman Committees of Public Health and Finance from 1902; primarily, a nationalist, as demonstrated by her membership of the LLL, the Gaelic League, Sinn Fein, first President of Cumann na mBan; involved in the suffrage campaign; participated in the 1916 Easter Rising; member of the Senate of Saorstát Eireann (Irish Parliament), 1922–36; despite her prevailing nationalism, she was 'the most persistent and determined champion of equal rights for women' (Clancy, 1990), as the only woman Senator to consistently champion the rights of homeless children, women's poverty, infant mortality; concerned with lack of representation by women on Dáil committees; involved in the debates for un-married women's protection in the Illegitimate Children (Affiliation Orders) Bill, 1929; made a significant contribution to defeating the Civil Service Regulation (Amendment) Bill which sought to prevent women's access to particular Civil Service posts, by highlighting the double-standard in practice with regard to the use of women's labour, 1925; objected to the Juries Bill which sought to exempt women from Jury service, 1927; again working to amend that part of the Conditions of Employment Bill which would restrict the employment opportunities of working class women, 1935.

s. Who Was Who (1941–50); Clancy (eds Luddy and Murphy, 1990); Luddy (1995a).

QUAILE, Mary T. JP (8 August 1886–16 December 1958) Trade Union pioneer organizer; *b.* Dublin; *do.* James Quail, mason and Bridget Lightholder; *e.* Elementary School; *r.* outdoor sports, walking, cycling; *c.* Clarion Club, Manchester, PLC; *a.* 23 Braithwaite Street, Dublin (1886); 20 Barlow Road, Levenshulme, Manchester (1927).

Fearless campaigner braving violent responses as she spoke for women workers' rights at factory gates in Manchester and London's East End; a lifelong pacifist; started work aged 12 as a domestic worker; worked as a waitress in a Manchester café in the 1900s and became interested in the TU movement when Margaret Bondfield (see entry) went to Manchester to organize women workers, Quaile then tried to organize the catering workers in Manchester; Assistant Organizer WTUC, Manchester, 1911–14; Organizing Secretary until Women's Group was formed by Manchester Trades Council, 1919; appointed National Woman Officer TGWU, 1919; Group Secretary Manchester Trades Council, 1923–6; Secretary of the Women's Group of the Manchester and Salford Trades Council, 1923–50s; member TUC General Council, 1923–6; Vice Chair NHI Section GFTU; took Margaret Bondfield's place as General Council representative on SJCIWO; delegate to NCLW, 1924: Chair Women's TU delegation to Russia, 1925; British woman representative on the new Women's Advisory Committee of the International Federation of Trade Unions, 1925; General Council represent-ative at TUC's Women's Conference, 1925; delegate to Women's Conference, moved a resolution on woman's TU Guilds, 1926; speaker at equal franchise demonstration, Hyde Park, 1928; appointed to Manchester magistrates bench, 1934; carried on her role as Treasurer of the Manchester Trades Council for many years into her retirement despite ill-health; awarded the TUC silver badge for her work, 1951; died in Withington, Manchester; 'her warm and loveable personality' ensured her 'many friends in the Labour and trade union movements' (*Manchester Guardian*).

p. assisted in writing the *Women's Report on Russia*.

s. Manchester Guardian, 17 December 1958; *Labour Who's Who* (1927); Office of the Registrar General, Dublin.

RACKHAM, Clara Dorothea (née Tabor), MA, JP (3 December 1875–11 March 1966) women's rights activist; *b.* London; *do.* Henry S. Tabor; *e.* Notting Hill High School, St. Leonards at St Andrews, Fife and Newnham College, Cambridge; *m.* Harris Rackham, Christ College Classics Lecturer, 1901; *r.* walking and cycling tours, tours abroad, swimming; *c.* PLC, Pioneer, Fabian Society, Half-Circle; *a.* 18 Hobson Street, Cambridge (1913), 9 Park Terrace, Cambridge (1924); Meadowcroft, Trumpington Road, Cambridge (1965).

Came from a Liberal background; went up to Cambridge, took Classics tripos 1895–8; at Newnham with and lifelong friend of, Susan Lawrence (see entry); worked as school manager on education committees, WEA lecturer, Chairman Eastern District, WEA; supporter of nursery schools from 1898; NUWSS member Executive Committee and Chairman Eastern Counties Federation, travelled extensively as activist, 1906–14; Chairman Executive Committee NUWSS, 1912–15; addressed NUWSS meetings on women's work in time of war, 1915; Poor Law Guardian, 1904–17; HM Inspector of Factories (temporary), 1915–19; President Cambridge Branch WCG; one of Labour's first Cambridge Town Councillors, 1919–57; Chairman Conference of Women's Organizations for Representation of Women at the LN, 1919; magistrate, Cambridge bench, 1920–50; Labour PPC Chelmsford early 1920s; member SJCIWO Sub-Committee on Birth Control, 1923; speaking tour of Scotland for NUSEC, 1926; speaker at Equal Franchise Demonstration, Hyde Park, 1928; Vice President BAWC, 1928; member Cambridge County Council, 1929; member of the Royal Commission on Unemployment Insurance 1930–2; Fellow and Associate of Newnham College; CND member and Aldermarston marcher in her eighties.

p. Great Britain Royal Commission on Unemployment Insurance. An Abridgement of the Minority Report: Signed by the Labour Members of the Commission, Councillor W. Asbury and Councillor Mrs C.D. Rackham (1933); *Factory Law* (1938).

s. List of Women Nominated for Service in Connection with the League of Nations (NUWT Archive, nd 1920–21?); *Labour Who's Who* (1924); *University Women's Review,* June 1954; *Guardian,* 25 October 1965; *The Times,* 16 March 1966; Bank and McDonald (1998).

RATHBONE, Eleanor Florence (12 May 1872–2 January 1946) politician, women's rights and social reformer; *b.* London; *do.* William Rathbone VI, Liberal politician & Emily Acheson Lyle; *e.* private, at home, Kensington High School, Somerville College Oxford; *a.* White Gables, Mossley Hill Road, Liverpool (1920–21), Oakfield, Penny Lane, Liverpool, 50 Romney St, London SW1 (1927).

Inherited the position of being the first woman representative of the Rathbone dynasty, a wealthy and influential Liverpool Quaker family; her father was a great philanthropist and Eleanor carried on the family tradition; graduated in Literae Humaniores (Classical Literature), 1896; Honorary Secretary Liverpool Women's Industrial Council, from 1897; a voluntary Friendly Visitor, appointed to the North Toxteth Committee, 1897; founder member and Honorary Secretary LWSS from 1898; Chair West Lancashire, West Chester and North Wales Federation of WSS; member Executive Committee NUWSS; shared her life with Elizabeth Macadam (see entry) whom she met in 1902; elected as the first woman member to Liverpool City Council, 1909–34; first woman JP Lancashire; initiated the Liverpool WCA, 1913; supported the establishment of the Department of Social Studies, University of Liverpool where she lectured and was a member of the University Council; during WW1 worked for the relief of women and children as Honorary Secretary to the Soldiers' and Sailors' Families' Association and then for the Local War Pensions Committee; it was this experience which fuelled her subsequent work for family

b: born; do: daughter of; e: education; m: married; r: recreation;
c: club; a: address; p: publications; s: sources

endowment; founded the FEC, 1917; Chairman of the Consultative Committee of Women's Societies since 1917; she had already written articles and reports on the results of Casual and Dock Labour, theory of woman's wages, technical education for women, conditions in various women's trades, the organization of widows' pensions, system of out-relief and more by 1920; succeeded Millicent Fawcett (see entry) as President of the NUSEC 1919–29; Independent PPC for Toxteth, Liverpool, 1922; her position as a significant economist was established with the publication of her most important work, *The Disinherited Family*, 1924; elected Independent MP for the Combined English Universities, 1928–46; member of the Duchess of Atholl's (Tory MP) Committee for the Protection of Coloured Women in the Colonies, 1929, and was particularly active in campaigns against female circumcision in Africa, as well as African women's 'slavery', and the taking of child brides (mui-tsai) in Hong Kong, challenging the government on these issues and those of education and welfare provision for women in Britain's colonies throughout the 1930s; Honorary President NUGC, 1931; worked in the interest of Indian women's political emancipation and for legislation to strengthen the Sarda Act to bring an end to child brides during the 1930s; became involved in the welfare and rights of Jewish and Arab women in Palestine, travelling there in 1934; the Spanish Civil War prompted her to initiate an all-party Committee for Spanish Relief, working with the Tory MP, the Duchess of Atholl, in 1936; an active pacifist in the promotion of LN work and opposed the government's appeasement policy, travelling to Balkan countries on a fact-finding mission, with Atholl in 1937; largely responsible for the Inheritance (Family Provision) Act to give widows and their children fairer access to property in wills, 1938; worked tirelessly for refugees throughout WW2, for aliens interned in this country, with Richard Grenfell she established and became Vice Chairman of the National Committee for Rescue from Nazi Terror; her greatest achievement was the success of the Family Allowance Bill for which she had campaigned since the end of WW1, although she still had to fight to the end to ensure that the money was paid to the mother and not to the father, it became law in 1945; died suddenly and the Rt. Hon. Sir Arthur Salter commented that she had been, 'a tenacious, gallant fighter all her days in the cause of the underprivileged'; the majority of her estate was left in bequests to charities and for refugees, notably those from Czechoslovakia and Spain.

    p. Memoirs of William Rathbone (1904); *The Disinherited Family* (1924); *The Ethics and Economics of Family Endowment* (1927); *Child Marriage: The Indian Minotaur* (1934); *The Tragedy of Abyssinia: What Britain Feels and Thinks and Wants* (1936); *War can be Averted: The Achievability of Collective Security* (1938); *The Case for Family Allowances* (1940); *False Facts about the Jews* (1944); see Alberti for a more detailed bibliography.

    s. List of Women Nominated for Service in Connection with the League of Nations (NUWT Archive, nd 1920–21?); Stocks (1950); Brookes (1967); Banks (1985); *Dictionary of Obituaries of British Radicals* (1993); see also Alberti (1996); Rathbone's papers are largely held by the University of Liverpool archive and the Fawcett Library.

ROLLS, Hon. Lady Eleanor Georgiana SHELLEY (née Rolls) (?–c.17 September 1961) engineering and aviation pioneer; *do.* First Baron Llangattock (John Allen Rolls) & Georgiana Maclean; *m.* Capt. Sir John Courtown Edward Shelley Rolls, landowner,

1898; *r.* music, reading, gardening; *a.* South Lodge, Knightsbridge, London SW7, The Hendre, Monmouth, Avington Park, Winchester (1927)

Assumed the additional name of Rolls when she inherited the family estates of her brother in 1917; early pioneer of aviation; President Woman's Pioneer Housing; school manager; member of WES; Co-Director of Atalanta, a women's engineering workshop, founded June 1920; member Advisory Council, WES Conference of Women, 1925; representative for WES on EAW; member of Council Industrial Co-partnership Association; member Air League; member Executive League of Empire.

s. Hutchinson (1934); *Women's Who's Who, 1934–5; The Lady's Who's Who* (1938–9).

ROYDEN, Agnes Maude (Mrs Hudson Shaw) DD, CH (23 November 1876–30 July 1956) preacher; *b.* Liverpool; *do.* Sir Thomas Bland Royden, shipowner and Tory MP & Alice Elizabeth Dowdall; *e.* Liverpool High School, Cheltenham Ladies' College, Lady Margaret Hall, Oxford; *m.* Rev. George William Hudson Shaw, 1944; *r.* motoring, bathing; *c.* UWC, 1917, Halcyon, Pioneer; *a.* Frankly Hall, Birkenhead, Cheshire (1913), 16 Rosslyn Hill, London NW3 (1920–21), 24 Rosslyn Hill, London NW3 (1927), 110 Hampstead Way, London NW11.

Came from a Conservative, Anglican Church family; graduated Second Class in the Honours School of Modern History, c.1900; on graduating, became one of the first women University Extension lecturers; Minister of Religion; worked in the Victoria Women's Settlement, Liverpool, 1901–03; curate to Hudson Shaw in South Luffenham, 1905; lecturer in English Literature and History for the Oxford University Extension Delegacy; she joined the NUWSS, 1908; joined the Executive Committee NUWSS, 1908; member Executive Committee LWSS; President Chester WSS; Vice President Oxford WSSS; took a course in maternity nursing in the South London Women's Hospital; editor of *The Common Cause*, 1908–14; wrote on the ethical, religious and economic aspects of the Women's Movement; resigned from the NUWSS Executive 1914; member WILPF, speaking in the cause of peace during WW1; visited America three times speaking and preaching; member of Rathbone's (see entry) FEC, 1917; the first public testimony of her religious future as a devout Anglo-Catholic came when she was invited to preach in the City Temple and then became assistant preacher there, 1917–20; first woman to preach in the Cathedral of St Peter, Geneva as part of the IWSA contribution to the Geneva Congress, 1920; President League Church Ministers, 1923; Vice President AMSH, 1923; NUSEC delegate Paris Congress of IAWSEC, 1926; speaker Peacemakers' Pilgrimage Rally, Hyde Park, 1926; SPG supporter; Vice President NUSEC, 1927; co-founder and minister of the Fellowship Services, Eccleston Square, London; regularly gave sermons and took services for various Women's Movement groups, eg. NUWT education conferences, 1926–7; Vice President Marriage Law Reform League, 1928; made a world tour, 1928–9; made a CH, 1930; peace crusader in the 1930s; awarded DD Glasgow University, 1931; first woman to preach in Glasgow Cathedral, 1932; regular speaker on feminist issues especially relating to women's industrial position and citizenship, social evils and the LN; attended the All India Women's Conference with Corbett Ashby (see entry), 1935; awarded Hon. LLD, Liverpool University, 1935; undertook preaching tours of the USA, Australia, New Zealand, India, China; preached on the radio; resigned her Guildhouse pastorate to dedicate herself to world peace, 1936; in the light of WW2, made a public renunciation of her pacifism, 1939–45.

p. pamphlets – *Votes and Wages; How Women Use the Vote* (1912); *Democracy and Physical Force; The True End of Government; The Great Adventure; The Church and Woman; Downward Paths: An Inquiry Into the Causes Which Contribute to the Making of the Prostitute* (1916); *Equality in the Spiritual World; The Future of Woman in Industry* (1919); books – *Women and the Sovereign State; Blessed Joan of Arc* (1918); *The Hour and the Church; Sex and Commonsense* (1922); *Political Christianity; Prayer as a Force; Beauty in Religion* (1923); *Here and Hereafter* (1933); *Myself When Young* (ed. Oxford, 1938); *A Threefold Cord* (1948); *If I had My Time Again: An Autobiography* (1950). Numerous writings on christianity and other aspects of her work and travels.

s. Labour Who's Who (1927); *List of Women Nominated for Service in Connection with the League of Nations* (NUWT Archive, nd 1920–21?); *Women's Who's Who, 1934–5*; Courtney (1934); *Dictionary of National Biography*, Williams and Palmer (1971); *Who Was Who*, 1951–60.

RUST, Tamara (née Kravetz) CP Women's Organizer; *m.* William Rust, editor *Daily Worker*, 1931; *a.* 45 Fitzroy Road, London NW1 (1949).

Member of the London District Committee of the CP; Secretary of the WAC of the CP; executed the idea of the WP, 1941; Treasurer and convenor of the Organizing Committee of the London WP, 1941; spoke at the 17th Party Congress about the necessity to ensure that women's abilities were used throughout society after the War, 1944; Executive Committee Member of the 17th, 18th, 19th, 20th, 21st Congresses.

p. pamphlets – *Where Women Enjoy Freedom* (between 1937–40); *Equal Pay for Equal Work – Your Questions Answered* (1944).

s. Branson (1997)

RYLAND, Beryl Stratheden (née Campbell) (c.1885–?) regional women's activist; *b.* London/India? *do.* Sir John Stratheden Campbell, KCSI, CIE & Honor Newmarch; *m.* Thomas Howard Ryland, farmer, 1909; one daughter, one son; *c.* Forum, Three Counties, Birmingham; *a.* Morton House, Kenilworth Road, Leamington.

Member of NUSEC; member Society Insurance Committee, 1927; member Sub-Committee Health Services, 1927: member Press and Publicity Committee, 1927; member Executive Committee, 1927; Chair Birmingham NCW Citizenship Subsection, 1926; Chairman Warwick Federation WI; member Executive Committee NFTG; Joint Honorary Secretary NUGC, 1932–3.

s. Hutchinson (1934).

SCHARLIEB, Mary Ann Dacomb (née Bird) DBE, MD, MS, JP (18 June 1845–21 November 1930) consultant gynaecologist; *b.* London; *do.* William Chandler Bird, branch manager & Mary Dacomb; *e.* boarding school, Manchester, private schools New Brighton and St John's Wood, LSMW, Madras Medical College, University of Vienna; *m.* William Mason Scharlieb, barrister, 1865; one daughter, two sons; *r.* foreign travel; *a.* 75 Park Street, Grosvenor Square, London W1 (1887), 149 Harley Street, London W1 (1887), 19 York Terrace, Regent's Park, London NW1 (1927).

Due to her stepmother's influence she received a good educational start in life; there was family resistance to her marriage which she overcame and on marrying she lived in Madras, India, 1865–c.1878; at first she assisted her husband with his work and through his clients discovered how poor the health and childbirth experiences of Indian women were, this motivated her to gain access for women to train as doctors in India and also to begin her own medical studies with midwifery, gaining access to the Lying-in Hospital, Madras, 1871; dissatisfied with her limited skills she enrolled at the Madras Medical College and qualified with a diploma in medicine, surgery and midwifery, 1878; returned to England to put her children into school and, despite her own ill health, through letters of introduction to Elizabeth Garrett Anderson and Florence Nightingale, to gain further qualifications, studied at the LSMW, gaining the degrees of MB and BS winning the gold medal and scholarship in obstetric medicine with honours in medicine, surgery and forensics, 1879–82; travelled to Vienna to obtain experience in operative midwifery, 1883; returned to Madras and was appointed Lecturer in Midwifery and Gynaecology, Madras Medical College, 1883; founded the Royal Victoria Hospital for Caste and Gosha Women; ill-health forced her to return to England, 1887; she began her medical practice in London, 1887; campaigned to raise money for the building of the New Hospital for Women in the Euston Road, London; became clinical assistant to Elizabeth Garrett Anderson at the New Hospital for Women and joint lecturer in medical jurisprudence, School of Medicine, 1888; first woman to be admitted to the University of London degree MD, graduated, 1888; became surgeon to the New Hospital, 1889–1902; lecturer on diseases of women, School of Medicine, 1889; passed the Mastership of Surgery examination, admitted, 1897; Senior Surgeon, New Hospital, 1899; appointed gynaecologist RFH, 1902; an enthusiastic suffragist, although she decried the use of militancy; engaged in medical relief work and lecturing on venereal disease in London during WW1; member of the birth rate commissions of 1916, 1919, 1922; CBE, 1917; President LSMW, 1917; one of the first women magistrates, working in the Juvenile Court and Visiting Justice at Holloway Prison, appointed 1920; President Women's Section, Congress of the Royal Institute of Public Health, Brussels (the British contingent included Lady Barrett [see entry], Dr C. Murrell [see entry], Dr W. Cullis [see entry], Margaret Haig Thomas [see entry]), 1920; Governor of St Mary's College Paddington; as a staunch Anglo-Catholic she opposed the birth control movement; member Expert Advisory Panel LSWS, 1923; Vice President SPG, 1925; Vice President NCUMC, 1925; DBE, 1926; one of her great friends was Dr Jane Walker (see entry); wrote a good deal on the health of women and children; regarded as one of the six best abdominal surgeons in the world; despite her poor health, she had boundless energy, lived a simple life and was a loyal friend and colleague; Louisa Garrett Anderson thought that Scharlieb's professional reputation had been an immense contribution to the women's cause; buried in the Brompton Cemetery.

p. 'Review of Surgery at the New Hospital for Women' in the BMA Journal, (1897); A Woman's Words to Women (1899); The Maternal Management of Children (1900); 'Alcoholism in Women' in ed. Dr Kelynack The Drink Problem (1905); The Seven Ages of Women (1915); The Hope of the Future (1916); How to Enlighten Our Children (1918); The Welfare of the Expectant Mother (1919); Straight Talks to Women (1923); ed. Sexual Problems (1924); Reminiscences (1924); The Psychology of Childhood (1927).

s. The Times, 22 November 1930; The Woman's Leader, 28 November 1930; The Vote, 5 December 1930; The Woman's Leader, 12 December 1930; British Medical Journal, 29 November 1930; Bank and McDonald (1998).

SEEAR, Beatrice Nancy (Baroness of Paddington) (7 August 1913–23 April 1997) politician; *do.* Herbert Charles Seear & Beatrice Maud Catchpole; *e.* Croydon High School, Newnham College, Cambridge, LSE; *a.* 189b Kennington Road, London SE11 (1994).

Took a first in History; worked in industry for ten years at C. and J. Clark, the Quaker shoe manufacturers, 1936–46; worked at Ministry of Aircraft production efficiency during WW2, 1943–5; Reader in Personnel Management at the LSE after the war, expert on women in employment 1948–78; unsuccessful Liberal PPC six times; proponent of equal pay; President of the Fawcett Society, 1970–85; President WLF, 1974; introduced an Anti-Discrimination Bill which was given its second reading on 7 November 1972; her Bill helped to pave the way and contributed to the Sex Discrimination Act, 1975; Chairman Council Morley College, President 1974–7; member Hansard Society Committee on Electoral Reform, 1975–6; retired from the LSE, 1978; Honorary Fellow LSE, 1980; Visiting Professor of Personnel Management City University, 1980–7; Deputy Leader of the Social and Liberal Democrats in the House of Lords, 1988–97.

p. Married Women Working (with P. Jephcott and J.H. Smith, 1962); *A Career for Women in Industry?* (with V. Roberts and J. Brock, 1964); *Industrial Social Services* (1964); *The Position of Women in Industry* (1967); *The Re-Entry of Women into Employment* (1971).

s. Guardian, 18 May 1988; *Who's Who* (1997).

SIMM, Elizabeth (Lisbeth) Emma (née Dodds) Labour movement organizer; *do.* George Dodds, Cramlington; *m.* Mathew Turnbull Simm, Labour MP, 1895; *a.* 29 Otterburn Avenue, Gosforth, Newcastle upon Tyne.

One of the key figures in the WLL, member Executive Committee and organizer, 1908–18; read a paper on working women in politics (later published) at the Annual Conference WLL, Glasgow 1914; member NUWSS; delegate to the TUC, 1918; representative of the NAUL on the WNAC, 1919.

p. The Working Woman in Politics (1914).

s. Who Was Who, 1916–28; *INW*, July 1956; Stenton and Lees, vol. 3 (1979); Colette (1989).

SKEFFINGTON, Johanna (Hanna) Mary Sheehy (née Sheehy) MA (24 May 1877–20 April 1946) suffragist, pacifist, women's rights activist; *b.* Kanturk, County Cork; *do.* David Sheehy, miller and MP & Elizabeth McCoy; *e.* Dominican Convent, Dublin, St Mary's University College; *m.* Francis (Frank) Skeffington, 1903; one son.

Strong political/nationalist/Catholic background, father imprisoned for his activities in the Land League, served as an MP for South Galway 1885–1900; her mother had imaginative ambition for her children and belief in women's public role; won a scholarship in 1897; graduated BA Hons. in Modern Languages, 1899; awarded an MA, 1902; French and German teacher, Rathmines Vocational School; founder member WGCGA, 1902; joined the IWSLGA, 1902; on marriage, in a gesture of equality, Hanna and Frank took one another's surnames; with Margaret Cousins (see entry), she formed the IWFL, November 1908; although a nationalist, she did not join any of the nationalist women's groups as women played a secondary role in them; in close contact both with the WSPU in Britain and with the BWSS in the North of Ireland; imprisoned in Mountjoy prison after breaking windows in government buildings, June 1912; managed *The Irish Citizen* suffrage paper with Frank from 1913; further imprisonment for attacking a policeman, December 1913; lost her teaching job as a result of her political activities; with Frank, became involved in the peace movement, due to the travel restrictions imposed by the British government, she was unable to attend the international women's peace conference in the Hague in April 1915; the turning point in her political activities came with the murder by the British of her husband during the Easter Rising, 1916; devastated, intent on securing an admission from the British authorities, after the officer responsible was court-martialled she left for America to lecture on the British position in Ireland and to fundraise for the nationalist cause, 1916–18; returned to continue her suffrage work; elected as Sinn Fein candidate for Dublin Corporation, end of 1919; Director of Organization for Sinn Fein, 1921; continued involvement with obtaining women's suffrage in the run-up to the Anglo-Irish Treaty, 1921; success for women's suffrage came with the Irish Free State Constitution, June 1922; during the Irish Civil War, fundraised in America for the Republican cause, 1922–3; founder member of the WPDL, 1922; delegate to the WILPF Dublin conference, 1926 and also at the Prague conference, 1929; part of the campaign to defeat the Juries Bill of 1927 (see also Jennie Wyse Power entry); kept herself and her son by lecturing, journalism and teaching; with Maud Gonne MacBride, Republican activist and Charlotte Despard (see entry) travelled to Russia with the Friends of Soviet Russia, 1930; a celebration in her honour held by the IWFL awarded her a medal from the WPDL, 1933; sustained her fight against the discriminatory legislation against women produced by the Irish Free State through-out the 1930s; key figure in the campaign by women's groups against the restrictions on women in de Valera's draft constitution, May 1937; launched the idea of the need for a women's party to defend women's rights, the WSPL formed in November 1937; as an Independent, supported by the WSPL, the WGA, IHA and the WCA, stood, unsuccessfully, for election in South Dublin in the general election, 1943; buried in Glasnevin cemetary, Dublin; Maud Gonne MacBride wrote, 'She is a great loss to Ireland' (Luddy, 1995b).

p. large number of articles in publications such as *Irish Citizen*, *Dublin*, *New Ireland Review*, *Irish Review*, *The Bell*.

s. Luddy (1995a); Luddy (1995b); Ryan (1996).

SMITH, Constance Isabella Stuart, OBE (?–26 March 1930) factory inspector, international labour campaigner; *do.* Rev. Hinton C. Smith; *e.* Belgium, Germany, King's College, London; *c.* Halcyon; *a.* 35 Hamilton Terrace, London NW8 (1929).

Her chief contribution was her persistent campaigning against the dangers of the industrial sweated trades employing women, involved with lead, phosphorus and night work; founding member of the British Section International Association for Labour Legislation, 1904; worked with Gertrude Tuckwell (see entry) in the CSU on the Sub-Committee of Research into sweating in women's industries; took over the Chair CSU from Tuckwell, 1911; shared a house with Tuckwell; worked on lead poisoning campaign; campaigned on several Factories Bills, particularly against sweating, resulting in the Trade Boards Act 1909; Chairman woman's committee on the National Health Insurance Bill; HM Senior Lady Inspector of Factories,

1913–21; HM Deputy Chief Inspector of Factories, 1921–5; Joint Secretary Women's Employment Committee, Ministry of Reconstruction 1917–19; Joint Honorary Secretary Committee Wage-Earning Children; member Industrial Law Committee; four time British delegate biennial conference International Association for Labour Legislation; Technical Adviser to British delegates, working with the pioneer socialist, Mary Macarthur (see entry), and Margaret Bondfield (see entry), at the first Conference of the ILO, Washington, 1919; also at the fifth conference, 1923; member LNU; Chair Independent Law Bureau of YWCA; attended Conference of Women, 1925; Executive Committee member NCW, 1927; despite ill health continued to work at full stretch, Tuckwell wrote of her 'tireless energy... the intensity of her labours hastened the end... she was a great public servant' (1 April 30); died at Hampstead General Hospital.

p. 'The Minimum Wage' in *Woman in Industry from Seven Points of View* (1908); *The Case for Wages Boards*; *The Workers' Handbook* (with Gertrude Tuckwell); *The Woman Factory Inspector in Industrial History* (1925); *Factory Conditions in China* (1927); articles in the *Nineteenth Century*, the *Economic Journal* and other journals; contributions to *Athenaeum*, 1906–11.

s. The Times, 29 March, 31 March, 1 April 1930; Weaver (1937); *Who's Who*, (1929).

SNOWDEN, Ethel (Mrs Philip Snowden) (née Annakin) (1881–22 February 1951) political lecturer and activist; *b.* Harrogate; *do.* Alderman Richard Annakin JP & Ethel Brown; *e.* Edge Hill College, Liverpool; *m.* Philip Snowden, Labour MP, 1905; *r.* music, reading, walking; *c.* Lyceum, Cowdray; *a.* 39 Woodstock Road, London NW4 (1920–21), 53 Carlisle Mansions, London SW1 (1924), Eden Lodge, Tilford, Surrey (1927), St Ermin's Court, London SW1 (1929), 206 Beatty House, Dolphin Square, London SW1.

Teacher for the Leeds School Board; when she was a student in Liverpool, her experiences of the slum conditions led her to become a member of the Christian Socialist movement which was campaigning for housing reform; temperance advocate; during this period she met her husband who was also engaged in this work, and during their married life she supported and cared for her husband as he was disabled; teaching in a school in Nelson, 1904; member NUT; she moved to London when her husband became an MP, 1906; her husband was Vice President MLWS and a leading champion of votes for women in the House of Commons due to his wife's influence who sincerely believed at the time that he could bring about votes for women single-handedly in Parliament; however, she was regarded by her suffrage colleagues as a very powerful orator for the cause on her own account; member Executive Committee and lecturer for the Fabian Society; Executive Committee NUWSS for six years; Vice President NUWSS; ILP delegate to LRC Conference, 1905; lecturer for ILP; joined and resigned WLL, 1906; worked at WILPF's HQ, Geneva in WW1; member of the Executive Committee of the LP; member of the Executive Committee of the UDC; member Executive Committee of the NPC; member Executive Committee NCCL; LP representative SJCIWO, 1919; delegate to the Socialist International Congress, 1919; delegate to the LN Conference in Berne, 1919; delegate to the WIL Conference, Zurich, where she put forward a resolution condemning the terms of the Treaty of Versaille and moving a resolution for a protest delegation to go to the peace conference in Paris which was seconded by

Emmeline Pethick-Lawrence (see entry), 1919; travelled and lectured extensively in the USA, Canada, New Zealand, Sweden, Holland, Switzerland, Germany and Austria; member Council SCF; member Labour Commission of Enquiry to Russia, 1920; member Women's Section NEC LP, 1920s; speaker WES Conference, 1925; Vice President SPG 1925; member Royal Commission on Food Prices, 1925; lectured on British life as guest of Canadian Education Association, 1925; Executive Committee Royal Institute for International Affairs; Executive Committee YWCA (Forward Movement); Executive Committee Victoria League; first woman Governor BBC 1927–33; member Advisory Committee on Films; director of Covent Garden Opera Syndicate; concentrated on temperance propaganda in the late 1930s and 1940s; member Royal Commission on Food; a stroke disabled her, 1947; died from the effects of a further stroke; proud to be a Yorkshirewoman and would speak in dialect with her Yorkshire friends; although some people found her aloof, her friend, Pethick-Lawrence wrote that 'she was a generous, warm-hearted, honest human being' (*The Times*).

p. *The Woman Socialist* (1907); *The Feminist Movement* (1913); *Through Bolshevik Russia* (1920); *A Political Pilgrim in Europe* (1921); *What We Want and Why* (c.1922)

s. *List of Women Nominated for Service in Connection with the League of Nations* (NUWT Archive, nd 1920–21?); *Labour Who's Who* (1924 and 1927); *Who's Who* (1929); *The Times*, 24 February 1951; Banks (1985).

SODDY, Winifred (Moller) (née Beilby) (1885–c.17 August 1936) women's rights campaigner; *do.* Sir George T. Beilby, FRS & Emma Clarke Newnam (see entry for Emma Beilby); *m.* Frederick Soddy, scientist, 1908; *a.* 131 Banbury Road, Oxford (1927).

Her mother (see entry) was a supporter of engineering employment opportunities for women; Honorary Treasurer NUSEC early 1920s; one of the 11 Executive Committee who resigned over protective legislation, 1927; Treasurer NUSEC; Executive Committee ODC, 1927–31; died in Oxford; the ODC obituary said that she had 'a beautiful gentleness with an inflexible firmness'.

s. *Who's Who*, 1929; *ODC Annual Report*, 1937.

SOLOMON, Daisy Dorothea, suffrage worker; *b.* South Africa; *do.* Saul Solomon, South African statesman and mining magnate & Georgiana Thompson (see entry); *a.* 7 Helenslea Ave, London NW11 (1934), 17 Buckingham Street, London WC2 (1934).

Member WSPU, 1908; suffered imprisonment; Organizing Secretary WSPU Hampstead Branch, 1912–13; member US, 1918; Literature Secretary of the BDWCU; member BCL, 1923; BCL representative at the IAWSEC Paris conference, 1923; Honorary Secretary EPRDC, 1926; member of WFL, 1926; Honorary General Secretary BCL, 1934.

s. Crawford (1999).

SOLOMON, Georgiana Margaret (Mrs Saul Solomon) (née Thompson) (18 August 1844–24 June 1933) equal moral standard and social purity campaigner; *b.* Haymount, Scotland; *do.* George Thompson & Margaret Stuart Scott; *m.* Saul Solomon, South African statesman and mining magnate, 1874; two daughters (see entry for Daisy) four sons; *a.* Les Lunes, Sumatra Road, London NW6.

Sunday School teacher from youth; temperance promoter; lifelong suffrage campaigner; left Britain to become Principal of the Good Hope Seminary, Cape of

Good Hope, 1873; elected President World Women's Temperance Union in South Africa; President Social Purity Alliance, Cape Town; led campaign against the re-introduction of the CD Acts at the Cape, which her husband had repealed in 1872; founded South African Women's Federation, Transvaal; returned to Britain on the death of her husband; President WLA, Sidcup, 1906; an active suffrage campaigner, suffered a vicious attack from the police when on a deputation to the House of Commons and was seriously injured, February 1909; also attended the Black Friday WSPU demonstration and spent one month in Holloway Prison, 1910; member WSPU; arrested twice, imprisoned, 1912; left WSPU, 1912; member AMSH; Executive Committee Anti-Slavery and Aborigines' Protection Society, 1913; Executive Committee LNSASRV and FCLWS, 1913.

    s. Women's Who's Who, 1913; The Times, 3 July 1933; Liverpool University Archive, D55/17/2/1–16.

SPURGEON, Caroline Francis Eleanor, DLitt, FRSL (24 October 1869–24 October 1942) Professor of English Literature; *b.* Norfolk?; *do.* Capt. Christopher Spurgeon, 36th Worcs Regiment; *e.* Cheltenham Ladies' College, Dresden, Paris, Kings College and University College London; *r.* walking, gardening, reading detective stories; *c.* Albemarle; *a.* 19 Clarence Gate Gardens, London NW1 (1929), Old Postman's Cottage, Alciston, Polegate, Sussex (1929), c/o Dean Gildersleeve, Barnard College, New York County (1942).

    Outstanding scholar, attended UCL 1896–1900 studying English; Second Class English (Senior), 1897; Quain Essayist and Morley Medallist for English Literature, 1898; First Class English Honours, Oxon, 1899; re-entered UCL for one year to study Icelandic, 1905; Docteur (Lettres) de l'Universite de Paris, 1911; awarded the first Research Fellowship, Federation of University Women, 1912; having spent several years travelling in her youth, she started University late and was 30 on graduation; Assistant Lecturer in English, Bedford College for Women, London, 1901–06; Lecturer English Literature, 1906–13; the first woman professor to be appointed in open competition in a British University Chair in English Literature to be held at Bedford College, 1913; Head of Department English Literature, Bedford College, 1913–29; Fellow King's College for Women, London; one of the two women members of the British Educational Union to go to America, October to December 1918; DLitt Michigan, 1918; on her return she published a report on women's university education in the USA; Visiting Professor Columbia University, New York 1920–21; after WW1 she initiated the IFUW 'to do what we can to see that such a war never happens again', at its first conference at Bedford College, unanimously elected President, 1921–5; prime mover in making Crosby Hall an international residence for university women; President BFUW, 1922–5; Vice President SPG, 1925; originated and inaugurated BUC; member Advisory Council Conference of Women, 1925; Hon. DLitt Michigan; Emeritus Professor of English Literature, London University, 1929?; moved to Tucson, Arizona, 1937; died in Arizona, Dean Virginia Gildersleeve was with her; Theodore Bosanquet (see entry) wrote that 'she enjoyed every good thing that life offered she had an abounding joie de vivre, coupled with a keen and discriminating sense of values' (UWR).

    p. Chaucer devant la critique en Angleterre at en France depuis son temps jusqu'a nos jours (1911); *Mysticism in English Literature* (1913); *Five Hundred Years of Chaucer*

Criticism and Allusion (1920–25); *Keats's Shakespeare* (1928); *Shakespeare's Imagery and What it Tells Us* (1935); contributions to *The Quarterly Review*, *Review of English Studies*, *Revue Germanique*, *Cambridge History of English Literature*; ed. – *Richard Brathwait's Comments* (1902), *The Castle of Otranto* (1908).

s. List of Women Nominated for Service in Connection with the League of Nations (NUWT Archive, nd 1920–21?); *Who's Who* (1929); *Women's Who's Who, 1934–5*; *New York Times*, 25 October 1942; *The Times*, 26 October 1942; *University Women's Review*, June 1943; UCL Records

STOCKS, Mary Danvers (Mrs J.L. Stocks), (née Brinton) (25 July 1891–6 July 1975) economist, writer and broadcaster; *b.* London?; *do.* Dr Roland Danvers Brinton, GP & Helen Constance Rendel; *e.* St Paul's Girls' School, London, LSE, University of London; *m.* John Leofric Stocks, academic, 1913; two daughters, one son; *r.* reading, attending the House of Lords; *c.* BBC; *a.* 22 Wilbraham Road, Fallowfield, Manchester (1929), 9 Croxteth Road, Liverpool 8 (1937), 37 Argyll Road, London W8 (1937), 10 Holland Park Court, London W14 (1938), Aubrey Lodge, Aubrey Road, London W8 (1952).

She took her degree in 1913; principally interested in economic issues; member NUWSS; tutor in economics at Oxford, 1913–16; Assistant Lecturer, LSE, 1914–18; member FEC, 1917; lecturer in Economics, King's College of Household Science; Lecturer Extra-Mural Department Manchester University, 1924–c.1936; active in the birth control movement, although she was an anti-abortionist; wrote a pamphlet on birth control advice at maternity clinics in support of NUSEC's campaign, 1925; first Chair Manchester, Salford and District Mothers' (Birth Control) Clinic, c.1926; Manchester JP; member NUSEC; NUSEC delegate at IAWSEC Paris Congress, 1926; NUSEC Annual Report gives special thanks for her work, 1926; Society Insurance Committee, 1927; member NUSEC Press and Publicity Committee, 1927; member NUSEC Executive Committee, 1927; member NBCC (later FPA); close friend, colleague and biographer of Eleanor Rathbone (see entry), also worked closely with Lady Denman (NFWI) and Eva Hubback (see entry); member Executive Committee NCEC, 1931; joint editor NUSEC paper, *The Woman's Leader*; lived in Liverpool, 1936–7; General Secretary London Council of Social Service, 1937–9; member Royal Commission on Betting and Gambling and of the Home Office Departmental Commission on Persistent Offenders; member Statutory Committee on Unemployment Insurance; appointed as the Principal Westfield College, London, giving the College a higher profile, 1939–51; awarded Honorary degrees, LLD University of Manchester, 1955; DLitt University of Liverpool, 1956; member LP; she was involved in working for the BBC as a scriptwriter, broadcaster and BBC panellist on the *Brains' Trust* and *Any Questions*, from 1936 to the 1960s; advocate of euthanasia; Deputy President WEA, maintaining her interest in its work into her retirement; in her retirement a member of the Unemployment Statutory Committee; a practising Christian; created a life peer, 1966; accepted the Labour whip; left the LP unhappy with Wilson's leadership and the Government's policies, 1974; regarded very much as an individualist, forthright and independent.

p. The Industrial State: A Social and Economic History of England (1921); *The Case for Family Endowment* (1927); *Everyman of Everystreet: A Nativity Play* (1929); *Equal Pay for Equal Work*; *Hail Nero! A Reinterpretation of History in Three Acts*

(1934); *Dr Scholefield: A Play* (1936); *The Victorians* (1941); *Fifty Years in Every Street: The Story of the Manchester University Settlement* (1945); *Eleanor Rathbone* (1949); *History of the Workers' Educational Association* (1953); *A Hundred Years of District Nursing* (1960); *Josephine Butler and the Moral Standards of Today* (1961); *Ernest Simon of Manchester* (1963); *Where is Liberty?* (1968); *My Commonplace Book* (1970); *Still More Commonplace* (1974).

s. The Times, 9 December 1938; *Guardian*, 16 February 1966; *The Times*, 7 July 1975; *Who Was Who* (1971–80); Blake and Nicholls (1986); BBC Written Archive Talks Files, 1936–62.

STRACHEY, Philippa (Pippa) CBE (1872–23 August 1968) women's rights campaigner; *b.* London; *do.* Lt. Gen. Sir Richard Strachey & Jane Maria Grant; *c.* Lyceum; *a.* 51 Gordon Square, London WC1, Lord's Wood, Marlow, Buckinghamshire (1968).

Her mother was a signatory to the first women's suffrage petition to Parliament in 1867 and was a member of the NUWSS and Vice President of the CUWFA; the family were part of the famous Bloomsbury set, Lytton Strachey, the writer, being Pippa's brother; member Executive Committee LSWS, 1906; Secretary LSWS, 1907–51; organized the NUWSS' first open-air rally, the 3000-women 'Mud March' of 1907; Secretary Women's Service Bureau for War Workers, 1914–20; member Committee London Units Scottish Women's Hospitals, 1914–19; Secretary to the Women's Service Bureau, 1914–22?; travelled a good deal in Europe and in India; spoke French, Italian and German; Secretary LSWS, 1917–19; worked with Ray Strachey to ensure the successful outcome of the first suffrage bill for women, 1917; Secretary LSWS from 1920; Secretary and later Honorary Secretary WEF; delegate WSIHVA Conference, 1928; nursed her mother and her brother in the late 1920s and early 1930s; she was the backbone of the LSWS with her invaluable supply of procedural knowledge and information, possessing a remarkable memory for detail and the history of the movement, she regarded herself as a 'backroom' person who was not interested in taking a public role, yet she was a great conversationalist; worked closely with her sister-in-law, Ray, to whom Pippa's long experience was invaluable in campaigning; Honorary Secretary, Fawcett Society, 1951; became CBE, 1951; Governor of Bedford College for Women; died in a Putney nursing home.

p. Memorandum on the Position of English Women in Relation to that of English Men (1935).

s. Women's Who's Who, 1913; Who's Who (1929); *The Times*, 26 August 1968; *Guardian*, 26 August 1968.

STRACHEY, Ray – Rachel Conn (Mrs Oliver Strachey) (née Costelloe) (4 June 1887–16 July 1940) women's rights campaigner and writer; *b.* London; *do.* Benjamin Francis Conn Costelloe, barrister & Mary Pearsall Smith; *e.* Kensington High School, Newnham College, Cambridge, Bryn Mawr College, USA; *m.* Oliver Strachey, civil servant, 1911; one daughter, one son; *r.* brickwork; *a.* 96 South Hill Park, London NW3 (1920–1), 42 Gordon Square, London WC1 (1922), 53 Marsham Street, London SW1 (1934).

Brought up by her American feminist grandmother, Hannah Whitall Smith, a preacher and writer; gained a third class degree in mathematics, 1905–08; member

NUWSS as a student, assisting Millicent Fawcett (see entry); studied electrical engineering at Oxford University, 1910; particularly engaged in employment issues for women, especially access and equal pay; also a builder, funded Women Builders' Corp; Parliamentary Secretary NUWSS, 1915–19; Chairman Employment Committee, LSWS, 1915–22; President Society Women Welders, 1916–18; member Executive Committee NCW, 1917–22; Chairman Women Services Bureau, WW1; member Committee LNU, Vice Chairman of Women's Committee; Parliamentary Secretary to Lady Astor MP for six months after her election, 1919; Editor of *The Common Cause*; Secretary, later Chairman WEF; British delegate Women War Workers Conference Paris, 1918; delegate to French WSU re. Peace Treaty, 1919; spoke at NCW Annual Conference Leicester, saying there should be no restrictions on women's work in the Restoration of Pre-War Practices Bill, 1919; Honorary Secretary Committee for Opening the Legal Profession to Women; Joint Committee on women employed in the Civil Service; Chairman Cambridge University Women's Appointments Board; Chairman Emergency Open Air Nursery Committee; Executive Committee British Institute of International Affairs, 1920–22; Independent PPC Brentford and Chiswick, 1918, 1922, 1923; LSWS representative at the Conference of Women, 1921; LSWS representative at Consultative Committee, 1921; delegate to the Equal Pay and Right to Work Conference, Rome, 1923; member of IWSA; Vice President Council for Representation of Women in the League of Nations, 1928; Executive Committee LNU and Vice Chairman Women's Committee; first Chairman Cambridge University Women's Employment Board, 1930–9; initiated the Women's Employment Federation, 1934; working with women MPs to relieve unemployment among professional women during 1939; sudden death.

p. The World at Eighteen (1907); *Frances Willard, Her Life and Work* (1912); *A Quaker Grandmother* (1914); *Marching On* (1923); *Keigwin's Rebellion: An Episode in the History of Bombay* (with Oliver Strachey, 1916); *Shaken by the Wind: A Story of Fanaticism* (1927); *Women's Suffrage and Women's Service: The History of the LNSWS* (1927); *Religious Fanaticism: Extracts from the Papers of Hannah Whitall Smith* (1928); *The Cause, A Short History of the Women's Movement* (1928); *Millicent Garrett Fawcett* (1931); *Group Movements of the Past and Experiments in Guidance* (with H.W. Smith, 1934); *Careers and Openings for Women* (1937); ed. – *Our Freedom and Its Results by Five Women* (1936); many campaigning pamphlets.

s. Who's Who (1929); *The Lady's Who's Who* (1938–9); Crawford et al. (1983); Banks (1985); Nicholls (1993); *Penguin Biographical Dictionary of Women* (1998).

STREATFEILD, Lucy Anne Evelyn Deane CBE, JP (1866–3 July 1950) *do.* Colonel Bonar Deane & Hon. Lucy Boscawen; *m.* Major Granville Edward Stewart Streatfeild, DSO, OBE, architect, 1911; *c.* University Women's; *a.* The Cottage-on-the-Hill, Westerham, Kent (1934)

HM Senior Inspector of Factories; member War Office Commission of Enquiry to Concentration Camps During the Boer War; member Royal Commission on Civil Service; first woman Organizing Officer, National Health Insurance Commission, London; member various Trades Boards under Trade Boards Act; Commission of Enquiry into Conditions of the WAAC in France; member Kent Executive Committee Women's Land Army; CBE, 1918; President WSIHVA, 1918–19; strongly in favour of trade union membership for WSIHVA; Vice

Chairman Kent Council of Social Service; member NFWI; died at her home and was buried at Westerham Parish church.

s. *Who's Who* (1929); *Who Was Who*, vol. 4; *The Times*, 8 July 1950.

SUMMERSKILL, Dr Edith Clara (Baroness) (19 April 1901–4 February 1980) Labour politician; *b.* Bloomsbury, London; *do.* William & Edith Summerskill; *e.* King's College, University of London, Charing Cross Hospital; *m.* Dr Jeffrey Samuel, 1925; one daughter (Shirley, a doctor, Labour MP Halifax 1964); one son (both took their mother's surname); *a.* Pond House, Millfield Lane, Highgate, London.

Summerskill's father was a doctor with beliefs in women's rights, radical politics and innovative medicine, she often accompanied him on his visits to his poorest patients; studied Chemistry, Physics and Biology at King's, 1918; followed her father's profession, qualifying in 1924, with a practice in London; involved in local government when a member of the Maternity and Child Welfare Committee of the Wood Green UDC, 1933; as a LP candidate she contested and won the safe Tory Green Lanes Ward of Harringay at the local government elections for the MCC elections, 1934; Labour PPC in a Putney by-election, 1934; difficult time as Labour PPC for Bury where her feminism and promotion of birth control caused great antagonism among the local Catholic community, 1935; successful Labour by-election candidate for Fulham West 1938–55; on marriage, she retained her maiden name and fought elections using this name, but her right to take her seat in the Commons as a married woman using her maiden name was unofficially questioned as she was the first woman to do this, this was resolved in 1938; both her children were given their mother's surname with the support of her husband; in the Commons she spoke first on raising nurses' pay and reducing their hours to a 48-hour week; her parliamentary concerns were soon aired on the weakening of the LN, pain-relief in childbirth and economic issues which affecting social services and the consumer; advised on parliamentary tactics by Eleanor Rathbone (see entry) in her campaign for women to be allowed access to anaesthetic during childbirth; used the opportunity of the Cancer Bill debate and criticized the position of poorer women who were unable to afford medical treatment and called for a State medical service, 1938; continued to use the opportunity in every medical debate to call for the introduction of a NHS; invited by the Spanish government to analyse the position of Spanish refugee women and children during the Civil War, 1938; invited to the USA to inform women's organizations of the Spanish conditions, 1938; after the fall of France, with other women colleagues, founded the Women's Home Defence Unit, for women who wished to learn to shoot to defend their country as women were not allowed into the Home Guard as combatants; also involved in pressurizing the government to utilize women in wartime employment during WW2 and was one of the initiators of the CWP in 1940; complained about men being appointed to deal with issues which affected women, and was one of five women subsequently appointed to the WCC to deal with these matters from March 1941; continued her defence of women's position during WW2 when she complained about the ethos betrayed by the discriminatory wartime poster, 'Be like Dad, Keep Mum'; first woman in a Commonwealth parliamentary delegation, going to Australia and New Zealand, 1944; Parliamentary Secretary for the Ministry of Food, 1945–50 with the fraught task of implementing rationing; led the British delegation to the UN's Food and Agriculture Organizations' (FAO) Conference, Washington, 1946; outlined

b: born;   do: daughter of;   e: education;   m: married;   r: recreation;   **141**
c: club;   a: address;   p: publications;   s: sources

Britain's part in tackling the dilemma of global food provision, 1947; successfully steered the Milk (Special Designations) Bill through the Commons, making the tuberculin-testing or pasteurization of milk compulsory, Nancy Astor (see entry) and Margaret Wintringham (see entry) had worked on this since the 1920s, Summerskill thought it her own greatest achievement, 1949; appointed as a Privy Councillor, 1949; member Political Honours Scrutiny Committee; chose a woman, Mrs Dorothy Rees, as her PPS when she became Minister of National Insurance, 1950–51; President of the MWA, succeeded by Vera Brittain (see entry); supported the Deserted Wives Bill, 1951; involved in the equal pay campaigns of the early 1950s, working with the Fawcett Society; twice attempted to get a bill through parliament concerning the rights of married women, moved the second reading of the Woman's Disabilities Bill in April 1952 and again in 1953; advocate of banning boxing and prize-fighting; Chairman of the LP, 1954–5; Labour MP for Warrington, using the new campaigning medium of television where she discussed food prices, 1955–60; spoke on the motion supported by eight Labour women members in a debate concerning the threats of nuclear weapons, 1955; with Joyce Butler (see entry) and Vera Brittain (see entry) she addressed a woman-only march against nuclear weapons' tests in Trafalgar Square, 1957; her visit to Egypt and subsequent condemnation of the British government's role in the Suez crisis resulted in threats and the loss of her Shadow Cabinet post and place on the LP's NEC; voted against the Street Offences Bill, 1959; voted in favour of consenting male homosexuals not being prosecuted, 1960; life peer, 1961; drafted a PMB, the Married Women's Savings Bill, one of a series of her Women's Disabilities bills, which later provided the substance of the Married Women's Property Act which she steered through the Commons, 1963; against hereditary and 'spiritual' peers; supported the Matrimonial Causes and Reconciliation Bill, 1963; supported the reform of the Abortion Law, 1965; supporter of the formation of the National Council for the Single Woman and her Dependants, 1965; successfully steered the Matrimonial Homes Bill through the Lords, 1966; CH, 1966; Phillips found her 'a stern, uncompromising, forbidding figure' .

p. *Babies Without Tears* (1941); *Wanted – Babies* (1943); *The Ignoble Art* (1956); *Letters to My Daughter* (1957); *A Woman's World* (1967); pamphlets: *Women Fall In* (1941).

s. Brookes (1967); Summerskill (1967); Phillips (1980); Crawford et al. (1983); Summerfield (1987); Pugh (1992); *Penguin Biographical Dictionary of Women* (1998).

SUMMERSKILL, Dr Shirley Catherine Wynne (9 September 1931–) feminist, MP; do. Dr E.J. Samuel & Edith Summerskill MP (see entry); e. St Paul's Girls' School, Hammersmith, Somerville College, Oxford, St Thomas's Hospital; m. John Ryman, MP, 1957.

Joined the LP, 1948; member Medical Practitioners' Union; Treasurer Oxford University Labour Club, 1952; practising doctor before becoming an MP; resident House Surgeon, later House Physician, St Helier Hospital, Carshalton, 1959; partner in general practice, 1960–68; Labour PPC Blackpool North by-election, 1962; Labour MP for Halifax, 1964–83; Opposition Spokesman on Health, 1970–74; with Barbara Castle (see entry) and Joan Vickers (see entry) opposed the government's attempt to transfer Family Allowances paid to mothers to tax credits paid to father's,

1973; Party Under-Secretary of State, Home Office, 1974–9; Opposition Spokesman on Home Affairs, 1979–83; Vice-Chairman PLP Health group, 1964–9; Chairman 1969–70; member LP NEC, 1981–3; UK delegate UN Status of Women Commission, 1968–9; member British delegation CoE and WEU, 1968 and 1969.
p. A Surgical Affair (1963); *Destined to Love* (1986).
s. Brookes (1967); *Who's Who* (1999).

SUTHERLAND, Mary Elizabeth, MA Hons, JP (30 November 1895–19 October 1972) Chief Woman Officer LP; *b.* Burnhead, Aberdeenshire; *do.* Alexander Sutherland, crofter & Jessie Henderson; *e.* Elementary, Girls' High School Aberdeen, University of Aberdeen, Aberdeen Training College; *a.* 108 Regent Street, Glasgow (1927), 63 Dunlop Towers, Telford Road, East Kilbride (1970s).

Her father was a Radical; scholarships enabled her to attend secondary school and university; her mother died in 1911, she took responsibility for the family; discovered her political affiliations whilst she was at secondary school; graduated with an MA Honours degree in History, 1917; qualified as a teacher, taught for a year at Aberdeen Girls' High, became involved in campaigning for a minimum wage and increased training provision; Assistant Secretary Departmental Committee on Women in Agriculture in Scotland, 1919–20; Organizer for the SFSU, with particular interest in women workers, 1920–22; Vice Chairman Stirling Trades and Labour Council, 1921–2; Editor *Scottish Farm Servant*; sub-editor *Forward*, the Glasgow ILP paper, 1923–4; Scottish Women's Organizer for the LP, 1924–32; Chief Woman Officer, LP, 1932–60; Secretary SJCIWO, 1932–60; correspondent British Section, Women's Committee of Labour and Socialist International, 1932–9; Editor of *Labour Woman*; member of the Ministry of Labour's WCC, from 1941–65; demanded greater specialist support for married women if they were to be involved in the WW2 war effort including the provision of nurseries; as a member of the FWG she contributed to its evidence to the Royal Commission on Equal Pay, 1945–6; involved in working for refugees during and after WW2; member Board of Directors NIH, 1946–66; British representative UN Commission on the Status of Women, 1947–52; CBE, 1949; member of and contributor to the *Bulletin* of the International Council of Social Democratic Women, 1955–64; her other international interest was in Scandinavian women, attending the Swedish Social Democratic Women's League congress in 1960; Secretary and trustee of the Houseworker Trust, 1964–5; died from a second stroke in East Kilbride; like her predecessor Marion Phillips (see entry), she was very much a Party woman, believing that women should work through the same structures as men to gain office.
s. LWW (1927); *LWW* (1938); *Dictionary of Labour Biography*, vol. 6; Summerfield (1987); *Who Was Who*, vol. 7; Pugh (1992).

SWANWICK, Helena Maria Lucy (née Sickert) CH, MA (30 June 1864–16 November 1939) feminist, pacifist, international journalist; *b.* Munich; *do.* Oswald Adalbert & Eleanor Sickert, artist; *e.* Neuville, France, Notting Hill High School, Girton College, Cambridge; *m.* Prof. Frederick Tertius Swanwick, academic, 1888; *r.* gardening, music, reading; *c.* University Club for Ladies, 1917; *a.* 26 Lawn Crescent, Kew Gardens, Surrey (1920–21), Satis, Maidenhead (1934)

Came to live in England, 1868; took second class Honours Moral Sciences tripos, 1885; later she took an ad eundem MA at Dublin; part-time lecturer in Psychology,

Westfield College, Hampstead, 1885; involved in working for working girls' clubs in Manchester, 1888–1909; member WTUC; lectured to the WCG; Victoria University Extension Lecturer on Economics and Sociology, Manchester and WEA; Honorary Secretary Manchester SWS and Knutsford WSS; member Committee Stowe Street Girls' Club, Manchester; earned money when she married as a writer for various magazines, journals and as a contributor to *Manchester Guardian* from 1894; first became involved in the suffrage movement subscribing to the WSPU, 1905; member of the NEWSS, 1905; first editor *The Common Cause*, 1909–12; member Executive Committee NUWSS; member LSWS; Vice President Richmond LP; resigned from the NUWSS on the pacifist issue, 1914; Honorary Secretary Committee of Organized Women, under Richmond Town Council 1914–15; first Chairman Richmond Day Nursery, 1914–15; played a leading role in founding the British Section of WILPF and was its Chairman for seven years; member Executive UDC, from 1915; joined the ILP, 1914; after WW1 the organization of international peace was her prime interest; member Committee of Inquiry into Sexual Morality; protested at the blockade of Germany and intervention in Russia and was heavily involved in the LN opposing government policy on these issues; made a member British delegation to LN Assembly, Geneva by Ramsay MacDonald, where she protested at the restriction of women to the one area of the protection of women and children and drug trafficking, 1924; Chairman BWIL for seven years; National President WIL, 1926; editor *Foreign Affairs*, journal of the UDC, 1924–8; appointed British delegate to LN Assembly, 1929; WIL representative on NUSEC/ERGECC deputation to Ramsay Macdonald, spoke on constructive peace policy, 1929; accepted invitation of SPG to White Press Luncheon, Equal Franchise Celebration, 1929; CH, 1931; it appears likely that she committed suicide at her home in Maidenhead suffering from depression, her husband had recently died, she had been suffering from heart problems and had had an operation for cancer, after a lifetime of working in the peace movement she was deeply distressed at the outbreak of WW2.

p. The Small Town Garden (1907); *The Future of the Women's Movement* (1913); *Women in the Socialist State* (1921); *Builders of Peace: Being a Ten Years' History of the UDC* (1924); *New Wars for Old* (1934); *Some Points of English Law; Frankenstein & His Monster* (1934); *Pooled Security: What Does it Mean?* (1934); *I Have Been Young* (1935); *Collective Insecurity* (1937); *The Roots of Peace* (1938); pamphlets – numerous, on women's issues and peace work, including, *Women & War* (UDC pamphlet 1915).

s. Women's Who's Who, 1913; List of Women Nominated for Service in Connection with the League of Nations (NUWT Archive, nd 1920–21?); *Labour Who's Who* (1927); *Women's Who's Who, 1934–5; The Ladies Who's Who* (1938–9); *Manchester Guardian*, 18 November 1939, 25 November 1939; *Who Was Who* (1929–40); Banks (1985).

SYMONS, Madeleine Jane (Mrs Robinson) JP (28 July 1895–21 March 1957) Trade Union and Labour activist; *b.* London; *e.* Newnham College Cambridge; *a.* 18 Pelham Crescent, London SW7 (1934).

She took the Economics tripos Part 1 Class 3, Part 2 Class 2:2, attending Newnham 1913–16; Negotiations Officer, NFWW, arbitrating with the government for increased wages for women munitions' workers, she was said to have won over

80% of her cases, 1916–20; delegate TUC, 1918; Negotiations Officer, Women's Section NUGMW, from 1920; member Women's Advisory Committee of Ministry of Reconstruction, 1919; worked on the establishment of the Trade Boards; member Executive Committee LP, 1922–3; delegate IFWW's Congress in Vienna, 1923; member Catering Trades Council, 1923; member Royal Commission Lunacy and Mental Disorder, 1924–6; representative of staff on Civil Service Arbitration Court, 1925–6; Chairman of the Mary Macarthur Scholarship and Holiday Home Committee; member WTUL; spoke to WSIHVA about their affiliating to her organization; member SJCIWO; JP County of London, Kensington Bench; member London Rota Justices for Juvenile Courts; friend of Susan Lawrence (see entry).

s. Labour Who's Who (1927); *Labour Woman*, May 1957; Newnham College Archive.

TATE, Maybird (Mavis) Constance (Mrs H.B. Tate) (née Hogg) JP (17 August 1893–5 June 1947) MP; *do.* Guy Weir Hogg; *e.* private, St Paul's Girls' School, Hammersmith; *m.* Capt. G.E. Gott, 1915, divorced, 1925; Henry Burton Tate, sugar manufacturing family, 1925, divorced, 1944; *a.* 39 Cadogan Square, London SW1.

Her interest in politics was first aroused on assisting her cousin, Sir Douglas Hogg to fight an election; knowledge of motoring and being a pilot equipped her to specialize in trade and commerce; member of the WFL; Municipal Reform candidate for LCC, West Islington, 1931; JP for Middlesex; entered House of Commons as Conservative member for Willesden West, 1931–5; spoke in the Commons against the removal of married women from the insurance scheme and against the marriage bar; went to Berlin and successfully secured the release of the wife and child of a socialist politician from Rosslau concentration camp, 1934; presented a petition on women's equal nationality rights with men to the Commons from over 100 Commonwealth women's organizations, 1935; subsequently became Conservative MP for Frome, 1935–45; member of the CWP during WW2; her flying experience contributed to her knowledge on defence issues, participated in defence debates, 1935–9; perhaps it was her recent personal experience of marital breakdown that led her to support a PMB on simplifying divorce, 1936; promoter of birth control and an abortion law reform supporter, particularly for rape cases; to support women's employment in the war effort, Tate revealed some of the inadequacies of men working in an aircraft factory which she had witnessed when she visited the factory disguised as a man, 1941; most significant success as a backbencher was leading the campaign on equal compensation for civilian war injuries on behalf of the Woman Power Committee, 1942; involved in trying to secure equal pay for the civil service and for teachers, as a member and in her role as Chairman of the EPCC, 1944–7; in the wake of her 1934 exploit, only woman member of a cross-party delegation to Belsen concentration camp just after the German surrender, 1945; put her noted public speaking ability to good use tackling issues of maternal mortality, mental health, abortion and suicide; inquest on her suicide from gas inhalation concluded that depression caused by financial problems, stress and an illness contracted at Belsen, had contributed to her state of mind; Edith Summerskill's (see entry) evaluation of Tate was as an 'outspoken feminist' (1967:60).

p. Equal Work Deserves Equal Pay (1945)

s. Women's Who's Who, 1934–5; LWW (1938); Brookes (1967); Stenton and Lees, vol. 3 (1979); Banks (1990); Pugh (1992).

TAVENER, Grace, LP WS Organizer; *b.* Yorkshire?; *e.* Canning School, Highgate; *a.* 43 Jessel House, Judd Street, London WC1 (1927).

'Brilliant organizer... beloved GT'; London and Home Counties Organizer for LP Women's Sections, covering Kent plus nine other counties, 1921–51; when she started her work there was only one group of women in this region, in Willesden, in 1921; her job was to establish new Women's Sections, to assist with section planning, to train and educate the membership and disseminate LP information; the burden of her workload caused a breakdown, 1925; WLL organizer for Southern and Home Counties, 1940; when she retired there were 350 Women's Sections, 9 Advisory Councils, 60 Constituency Central Committees and 50,000 women LP members in her district, 1951.

s. Labour Who's Who (1927); *Hutchinson* (1934); *Labour Woman,* January 1951.

TENNANT, Winifred Margaret Coombe, (née Pearce-Serocold) (Mam o Nedd) JP (1875–31 August 1956) social worker; *do.* Lieutenant George Pearce-Serocold, RN & Mary Clarke Richardson; *e.* private schools, England, France, Italy; *m.* Charles Coombe Tennant, landowner 1895; one daughter, three sons; *r.* travel; *c.* Ladies' Empire; *a.* Cadoxton Lodge, Vale of Neath, Glamorganshire, 73 Portland Place, London W1 (1934), 18 Cottesmore Gardens, London W8 (1938).

Member Executive Committee NUWSS; Vice Chairman Glamorgan Women's Agricultural Committee, 1914–18; Chair Neath & District War Pensions Committee, 1917; Gorsedd Mistress of the Robes; Honorary Bardic degree, 1918; elected member Executive Committee at the Llandrindod Conference on Self-Government for Wales, 1918; member Joint Committee for coordinating the Welsh National Movement, 1919; first woman to be appointed as magistrate to Glamorgan County Bench, 1920; visiting justice Swansea prison, 1920–31; first woman substitute delegate Great British Assembly LN, 1922; Liberal PPC Forest of Dean, 1922; member Central Committee and Chairman of the House Committee, ESU; member Institute International Affairs; Vice President Welsh National Liberation Council; member Court of Governors, University College, Cardiff; member Council Aberdare Hall, Cardiff; President Women's Section of the Welsh School of Social Service; involved in lobbying government to utilize the Geneva Convention for the benefit of British POWs, WW2; owner of the Coombe Tennant Collection of Modern French pictures; member Executive Committee Swansea Art Gallery; died in her London home.

p. Women and Welsh Housing (1919); contributions to the suffrage press.

s. Women's Who's Who, 1934–5; Hutchinson (1934); *Who's Who in Wales* (1937); *The Lady's Who's Who* (1938–9); *The Times,* 1 September 1956.

THOMAS, Margaret Haig (Second Viscountess Rhondda) (12 June 1883–20 July 1958) women's rights campaigner and magazine proprietor; *b.* London; *do.* David Alfred Thomas, Viscount Rhondda, coal owner and politician & Sybil Margaret Haig, WSPU; *e.* by governesses, Notting Hill High School, St Leonards and St Andrews, Somerville College, Oxford; *m.* Sir Humphrey Mackworth, landowner, 1908; *r.* gardening; *a.* 15 Chelsea Court, London SW3 (1927).

Influenced by her aunt Janetta and a cousin who were militant suffragettes, she and her mother joined the WSPU, 1908; Secretary Newport Branch WSPU; arrested and imprisoned in Usk for a chemical attack on a pillar box; bored and frustrated by the social expectations of her position, she wanted to play a public role; during WW1 Commissioner of Women's National Service in Wales; Chief Controller of Women's Recruiting, 1918; her father wanted a 'right-hand man' and the closeness of their relationship made Margaret perfect for the job and she became his personal assistant, thereby learning the business despite the astonishment of the exclusively male Cardiff business world; when her father became controller at the Ministry of Food in WW1, she acted as his substitute running his business empire; on his death she inherited her father's title and business, 1918; on the Board of *The Western Mail*, Director of 15 colliery boards, Director of 5 companies exporting or trading in coal, 1920; President WIL, 1918; Treasurer for the New Hospital for Women and Children, Brighton working with Louisa Martindale (see entry); founded *Time & Tide* magazine, 1920; Chair and founder member SPG, 1921; SPG representative Conference of Women, 1921; SPG representative CCWO, 1921; President NWCA 1921–4; failed to succeed with her campaign to take her seat in the House of Lords, 1922; shared a London flat and a country home with Helen Archdale until the relationship started to deteriorate in the late 1920s, severing when Rhondda's new companion, Theodora Bosanquet (see entry), and she decided to live together from 1933; member Council SWJ, 1922–3; offered office accommodation and advice on salaries, campaigning to WSIHVA; President WSIHVA, 1922, 1923, 1924, 1929; President/Chair NWCA, 1923; speaker on commerce, WES Conference, 1925; Chair EPRDCC, 1926; attended the initial meeting of the ODC, 1926; director of nearly 40 companies by 1927; Chair International Committee SPG, 1928; speaker on behalf of CS at Equal Pay Demonstration 1928; inaugurator and chair of BUC; speaker equal franchise demonstration, Hyde Park, 1928; President of WIL; Vice President of EAW, 1934; died from stomach cancer exacerbated by personal neglect as she spent over a quarter of a million pounds preoccupied with keeping her journal, *Time & Tide* afloat; regarded by many as one of the most extraordinary figures of the Women's Movement.

p. D.A. Thomas, Viscount Rhondda (1921); *This Was My World* (1933).

s. This Was My World, Viscountess Rhondda (1933); Courtney (1934); Williams and Palmer (1971); Eoff (1991).

THOMPSON, Edith Marie CBE (1879–25 August 1961) public service; *do.* W.F. Thompson; *e.* Norland Place School, Cheltenham Ladies' College, King's College University of London; *r.* travel, hockey; *c.* Forum, Ex-Service Women's; *a.* Gables, Aldeburgh, Suffolk (1934).

Played for the King's College Hockey Club at the end of the nineteenth century; founder/Editor *The Hockey Field* weekly journal, 1901–20; VAD, WW1; Assistant Chief Controller of Inspection QMAAC, 1918–20; helped to establish Ex-Service Women's Association, 1918; OBE, 1919; CBE, 1920; member Aldeburgh Town Council, 1921–7, 1929–32; member East Suffolk County Education Committee; member Executive Committee SPG, 1921; member WSIHVA; signatory to WSIHVA Rules, 1921; representative on SPG delegate on Child Assault, 1923; attended NCM Conference 1923; WSIHVA representative RSI Congress, Hull, 1923; Fellow University of London; County Organizer NFWI; member Lancet Commission on Nursing, 1932–3; Chair Executive Overseas Settlement of British Women, 1936–46; President All England Women's Hockey Association, 1923–8, 1946–7; managed women's hockey teams all over the world, Honorary Life member

Women's Hockey Association England, USA, Australia, NZ, South Africa; Executive Committee National Playing Fields' Association; HQ Organizer Women's Land Army, start of WW2; Liaison Official Children's Overseas Reception Board, South Africa, 1940–45; Governor Bedford College and St Felix School, Southwold, 1961.

p. Hockey as a Game for Women (1904); History QMAAC.

s. Hutchinson (1934); *Women's Who's Who, 1934–5*; *The Times*, 26 August 1961, 1 September 1961.

TUCKWELL, Gertrude Mary, CH, JP (25 April 1861–5 August 1951) trade unionist; *b.* Oxford; *do.* Rev. William Tuckwell, Master New College School & Rosa Strong; *e.* at home by father, then Bishop Otter's College, Chichester, Teacher Training College, Liverpool; *a.* 13 Chester Terrace, London SW1 (1929), Little Woodlands, Wormley, Godalming (1931).

Influenced by her father, a 'radical parson' who tried to improve the conditions of agricultural workers, and her aunt Mrs Mark Pattison (Lady Dilke), the trades union pioneer; Elementary School teacher London School Board, Chelsea 1885–92; joined the teachers' organization and addressed some of its meetings; member the Women's Protective and Provident League which later became the WTUL; Honorary Secretary WTUL and her aunt's secretary, 1892–1904; Honorary Secretary, WTUL; at aunt's death, President WTUL, 1904–21; worked closely with Mrs Tennant (see entry), Mary Macarthur (see entry), Lucy Deane Streatfeild (see entry), Adelaide Anderson (see entry), campaigning on protection of women workers from wage exploitation and industrial injury, resulted in Factory Act, 1895 and Factory and Workers Act, 1901; member Advisory Committee Ministry of Health, 1905–23; led foundation of Industrial Law Committee and National Anti-Sweating League for campaigns against lead poisoning, setting up exhibition on sweated industries (1906), in turn, contributed to Trade Boards Act, 1909; President NFWW, 1908–18; member Department Committee to Enquire into Lead Poisoning in China and Earthenware, 1908–10; member LP; member Committees of Ministry of Reconstruction; supposedly 'retired' in 1918; appointed to the Labour Advisory panel of the Engineering Trades Committee, Ministry of Reconstruction, 1918; after WW1 worked on maternal mortality, maternal and child welfare; member Advisory Committee to Lord Chancellor for Selecting Women JP, 1921–2; first woman JP for the County of London, 1920; President WPHOA 1921, 1922, 1927, 1928, 1929; assisted with negotiations for WSIHVA's entry to the TUC; member Women's Central Committee on Women's Training and Employment, 1920–22; Vice President WSIHVA, 1924; President WSIHVA, 1922 and 1929; with Mrs Tennant she established and was Chair Maternity Mortality Committee, 1927; member Royal Commission on NHI, 1924–8; Chair National Association Probation Officers; launched Maternal Mortality Conference, 1928; founder member Magistrates' Association; Vice Chairman YWCA's Industrial Law Bureau; member SJCIWO; supported Labour PPC Mary Carlin's campaign, 1930; CH, 1930; awarded the TUC Gold Badge and an illuminated address in album form for her 25 years work for the WTUL; died at the Royal Surrey Hospital.

p. The State and Its Children (1894); *The Workers' Handbook* (1908); *Life of Sir Charles Dilke* (with Stephen Gwynn, 1917); 'The Regulation of Women's Work' in *Woman in Industry from Seven Points of View* (1908); articles on industrial issues in

Nineteenth Century, *Fortnightly Review* and numerous other publications. See the *Dictionary of Labour Biography* for a complete list of her publications.

s. *Who's Who* (1929); *The Lady's Who's Who* (1938–9); *The Times*, 6 August 1951; Williams and Palmer (1971); *Dictionary of Labour Biography*, vol. 4; *Who Was Who*, vol. 5.

TURNER, Ethel Margaret (Madge) (24 July 1884–19 February 1948) equal moral rights campaigner; *r.* gardening, painting; *a.* Kenardington, Kent (1945).

Member WFL, imprisoned for her suffrage activities; introduced to the AMSH by Alison Neilans (see entry), a friend and suffrage colleague with whom she shared her life; AGS and Librarian AMSH, 1919–41; member NUSEC Sub-Committee on Health Services, 1926; collaborated with Millicent Fawcett (see entry) on a memorial volume on Josephine Butler, 1928; succeeded Neilans as General Secretary, 1941; Joint Editor, later sole Editor *The Shield*; nursed Neilans through her final illness until her death, 1941–3; retired to pursue her second love of growing and studying flowers, 1945; died in her London home after a sudden illness.

p. *Josephine Butler: Her Work and Principles and their Meaning for the 20th Century* (1928); *Common British Flowers* (1948).

s. *The Shield*, October 1945, November 1948.

TWEEDY, Hilda (née Anderson); social rights and welfare activist; *b.* (26 August 1911–); *b.* Clones, County Monaghan; *do.* Rev. James Ferguson Anderson & Muriel Frances Victoria Swayne; *e.* Alexandra School and College, Dublin; *m.* Robert Tweedy, 1936; three children.

The eldest of three girls, her father brought them up to believe that they should never let being a girl get in their way and should also never give a second-class performance because they were female; after finishing school went out to Egypt to join her parents, 1929; started a PNEU school in Alexandria, whilst simultaneously reading for an external University of London mathematics degree by correspondence course, 1929–36; married in Egypt; on her return to Dublin as a married woman she was refused a job as a teacher on the grounds that if she became pregnant it would not be nice for the girls she taught; decided to tackle the extreme effects on children of the food shortages resulting from WW2, came together with four other women resulting in the Houswives' Petition, 1941; this developed into the IHC with Tweedy as joint honorary secretary, 1942; finally becoming the IHA, 1946; delegate to the IAW Amsterdam conference, 1949; subsequently became Chair of the IHA; member WAC, 1964; involved in the establishment of the National Commission on the Status of Women, Honorary Secretary of the first ad hoc committee, 1968; Chairwoman of the CSW, 1972; served on the IAW board, 1961–3, 1973–89; convenor of the IAW Commission on International Understanding (Peace through Human Rights and IU), represented the IAW as an observer at many UN meetings on disarmament and peace, 1982–6; awarded Doctor in Laws, honoris causa, Trinity College, Dublin partly in recognition of her work for women's rights, 1990; currently, a supportive honorary board member of the IAW and the NCW in Ireland, as well as taking an active interest in the struggle against the renewed rise in global racism.

p. *A Link in the Chain: The Story of the Irish Housewives' Association 1942–92* (1992).

s. Tweedy (1992); conversation with Hilda Tweedy 17 May 2000.

b: born;   do: daughter of;   e: education;   m: married;   r: recreation;   **149**
c: club;   a: address;   p: publications;   s: sources

UNDERWOOD, Florence Ada (c.1875–19 January 1942) women's rights campaigner; *c.* International Suffrage.

General Secretary WFL from its inception for thirty years, 1907–c.1937; in the early days of the WFL she worked in the Clapham Branch; attended the initial meeting of the ODC, 1926; Editor *The Vote/WFL Bulletin*; the continuance of the WFL as an organization into the 1940s was credited to her, although she was extremely modest about her achievements; after full suffrage had been achieved she concentrated her efforts on the abolition of the mui tsai (child brides) system in Hong Kong; member SJSPA; one of her lifelong friends was Edith Zangwill (see entry) and she was also a close friend of Elizabeth Knight (see entry); her health was never good and she suffered a long and debilitating illness.

s. Women's Who's Who, 1913; WFL Bulletin, 30 January 1942, 30 February 1942.

VARLEY, Julia, OBE (16 March 1871–24 November 1952) Trade Union Official; *b.* Bradford; *do.* Richard Varley & Martha Ann Alderson; *e.* Elementary School; *r.* photography; *a.* 1 Loveday Street, Birmingham (temporary 1927), 42 Hay Green Lane, Bournville (1927).

Her great grandfather, a Peterloo veteran imprisoned for Chartist activism (working-class political reform movement, 1838–48), had influenced her to 'work for the people' (*Dictionary of Labour Biography*); she began work in a textile mill as a half-timer at the age of ten; by the age of fourteen she was a full-time weaver; first Union membership, 1888; when her mother died she had to give up work to care for her younger siblings, but maintained her union activities; member Executive Committee Bradford Trades Council; with the pioneer trade unionist, Mary Macarthur (see entry), she helped to unionize the women chainmakers at Cradley Heath who were paid one penny an hour, into an NFWW branch, 1907; Secretary Bradford Branch Weavers' and Textile Workers' Union, 1900; Bradford Board Gardens, 1904; member WTUL; member WSPU; imprisoned twice for suffrage activities, 1907; Senior Woman Organizer, Workers' Union, 1913 to 1920s; member Executive Committee and Council of Overseas Settlement of British Women; Executive Committee Industrial Welfare Society; Executive Committee Industrial Welfare Alliance; undertook research on women in tramp wards and lodging houses; worked on the SOSBW and visited some of the women settlers in Canada, 1925; member SJCIWO; member of the Commission investigating allegations against the WAAC in France, 1918; member of the Departmental Committee on the Employment of Women and Young Persons on the Two-Shift System (used as a means of evading legislation on industrial working hours), 1920 and 1934; Chief Woman Organizer WU, and subsequently the TGWU, 1920s to 1935; served on the General Council TUC with one year's break (1925–6), 1921–36; delegate IFWW Conference, 1923; member Ministry of Labour Committee on the Supply of Domestic Servants, 1923; Vice Chairman SJCIWO, 1923, 1927; member Advisory Council WES Conference of Women, 1925; awarded OBE, 1931; main speaker at an international conference on the status of women in Geneva, 1935; presented with the TUC gold medal on her retirement from the General Council, 1935; retired from the TGWU, 1936; during her retirement, despite losing her sight, she attended the TUC Women's Conferences and TUC until 1951; eventually went to live with her sisters in Bradford where she died; Marion Phillips (see entry) said at her retirement that she was 'a good colleague, a good citizen, a good friend' (*Dictionary of Labour Biography*).

p. articles and reports, see the *Dictionary of Labour Biography* entry for a complete list.

s. Labour Who's Who (1927); *The Lady's Who's Who*, 1938–9; *Dictionary of Labour Biography*, vol. 5; see also her private papers, University of Manchester.

VEITCH, Marian (Mrs Donald Barnie) (8 July 1913–24 July 1973) trade unionist; *do.* Arthur Edward & Elizabeth Veitch; *e.* Huntsman's Gardens School, Sheffield, Ruskin College, Oxford; *m.* Donald Barnie, Hendon Polytechnic lecturer, 1965.

Sheffield City councillor, 1945–56; working as a clerk until 1956; Yorkshire District Official, GMWU, 1957–60; member of the Food Standards Committee, 1965–8; only woman Executive Committee member Confederation of Shipbuilding and Engineering Unions, 1962–70; member International Metal Workers Federation of Women Workers, 1962–70; member International Union of Food and Allied Workers' Association, 1964–70; member Food Standards Committee, 1965–8; Chairman International Federation of Industrial Organizations Women's Committee, 1969–70; National Woman Officer GMWU from 1960–70; member Engineering Training Board, 1968–70; it was with her eight male Executive Committee colleagues of the CSEU that she battled on the issue of equal pay during the national strike of women engineering workers, accusing them of 'selling women workers down the river' she was supported in her strike threat by Barbara Castle (see entry) in October 1968; a childhood heart complaint forced her into premature retirement at 57; her death prevented completion of her autobiography, *She's 'Ere!*

s. Who Was Who, vol. 7; *The Times*, 24 October 1968, 27 July 1973.

VICKERS, Joan Helen (Baroness of Devonport) (1907–23 May 1994); *do.* Horace Cecil Vickers & Lilian Morro Lambert Grose; *e.* St Monica's College, Burgh Heath, Surrey and Paris; *a.* Albemarle Villas, Devonport, the Manor House, East Chisenbury, Pewsey, Wilts (1994).

LCC member Norwood, 1937–45; MBE for her work with prisoners-of-war in South East Asia with the Red Cross; Conservative PPC for Poplar South, 1945; served in the Colonial Service in Malaya, 1946–50; Conservative MP Plymouth, Devonport, 1955–74 when she was defeated; interested in welfare issues; voted for the abolition of the death penalty, 1956; carried on from Edith Summerskill (see entry), introduced her PMB Maintenance Orders (Attachment of Income) Bill to legislate for maintenance arrears to be deducted directly from a man's earnings, the Bill failed opposed by MPs who were lawyers, 1957; her Bill was taken up by the government, she steered it through the Commons, Maintenance Orders (Attachment of Income) Act, 1958; UK delegate UN Status of Women Commission, 1960–64; President Status of Women Committee, 1962; Honorary Secretary of the Conservative backbench Naval Sub-Committee; with Judith Hart (see entry) successfully opposed the Employment of Women Bill, 1963; succeeded in getting her second PMB, the Young Persons (Employment) Bill passed, improving their working conditions, 1964; DBE, 1964; worked with Barbara Castle (see entry) and Shirley Summerskill (see entry) opposing the government's attempt to replace Family Allowances paid to mothers with a tax credit included in the father's salary, 1973; UK delegate Chairman of CoE and WEU, 1967–74.

s. Brookes (1967); Stenton and Lees, vol. 3 (1979); *Who's Who*, 1994.

WALKER, Dr Jane Harriett, CH, LLD, LRCP, LRCSE, MD (24 October 1859–17 November 1938) tuberculosis treatment pioneer; *b.* Dewsbury, Yorkshire; *do.* John Walker, blanket manufacturer & Dorothy Ann Clay; *e.* Southport, London School of Medicine for Women, Vienna; *r.* music, painting, bridge; *c.* Albemarle, Cowdray, National Labour; *a.* 122 Harley Street, London W1 (1920–21), East Anglian Sanatorium, Maryland, Suffolk (1901).

LRCPI and LM, 1884; MD Bruxelles, 1890; LRCSEd. 1889; pursued her training gaining an MD (Brussels), because she was unable to obtain a doctorate in medicine at a British university, 1890; member of the BMA from 1893; clinical assistant in paediatrics at the East London Hospital and subsequently, resident medical officer at the Wirral Children's Hospital; although she was in general practice until 1901, her life's work began with a visit to the Nordrach Colony in the Black Forest, which made her a supporter of the open-air treatment of tuberculosis; specialized in the treatment of tuberculosis and was the first person to introduce the open-air treatment of consumption into England, when she opened a small sanatorium in a farmhouse in Downham market, Norfolk, 1892; this expanded and she started the East Anglian Sanatorium, Nayland, Suffolk, 1901; a section for the poorest patients was opened in 1904; a children's ward in 1912; a department for soldiers, 1916; finally provision for officers, 1919; Consultant Physician Ministries of Food and Munitions; member of the Departmental Committee on provision for the Treatment of Tuberculosis; member of Government Advisory Commission on Research; founder, first President, Treasurer and Honorary Secretary, MWF; Fellow Royal Society of Medicine; Physician of New Hospital for Women; Medical Superintendent of the East Anglian Children's Maltings Farm Sanatorium; delivered a series of lectures in the USA on Tuberculosis, 1923; Vice President of the Section of Tuberculosis at the BMA's Annual Conference, 1923; JP County of Suffolk; Fellow Royal Institute of International Affairs; many interests outside medicine and served on the West Suffolk Agricultural Committee and other public bodies; a LP supporter; a suffrage activist from the early years of the movement she was also Treasurer of the AMSH for eighteen years; she was recognized as a CH and an honorary LLD from Leeds University, 1931; great personal friend of Millicent Fawcett (see entry); she was still at work, the oldest woman practitioner in the country, even days before her death and due to celebrate the diamond jubilee of her career in medicine; died at her Harley Street home; Lady Barrett (see entry) spoke of her as 'a lovable friend and pioneer for the equal rights of men and women' (BMA).

p. A Handbook for Mothers (1893); *A Book for Every Woman* (1895); *Open-Air Treatment of Consumption, 7 Years' Experience* (1899); *Modern Nursing of Consumption* (1904).

s. List of Women Nominated for Service in Connection with the League of Nations (NUWT Archive, nd 1920–21?); *Who's Who* (1929); *Women's Who's Who, 1934–5*; *The Lady's Who's Who* (1938–9); *British Medical Journal*, 26 November 1938, Dewsbury Reference Library.

WARD, Irene Mary Bewick (Baroness of North Tyneside) CBE (1895 –26 April 1980) politician; *do.* Alfred J. Bewick Ward & Elvira Mary; *e.* Newcastle Church High School; *a.* 6 Roseworth Terrace, Gosforth, Newcastle upon Tyne (1938).

Her father died was she was young, her childhood was marked by poverty; first attempt as Conservative PPC for Wansbeck, Northumberland was thwarted, she was forced to concede as Party members did not want a woman candidate, 1923; contested Morpeth, 1924, 1929; worked on a voluntary basis for the Conservatives; CBE, 1929; held Wallsend for the Conservatives, 1931–45; became conversant with mining and shipbuilding issues in her constituency, the poverty and hardship of her constituents influenced her; gave her maiden speech during the Coal Mines Bill, criticising the government's failure to ensure miners' wages, 1932; Honorary Member Executive Committee NCW; together with Nancy Astor (see entry) and Eleanor Rathbone (see entry) she voted for amendments to improve the position of Indian women in the new Constitution, 1935; succeeded in awarding elderly people in Poor Law Institutions pocket money under the Poor Law (Amendment) Bill, 1937; Chaired the WPC; Chairman of the CWP initiated by Nancy Astor (see entry) and Caroline Haslett (see entry) which met throughout WW2 at Astor's home monitoring women's wartime employment position; part of the manpower debate discussing women's employment take-up during the Second World War, 1941; appointed to WCC by Lloyd George to advise him, 1941; great friends with Ellen Wilkinson (see entry): JP Newcastle upon Tyne, 1949; lost her seat in 1945, returned as Conservative MP for Tynemouth, 1950–74; her priority was equal pay, tabled an amendment to the King's Speech, which had omitted equal pay, 1950; championed people like pensioners, who lived on a fixed income; supported the Deserted Wives Bill, 1951; signatory to a letter to *The Times* on the Conservative Party's failure to choose enough women PPCs, 1952; PMB success with the Rights of Entry (Gas and Electricity) Boards Bill, 1953; DBE, 1955; true to her promotion of women's interests, questioned why the Commons' Librarian was advertising for male personnel only, due to her persistence women librarians were employed, 1955; third legislative success with the Nurses (Amendment) Bill, 1960 and finally, Penalties for Drunkenness Bill, 1962; CH, 1973; Honorary Fellow Lucy Cavendish College, Cambridge; retired, 1974; Baroness Ward of North Tyneside, 1974, participated in the House of Lords for some years.

p. F.A.N.Y. Invicta (1955)

s. LWW (1938); Brookes (1967); Stenton and Lees, vol. 3 (1979); *Who Was Who*, vol. 7; Banks (1990); Pugh (1992).

WATSON, Dr Alexandra (Mona) Mary Campbell Chalmers (née Geddes) MD, CBE (31 May 1872–7 August 1936) physician; *b.* India; *do.* Auckland Campbell Geddes, civil engineer & Christina Helen Macleod Anderson; *e.* Sandys House, St Leonard's School, St Andrews, Edinburgh School of Medicine; *m.* Chalmers Watson, MD, FRCP, 1898; two sons; *c.* Women's United Services, Caledonian Ladies', Edinburgh; *a.* Fenton Barns, Drem, East Lothian.

Connected to the Garrett Andersons (see entries) through her mother; attended St Leonard's School 1888–90; as the first woman medical graduate of the University of Edinburgh, she suffered prejudice and opposition during her training; graduated MB, CM, 1896; gained MD, 1898; a suffragette; spent a year working in a maternity hospital and district nursing institute in Plaistow, London; six months in Dr Barnardo's Homes, Kent; Physician Edinburgh Hospital and Dispensary for Women and Children, from c.1900; in practice in Edinburgh with her husband until 1914; Manager Royal Infirmary, Edinburgh; Honorary Secretary Queen's Institute of District Nursing; Honorary Secretary Queen Victoria's Jubilee Nurses Scottish Central Council; President Scottish Women's Medical Association; President

Women's United Services Club; founder and first Chief Controller of the WAAC, 1917–18; CBE, 1917; President Edinburgh WCA; member Standing Committee on Health Services, Department of Health for Scotland; first President Scottish Women's Hockey Association; assisted her husband with editing the *Encyclopaedia Medica*; ran Fenton Barns, a large dairy farm researching the application of scientific principles to farming and its suitability for women, 1923–33 to c.1936; member SPG, 1925; Chair *Time & Tide* Publishing Company Board of Directors, c.1929; President MWF, 1935; involved in numerous Scottish women's organizations; died at her brother's home, Rolvenden, Kent.

p. 'Invalid Feeding' in *Encyclopaedia Medica* (1900).

s. The Times, 15 May 1928; *Who's Who*, 1929; *Daily Telegraph*, 10 August 1936; *Manchester Guardian*, 10 August 1936; *Time & Tide*, 15 August 1936; *British Medical Journal*, 15 August 1936; St Leonard's School Archive.

WHATELY, Mary Monica, BA (1890–12 September 1960) Organizer and Public Speaker; *b.* London; *do.* Major Reginald Pepys Whately and Maud Isobel Davies; *e.* at home, LSE; *r.* music, dancing; *c.* PLC; *a.* 75 Harcourt Terrace, Redcliffe Square, London SW10 (1913), 31 Brookfield, London N6 (1927), Moyle Towers, Hythe, Kent (1927).

BA in Politics; Honorary Treasurer CWSS since its foundation, 1911; member of WSPU; friend of Dorothy Elizabeth Evans (see entry) and Emmeline Pethick-Lawrence (see entry), who called her an 'outstanding leader of the world movement for women's status'; after WW1 she was involved in famine relief work in Austria, Germany, Poland, Russia; visited Germany on behalf of hostage prisoners; subsequently member SJSPA; member Executive Committee NUSEC, one of the 11 members who resigned over the protective legislation issue (the support of industrial legislation to 'protect' working women was viewed by equalitarian feminists as a dilution of their struggle for total equality), 1927; member SPG; member ODC; member SWM; member SJSPA; member Peace Army; member Committee for Information on India; member LP; Associate of Women Police; Labour PPC for St Albans, she polled 12,000 votes, Vera Brittain (see entry) and Winifred Holtby (see entry) worked for her campaign, 1929; member LNU; Honorary Secretary St Pancras SEC; Labour PPC for St Albans and LCC candidate for West Fulham, 1930; member NMW; spoke at a rally for Labour PPC Mary Carlin, 1930; member Women Candidates' Association, represented this group at Ethel Bentham's (see entry) funeral, 1931; Chairman St Pancras SEC, 1931; member LCC for Limehouse; met Ghandi, 1933; her meetings during the LCC elections in Stepney were constantly disrupted by Fascists, 1937; visited India as member Indian League Delegation; visited USA to study the conditions of workers under prohibition; member of a delegation to Spain after the Civil War; Chair SPG after WW2; campaigned for equal rights with regard to race as well as gender, on a visit to South Africa after WW2 she was appalled at the discrimination she witnessed; also opposed to blood sports and the use of performing animals.

p. articles and reviews.

s. Women's Who's Who, 1913; *Labour Who's Who* (1927); *The Lady's Who's Who* (1938–9).

WHITE, Amber Blanco (née Reeves) (pen-name Amber Reeves) OBE (1 July 1887–26 December 1981) writer; *b.* New Zealand; *do.* William Pember Reeves, NZ Agent General to London & Magdalen (Maud) Stuart Robison; *e.* Kensington High School, Newnham College Cambridge; *m.* George Rivers Blanco White, lawyer, 1909; one daughter, two sons; *r.* reading, gardening; *c.* PEN; *a.* Pembroke Gardens, London NW3, 44 Downshire Hill, London NW3 (1927), Bedham, Fittleworth, West Sussex (1938).

Her mother was a member of the Fabian Women's Group; White was a brilliant student at Newnham, awarded the Marion Kennedy scholarship, 1905–08; Treasurer CUFS, 1906; befriended Rachel Costelloe (see entry) at Cambridge; although she spent her university life disregarding the rules and conventions, she took a double first in the Moral Sciences tripos; she gave a talk on women's suffrage at Morley College, 1909; became intimate with H.G. Wells while she was still a student and is thought to have been the inspiration for his novel, *Ann Veronica*, this relationship resulted in an illegitimate daughter, Anna Jane, 1909, (despite her mother's suggestion that Amber have an abortion); a marriage was arranged for her in the same year, 1909; during WW1 she joined the ATS; Director of Women's Wages, Ministry of Munitions, 1916–19; worked briefly at the Board of Trade researching the position of women's wages in the Midlands light metal trades, however, she was dismissed from this post, Fry concluded it was due to a combination of the Board's prejudice against women in the civil service and her married state, 1921; member National Whitley Council for Civil Service, 1919–20; OBE, c.1922; having met her at Cambridge, Amber became a lifelong friend of and adviser to Eva Hubback (see entry) in her job as NUSEC's Parliamentary Secretary; joined the LP, 1924; member NUSEC's Sub-Committee on Health Services, 1927; member of NUSEC's Press and Publications Committee, 1927; member Executive Committee NUSEC, 1927; philosophy and psychology lecturer Morley College, London 1928–65; Editor *The Woman's Leader*, 1929; Honorary Secretary to Morley College Council, 1929; representative NUSEC on deputation to Ramsay MacDonald, spoke on equal pay in civil service and dismissal on marriage, 1929; member Fabian Society, regularly involved in Fabian summer schools; worked with Eva Hubback on establishing the Townswomen's Guilds; member executive committee NUGC, 1931; Editor *The Townswoman*, 1933; Labour PPC Hendon, 1933, 1935; member Council PEN; an authority on economic issues; Acting Principal, Morley College, 1946–7; she retired in 1965; left an estate of £175,672; it was felt that she had not fulfilled the early promise of her remarkable intellect in her professional life.

p. The Reward of Virtue (1911); *A Lady and Her Husband* (1914); *Helen in Love* (1916); *Give and Take* (1923); *The Work, Wealth and Happiness of Mankind* (with H.G. Wells, 1932); *The Nationalisation of Banking* (1934); *The New Propaganda* (1938); *Worry in Women* (1941); *Ethics for Unbelievers* (1947); also articles for *Fabian News, Saturday Review, Queen, Vogue*.

s. The Lady's Who's Who (1938–9); *The Times*, 6 January 1982; *Ham & High*, 21 May 1982; *Who Was Who*, vol. 7; Fry (1992); see also private papers held by the family.

WHITE, Eirene Lloyd (Baroness of Rhymney) (née Lloyd Jones) (7 November 1909–23 December 1999) Labour politician; *b.* Belfast; *do.* Dr Thomas Jones, politician & Eirene T. Lloyd, Co-operative Movement activist; *e.* St Paul's Girls'

School, Hammersmith, Somerville College, Oxford; *m.* John Cameron White, journalist, 1948; *a.* 22 Bailey Court, Hereford Road, Abergavenney, Gwent (1999).

Influenced by parental background towards a political career, her father's experiences as Deputy Secretary to the Cabinet ensured a healthy scepticism; Ministry of Labour officer, 1933–7 and 1941–5; spent some time in America studying library provision, the discrimination of not being able to eat in the same restaurant as the black singer and political activist, Paul Robeson, made her an anti-racist campaigner; first woman political lobbyist, *Manchester Evening News*, where she worked with Mary Stott (see entry), 1945–9; member LP NEC, 1947–53, 1958–72; successful on her second attempt as Labour candidate for East Flint, North Wales, 1950–70; specialist issues were overseas, industrial matters, education, child welfare; introduced Matrimonial Causes Bill to liberalize divorce laws, eventually dropped as Party feared the alienation of Catholic voters at the election, 1951; supporter of the EPCC; voted against the Street Offences Bill, 1958; opposition spokesman on education, 1959; Chairman Fabian Society, 1958–9; Parliamentary Secretary to the Colonial office, 1964–6; Minister of State at the Foreign Office, 1966–7; Chairman NEC 1968–9; Minister of State at the Welsh Office, 1967–70; Chairman LP, 1968–9; President NCW, sat until she retired, 1970; President Nursery Schools Association, 1964–6; created Baroness White, 1970; Member Royal Commission on Environmental Pollution, from 1974; Governor National Library of Wales; sat in the Lords from 1979; Deputy Speaker House of Lords, 1979–89.

p. *The Ladies of Gregynog* (1985)

s. Brookes (1967); Phillips (1980); Stenton and Lees, vol. 4 (1981); *Who's Who*, 1999; *Guardian*, 27 December 1999.

WHITTY-WEBSTER, Dame May (Mrs Ben Webster) DBE (19 June 1865–29 May 1948) actress; *b.* Liverpool; *do.* Alfred Whitty, founder of the Liverpool Post & Mary Ashton; *e.* private; *m.* Ben Webster, actor, 1892; one daughter; *c.* Cowdray, Three Arts, Arts Theatre; *a.* Church Place, 31 Bedford Street, London WC2 (1934), Hollywood (1937–48).

Made her first appearance on stage, 1881; prominent member AFL during WW1, working in the AFL to organize the Women's Emergency Corps; Chair British Women's Hospital which raised £150,000 to build the Star and Garter Home for disabled solders and £13,000 for the Scottish Women's Hospital; Chairman Era War Distress Fund; member of the Entertainments Committee of the Endell Street Hospital (see Flora Murray entry), 1915–19; after the War, awarded the OBE and DCO; Chairman Theatrical Ladies Guild; Chairman AFL, 1926; worked for the extension of the franchise with AFL in the 1920s; speaker at an AFL 'at home', 1926; Chairman Three Arts Women's Employment Fund; Vice President the actors' union, British Actor's Equity, which was inaugurated in the Webster's flat; Vice Chairman Appeal Committee, Children's Country Holiday Fund; moved to Hollywood, 1937; Vice President British War Relief in Los Angeles, during WW2; she did not retire, her theatre and film career spanned over 62 years; died in Hollywood.

s. *Who's Who* (1929); *Women's Who's Who, 1934–5*; *The Lady's Who's Who*, (1938–9); *New York Times*, 30 May 1948, 31 May 1948, 6 June 1948; *Manchester Guardian*, 31 May 1948; *Daily Herald*, 30 May 1948.

WILKINSON, Ellen Cicely (Red Ellen/The Fiery Particle) MA (8 October 1891–6 February 1947) Trade Union Official and Labour politician; *b.* Manchester; *do.* Richard Wilkinson, cotton operative & Ellen Wood; *e.* Church Elementary School Manchester, Ardwick Higher Elementary School, Manchester Day Training College, Manchester University; *r.* reading, walking, golf, theatre; *c.* PLC, NTU; *a.* 30 John Street, London WC1 (1927), 18 Guildford Street, London WC1 (1934), Twixtlands, Penn, Buckinghamshire (1947).

From a Methodist, temperance family; won a scholarship to Secretarial School, 1902; won pupil teaching bursary, 1906; joined the ILP, 1907; attended College for half the week, taught for the other half for two years to gain a teaching qualification; active in the suffrage movement in Manchester while at training college; matriculated, 1909; won Jones Scholarship in History to go to university, 1910; joined the Manchester University Fabian Society, University Socialist Federation and was involved with the Fabian Women's Group; joined MSWS, 1912; graduated MA History and Economics; her original ambition was to become a journalist; full-time organizer NUWSS, Manchester, 1913–14; seconded by the NUWSS to the Stockport Relief Committee, 1914; first AUCE, 1915; joined WILPF, 1915; led a strike of women shop assistants being paid 7–8 shillings a week, in Plymouth, Nancy Astor (see entry) helped to get some of them jobs after the strike, 1915; there was an unlikely lifelong friendship and working relationship between Wilkinson and Astor; she set up a women's department in the union, 1915; did a lot of work with women workers especially in laundries, biscuit and soap works; supported the value of women-only conferences; appointed to several Trade Boards, 1920–21; continued as National Woman Organizer when AUCE became NUDAW, 1921; writing for her union journal and political papers; active participant in the formation of the Communist Party of Great Britain, 1920; elected Manchester City Council, 1923; persuaded the Council to take measures to assist unemployed women, 1923; Labour PPC Ashton-under-Lyme, 1923; resigned from the Communist Party, 1924; NUDAW-sponsored, she became Labour MP for Middlesborough, the youngest woman to enter the Commons, her campaign also supported by the WFL of which she was a member, 1924–31; as an MP she actively supported Women's Movement campaigns both in and out of Parliament, for instance she was involved with NUSEC, AFL, EAW, IWSA, BAWC, particularly the franchise extension and equal pay; seconded a Bill to extend the franchise, 1925; worked passionately for the causes of working people, women, children and the peace movement and was ordered to rest on several occasions; an example of part of her workload for one month – she motored 2000 miles, addressed 41 mass meetings – each with an average audience of 2000 – speaking for 45 minutes at each, June 1926; PPS to Susan Lawrence, Parliamentary Secretary to the Ministry of Health, 1929; she lost her parliamentary seat, 1931; involved with the anti-Fascist international underground movement, early 1930s; visited Spain on a relief mission, 1934; member WAWF, 1934; worked in NUDAW and as a journalist, especially for *Time & Tide*, 1931–5; Labour MP, Jarrow, 1935–47; supported the hunger march, the Jarrow Crusade, from Jarrow to London, walking with the men for long stretches and addressing meetings organized each night en route, 1936; made several further visits to Spain including one to study the work of relief agencies, with the Tory MP the Duchess of Atholl, Eleanor Rathbone (see entry), Dame Rachel Crowdy (see entry), 1937; involved with the founding of the weekly Labour paper, *Tribune*, 1936;

Parliamentary Secretary, Ministry of Pensions, 1940; Parliamentary Secretary, Ministry of Home Security, 1940–45; Minister of Education, 1945–7; as Minister of Education she raised the school-leaving age to 15, 1947; visited Germany, 1945; member British Delegation at the founding of UNO, San Francisco, 1945; Joint President First Plenary Session UNESCO in London, 1945; responsible for the provision of free school milk and for enabling the provision of school meals; died from a heart attack after taking an 'accidental' overdose of medication in the wake of a bout of bronchitis, died alone in her flat, she was buried at Penn, Buckinghamshire; it was the popular consensus that her early death was induced by overwork because of her passionate convictions and dedication to others.

p. A Workers' History of the General Strike (with Raymond Postgate, J.F. Horrabin, 1927); *Clash* (1929); *Peeps at Politicians* (1930) *Division Bell Mystery* (1932) *Why Fascism?* (with Dr Edward Conze, 1934); *Why War?* (1934); *The Town that Was Murdered* (1939); articles for a wide range of union and political papers including *Labour Leader, New Leader, Lansbury's Labour Weekly, Sunday Worker, Time & Tide, Co-operative Employee, New Dawn.*

s. Manchester Guardian, 7 February 1947; *The Times*, 7 February 1947; Oxford (1938); Brookes (1967); Vernon (1982).

WILLIAMS, Dr Ethel Mary Nucella, MD (Lon), DPH (Cantab), JP (1863–29 January 1948) public health worker; *b.* Cromer, Norfolk; *do.* Charles Williams, country squire & Mary Elizabeth Ketton Williams; *e.* Norwich High School, Newnham College, Cambridge, LSMW; *r.* gardening, walking; *c.* BMWF, BMA; *a.* 3 Osborne Terrace, Newcastle upon Tyne (1920–21) Low Bridges, Stocksfield, Northumberland (1948).

Women were not able to take degrees at Cambridge, although she attended lectures there from 1882–5; also as women could not undertake hospital training in this country she studied clinical work in Vienna and Paris, travelling extensively in Italy and Switzerland studying public health methods; qualified with a London MB, 1891; joined the BMA, 1891; became MD, 1895; took a Cambridge DPH, 1899; began her medical career as resident Medical Officer at the Clapham Maternity Hospital and the Blackfriars Dispensary for Women and Children; went to live in Newcastle upon Tyne setting up in general practice with her friend and colleague, Dr Ethel Bentham (see entry), until Bentham returned to London, 1909; one of the first women to drive a car in the North-East, 1906; as a prominent feminist, her involvement with the suffrage campaign began with her participation in the NUWSS' celebrated 'Mud March' in London, 1907; Chairman North-Eastern Federation NUWSS; active in the establishment of several women's organizations; took over from Beatrice Webb as director of research into the Commission into the working of the Poor Law, which Marion Phillips (see entry) was working on, 1907; interested in the organization of a health service and in public health in general; magistrate for Northumberland; became a JP, 1931; member of the Panel for Juvenile Courts; Crown Member of the University of Durham Senate, 1936; member Appeals Committee and Quarter Sessions; member BFUW; member BFMW; President BFMW, 1936; member LNU; member WIL; Medical Officer for the Women Students' Day Training Department of Armstrong College; member of the Newcastle School Board and of the Education Committee; President NFMW; presented with a portrait and a cheque by the Newcastle NCW in recognition of her public service, but donated the cheque to the Northern Women's Hospital, 1946; died at her home and was intered at Hindley churchyard.

p. papers in medical journals.

s. List of Women Nominated for Service in Connection with the League of Nations (NUWT Archive, nd 1920–21?); *Women's Who's Who, 1934–5*; *The Lady's Who's Who* (1938–9); *British Medical Journal*, 21 February 1948; Newnham College Archive.

WILSON, Emelye Ethelreda SRN; health activist; *e.* Church of England School, St Ives, Girls' Modern School, Bedford; *r.* music; *c.* Soroptimist; *a.* 77 Hagley Road, Edgebaston, Birmingham (1934).

Superintendent Women Workers, Metropolitan Vickers Electrical Company, Manchester; Chair Peace Crusade Branch, LN, Birmingham; Council Member New Health Society; member College of Nursing; Executive Committee Institute of Labour Management; spoke at WES Conference of Women in Science, Industry and Commerce on 'The Possibilities of Advancement for Women in Industry', 1925; member Institute of Industrial Welfare Workers.

s. Hutchinson (1934); *The Woman Engineer*, ii/3 (June 1925).

WILLSON, Laura Ann, MBE (c.1878–17 April 1942) engineer; *b.* Yorkshire; *e.* Elementary School; *m.* E.A. Willson, industrialist; one daughter; *a.* 8 Park Road, Halifax.

Started work as a 'half-timer' in a textile factory at 10 years old; her early years were devoted to the TU movement to improve women's working conditions; Branch Secretary Halifax WLL, 1907; a suffragette, she was imprisoned; during WW1 Willson became manager of the new women's section of Messrs Smith, Barker & Willson, her husband's lathe-making factory (he was a self-made man); awarded an OBE for her war-time munitions work; as a result of her war-time experiences she helped found the WES to protect the position women had won for themselves in industry and to work for equal opportunities in engineering, she contributed to the initial funding of the organization, 1919; founder member EAW; chaired the 'Industrial Welfare and Factory Inspection' session of the WES Conference, 1925; interested in the concept of labour-saving as taken from industry and applied to housework, to this end she wanted to construct modern housing for working people to include the latest electrical and gas appliances; in Halifax she had 72 houses constructed, and 160 in progress from July 1925–6; first woman member Federation of House Builders; President WES, 1925–c.1928; during her Presidency she was vital to the organization's survival through her fund-raising activities; cremated at Woking.

s. The Woman Engineer, ii/5 (December 1925), ii/7 (June 1926), v/2 (June 1942); Collette (1989).

WINTRINGHAM, Margaret (née Longbottom) JP (4 August 1879–10 March 1955) teacher, Liberal MP, suffragist; *b.* Oldfield, Yorkshire; *do.* David Longbottom; *e.* Keighley Girls' Grammar School, Bedford Training College; *m.* Tom Wintringham MP, 1903; *r.* sport; *a.* Little Grimsby Hall, Louth, 30 St Thomas Mansions, London SE (1924), 21 Minster Yard, Lincoln (1955).

Headmistress of a school in Grimsby before her marriage; member Grimsby Education Committee; member Grimsby Committee for lodging and feeding

Belgian refugees, and responsible for administering the Prince of Wales fund for the relief of industrial distress, 1914; after her husband was adopted as PPC for Lincolnshire Louth, she became a VAD at Louth Auxiliary Hospital; Chairman of the Women's War Agricultural Committee; member of County Agricultural Committee for conserving and increasing food supplies; President Louth WLA; Honorary Secretary Lindsey Federation WI; JP for Lindsey; Vice President Lincolnshire Total Abstinence Association; first British woman to be elected to Parliament, on her husband's death in August, she contested his seat and was elected as Independent Liberal MP in a September by-election, 1921; co-operated in the Commons and became good friends with the only other woman MP at the time, Nancy Astor (see entry); spoke for the retention of women police, for legislation to enable women peers to sit in the Lords, representation of women on public bodies, criminal law amendments relating to women and children; campaigner for franchise extension, a pacifist and supporter of the LN; re-elected, 1922; sat on the Parliamentary Committee for Agriculture investigating the disparity between the price of food between the producer and the consumer; served on Standing Committees on the Universities Bill, Lady Astor's Bill on intoxicating liquor, the Equal Divorce Bill, 1922; sat on the joint select committees on the Nationality of Married Women and the Equal Guardianship of Children; supporter WES; attacked Stanley Baldwin in the Commons for his 'man-made Budget', 1923; lost her seat, 1924; Honorary Vice President Blue Triangle Forward Movement, YWCA, 1924; Vice President SPG, 1925; Vice President NUSEC, 1927; President WNLF; member Royal Commission on the Civil Service; with Astor during the Depression of the early 1930s, worked with the SCF to assist with the establishment of open-air nurseries in Wales and the North-East, where meals were provided and work found for the childrens' fathers making equipment for the schools; member County Council Lindsey, 1933; Vice President EAW, 1934; PPC Aylesbury, 1935; member Central Agricultural Wages Board; member Women's Central Committee on Women's Training and Employment; adopted as Liberal PPC Gainsborough, Lincolnshire, 1938; President Domestic Studies Association; died in a London nursing home.

s. *British Women MPs* (D.M. Northcroft, 1922–3); *The Lady's Who's Who*, (1938–9); *Manchester Guardian*, 31 May 1938, 11 March 1955; *The Times*, 11 March 1955, 23 March 1955, 24 March 1955; Brookes (1967).

ZANGWILL, Edith Chaplin Ayrton (Mrs Israel Zangwill) (née Ayrton) (1 October 1875–5 May 1945) writer; *do.* Prof. William Edward Ayrton, scientist & Matilda Chaplin, MD; *e.* Bedford College for Women, London University; *m.* Israel Zangwill, writer, 1903; one daughter, two sons; *a.* Far End, East Preston, Littlehampton, Sussex (1929).

Step-daughter of Hertha Ayrton (see entry); attended Bedford College, gaining a Matriculation Div. 1, 1889–92; active suffragist, 1906–13; her husband was also a prominent supporter of women's suffrage; she was a close friend of Florence Underwood (see entry); member Executive Committee BAWC, 1928; speaker at Equal Franchise Demonstration, Hyde Park, 1928; spoke at the UJW's annual conference to rouse Jewish women to become active in the Jewish women's peace movement, 1929; Honorary Treasurer Women's Peace Crusade, early 1930s; involved in the WIL's disarmament campaign 1931–2.

p. Barbarous Babes (1904); *The First Mrs Molivar* (1905); *Teresa* (1909); *The Rise of a Star* (1918); *The Call* (1924); *The House* (1928).

s. Who's Who (1929); *Women's Who's Who, 1934–5*; London School of Jewish Studies; The Bedford Centre for the History of Women.

ZIMMERN, Elsie Mary *a.* 406 Elm Tree Mansions, London NW8 (1934).

Part founder Nursery Training School, Golders Green, she was its Honorary Secretary and Warden, 1911–23; Organizing Secretary Child Welfare Exhibitions, NCW, 1917–28; member Maternity and Child Welfare Committee NCW, 1922; General Secretary ICW, 1925–30; Executive Committee NCW, 1927; Honorary Secretary Associated Countrywomen of the World, from 1929; Honorary Secretary Liaison Committee of Rural Women's Organizations, from 1931; member WIC; Executive Committee NCW, 1936; member British delegation at the ICW Conference at Dubrovnik, 1936; she represented the ACW at Ogilvie Gordon's (see entry) funeral and memorial service, 1939.

s. Hutchinson (1934); *The Lady's Who's Who* (1938–9).

ORGANIZATIONS

AGOWHMC – Anglican Group for the Ordination of Women to the Historic Ministry of the Church, 1932.
Object: To secure the admission of women to the Ministry.
   In 1952 it had approximately 200 men and women members.
   s. COI (1952).

ALRA – Abortion Law Reform Association, 1936
Formed with the intention of campaigning for legal abortion which would especially benefit working-class women who had no access to safe abortion and less access to effective birth control. It had strong links to the Workers' Birth Control Group with many of the same women activists, such as Stella Brown and Dora Russell, leading both organizations. It succeeded in contributing to the passing of the Abortion Act, 1967.
   s. ALRA Archive Wellcome Institute; Graves (1994).

AMSH – Association for Moral and Social Hygiene, 1915
This was the British Branch of the International Abolitionist Federation founded by Josephine Butler (who campaigned successfully against the Contagious Diseases Acts) in 1875 which was the successor to the Ladies' National Association for the Abolition of State Regulation of Vice and for the Promotion of Social Purity, also founded by Butler in 1870.
   Object: 'To promote the principles of the IAF, ie. the abolition of State regulation of prostitution and the condemnation of all "laws of exception" aimed at women, or any class of women, applied under pretext of morals, which do not equally apply to all persons'. Affiliated to the International Abolitionist Federation, Geneva.
   Still in existence as the Josephine Butler Society.
   Archive: National Library of Women, London.
   Paper: The Shield.
   s. Gates (1923).

AWKS – Association for Women Clerks and Secretaries, 1903
Because of its initials, this group adopted the bird, the Awk as its emblem, thereby changing the C in its acronym to a K.

p: publications;   s: sources

Objects:

1. To unite for their mutual industrial protection women clerical workers, to secure the abolition of sex differentiation in the clerical world and to co-operate with other bodies working for similar objects.

2. To secure increased opportunities of employment for members and to assist them when unemployed, and for this purpose to administer the Unemployment Insurance Acts.

3. To increase the technical efficiency of women clerical workers, to raise the standard of their training, and to assist members to train.

4. To improve the health standard of women clerical workers and to assist members when sick, and for this purpose to co-operate with the National Federation of Women Workers' National Health Insurance Society.

5. To provide social and residential Clubs for members.

The Association is affiliated to the International Federation of Trade Unions, through the Trade Union Congress at Amsterdam.

It had a feminist profile and by 1922 had a membership of 3000.

Archive: Working Class Library, Manchester.

Paper: The Woman Clerk.

s. Gates (1923).

BAWC – British-American Women's Crusade

Object: 'For the mutual renunciation of war as an instrument of international policy in favour of the pacific settlement of all international disputes'.

s. Astor Archive (Soc 4).

BCL – British Commonwealth League, 1925

The successor to the British Dominions Women Citizens Union (1923) and the British Overseas Committee of the International Woman Suffrage Alliance.

Object: 'To uphold the principles of democracy within the British Commonwealth of Nations and to secure, by co-operation between men and women, the full development of liberties, and equal status and opportunities for all its citizens.' Still in existence as the Commonwealth Countries League.

s. Astor Archive (MS 1416/1/1/830); BCL Conference Reports 1925–39 (Fawcett Library).

BFBPW – British Federation of Business and Professional Women, 1935–69

Started life as the British Federation of Business and Professional Women's Clubs in 1933. At a meeting in January 1935 the word, 'club' was discussed and it was decided to establish a new constitution for the BFBPW.

Object: To promote and safeguard the interests of business and professional women, to establish a closer co-operation between them, to secure effective and consistent co-ordination of action on matters affecting their mutual interests and also to promote and maintain such professional standards and training as would make a constructive contribution to the professional world and to the community at large. It was involved in the Committee for Equal Compensation for War Injuries which campaign succeeded by 1943. It then commissioned a report on women's position in national wage negotiation machinery, 1945. It was affiliated to the International Federation of Business and Professional Women and was active in the international arena.

By the 1950s its object had developed: To secure equal opportunity of training and employment for business and professional women in all spheres of public life, on the same basis with men where qualifications are equal.

s. Organization papers at the Fawcett Library; COI (1952).

BFUW – British Federation of University Women, 1907
Object: 'The Federation aims at creating an organization representative of British University women in all professions – endeavours to promote friendship and co-operation between university women at home and abroad. It encourages independent research work by university women, advises them as to training for work other than teaching and seeks to stimulate their interest in municipal and public life. It is affiliated to the International Federation of University Women.' Still in existence as the BF of Women Graduates, London.

s. Gates (1923).

BHA – British Housewives Association 1925
The importance of the Housewife as a consumer has never been sufficiently appreciated. The Housewife represents the greater part of the purchasing power of the nation; she is the principal consumer for whom trade exists and our national prosperity depends not only on what she buys but on how she uses her purchases.

1. To deal with matters appertaining to the home.
2. To discourage trade in adulterated food.
3. To encourage the clean handling of food.
4. To endeavour to obtain fair prices.
5. To increase trade within the Empire.
6. To raise the standard of efficiency in domestic work and the status of the domestic worker.
7. To obtain and distribute information on matters of importance to the Housewife.
8. To encourage –
    a) The building of labour-saving houses and the right use of labour-saving apparatus.
    b) The extension of the use of electric power, gas and the telephone.
    c) Any practicable schemes for the supply of communal hot water.
9. To open up new occupations for girls and women connected with varying forms and degrees of domestic service – in the household, in the institution, in commerce, and in the government of the country. In so doing, the Association would relieve congested occupations and professions, reduce the numbers of unemployed, relieve rates and taxes, and increase trade.

s. Astor Archive (MS 1416/1/1/834).

CBC – Society for Constructive Birth Control and Racial Progress, 1921
Founded by Marie Stopes, it held its meetings at Essex Hall, London. It opened a Mothers' Clinic for CBC in Holloway, later in the Tottenham Court Road.
    Objects:
    1. to bring home to all the fundamental nature of the reforms involved in conscious and constructive control of conception and the illumination of sex life as a basis of racial progress.

2. to consider the individual, national, international, racial, political, economic, scientific, spiritual and other aspects of the theme, for which purpose meetings will be held, publications issued, Research Committees, Commissions of Enquiry and other activities will be organized from time to time as circumstances require and facilities offer.

3. to supply all those who still need it with the full knowledge of sound physiological methods of control.

Paper: Birth Control News.

s. Astor Archive (MS 1416/1/1/838).

CCWO – Consultative Committee of Women's Organizations, 1922–28

This was originated by Nancy Astor in order to provide women's groups with an opportunity to network. A provisional meeting was called in 1921 and the organization was convened to co-ordinate women's political work and consisted of 65 affiliated organizations.

Object: 'To collect and communicate information of mutual interest to provide a centre which shall serve as a clearing house of ideas; to maintain a piece of machinery by which different groups can act together for a particular purpose without any dissenting societies.'

s. Gates (1923).

CMW – Council of Married Women, 1952–69

This was a break-away organization from the Married Women's Association formed by the MWA's President, Helena Normanton (see entry) with three other MWA members, Doreen Gorsky, Helen Nutting (see entry) and Evelyn Hamilton. The split was the result of a disagreement as to the nature of the evidence given by Normanton to the RC on Marriage and Divorce. The organization dwindled as the years progressed being kept alive in its later years by Nutting.

Objects:

1. To support the stabilization and dignity of marriage as an institution.

2. To promote the further equalization of the sexes in marriage and its consequences.

3. To promote legislation for legal and economic justice for wives, mothers and widows, for women who have obtained decrees of dissolution of marriage, separation orders, and for children and orphans.

s. CMW Papers, Fawcett Library.

CNM – Cumann na mBan (Women's Council), 1914

Formed in May 1914 as a subsidiary of the Irish Volunteers whose prime purpose was to achieve Irish independence from the British. However, many of its members, such as its first President, Jennie Wyse Power (see entry) also belonged to suffrage groups. Its members took part in the front-line fighting of the Easter Rising 1916. In 1918 it campaigned for those newly-enfranchised women to use their vote to support Sinn Fein.

s. Luddy (1995a).

CRWLN – Council for the Representation of Women in the League of Nations, 1919
This began as an organizing committee for a conference on the issue at Caxton Hall, London on 4 September 1919.

CWCS – Council of Women Civil Servants, 1920
It began life as the Standing Joint Committee of Higher Women in the Civil Service.

Object: 'To discuss the different urgent problems affecting women in the higher grades of the Civil Service.' They campaigned for equal pay for men and women in the same grades, entry to Departments from which women were still excluded and equality of opportunity in departments to which women were already admitted.

Archive: Fawcett Library.

CWP – Committee on Woman Power, 1940–45
It was formed as a cross-parliamentary group, initiated largely by Edith Summerskill (see entry), Irene Ward (see entry) and Nancy Astor (see entry) formed in May 1940 to pressurize the Government into recruiting women into work for the war effort which it was failing to do. The CWP liaised with other groups such as the FBPW (see entry). The CWP reaffirmed the understanding reached at the time the TUC representatives joined the Committee that this Committee would not encroach on matters recognized as the province of the Trade Union organization.

Objects:
1. To further in every possible way the fullest utilization of woman power in the war effort and to endeavour to secure equitable treatment of women so utilized.
2. To collect and consider facts concerning any matter that influences the use of woman power.
3. To make representations to the appropriate authorities where official action is necessary.
4. To prepare statements for the Press in connection with the use of woman power.
5. To co-operate with other Societies and bodies on special aspects of recruitment, employment and treatment of women.
6. To press for the inclusion of trained and experienced women in all stages of the war effort, from the framing of policy downwards.

s. Wood (1943); Summerfield (1987).

EAW – Electrical Association for Women, 1924
Began life as the Women's Electrical Association, but the acronym of WEA caused confusion with the Workers' Educational Association and was, therefore, altered.

Objects: To collect and distribute information on the use of electricity, more particularly as affecting the interests of women.

To secure the representation of women on Local Electricity Committees and other public bodies.

s. Astor Archive (MS 1416/1/1/829).

EPCC – Equal Pay Campaign Committee, 1944–56
After the BFBPW's success with equal compensation for war injuries in 1943, it called a meeting to discuss what the next campaign target should be. They decided it should be equal pay. The BF commissioned a report on women's position in national wage machinery. The report was ready by January 1944.

The Joint Committee on Women in the Civil Service provided basic information for the organization's work to campaign for equal pay in the public services. It issued the following press statement at its termination:

'In view of the Government's decision to implement equal pay in the Civil Service by seven stages starting from January 1955, followed by corresponding decisions of the Burnham Committee and other bodies, the Committee and Council believe that the further necessary work is best undertaken by the individual organizations in their own spheres.'

The EPCC had over 50 national organizations involved in its work when it disbanded.

s. EPCC Papers, Fawcett Library.

ERI – Equal Rights International, 1929–34
Object: To struggle against artificial restrictions on women's work. Across frontiers and states. They dealt with the married women's bar, exclusion from factory specialist work, unequal pay and restrictions in industry.

'As long as law and custom treat women as one race and men as another there will remain a woman question, and not until men and women, equal and united side by side, work together free and untramelled, will the Women's Movement be a thing of the past', (from *Status of Women*, a pamphlet issued by the ERI shortly before the Second World War).

s. TUC Collection.

FES – Family Endowment Society, 1924
This began life as the Family Endowment Committee in 1917, then became the Family Endowment Council in 1918 and, finally, the FES.

Object: 'It exists for the purpose of investigating the question of family endowment from various points of view.'

Founded, primarily by Eleanor Rathbone, the FE Committee was left-wing in tone, holding its early meetings at the 1917 Club, whereas the Society consisted of all-party and non-party members. They worked to collect and compile literature which they disseminated by providing expert advice to Royal Commissions and other interested bodies.

Archive: Fawcett Library.

s. Gates (1923).

FWG – Fabian Women's Group, 1908–52
Founded by Charlotte Wilson, an anarchist, who was one of the earliest members of the Fabian Society. Held its initial meeting at Maud Pember Reeves' (author of '*Round About a Pound a Week*') home in London. Despite the small membership, a maximum of 230 in 1912, its influence was greater than its size and it produced many significant pamphlets and reports.

Objects:

1. Equality in citizenship.
2. Economic independence.
Affiliated to the SJCIWO.
s. Alexander (1979).

IAWSEC – International Alliance of Women for Suffrage and Equal Citizenship, 1926
This was the successor to the International Woman Suffrage Alliance (see below) which changed its name at its 1926 Paris Congress in order to indicate the development and broadening of the Alliance's aims to work for issues such as equal pay, equal educational rights and protective legislation for the nationality rights of married women.
Object: Concentrates on equal suffrage in its member countries and on the establishment of liberty, status and opportunities between men and women in the international world.'
s. Brittain (1953); Crawford (1999).

ICW – International Council of Women, 1888
Franciska Plaminkova, a Czech feminist, was the first Chairman.
Object: 'To provide means of communication between women's organizations, and opportunities for women from all countries to meet and confer upon the welfare of the commonwealth, the family and the individual. Among its departments of work are those for Peace by Arbitration, Suffrage and the Rights of Citizenship, the Legal position of women, Emigration, Education and Health.'
Affiliated to the National Council of Women.
s. Gates (1923).

ICWG – International Co-operative Women's Guild, 1921
Formed at the International Co-operative Congress in Basle. It had branches in 15 countries.
Object: 'To unite co-operative women of all lands; to develop the spirit and further the practice of co-operation; to raise the status of women through the achievement of economic and political equality, and to improve the standard of family life; to promote the education of women co-operators, and to make them fit for practical tasks side by side with men; to work for international peace through security and friendly relations between all countries.'
s. Gates (1923).

ICWSA – Irish Catholic Women's Suffrage Association, 1915
Established 29 March 1915 in Dublin. Non-party and non-militant.
Object: 'Aims at educating public opinion and drawing into the suffrage movement Catholic women who have hitherto taken no interest in social work, nor realized how needful the vote is for women in these democratic days when it is the only way the voter can make his claim heard. We wish especially to prove that our religion makes it our duty to work for the common good, and therefore we desire the legal right to take our share in carrying our true social reform in our own country.'
s. Luddy (1995a).

IFBPW – International Federation of Business and Professional Women, 1930
Object: To promote the interests of business and professional women and to secure combined action by them; to work for high business and professional standards of service; to promote friendly relations and understanding among business and professional women of all countries; to make available, and ensure the use of the specialized knowledge and economic and technical skills of business and professional women in the promotion and support of the programmes and activities of the United Nations and other world government organizations.
    s. COI (1952).

IFUW – International Federation of University Women, 1919
Object: 'To promote understanding and friendship between the university women of the nations of the world, and thereby to further their interests and develop between their countries sympathy and mutual helpfulness.'
    By 1927, its members included graduates from 27 countries. Crosby Hall on the Embankment in London was its London centre.
    s. Gates (1923).

IHA – Irish Housewives Association, 1942
A small group of women met to discuss what they could do to tackle the difficulties being experienced by women and their families under the 'Emergency'. They organized the 'Housewives Petition' which was sent to the Government before Budget Day, 1941. Later that year over 600 additional signatures were collected. To capitalize on this action, a meeting was called and the IHA was formed, 12 May. Predominantly Protestant, middle-class membership campaigning on welfare, domestic and consumer issues. They also worked closely with the IWWU. Progressed and extended its influence on an international scale, becoming affiliated to the IAW, 1948. Organized a Symposium on Human Rights, 1968. In 1975 delegates attended the UN International Woman's Year conference in Mexico. The group is involved in an advisory capacity to Government and in supporting women's participation in local and national politics.
    s. Tweedy (1992).

IWCA – Irish Women Citizens' Association, 1923–47
This was a transformation of the first women's suffrage group in Ireland, the constituitonal IWSLGA. After women gained the vote in 1922, the aims and name of the IWSLGA were changed to work for the political education and encouragement of women in the use of the vote and its attendant responsibilities as citizens. In 1947 the IWCA was incorporated into the IHA.
    s. Tweedy (1992).

IWFL – Irish Women's Franchise League, 1908
Founded on 11 November 1908 as a militant alternative to the IWSLGA, women only. Men could only be associates. Worked with the British WSPU. Based in Dublin. IWFL members also tended to support the nationalist cause and its attendant interest in Irish culture.
    Object: to obtain the parliamentary vote for the women of Ireland on the same terms as men had it, or as it might be given to them; to educate by all forms

of propaganda the men, women and children of Ireland to understand and support the members of the League in their demands.

   s. Owens (1975); Luddy (1995a).

IWSA – International Woman Suffrage Alliance, 1902–26
Founded in America during an International Woman Suffrage Conference with participants from ten countries. It sought to encourage individual national organizations to seek and achieve enfranchisement for women. Object: 'To secure a real equality of liberties, status and opportunity between men and women'. In 1914 the IWSA sought to prevent the outbreak of WW1 by lobbying the Foreign Office and government embassies in London. In 1923, there were 39 associations affiliated to the IWSA.

   Paper: International Woman Suffrage News (Jus Suffragii).

   s. Gates (1923); Tweedy (1992); Crawford (1999).

IWSF – Irish Women's Suffrage Federation, 1911
All-Ireland umbrella group for non-militant suffrage societies. It held its first meeting in the Shelbourne Hotel, Dublin on 21 August. By 1912 it had twenty-six affiliated organizations.

   s. Fox (1958); Luddy (1995b).

IWSLGA – Irish Women's Suffrage and Local Government Association, 1876–1923
Originally known as the Dublin Women's Suffrage Association, established in February 1876 by Anna Haslam, one of the signatories to the first women's suffrage petition to the House of Commons in 1866. The DWSA became the IWSLGA in 1901, it was a non-militant, constitutional group whose membership was mainly Protestant and middle-class. When all women gained the vote in 1922, it changed its name and agenda to become the IWCA.

   s. Tweedy (1992); Luddy (1995a).

IWWU – Irish Women Workers' Union, 1911
Started in an attempt to counteract the discrimination evidenced by male trade unionists. James Larkin was its President and the original Secretary was his sister, Delia Larkin. As well as fighting for improved wages and conditions, it was intended to support the women's franchise struggle. Primarily became a union for women in the printing trades and laundry workers. Rapidly became a great success with two thousand members by 1918.

   s. Luddy (1995a).

LNSWS – London and National Society for Women's Service, 1926
Previously, the London Society for Women's Suffrage (1907) which became the London Society for Women's Service (1919) and subsequently, the LNSWS, which became the Fawcett Society in 1953 and plain, Fawcett in 1998.

   Archive: Fawcett.

LNU – League of Nations Union (Women's Advisory Council)
In the aftermath of the First World War, the League of Nations was established in 1919 in an attempt to establish international machinery for the resolution of future conflict and the promotion of peace.

Objects:

1. To consider and advise upon the best means of securing the support of women for the League and for the Union.
2. To keep the Executive Committee informed concerning the opinions of women's organizations on matters affecting the League of Nations.
3. To advise upon such matters affecting the league as are made a subject of special study by any of the constituent societies, or concerning which they have special knowledge and experience.

s. Hutchinson (1934).

MWA – Married Women's Association, 1938

Object: To raise the status of women, married or single, by enactments intended to secure full citizenship rights for all members of the family; especially to secure for wives a legal right to a share in the family income.

By the end of the 1940s the Object had evolved:

1. To create a legal financial partnership in marriage.
2. To establish a comprehensive medical service for the whole family.
3. To work for family allowances for all children (partly accomplished), social security (partly accomplished), equal guardianship rights, equal pay.
4. To ensure right of domicile and right of married women to earn.
5. To awaken women to their political responsibilities as citizens.

s. TUC Collection; SWC (nd post-WW2).

MWDL – Married Women's Defence League (Bolton), 1931

One of its aims was to assist women who were attempting to separate from their husbands about court procedures and to inform them of their legal rights.

s. Daily Herald, 15 July 1931.

MWF – Medical Women's Federation, 1916

The Association of Medical Women was first established in London with nine members in 1879. The existing local Associations of Registered Medical Women combined to form the MWF. By 1925, it had 1016 members.

Object: 'To safeguard and promote the professional interests of medical women; to enable them to speak as a body and so to exert a greater influence on public policy in regard to those matters, such as health administration, in which they are directly concerned.' By 1952 the object had been redefined as 'The promotion of the medical and allied sciences, including medical research, and the furtherance of their study teaching and practice; and to watch the interests of medical women and to express their views – women being a minority in the medical profession.' Still in existence, London.

Archive: Wellcome Institutes.

s. Introduction to Archive Collection.

NAWL – National Association for Women's Lodging-Homes, 1909

Established as a result of a meeting at the British Institute for Social Service on February 24.

Objects:

1. To link together all organizations and individuals interested in opening or

maintaining Lodging-Homes, Lodging-Houses, or Shelters for Women and Girls in the United Kingdom.

2. To collect and disseminate information as to existing accommodation and the need for more, by publication, conferences, deputations to public authorities, etc.

3. To promote legislation for the better regulation of Common Lodging-Houses in so far as they affect women.

4. To encourage the formation of local committees affiliated with the parent Association.

s. Higgs (1910).

NBCC – National Birth Control Committee/Council, 1930
Formed to co-ordinate the work of the five existing birth control societies. It began to emphasize clinic advice for sterility and the positive side of planned parenthood. It avoided the abortion issue as being too controversial. Its Chairman was Lady Denman. Mary Stocks (see entry) was a prominent member and Marie Stopes, the birth control pioneer was a member for a brief period. It changed its name to the Family Planning Association in 1939 to present a more positive image.
s. Banks (1985 and 1990).

NCEC – National Council for Equal Citizenship, 1932–49
This association was a result of the reorganization of the NUSEC into two separate bodies in 1932, the NUGC and the NCEC. The NCEC was to work on a 'feminist, political programme'.
Object: To obtain all such reforms as are necessary to secure a real equality of liberties, status, and opportunities between men and women.
In 1949 it combined with the NWCA.
s. *The Woman's Leader*, April 1932; Pugh (1992).

NCUMC – National Council for the Unmarried Mother and Her Child, 1918
Object: 'To obtain reform of the existing Bastardy Acts and Affiliation Acts. To secure the provision of adequate accommodation to meet the varying needs of mothers and babies throughout the country, such provision to include hostels with nurseries attached where mother can live with her child whilst continuing her ordinary work. To deal with individual inquiries from, or on behalf of, unmarried mothers.
s. Gates (1923).

NCW – National Council of Women of Great Britain and Northern Ireland, 1895
Originated from a movement of women for the care of girls and the formation of Ladies' Associations for the Care of Friendless Girls. Realizing that poor working conditions caused many of these young girls' problems, they formed small groups known as Unions of Women Workers. By 1895, there were 125 Ladies' Associations and 15 unions; in that year a national organization was formed, the National Union of Women Workers. At a Conference in 1895, the NCW came into being as a co-ordinating body for all these activities. In 1898, the title of the organization became the combined one of the NUWW and the NCW. By the end of 1918 there were 126 branches and 156 affiliated societies.

Object: 'To promote the welfare of the community; to co-ordinate organizations; to work for the removal of women's disabilities, and to collect and redistribute information.'

It had a Junior Branch and was affiliated to the International Council of Women. Still in existence, London.

    s. NCW (1955).

NFBPWC – National Federation of Business and Professional Women's Clubs of Great Britain and Northern Ireland, 1938
Object: To encourage in business and professional women a realization of their responsibilities in their own country, and consequently in world affairs; to give them opportunities to meet together and assess matters which are their common concern; to encourage international goodwill; to work for the removal of sex discrimination in all spheres of business and in the professions.

    s. COI (1952).

NFWI – National Federation of Women's Institutes, 1915
First WI in Britain was formed in Anglesey, North Wales; WIs originated in Canada.

    Object: 'To improve conditions of rural life by various means.'

    'Looking back... it is difficult to recapture in imagination the repressive atmosphere which still enclosed British women. This was particularly true in the country...' There was opposition to the formation of Institutes by 'Church, Chapel, or manor-house' because of the radical concept of women organizing themselves into their own movement and because of the democratic principles adopted by the WIs which ran counter to rural feudalism (1953:13). Several ex-suffragettes were involved in the early days and Grace Hadow (see entry) contextualized the wider meaning of the NFWI's work 'I fail to see how anyone can take even the most elementary interest in children and cooking without inevitably taking an interest in politics.' (*The Woman's Leader*, 1 August 1924, p. 215). By 1923 it had 2600 branches. Still in existence, London.

    Archive: NFWI, 104 New Kings Rd, London SW6 4LY.

    s. Jenkins (1953).

NFWW – National Federation of Women Workers, 1906–20
Initiated by Mary Macarthur (see entry), trade unionist pioneer, as a response to the difficulty of the union organization of low-income women workers unable to afford to contribute to the multiplicity of trades in which they worked. She circumvented this problem with an organization that could represent all women workers.

    Objects:

1. To unite, for their mutual protection, work-women who are engaged in unorganized trades.
2. To improve the conditions of employment of working women; to watch their interests, and to secure the redress of individual or collective grievances.
3. To regulate the relations between employer and employed.
4. To secure fair payment for services rendered.
5. To give legal aid to members as far as the law allows.
6. To provide a weekly allowance for members when ill or in distressed circumstances.

7. To financially support members who may be involved in a dispute, with the sanction of the Federation.
8. To administer benefits under the National Insurance Act.

As a socialist, Macarthur believed in the common goals of men and women and in 1920 negotiated the amalgamation of the NFWW with the National Union of General Workers, with the provision of a Women's department and a Chief Woman Officer; Women Organizers and a Women's National Committee.

Archive: TUC Library, University of North London.

s. Cole (1949), Brittain (1953), NFWW Eighth Annual Report (October 1915).

NIH – National Institute of Houseworkers, 1946
This was established by the Government as a result of a report into the post-WW2 organization of private domestic workers produced by Violet Markham and Florence Hancock (see entry). They recommended the foundation of this organization in order to improve the status of domestic workers. Dorothy Elliott (see entry) was seconded as head of the organization.

s. Elliott (unpublished MS).

NJCWWO – National Joint Committee of Working Women's Organizations, 1941
This was previously the Standing Joint Committee of Industrial Women's Organizations (SJCIWO).

NJCWWO – National Joint Committee of Working Women's Organizations, 1941
This was previously the Standing Joint Committee of Industrial Women's Organizations (SJCIWO).

NSPA – National Spinsters' Pensions Association, 1935
Object: To secure pension for insured spinsters at 55.

s. TUC Collection.

NUSEC – National Union of the Societies for Equal Citizenship, 1919–32
The largest non-party co-ordinating body of suffrage groups, the National Union of Women's Suffrage Societies (NUWSS) developed its constitution and changed its name to reflect the post-1918 suffrage position and the new political goals of women, to become the NUSEC.

Object: 'To obtain all such reforms as are necessary to secure a real equality of liberties, status, and opportunities between men and women.'

In 1923 there were 130 branches and it was affiliated to the International Women's Suffrage Alliance.

Archive: National Library of Women.

Paper: The Woman's Leader.

s. Gates (1923).

NUTG – National Union of Townswomen's Guilds, 1932
The joint brainchild of Eva Hubback (see entry) and Margery Corbett-Ashby (see entry) the intention was to provide new women voters in urban areas with an organization to combine 'comradeship, arts and crafts and citizenship'. It started life as an offshoot from the NUSEC. A meeting at St George's Hall, London in 1928 to

arrange for the disposal of the remaining suffrage funds passed the motion for the establishment of the new Guilds. Four initial Guilds were created in 1928 – Haywards Heath, Burnt Oak, Moulsecomb and Romsey, this grew to 26 Guilds in a year. In 1932 the NUSEC divided into the National Council for Equal Citizenship (NCEC) and the National Union of Guilds for Citizenship (NUGC).

Object: 'To encourage the education of women to enable them as citizens to make their best contribution towards the common good'. The NUGC represented the rapidly growing number of Guilds. In 1933 the NUGC became the NUTG. Its additional objective being 'To serve as a common meeting ground for women irrespective of creed and party, for their wider education, including social activities'.

s. Stott (1978).

NUWSS – National Union of Women's Suffrage Societies, 1897–1919
See NUSEC.

NUWT – National Union of Women Teachers, 1920
This organization began as the Equal Pay League (1904), it then became the National Federation of Women Teachers (1906) and finally, the NUWT at its Bath Conference. It was a highly militant organization, with a large proportion of its membership having been suffragettes.

Objects:
1. To convene conferences on educational subjects and to promote such questions as have for their object the well-being of women and children
2. To secure equal pay for men and women teachers of the same professional status
3. To secure that all the higher educational posts and the headships of mixed schools shall be open to women equally with men, and with equal remuneration.

Archive: Institute of Education, University of London.

s. Phipps (1928).

NUWW – National Union of Women Workers, 1895
See NCW.

NWAC – National Women's Advisory Council, 1943
Established shortly after the 16th Communist party Congress of August 1943 when five women were elected on to the new Executive Committee. The NWAC was to instigate campaigns on women's issues. The Council's members then visited District Committees to assist with establishing women's sections of the CP. A monthly magazine, *Woman Today*, was launched.

s. Branson (1997).

NWCA – National Women Citizens' Association, 1917
This was a 'daughter' organization of the NCW and was a response to the women's suffrage success of the Representation of the People Bill. A model was provided in the form of the Liverpool WCA formed by Eleanor Rathbone (see entry) in Liverpool in 1913. These groups flourished in the 1918 post-suffrage movement as an educating forum for women.

Object: 'To bring together on non-party, non-sectarian, and democratic lines, women's societies and individual women, in order to foster a sense of citizenship in women; to encourage the study of political, social and economic questions, and to secure the adequate representation of women in local administration, and in the affairs of the nation and of the Empire.' The Associations were affiliated to the NCW and the ICW.

Archive: National Library of Women.
Paper: The Woman Citizen.
s. Gates (1923).

ODC – Open Door Council, 1926

The first meeting to discuss the formation of this group was held on 5 May 1926 at Chrystal Macmillan's (see entry) house.

Object: 'To secure that women shall be free to work and protected as workers on the same terms as men, and that legislation and regulations dealing with conditions and hours, payment, entry and training shall be based upon the nature of the work and not upon the sex of the worker. And to secure for women, irrespective of marriage or childbirth, the right at all times to decide whether or not they shall engage in paid work, and to ensure that no legislation or regulation shall deprive them of this right.'

A militant, feminist group who were wedded to the concept of equal citizenship, they were to have many bitter disputes with working-class industrial women's groups and, as middle-class women, were accused of assisting employers in their exploitation of the working-class. In 1927, 11 ODC members who were on the Executive Committee of the NUSEC were to resign over what they perceived as a dilution of the NUSEC's objective of equal citizenship in favour of social reform issues.

Archive: National Library of Women.
Paper: The Open Door.
s. ODC Annual Report 1926–7.

ODI – Open Door International, 1929

It had its beginning at the IWSA Congress in Paris in June, 1926 where restrictive legislation was one of the main debates. The ODC held three meetings for sympathizers and in the ODC's opinion the IWSA had failed to give a satisfactory lead on the restrictive legislation issue and an international committee was needed to protect women's right to work. A meeting decided that such an International Committee should be formed adopting the ODC's object with two members from each country present: Britain, Belgium, Egypt, France, Germany, Greece, Hungary, Norway, Palestine, Sweden and the USA. The weekend before the IAWSEC's Triennial Meeting in Berlin in June 1929, a Conference was held inviting all those women concerned with economic equality, which took place on June 15/16. A constitution, manifesto and Woman Worker's Charter of Economic Rights adopted. The HQ of the International to be in London. By 1938 it had National Branches in Austria, Belgium, Czech republic, Denmark, France, Norway, Sweden, Uruguay; Affiliated Societies in Finland, France, Hungary, Sweden, USA.

Archive: Fawcett Library.
s. ODC Annual Reports 1926–7, 1929–30.

OTA – Over-Thirty Association, 1934
This was a development from the Fitzroy Club for Unemployed Women which was opened in 1933. The demand for the Club's services was so great, it was felt that the women needed 'more than a club could offer'.

Object: To assist and promote the interests of lower-paid older women workers and to achieve fully public recognition for their needs and to make a concerted and constructive effort to ensure for them a reasonable standard of life and the opportunity of rending to the community that service which they are specially qualified to give. To alleviate the suffering which unemployment, irregular employment, insecurity of livelihood, low wages and bad housing conditions cause to older women workers of low-income groups. In 1945 it became the Over-Forty Club.

s. TUC Collection.

RWG – Railway Women's Guild
Based in Bristol. Object: 'The Guild is formed for the purpose of affording means of social intercourse amongst the wives and daughters of railway workers; to render such assistance to any of its members as may be necessary; to co-operate with the local branch of the Amalgamated Society of Railway Servants (ASRS) in any worthy object it may undertake, to organize on behalf of the ASRS, to study and spread the principles of Trade Unionism among women, to keep in touch with other women workers, and to help the cause of the workers generally.' In 1907, the Guild had 76 branches. Affiliated to the Standing Joint Committee of Industrial Women's Organizations.

Archive: Some papers at TUC Collection and Labour Party Archive.

s. Report of the RWG, 1907.

SF – Suffragette Fellowship, 1931
Intended to continue the memory of the work of feminist pioneers in the Women's Movement, especially the militant suffrage workers. It also worked to continue women's economic, political, social and educational emancipation on an equal basis with men.

s. Tuttle (1986).

SJCIWO – Standing Joint Committee of Industrial Women's Organizations, 1916–41
Objects: To forward the interests of working women and to assist in securing their representation on any local, national, or international committees or similar bodies established by government or other authorities to deal with matters in which women have a special interest; to set forth a policy for working women on such committees, and to keep them informed on matters important to them in their work; to conduct joint campaigns by means of publications in the press, meetings, deputations, and other methods, on any subject of national importance on which combined action by working women may be beneficial; to act as an advisory committee on women's questions to the Executive Committee of the LP. The SJC consisted of representatives from the LP, General Council of the Trades Union Congress, Co-operative Union, Women's Co-operative Guild, Railway Women's Guild, Workers' Union, National Union of General Workers, Railway Clerks' Association, National Union of Distributive and Allied Workers, Transport and General Workers Union,

Association of Women Clerks and Secretaries, National Union of Clerks, National Amalgamated Union of Shop Assistants, Fabian Society, Union of Post Office Workers, National Union of Boot and Shoe Operatives, Association of Civil Service Sorting Assistants, Tailors' and Garment Workers' Trade Union, National Society of Pottery Workers, the Actors' Association, Power Framework Knitters' Society, Municipal Employees' Association, Independent Labour Party. Despite some points of contention (see ODC) the SJC worked with the non-party women's groups on many campaigns throughout this period.

   Archive: TUC Library Collection, University of North London.

   s. Gates (1923).

SJISPA – St Joan International Social and Political Alliance, 1931
Object: To secure the political, social and economic equality of women with men and to further the work and usefulness of Catholic women as citizens.

   s. COI (1952).

SJSPA – St Joan Social and Political Alliance, 1923
This was the successor to the Catholic Women's Suffrage Society (1911) which, like many other suffrage groups, responded to the political and social developments in the Women's Movement of the 1920s, and changed its name. The Committee decided on 24 January 1918 to present a resolution to its annual meeting concerning 'the continuation of the Society with the intention of working for the further extension of the franchise to women on the same terms as it is, or may be, given to men; to establish the political, social and economic equality between men and women, and to further the work and usefulness of Catholic women as citizens'.

   Archive: National Library of Women.

   Paper: The Catholic Citizen.

   s. The Catholic Women's Suffrage Society (nd).

SMW – Society for the Ministry of Women, 1929
Object: To secure equal opportunities for men and women in the official service of the Church.

   It became the Society for the Equal Ministry of Men and Women in the Church, in 1942 . 'The new title does not denote a change of policy, but it formulates more explicitly the aim of the earlier Society.'

   s. SWC (nd post-WW2).

SPBCC – Society for the Provision of Birth Control Clinics, 1921–2
The Walworth Women's Welfare Centre opened in 1922, in its first four years it dealt with 7000 cases; there was also the North Kensington Women's Welfare Centre and the East London Women's Welfare Centre. Provincial centres were opened in Cambridge, Wolverhampton, Salford and Liverpool.

   In 1926, Mrs Evelyn Fuller was Honorary Secretary and Mrs Evelyn Graham Murray, Chairman.

   s. Wellcome Institute.

SPG – Six Point Group, 1921–81
Founded by Margaret Haig Thomas, Lady Rhondda (see entry). With a membership consisting of many ex-suffragettes, the group was militant in tone and its driving force was action not education. It, therefore, set itself a six-point practical agenda:

1. Satisfactory legislation for Child Assault.
2. Satisfactory legislation for the Widowed Mother.
3. Satisfactory legislation for the Unmarried Mother and her Child.
4. Equal rights for guardianship for Married Parents.
5. Equal pay for Teachers.
6. Equal opportunities for Men and Women in the Civil Service.

It was a dynamic force in the 1920s movement, not limiting itself to the stated agenda but organizing and participating in the major campaigns of the period including the franchise extension.

Paper: Time & Tide. Although the paper was originally used as a political vehicle, it developed into a voice for the cultural and artistic world and eventually became establishment in tone until its closure.

Archive: National Library of Women.
s. SPG Leaflet (nd 1921? JN925 TUC Collection).

SWC – Status of Women Committee, 1935–82
It was a co-ordinating committee, although it also had individual members. It was formed under the Chairmanship of the President of the NCW to study and where necessary to supplement the reports of the British Government on the position and rights of British women to the League of Nations Committee of Experts. Such supplementary reports being forwarded through the ICW.

Before WW2 the Committee's work was confined to fact-finding and reporting. Members decided that in future it should become a propaganda committee for equal status of men and women, working for the removal of the disabilities and discriminations of women in all spheres, economic, civil and political. By 1946 it consisted of 17 organizations and a further five observer organizations. As the Committee worked for legislative change, it deemed its function to have been fulfilled after the sex discrimination legislation of the 1970s had been passed.

s. SWC (nd post-WW2); SWC papers, Fawcett Library.

SWJ – Society of Women Journalists, 1895
Founded for the association of women engaged in journalism, either as writers, or artists in black and white, in the UK, the Colonies, and abroad.

Object: 'For promoting and protecting the personal and professional interests of its members and to maintain and improve the status of journalism as a profession for women.'

Paper: The Woman Journalist.
s. The Woman Journalist, 1928.

UJW – Union of Jewish Women, 1902
Object: 'To promote the welfare of Jewish women throughout the United Kingdom and British Empire.' The Union advises and informs Jewish girls and women who desire to train for professional or skilled employment, and for this purpose

administers a Loan Training Fund. The Union keeps a register of professional and voluntary workers. It was affiliated to the NUSEC.

s. Gates (1923).

UTG – Union of Townswomen's Guilds, 1928
It became the National Union of TGs in 1932.

WBCG – Workers' Birth Control Group, 1924
Originated from the LP to provide assistance for the working-class in opposition to the Malthusians and Eugenicists who thought the poor were inferior. Women such as Dora Russell and Stella Browne were leading proponents.

Objects: Tto pressure the Government into providing birth control advice for all women in state maternity clinics, most particularly for working-class women.

s. Russell (1977).

WCAWF – Women's (World) Committee Against War and Fascism, 1934
An international movement, it had branches in most countries in the world. Some of the leading members of the British branch were Charlotte Despard (see entry), Vera Brittain (see entry), Ellen Wilkinson (see entry), Evelyn Sharpe, a former suffragette, Sylvia Pankhurst, suffragette daughter to Emmeline Pankhurst (see entry), Mrs Corbett-Ashby (see entry), Storm Jameson, the feminist author, Sybil Thorndike, actress and AFL member together with women from the CP. They drew up a Women's Charter which demanded the repeal of the Anomalies Act and Means Test, a rent exemption for the unemployed, married women's right to work, free maternity hospitals, birth control at local clinics, legalization of abortion, the release of all women imprisoned for abortion. The final section of the charter demanded the disbanding of all Fascist organizations, support for Russia's demand for total disarmament and all armament production to be turned to production for social use. In Britain, it had *Women Today* Readers' Groups to promote its campaigning. As well as women's rights in Britain, members campaigned against the war in Spain and the massacre of the Chinese by Japan during 1937.

Paper: Woman Today.

s. Liddington (1989); *Woman Today.*

WCC – Women's Consultative Committee, 1941
Established by the Minister of Labour, Ernest Bevin, after considerable lobbying by women MPs (see Edith Summerskill entry), to advise the MOL on the recruitment of women and their assimilation into industry during WW2.

s. Summerfield (1987).

WCG – Women's Co-operative Guild, 1883
Object: 'To organize women for the study and practice of co–operation and other methods of social reform, and improved conditions of domestic life.'

During its first ten years, the Guild became increasingly aware that although an organization largely for married women, its work was not of the 'mothers' meetings variety, but that women had public responsibilities and that the Co-operative Movement could train women for citizenship, as well as men. It became increasingly radical in its campaigning, highly organized and professional with a massive membership. It often came into contention with the Central Board of the Co-op because it was so radical. In 1910, it had 25,942 members in 521 branches and by 1924, 51,000 members in 1100 branches. Still in existence as the Co-operative Women's Guild, Enfield.

Archive: British Library of Economics and Political Science/University of Hull.

s. Gates (1923); WCG (1932).

WEC – Women's Election Committee, 1920

Object: To assist or run women parliamentary candidates of all the recognized political parties in Parliament and suitable women standing independently, provided that all candidates thus assisted:

1.   Stand for equality of men and women in the State.
2.   Have a reasonable amount of support in the constituencies they desire to represent.

By 1927 they were working for the total legislative equality of men and women in the State.

s. Gates (1923).

WEF – Women's Employment Federation, 1934

Officially came into being in 1934 but the process had started in 1932. It was financed by money from the Carnegie Trust and appeals made by the heads and former heads of women's colleges. Philippa Strachey (see entry) was the Honorary Secretary of the Executive Committee and Ray Strachey (see entry) was the Chairman. It indexed and disseminated careers information, interviewed employers and potential employers and sent out its officers to visit schools, employers and universities. Concentrated on careers for middle-class women, it aimed to supplement the Labour Exchange's function.

It still survives as the National Advisory Centre on Careers for Women?

s. Fawcett Library.

WES – Women's Engineering Society, 1919

This organization was founded in order to maintain the gains that women had made in engineering employment during WW1. It was founded and sustained by three wealthy women, Lady Parsons, Mrs Willson and Lady Moir.

Object: 'To promote the training (academic and workshop) and employment of women in the engineering profession and allied trades and industries, and to work for the admission of women to membership of engineering institutes.'

They worked to put pressure on employers and the Unions to let women back into engineering and to assist with the difficulties that were being caused by legislation such as the Pre-War Trade Practices Act (1919).

Paper: The Woman Engineer. Still in existence, London.

s. Gates (1923).

WFL – Women's Freedom League, 1907–61

As a breakaway group from the WSPU, it was militant in its tactics and had continued to fight for the vote throughout the First World War. It was in the forefront of the inter-war campaigns.

Object: 'To secure for women the parliamentary vote as it is or may be granted to men; to use the powers already obtained to elect women to Parliament and upon other public bodies for the purpose of establishing equality of rights and opportunities between the sexes; to organize women (voters and non-voters) and to promote the social and industrial well-being of the community.

Archive: National Library of Women.

Paper: The Vote.

s. Gates (1923).

WGCGA – Women Graduates' and Candidate Graduates' Association, 1902
It aimed to advance 'the interests of women in any scheme of university education in Ireland and to ensure that all advantages of such education shall be open to women equally with men'. It expanded its remit to supporting work for the political rights for women.

s. Luddy (1995b).

WGE – Women's Guild of Empire
An 'unofficial' Conservative women's organization. It was right-wing in character and had some ex-WSPU members. As well as such pro-Government, right-wing activities as leading the Procession of Women against strikes and lock-outs in 1926, it was also involved in some aspects of the Women's Movement such as the CCWO and it was affiliated to the SPG.

s. various women's papers.

WIL – Women's International League, 1915
This was the British section of the Women's International League for Peace and Freedom (WILPF) in Geneva, founded during the International Congress of Women (which issued from the International Suffrage Alliance) at The Hague in April as a courageous response to the outbreak of WW1.

Object: To establish the principles of right rather than might, and of cooperation rather than conflict, in national and international affairs, and for this purpose to work for:
  1. the development of the ideals underlying modern democracy in the interests of constructive peace.
  2. the emancipation of women and the protection of their interests.

By 1923 there were 30 branches in Britain and 27 in other countries. Still in existence, Bromley.

Paper: Pax International.

s. Gates (1923).

WLL – Women's Labour League, 1906–18
Object: 'To form an organization of women to work for independent Labour representation in connection with the Labour Party, and to obtain direct Labour representation of women in Parliament and on all local bodies.'

Membership was limited to women members and the wives and daughters of members of societies eligible for affiliation to the LP. Their intention was to educate themselves on political and social issues and to protect the interests of working women by improving their social and industrial conditions. They were immensely successful in attracting women and their membership soared. Under the newly organized LP constitution, the WLL were subsumed into the LP as Women's Sections, losing their independent political voice.

Archive: Labour Party Archive, Manchester.

s. NWLL leaflet (1914).

WNLF – Women's National Liberal Federation, 1919
The Women's Liberal Federation (1886) and the Women's National Liberal Association (1892) joined forces in April to form the WNLF.

Objects:

1. To promote the adoption of Liberal principles in the government of the country.
2. To promote just legislation for women and the removal of all their legal disabilities as citizens, and to protect the interests of children.
3. To advance political education by meetings, lectures, and the distribution of literature.
4. To promote Women's Liberal Associations in every constituency with a view to their affiliation to the WNLF, such Women's Liberal Associations to be self-governing bodies, controlling their own policy for the furtherance and maintenance of the above objects.
5. To bring into union all Women's Liberal Associations, and to promote the admission of women to membership in every Liberal Association on equal terms with men electors or members, and entitled to equal privileges.

s. Gates (1923).

WP – Women's Parliament, 1941
The object was to equalize the economic and social status of women.

In 1941, Tamara Rust (see entry) and Ted Bramley, London District Secretary, of the CP, sought to expand the movement for women's rights through a Women's Parliament. The idea was taken up and on 13 July 1941 the first meeting of the London Women's Parliament took place with 345 delegates discussing issues on women's work, welfare and pay. This first session was sponsored by the Peoples' Convention. Other Women's Parliaments existed in Lancashire, Yorkshire, South Wales and Scotland.

s. Branson (1997).

WPDL – Women Prisoners' Defence League, 1922
Formed in Ireland in August 1922 with the intention of providing the families of those imprisoned without trial by the Provisional Government during the Civil War 1922–3, with assistance in the way of food, clothes and money. In January 1923 it was declared an illegal organization and prohibited, but its members continued with their work.

s. Luddy (1995b).

WPH – Women's Pioneer Housing, 1920
In the postwar world of increasing numbers of women entering employment and leaving home, there was an urgent need for suitable housing for professional women.

Object: 'To provide small self-contained flats or unfurnished rooms for women workers.' Still in existence, London.

s. WPH Report, November 1921.

WPHOA – Women Public Health Officers Association, 1930
Formerly the WSIHVA.
Object:
1. To safeguard the interests and improve the status of women officers in the Public Health Service as specified in Rule IV.
2. To promote the interchange of such knowledge of Sanitary and Social Science as is likely to be of assistance to them and others.
s. Wellcome Institute.

WPPA – Women's Publicity Planning Association, 1939–56
Object: To promote, encourage and further friendly relations and co-operation of every kind, in the case of women's status, both within and outside the British Commonwealth of Nations. It was involved in the Equal Compensation for War Injuries campaign and in the formation of Women for Westminster. It also contributed to the Equal Citizenship Campaign, employing Dorothy Evans (see entry) as national organizer and publishing her writing on the Equal Citizenship (Blanket) Bill. It also published Vera Douie's (see entry) research.
s. TUC Collection; WPPA Papers, Fawcett Library.

WSIHVA – Women Sanitary Inspectors and Health Visitors' Association, 1896
A radical organization which realized the significance of organization and training the membership in order to professionalize their work. They affiliated to the TUC in 1924 and were active in their support of the non-party women's organizations, consistently active in equality campaigns throughout the period.
Object: 'To safeguard the interests and improve the status of Women Sanitary Inspectors and Health Visitors and to promote the interchange of such knowledge of sanitary and social science as is likely to be of assistance to them and others.' Still in existence, although it merged to become a part of Manufacturing, Science, Finance (MSF) in August 1990.
Archive: Wellcome Institute.
s. Annual Report 1923.

WSPL – Women's Social and (Progressive) Political League, 1937
Initially named the Women's Social and Progressive League, this was later renamed, with 'Political' substitued for 'Progressive'. Non-party and non-sectarian Irish. This was the vision of Hanna Sheehy Skeffington (see entry) to see the emergence of a women's party. It was established in the period of Eamonn de Valera's introduction of a new Constitution. The extension of the economic, social and political rights of women together with women's participation as active citizens formed its remit. Membership was open, it held weekly discussion meetings. Its objects were:
1. Organization of women voters throughout the country.
2. United effort to secure the principle of equal opportunities for men and women, and equal pay for equal work.

3. Promoting the candidature of women as independent members of the Dáil, Senate, and Public Boards, and securing a fair proportion of women representatives on all commissions set up by the government.
4. Constant vigilance and united action on all legislation affecting the interests of women.

p. An Open Letter to Women Voters (1938)
s. Tweedy (1992); Luddy (1995b).

WTUL – Women's Trade Union League, 1874–1920
Founded by Emma Paterson (née Ann Smith), Secretary of the Women's Suffrage Association. It was originally known as the Women's Protective and Provident League but was restructured in the late 1880s after Paterson's death in 1886. Its original aims were:
1. To protect the trade interests of the members by endeavouring, where necessary, to prevent the undue depression of wages, and to equalize the hours of work.
2. To provide a fund from which members may obtain allowance weekly in sickness or when out of employment.
3. To arrange for registration of employment notices, so that trouble in searching for work may be avoided, and to collect useful trade information.
4. To promote arbitration in cases of dispute between Employers and Employed.

Operating as a Women's TUC the majority of its members came from the textile industry. The TUC took over the work of the WTUL in 1920 with the Women Workers' Group operating as a committee of the TUC General Council.
s. Boston (1980).

WWM – Women for Westminster Movement, 1942–49
This organization was launched by the WPPA.
Object:
1. To stimulate women to a fuller sense of citizenship.
2. To educate women by organizing lectures, debates, study groups and other activities leading to a wider understanding of national and international affairs.
3. To assist women to take part in Local and Parliamentary Government.
4. To press for the inclusion of women on Reconstruction Committees and all bodies dealing with public affairs..
5. To secure the attainment of full citizenship for women in this country and throughout the united nations and the world by propaganda, publicity and Parliamentary action.

It joined the NWCA in 1949.
s. SWC (nd post-WW2).

PART 2

1968–84

BIOGRAPHICAL SKETCHES

Summary

Abdela, Lesley	(UK/journalist, broadcaster)
Abzug, Bella	(US/activist, politician)
Adams, Carol	(UK/educationist)
Alexander, Sally	(UK/academic)
Amos, Valerie	(UK/public service)
Archer, Robyn	(Australian/creative artist)
Atkinson, Ti-Grace	(US/rad. fem. activist)
Bacon, Wendy	(Australian/journalist)
Bandler, Faith	(Australian/writer, Aboriginal activist)
Banotti, Mary	(Irish/MEP)
Barnes, Monica	(Irish/politician)
Barrett, Michele	(UK/academic)
Bellos, Linda	(UK community activist/politician)
Brown, Rita Mae	(US/writer)
Brown, Wilmette	(US/UK activist)
Brownmiller, Susan	(US/activist)
Bryan, Beverley	(UK/teacher)
Bunch, Charlotte	(UK writer and organizer)
Byrne, Eileen	(UK/educationist)
Callil, Carmen	(Australian/UK publisher)
Campbell, Beatrix	(UK/journalist, broadcaster)
Charlton, Valerie	(UK/childcare activist)
Chicago, Judy	(US/artist)
Chisholm, Shirley Anita	(US/politician)
Churchill, Caryl	(UK/dramatist)
Colquhoun, Maureen	(UK/politician)
Coote, Anna	(UK/journalist)
Cox, Eva	(Australian/political activist, academic)
Curtis, Zelda	(UK/older women)
Dadzie, Stella	(UK/black education)
Daly, Mary	(US/rad. fem. theologian)
De Lanerolle, Ros	(UK/publisher)
Doyle, Mikki	(US/UK journalist)
Dworkin, Andrea	(US/rad. fem. theorist/activist)
Fairbairns, Zoe	(UK/writer)

Fell, Alison	(Scottish writer)
Fennell, Nuala	(Irish politician)
Ferraro, Geraldine	(US/politician)
Firestone, Shulamith	(US/rad. fem. activist)
Freeman, Joreen	(US/lawyer/writer)
Friedan, Betty	(US/public service)
Garner, Helen	(Australian/writer)
George, Jenny	(Australian/trade unionist)
Gill, Tess	(UK/lawyer)
Gilligan, Carol	(US/psychologist)
Ginsberg, Ruth Bader	(US/lawyer)
Gould, Joyce	(UK/politician
Greer, Germaine	(Australia/activist)
Heathfield, Betty	(UK/trade unionist)
Hewitt, Patricia	(UK/politician)
Hobbs, May	(UK/activist)
hooks, bell	(US/writer, academic)
Hutt, Jane	(UK/community activist, politician)
Jackson, Stevi	(UK/activist/academic)
James, Selma	(UK/activist)
Jeffreys, Sheila	(Australian/lesbian activist, academic)
Kenny, Mary	(Irish/journalist)
Kennedy, Mary	(UK/activist, academic)
Koedt, Anna	(US/activist, artist)
Kroll, Una	(UK/women's ordination)
Lorde, Audre	(US/writer)
McCafferty, Nell	(Irish/journalist)
McCartan, Joyce	(Irish/community, peace campaigner)
MacKinnon, Catharine	(US/lawyer)
McWilliams, Monica	(Irish/academic)
Maher, Mary	(Irish/journalist)
Maitland, Sara	(UK/writer, theologian)
Millett, Kate	(US/activist, artist, academic)
Mitchell, Juliet	(New Zealand/UK psychoanalyst)
Morgan, Robin	(US/rad. fem. writer, editor)
Morgan, Sally	(Australian/Aboriginal rights, writer)
Mullarney, Máire	(Irish/journalist, activist)
Norton, Eleanor Holmes	(US/lawyer)
Oakley, Ann	(UK/academic, writer)
O'Connor, Sandra Day	(US/lawyer)
Parmar, Pratibha	(UK/activist, media)
Patel, Pragna	(UK/activist)
Pettit, Ann	(UK/peace activist)
Pizzey, Erin	(UK/domestic violence activist)
Reid, Elizabeth	(Australian/politician)
Rich, Adrienne	(US/lesbian fem. poet)
Richardson, Jo	(UK/politician)
Roberts, Michele	(UK/writer)

Robinson, Mary	(Irish/human rights lawyer, politician)
Rowbotham, Sheila	(UK/academic, historian, writer)
Ryan, Edna	(Australian/trade unionist)
Ryan, Susan	(Australian/politician)
Sandler, Bernice	(US/academic/public policy)
Sarachild, Kathie	(US/rad. fem. activist)
Scafe, Suzanne	(UK/black community education)
Segal, Lynne	(Australia, activist/academic)
Sloan, Margaret	(US/Black fem. activist)
Smith, Barbara	(US/Black fem. activist)
Smyth, Ailbhe	(Irish activist/academic)
Spender, Dale	(Australia/UK writer, academic)
Steinem, Gloria	(US/journalist)
Stott, Mary	(UK/journalist)
Sykes, Roberta	(Australian/Aboriginal activist, writer)
Tweedie, Jill	(UK/journalist)
Wainwright, Hilary	(UK academic)
Walker, Alice	(US/writer)
Wallace, Michele	(US/writer, teacher)
Wandor, Michelene	(UK/playwright)
Willis, Ellen	(US/rad. fem. activist)
Wilson, Amrit	(UK/activist, writer, academic)
Wilson, Elizabeth	(UK/academic)
Wise, Audrey	(UK/politician)

BIOGRAPHICAL
SKETCHES

ABDELA, Lesley (UK journalist and broadcaster).

Attended art school; worked in advertising; Research Assistant to Liberal MPs, David Penhaligon and John Pardoe; stood as Liberal PPC for East Herts, 1979; founder of the 300 Group, 1980; member FS.

p. Women with X Appeal: Women Politicians in Britain Today (1989); *What Women Want* (ed. 1994).

s. Guardian, 2 March 1981; Abdela (1989).

ABZUG, Bella (US lawyer, women's rights politician and activist) 1920–98.

Educated at Hunter (Women's) College; worked in a shipyard during WW2; graduated from the Columbia University Law School, 1947; practising lawyer in New York, 1944–70; as a lawyer, represented people from the Civil Rights Movement and those persecuted by the McCarthy trials; instigated the feminist, anti-nuclear Women Strike for Peace, 1961–70; campaigned for the Civil Rights Act, 1964 and the Voting Rights Act, 1965; founded the WSP, 1962 and the NWPC, 1970; campaigned for 24-hour childcare facilities, 1971; introduced the first lesbian/gay civil rights bill, 1975; as a member of the House of Representatives from 1971–6, lobbied for the ERA, was officer for the national commission for IWY, raising funding for the NWC, 1977; ran for New York mayor, 1977; founded the IWEDO; President WFPC; although disabled, she participated in the NGO Conference which was complementary to the UN Fourth World Conference on Women in Beijing, 1995; 'a pioneer in making women's and gay rights issues of social policy and governance' (Dworkin in *Guardian* 1998).

p. Bella! (1972); *Gender Gap* (with Mim Kelber, 1984).

s. Tuttle (1986); Schneir (1995); Cullen-DuPont (1996); *Guardian*, 2 April 1998; *The Times*, 2 April 1998; *Independent*, 4 April 1998.

ADAMS, Carol (UK educationist) *b.* 1948.

Graduated in history; in her twenties she was a history and social studies teacher in a London comprehensive; as an ILEA EO Inspector, she was heavily involved in the ILEA's ground-breaking anti-sexist education initiatives; member of Virago's advisory group.

p. The Gender Trap: Education & Work/Sex & Marriage/Messages & Images (with Rae Laurikietis, 1976); *Ordinary Lives: A Hundred Years Ago* (1982); *Her Studies: A Resource List* (with Diana Hargreaves, 1983); *Under Control: Life in a*

p: publications;   s: sources

Nineteenth Century Silk Factory (1983); *Investigating Gender in the Primary School: Activity Based INSET Materials* (with Valerie Walkerdine, 1986); *Investigating Gender in the Secondary School: Activity Based INSET Materials* (1986); *Visiting Teachers for Equal Opportunities at the Institute of Education 1986–7* (Adams et al., 1987); pamphlets – *From Workshop to Warfare: The Lives of Medieval Women* (Adams et al., 1983).

s. Adams (1976).

ALEXANDER, Sally (UK activist and historian) *b.* 1943.

Originally trained as an actress at RADA from the age of sixteen; worked on the radical newspaper, *Black Dwarf*; studied History at Ruskin College, Oxford, 1968–70, and UCL; one of the organizers of the first NWLC, 1970; activist in the WLM, involved with *Red Rag*; co-founder and member of the Editorial Board of the socialist/feminist HWJ; taught history for the WEA in London and at Birkbeck College; member of the advisory group of Virago; Principal Lecturer in History and Cultural Theory, University of East London, from 1992; Professor of Historical and Cultural Studies, Goldsmith's College from 1997.

p. St Giles Fair, 1830–1914: Popular Culture and the Industrial Revolution in Oxford (1970); *In Defence of 'Patriarchy'* (with Barbara Taylor, 1980); *Women's Work in Nineteenth Century London: A Study of the Years 1820–50* (c.1983); *Studies in the History of Feminism, 1850s–1930s* (1984); *Women's Fabian Tracts* (1988); *Women's Voices from the Spanish Civil War* (ed. Jim Fyrth, 1991); *Becoming a Woman and Other Essays in Nineteenth and Twentieth Century Feminist History* (1994).

s. Campbell and Coote (1982); Alexander (1994); Purvis (ed. 1995).

AMOS, Valerie (Baroness Amos of Brondesbury) (UK public service) *b.* 1954.

Educated at the University of Warwick, BA Sociology, MA Cultural Studies from University of Birmingham, doctoral research at University of East Anglia; member of the Race and Politics group at the Centre for Contemporary Cultural Studies at the University of Birmingham; one of the women who established the Birmingham Black Women's group; went into local government with London boroughs of Lambeth (1981–2), Camden (1983–5), Hackney (1985–9); also worked as a management consultant from 1984–9; Chief Executive EOC, 1989–94; Chair Afiya Trust, from 1995; created a life peer, Baroness Amos of Brondesbury in 1997.

p. Many Voices, One Chant (ed. with Gail Lewis, Amina Mama, Pratibha Parmar, 1984); 'Challenging Imperial Feminism' in *Many Voices, One Chant* (1984).

s. Feminist Review, (Autumn 1984); *Who's Who*, 1999.

ARCHER, Robyn (Australian feminist and creative artist) *b.* 1948.

Born and educated in Adelaide; after gaining her DipEd she taught English for three years; a singer, actress and writer, after successful appearances in Brecht, became known for her one-woman feminist, political cabaret she wrote, such as *A Star is Torn* and *Pack of Women*, has written 20 theatrical pieces; promoted lesbian culture with many songs written especially for lesbian events; developed as a writer/producer/manager; Director of the WCNTTLC May day March and Pageant, 1990; Chair of the Australian Council Community Development Board, 1992; artistic director National Festival of Australian Theatre, 1993; awarded the Australian Creative Fellowship 1991–3; recorded 14 albums; Executive Woman of the Year, 1998.

p. Seven Deadly Sins (1974); *Kold Komfort Kaffee* (1978); *The Pack of Women* (1981); *Mambo* (opera, 1989); *The Robyn Archer Songbook*.

s. Who's Who in Australia (1980); Arnold and Morris (1994), Caine (1998).

ATKINSON, Ti-Grace (US radical feminist activist) *b.* 1939.

One of the early members of the WLM; her attempts to introduce democratic methods to NOW resulted in her giving up her Presidency of the New York Chapter; went on to found one of the early WLM groups in the US, the Feminists, 1968; she divined the concept of women as the first exploited class with 'the institution of sexual intercourse' having been created to subordinate women; placed lesbians as the central liberators of the WLM as their sexuality enabled them to destroy confining stereotypes most famously she devised the axiom, 'Feminism is the theory, lesbianism is the practice'; co-founder of HRWI; working to coordinate feminist activism in New York, 1985.

p. Amazon Odyssey (1974).

s. Tuttle (1986); Humm (1989).

BACON, Wendy (Australian activist and journalist) *b.* 1946.

Bacon was born in Melbourne and read history at her home town university; she went on to study law at the University of NSW; as a student she spent a week in jail on obscenity charges in her capacity as editor of the student paper, *Tharunka*; this experience led her to assist in forming the groups, PAG and WBB; spent many unsuccessful years involved in legal action, contesting the rejection of her application to be admitted to the NSW Bar; became an investigative journalist with the *National Times*, revealing extensive legal and political corruption in the NSW systems; a film and TV researcher and writer; went on to become an academic at the Australian Centre for Independent Journalism, University of Technology, Sydney.

s. Arnold and Morris (1994); Caine (1998).

BANDLER, Faith (Ida Lessing) (Australian writer and Aboriginal activist) *b.* 1918.

Born in Tumbulgum, NSW; her father was a Hebridean Islander brought to Queensland by slave traders in 1883; founder of the Aboriginal Australian Fellowship, with Faith Gibbs, 1956; NSW State Secretary, 1962–70; Director of the Referendum Campaign to achieve a Federal Referendum to remove sections of legislation discriminating against aboriginals, 1967; General Secretary Federal Council for the Advancement of Aboriginals and Torres Straits Islanders, 1970–73; founder of the National Commission of Australian South Sea Islanders, 1974; she refused MBE in 1976; member Senate Sydney University, 1978–81; awarded the Human Rights medal, 1997.

p. Wacvie (1976); *Marani in Australia* (with L. Fox, 1980); *The Time Was Ripe* (with L. Fox, 1980), *Werou, My Brother* (1984); *Turning the Tide* (1988).

s. Buck (1992); Arnold and Morris (1994); *Who's Who of Australia* (2000).

BANOTTI, Mary (Irish politician) *b.* 1939.

Born Dublin; grandniece of Michael Collins (Nationalist leader); trained as a nurse; worked as an industrial welfare officer; founder member of ADAPT and Irish Women's Aid; member of AIM; elected as Dublin Euro Constituency MEP, European Parliament, 1984; re-elected 1989, 1994, 1999; membership of European

Parliament Committees including Citizens' Freedoms and Rights, Justice and Home Affairs, Women's Rights and EO; Fine Gael candidate for the presidential election in 1997; European Parliament President's Mediator for Trans-nationally abducted children; appointed a UNFPA Goodwill Ambassador for Ireland in the area of reproductive health care and family planning services, 1999

   s. www.finegael.com/constituencies/meps/banotti_mary_mep.htm.

BARNES, Monica (Irish politician) *b.* 1936.

   Born Carrickmacross, County Monaghan; educated St Louis Convent, County Monaghan and Oranges Academy, Belfast; previously a lecturer; went into politics from the Women's Movement; founder member of the CSW in 1973; Vice Chairperson WPA, 1973–4; administrator for CSW, 1978–81; member Dun Laoghaire BPWC; member Women's Representative Committee, 1974–8; formed, Women Elect, a group of councillors to assist women with election expenses, 1975; member Employment Equality Agency, 1977–82; member Femscan Committee; member ICCL, Irish AAM, CND; Vice President Women's Federation, European People's Party; first woman Vice President of Fine Gael, 1980; spoke out against the abortion amendment and in favour of divorce in the 1980s; Fine Gael spokesperson on Law Reform and Assistant Whip in the Seanad, 1982; Dáil Deputy, 1982–92; Fine Gael opposition spokesperson on Women's Rights, Chairperson Joint Oireachtas Committee on Women's Rights; European elections Leinster candidate 1979 and 1984; Fine Gael general election candidate 1981, 1982, 1992; TD (member Irish Parliament) for Dun Laoghaire.

   s. Guardian, 10 February 1987; Mahon (1996); www.finegael.com/constituencies/firstmem/monicabarnesdunloagh.htm.

BARRETT, Michele (UK feminist sociologist) *b.* 1949.

   According to Humm (1989), Barrett has, 'widened the definition of women's politics'; read sociology at Durham and Sussex Universities; Sociology lecturer at the City University from 1977; member of the editorial collective, *Feminist Review*; member of the Feminist Anthology Collective; Professor Modern and Cultural Literary Theory, School of English and Drama, Queen Mary and Westfield College, University of London.

   p. Ideology and Cultural Production (ed. 1979); *Women's Oppression Today: Some Problems in Marxist Feminist Analysis* (1980); *Virginia Woolf, Women and Writing* (ed. 1980); *The Anti-Social Family* (ed. with M. McIntosh, 1982); *The Politics of Diversity* (ed. with Roberta Hamilton, 1986); *Women's Opposition Today: The Marxist/Feminist Encounter* (1988).

   s. Barrett and McIntosh (1982); Campbell and Coote (1982); Humm (1989).

BELLOS, Linda (UK community activist and politician) *b.* 1951.

   Black Marxist lesbian radical feminist; born in Lambeth; parents both LP members; attended Brixton Comprehensive school, leaving with an A-level in music, played the clarinet; lost custody of her children in her divorce as a result of her lesbianism; politics degree from University of Sussex, 1981; returned to Lambeth, activist in radical feminist groups, black women's groups and WAVAW; member Lambeth Council's Lesbian and Gay Working Party, 1983; joined the LP to support the struggle for the establishment of black sections, 1984; member hard left; elected as Leader of Lambeth Council, 1985; controversial period of office because her priorities were attempting to deliver social justice Lambeth residents and addressing the multiple discriminations which exist in local government; due to mounting contention about service delivery and budgetary issues, resigned as Lambeth leader, April 1988; involved in community activism, writing, teaching, broadcasting.

p. 'For Lesbian Sex, Against Sado-Masochism' in Kanter, Hannah et al. (eds), Sweeping *Statements: Writings from the Women's Liberation Movement 1981–3* (1984); numerous journal and newspaper articles.

s. Evening Standard, 16 May 1986; *Guardian,* 11 May 1987; Cooper (1994).

BROWN, Rita Mae (US writer) *b.* 1944.

Born in Pennsylvania; brought up in Florida; her civil rights activism coupled with her lesbianism resulted in expulsion from the University of Florida; completed her BA history degree at New York University; joined NOW in 1969 but left in 1970 as a result of the alienation she experienced as a lesbian; member of the Harriet Tubman Brigade of the Redstocking Sisterhood; among a group of lesbians who originated the group, Radicalesbians and produced a paper, *The Woman-Identified Woman* analysing the political position of lesbianism; she held to the concept that only lesbians could create a successful feminist movement.

p. The Hand that Cradles the Rock (1971); *Rubyfruit Jungle* (1973); *Songs to a Handsome Woman* (1973); *The Plain Brown Rapper* (1976); *In Her Day* (1976); *Six of One* (1978); *Southern Discomfort* (1982); *Sudden Death* (1983); *High Hearts* (1986); *Bingo* (1988); *Starting from Scratch* (1988).

s. Morgan (1970); Tuttle (1986); Buck (1992).

BROWN, Wilmette (US/UK activist) *b.* 1947.

Born in Newark, New Jersey; began studying at Wellesley University but transferred to the University of California, studying History and Russian; involved in the American civil rights movement in anti-Vietnam and black power demonstrations; worked as a teacher, social worker and youth organizer; emigrated to Britain; co-cordinator of the King's Cross Women's Centre with Selma James (see entry); established the Wages for Housework and the English Collective of Prostitutes groups; involved in the Greenham Common women's peace camp; member CND General Council; believed in the use of anti-racist strategies as a key campaigning tool.

p. Wages for Housework International Campaign Journal (Spring 1982); *Black Women and the Peace Movement* (1983); *Time Off for Women* (with Selma James, 1984); *Roots: Black Ghetto Ecology* (1986).

s. Guardian, 23 November 1987, 23 December 1987.

BROWNMILLER, Susan (US feminist activist) *b.* 1935.

A journalist, she had worked in the civil rights movement before becoming active in the WLM; member of the NYRF, 1969; known for her seminal text on rape published in 1975 which analysed the issues around sexual violence against women and has been referenced in campaigns for legislative and societal change; co-founder with Robin Morgan (see entry) and others of WAP in 1979.

p. Against our Will: Men, Women and Rape (1975); *Femininity* (1984); *Waverly Place* (1989).

s. Tuttle (1986); Humm (1989); Schneir (1995); Cullen-DuPont (1996).

BRYAN, Beverley (UK black activist) *b.* 1949.

Born in Jamaica; came to England in 1959; primary and further education teacher; involved in black, community and women's politics from the late 1960s; founder member of the Brixton Black Women's Group; taught adults in south London.

p. The Heart of the Race: Black Women's Lives in Britain (1985).

s. Bryan, 1985.

BUNCH, Charlotte (US writer and organizer) *b.* 1944.

Civil rights activist; member of the WLM from its earliest days; one of the originators of the lesbian newsletter, *The Furies* and also founder and editor of *Quest: A Feminist Quarterly*; also founded DC Women's Liberation group; consultant to the UN Secretariat for the World Conference of the UN Decade for Women, 1975–85; subsequently, her work has been instrumental in devising the concept of women's rights as human rights and campaigning for the inclusion of a women's agenda in the policy and practice of human rights; founding director of the Public Resource Center, tenured fellow at the Institute for Policy Studies; founder and executive director of the Douglas College Center for Women's Global Leadership (Global Center) in 1989; Professor in the Bloustein School of Planning and Public Policy, Rutgers University; on the board of Ms Foundation; member of Human Rights Watch's Women's Rights Division; received the Eleanor Roosevelt Award for Human Rights, December 1999.

p. books – *The New Women: A Motive Anthology on Women's Liberation* (ed. with Joanne Cooke, 1970); *Women Remembered: Short Biographies of Women in History* (ed. with Nancy Myron, 1974); *Class and Feminism* (ed. Nancy Myron, 1974); *Lesbianism and the Women's Movement* (ed. Nancy Myron, 1975); *Building Feminist Theory: Essays from Quest* (et al., 1981); *Feminism in the Eighties: Facing Down the Right* (1981); *Learning Our Way: Essays in Feminist Education* (ed. with Sandra Pollock, 1983); *International Feminism: Networking Against Female Sexual Slavery, Report on Global Feminist Workshop Against Traffic in Women* (ed. with Barry and Castley, 1984); *Passionate Politics: Feminist Theory in Action* (1987); *Demanding Accountability: The Global Campaign and Vienna Tribunal for Women's Human Rights* (with Niamh Reilly, 1994); a vast output of publications, see website for complete list.

s. Tuttle (1986); Peters and Wolper (1995); www.cwgl.rutgers.edu/staff.html (2000).

BYRNE, Eileen (UK educationist) *b.* 1934.

Her research was instrumental in analysing the discrimination inherent in educational curriculi and management structures and was used for devising a critique of pedagogical practice; as a Deputy Chief Education Officer, gave evidence on discrimination in secondary school timetabling and the employment of education officials to the Select Committee on Nancy Seear's (see entry) Anti-Discrimination Bill, 1972; Education Officer UK EOC; Education Consultant to the Commission of the EC; took up a post at the University of Queensland.

p. Planning and Educational Inequality: A Study of the Rationale of Resource Allocation (1974); *Women & Education* (1978); *Equality of Education & Training for Girls (10–18 years)* (1979); *They Took Away the Sky* (1983); *Women & Engineering: A Comparative Overview* (1984); *University of Queensland, Senate Working Party on the Status of Women in the University: A Policy Report* (1987); *Gender in Education* (1990); *Investing in Women: Technical and Scientific Training for Economic Development* (1991); *Women & Science: The Snark Syndrome* (1993).

s. *Women Speaking* (1979); Campbell and Coote (1982); University of London Library catalogue.

CALLIL, Carmen (Australian/UK resident, publisher) *b.* 1938.

Attended the Star of the Sea Convent and Loreta Convent in Melbourne before entering Melbourne University and gaining a BA; Buyer's Assistant for Marks & Spencer, 1963–5; she then went into publishing as editorial assistant with Hutchinson, 1965–6, Batsford, 1966–7; publicity manager for Panther Books, then Granada Publishing, 1967–70; Andre Deutsch, 1971; publicity for Ink newspaper, 1972; founded her own book publicity company, Carmen Callil Ltd, 1972; with all this publishing experience she founded the first British feminist publishing house of the 'Second Wave', called Virago, in 1972, which became incorporated as a company in 1973; Managing Director of Virago from 1972–82; went on to become managing director and publisher-at-large for several large international publishing companies; on the managing board of Channel 4 1985–91; Chair of the Booker Prize for Fiction from 1997.

s. *Who's Who* (1999).

CAMPBELL, Beatrix (Bea) (UK journalist, author, socialist feminist activist, social commentator) *b.* 1947.

Originally a CP member and journalist on the Morning Star; became active in the WLM in 1970; founder member of the WL journal, *Red Rag* in 1971; member of Virago's advisory group; worked extensively in propagating feminist perspectives through her campaigning and writing; *Guardian* columnist, television and radio contributor; Visiting Professor of Women's Studies, University of Newcastle upon Tyne.

p. *Sweet Freedom: The Struggle for Women's Liberation* (with A. Coote, 1982); *Wigan Pier Re-Visited: Poverty and Politics in the Eighties* (1984); *The Iron Ladies: Why do Women Vote Tory?* (1987); *Unofficial Secrets: Child Abuse* (1988); 'Feminist Politics After Thatcher' in *Working Out* (ed. H. Hinds, 1992); *Goliath: Britain's Dangerous Places* (1993); *Diana, Princess of Wales: How Sexual Politics Shook the Monarchy* (1998).

s. Campbell (1982); Tuttle (1986).

CHARLTON, Valerie (UK child-care activist).

Originally a member of the CP, which she left because of its discriminatory policies against women; activist in one of the first WLM groups in London; member of the *Red Rag* collective; one of a small group of women to establish the Camden Children's Community Centre in Dartmouth Park Hill in London to provide free, full-time nursery care for children from two-and-a-half to five years old; the nursery was run by the parents on non-sexist, collectivist principles in line with one of the key demands of the WLM for twenty-four hour childcare provision; subsequently a sculptor working on special effects in the film industry.

p. *The Patter of Tiny Contradictions* in *Red Rag*, no 5, 1973.

s. *Red Rag*, Nos 1 and 5; Campbell and Coote (1982); Wandor (1990).

CHICAGO (COHEN), Judy (US feminist artist).

Took her home town for her name. Co-founder of the Feminist Studio Workshop at the California Institute of Arts and the Women's Building, successor to the FSW. The work which gave her international fame was *The Dinner Party*, a multimedia work to acknowledge the contributions of 999 women from myth and history, which opened in San Francisco in 1979. Some of her other work has been *Menstruation Bathroom* (1971), *The Birth Project* (1984), *The Holocaust Project* (1993). She has also made films and written books to record the artistic process.

Films: Womanhouse (1972); *Right Our of History: The Making of the Dinner Party*; *Holocaust Project: From Darkness into Light*.

p. Through the Flower: My Struggle as a Woman Artist (1975); *The Dinner Party: A Symbol of Our Heritage* (1979); *Embroidering Our Heritage: The Dinner Party Needlework* (1980); *The Birth Project* (1985); *Holocaust Project: From Darkness into Light* (1994).

s. Campbell and Coote (1982); Cullen-DuPont (1996); Penguin (1998).

CHISHOLM, Shirley Anita (US politician) *b.* 1924.

Took an MA in Education at Columbia University; her career began as a child care centre administrator; gained a State Assembly seat, 1964, 1965, 1966 and was particularly interested in campaigning for domestic workers; she became the first African-American woman to win a seat in the House of Representatives, from 1968–82, championing the rights of poor women from minority groups; she ran in the Democratic Party's primary for the Presidential nomination as a way of staking a claim for the future for others, 1972; she was also the first woman and the first African-American woman to be on the House Rules Committee, 1976; after leaving politics in 1982 she later became Purrington Professor of Political Science at Mount Holyoke College (America's first women's college).

p. Unbought and Unbossed (1970); *The Good Fight* (1973).

s. Cullen-DuPont (1996).

CHURCHILL, Caryl (UK playwright) *b.* 1938.

Attended Trafalgar School, Montreal and whilst a student at Lady Margaret Hall, Oxford she had her first two plays produced; gained a BA, 1960; several of her feminist plays have focused on the issue of women hidden from history and examine historical aspects of women's lives, as well as other political aspects of feminism; she has written for the theatre, radio and television; resident playwright at the Royal Court, London during the 1970s; also worked with the feminist theatre company, Monstrous Regiment; regarded as one of the most significant playwrights of her generation.

p. Downstairs (1958); *Having a Wonderful Time* (1960); *Schreber's Nervous Illness* (1972); *Owners* (1972); *Moving Clocks Go Slow* (1975); *Objections to Sex and Violence* (1975); *Vinegar Tom* (1976); *Traps* (1977); *Floorshow* (1977); *Cloud Nine* (1979); *Three More Sleepless Nights* (1980); *Top Girls* (1982); *Crimes* (1982); *Fen* (1983); *Softcops* (1984); *A Mouthful of Birds* (1986); *Serious Money* (1987); *Light Shining in Buckinghamshire* (1976); *Cloud Nine* (1978).

s. Tuttle (1986); Buck (1992); *Who's Who* (1999).

COLQUHOUN, Maureen (UK MP and activist) *b.* 1928.

Committed lesbian feminist; original member of ALRA; member of the LP since 1945; worked in local government politics before becoming a Labour MP for Northampton North, 1974–9 working on bills and speaking on abortion, equal rights, pensions and protection of prostitutes; in 1975 the first woman MP to come out as a lesbian and suffered prejudice and abuse from parliamentary colleagues, the press and public; lost her seat in the 1979 general election; became a political researcher and writer after leaving Parliament; Information Officer Gingerbread, the organization for single-parent families, 1980–82; Honorary Secretary All Party Group on AIDS, 1987–8; Chair Secretaries' and Assistants' Council, House of Commons, 1992–3; Chief Executive North West Government Relations since 1994.

p. Get Yourself Selected / Elected: A Handbook of Opportunities in Public Life for Self-Help Gingerbread Groups (1981); *A Woman in the House* (1980); *Inside the Westminster Parliament* (1992); *New Labour – New Lobbying* (1998).

s. Women's Report, vol. ii, Issue 3; *Who's Who* (1999).

COOTE, Anna (UK feminist journalist).

Studied Modern History and Politics, University of Edinburgh, graduating 1968; journalist on the *Observer*, freelance writer; campaigner for equal rights in her profession and in the WLM; also a broadcaster; notably, presented the motion against the issue of pin-ups against NUM leader, Arthur Scargill at a debate held by the Trade Union Journals' Section of the NUJ, 1979; member of Virago's advisory group; took El Vino to the Court of Appeal with Tess Gill (see entry) in a case sponsored by the EOC to challenge the wine bar's discriminatory practice of only serving women who were seated, 1981.

p. Civil Liberty: The NCCL Guide (1973); *Women's Rights: A Practical Guide* (1974); *Women Factory Workers: The Case Against Repealing the Protective Laws* (1975); *Battered Women: How to Use the Law* (with Tess Gill, 1975); *The Rape Controversy: The Laws, The Myths, The Facts* (with Tess Gill, 1975); *Equality and the Curse of the Quango* (1978); *Equal at Work? Women in Men's Jobs* (1979); *Why Girls Don't Like Maths* (1980); *Women Pay the Price for Economic Growth* (1980); *Powerlessness and How to Fight It* (1980); *Hear this Brother: Women Workers and Union Power* (with Peter Kellner, 1980); *The Family in the Firing Line: A Discussion Document on Family Policy* (with Jean Coussins, 1981); *Sweet Freedom: The Struggle for Women's Liberation* (with B. Campbell, 1982); *Under the Carpet of History* (1982); *Power & Prejudice: Women and Politics* (with Polly Pattullo, 1990); *Families, Women and Crime* (ed. 1994).

s. Coote and Gill (1974); Campbell and Coote (1982).

COX, Eva (Australian academic and political activist) *b.* 1938.

Born in Austria, came to Australia in 1948; took a BA Hons from University of NSW; member Women's Economic Think Tank and founding member of the Women's Electoral Lobby in the early 1970s; also involved with the Media Women's Action Group; Director NSW Council of Social Service, 1977–81; participated in the Alternative Economic Summit on the exclusion of women in corporate and public life, 1983; Senior Assistant Director NSW Department of Youth and Community Services, 1984–8; Senior Lecturer in the Department of Humanities and Social Science, University of Technology, Sydney from 1995; has a consultancy company, Distaff Associates.

p. A Truly Civil Society (ABC Boyer lecture, 1995); *Leading Women* (1996). *s.* Caine (1998); *Who's Who in Australia* (2000).

CURTIS, Zelda (UK activist) *b.* 1923.

From a Jewish immigrant family, joined the CP during WW2, later working at the *Daily Worker* and the *Morning Star*; involved with the WLM from its beginnings at the Ruskin conference; after much dissent about the Party's attitude towards women's issues, left the CP in 1981; became involved in women's projects internationally in the NGO, War on Want; dominance of young women's issues in the WLM led her to form the OWG; paid worker of Pensioners' Link Older Women's Project which was funded by the GLCWC from 1984, now Association of Greater London Older Women (AGLOW); co-opted member GLC's WC; member IWG.

s. Feminist Review, no 31, Spring 1989.

DADZIE, Stella (UK black education) *b.* 1952.

Modern languages teacher in a London comprehensive for six years; taught in a centre for young offenders; lecturer in Black Studies in a North London College working with women and the unemployed for four years; took an MA in Afro-Caribbean/Afro-American studies; founder member of OWAAD.

p. The Heart of the Race: Black Women's Lives in Britain (with Beverley Bryan, Suzanne Scafe, 1985); *Educational Guidance with Black Communities: A Checklist of Good Practice* (1990); *Essential Skills for Race Equality Trainers* (with Gurnam Heire, Andy Forbes, 1992); *Older & Wiser: A Study of Educational Provision for Black and Ethnic Minority Elders* (1993); *Survey of Numbers of Black Adults with Professional Qualifications Gained Overseas* (1993); *Working with Black Adult Leaners: A Practical Guide* (1993); *Equality Assurance: Self-Assessment for Equal Opportunities in Further Education* (1998); *Making a Difference: A Resource Pack for People Who Want to Become More Active Citizens* (1999).

s. Dadzie (1985); Bodleian Catalogue.

DALY, Mary (US radical feminist theologian and philosopher).

Graduated with a PhD and ThD from the University of Fribourg, Switzerland and became associate Professor of Theology at Boston College, Massachusetts; when her first book was published, she was dismissed from Boston College, but was allowed to return as her students championed her cause; her challenging work analyses patriarchy within religion and her feminist philosophy seeks to deconstruct language to enable a woman to redefine her own reality as a woman-identified woman; to this end she has coined a new language which gives her work an added complexity.

p. The Church and the Second Sex (1968); *Beyond God the Father: Toward a Philosophy of Women's Liberation* (1973); *Gyn/Ecology* (1978); *Pure Lust: Elemental Feminist Philosophy* (1984); *Webster's First New Intergalactic Wickedary of the English Language* (with Jane Caputi, 1987); *The Be-Dazzling Voyage: Containing Recollections from My Logbook of a Radical Feminist Philosopher* (1992).

s. Daly (1978); Schneir (1995); Cullen-DuPont (1996).

DE LANEROLLE, Ros (UK publisher) died 1993.

Originally from South Africa, a socialist, involved in radical politics, was a founding member of the AAM in Britain; Editor of *Revolution Africaine* in London; writer, radical editor; founder member of Women in Publishing; Editor at Souvenir Press before becoming Managing Director of the Women's Press from 1981–90; won the 'Women in Publishing Pandora Award' for 'raising the status of women in publishing', 1992; co-originator of the 'Orange Prize for Fiction' for women writers; died from cancer.

s. Guardian, 13 April 1988; Women in Publishing.

DOYLE, Mikki (US journalist) 1916–95.

Born in New York; joined the CP at 16; a lifetime of activism; deported from the US and came to Britain, 1953; Secretary of the CP SW London women's committee; worked briefly in a factory, then advertising, trade attaché in Cuba before becoming Women's Editor on the *Morning Star* from 1967 until she retired in 1987; a 'practical' feminist, she revolutionized the women's page from domestic concerns to Women's Movement issues; founder member of the group, Women in Media; also an anti-racist campaigner.

s. Link, no 40; *Guardian*, 9 May 1980; *Independent*, 12 December 1995; *Guardian*, 18 December 1995.

DWORKIN, Andrea (US radical feminist theorist and activist) *b.* 1946.

Graduated from Bennington College, 1968; before her work in the WLM she was a waitress, factory worker and receptionist; she has largely concentrated her campaigning against the sexual oppression of women emanating from pornography; she has worked with the lawyer, Catharine MacKinnon (see entry) to effect legislative change in several US states; she has also taught a course about pornography with MacKinnon at the University of Minnesota.

p. Woman Hating (1974); *Our Blood: Prophecies and Discourses on Sexual Politics* (1976); *The New Woman's Broken Heart* (1980); *Take Back the Night: Women on Pornography* (1980); *Pornography: Man Possessing Women* (1981); *Right-Wing Women* (1983); *Ice & Fire* (1986); *Intercourse* (1987); *Pornography and Civil Rights: A New Day for Women's Equality* (1988); *Letters from a War Zone: Writings 1976–89; Mercy* (1991).

s. Schneir (1995); Cullen-DuPont (1996); Penguin (1998).

FAIRBAIRNS, Zoe (UK writer) *b.* 1948.

Read history at the University of St Andrews and the College of William and Mary in Virginia, USA; member of the *Spare Rib* collective and acted as the poetry editor; information officer at the WRRC collective, 1975–7; predominant contribution as a writer of political novels and poetry; writer in residence at various secondary schools, including Rutherford School, North London, 1977–8; also a freelance journalist and member of the Virago advisory group; won the Fawcett Society's book award with *Here Today* in 1984.

p. Study War No More: Military Involvement in British Universities (1974); *Women's Studies in the UK* (ed. 1975); *Tales I Tell My Mother* (with Maitland, Roberts, Wandor, 1978); *Benefits* (1979); *Stand We at Last* (1983); *Here Today* (1984); *Closing* (1987); *More Tales I Tell My Mother* (1987); *Daddy's Girls* (1992).

s. Fairbairns (1978–79); *Spare Rib* (1979); Tuttle (1986); Buck (1992).

FELL, Alison (UK/Scot, writer) *b.* 1944.

Poet, novelist, journalist; attended Edinburgh Art College; Marxist feminist; active in the WLM from 1969; co-founder the Women's Street Theatre Group after moving to London, 1970; worked on the underground paper, *Ink*, then the *Islington Gutter Press*, member of the *Red Rag* collective; member of the *Spare Rib* collective from 1975.

p. Hard Feelings: Fiction and Poetry from Spare Rib (1979); *The Grey Dancer* (children's novel, 1981); *At the Edge of Ice* (1983); *Kisses for Mayakovsky* (1984); *Every Move You Make* (1984); *The Bad Box* (1987); *The Seven Deadly Sins* (1988).

s. Tuttle (1986); *One Foot on the Mountain* (1970); Buck (1992).

FENNELL, Nuala (Irish journalist and politician).

One of the founding members of the IWLM, 1970; broke away from the original WLM group in 1971, wanted to make a practical difference to the lives of Irish women who needed emancipation most, formed a liberal reformist group, AIM in 1972 largely concerned with legal reform; instrumental in the formation of Irishwomen's Aid to combat domestic violence, 1974; unsuccessful as an independent candidate in the 1977 election; joined Fine Gael, elected in 1981; made Minister of State for Women's Affairs, 1982; continued to engage in law reform, chaired an Interdepartmental Working Party on Women's Affairs and Family Law Reform, set up by theTaoiseach, 1983; her office sponsored seminars, open days, information and a freephone advice line on health and entrepreneurship; also enabled an extensive number of women's groups to have access to financial assistance; lost her seat in the 1987 election.

p. Can You Stay Married? (with Deirdre McDevitt, Bernadette Quinn, 1980).

s. Mahon (1996).

FERRARO, Geraldine (US lawyer and Democrat member of Congress) *b.* 1935.

Graduated with a BA in English, Marymount College, 1956; she was a teacher in New York while studying for a law degree in the evenings; worked as a private practice lawyer before becoming an assistant district attorney, 1974–8; won a seat in Congress, 1978, 1980, 1982; she co-sponsored the Economic Equity Act, which would have ensured many of the equality demands of the rejected ERA, but it also failed, 1982; first woman to be appointed Chair of the National Platform Committee of the Democratic Party, 1984; first woman to become a Vice Presidential nominee, 1984.

p. Ferraro: My Story (with Francke, nd).

s. Cullen-DuPont (1996).

FIRESTONE, Shulamith (Canadian radical feminist) *b.* 1945.

She gained a degree in fine art from the Art Institute of Chicago; the first WLM group she organized was the Chicago Westside Group in 1967; went on to co-found the NYRW, a breakaway from the Stanton-Anthony Brigade, 1967; after splitting from NYRW, she was involved in 1969, with Ellen Willis, in founding, and naming the group Redstockings and eventually the NYRF; with Anna Koedt (see entry) editor of *Notes From the First Year*; her book provided a fundamental contribution to the WLM.

p. Notes From the First Year (1968); *Redstockings Manifesto* (1969); *The Dialectic of Sex: The Case for Feminist Revolution* (1970); *Coinage of Redstockings* in *Feminist Revolution* (1975).

s. Kramarae and Treichler (1985); Schneir (1995); Tuttle (1986); Cullen-DuPont (1996).

FREEMAN, Jo (pen-name Joreen) (US political scientist and lawyer) *b.* 1945.

Brought up in Los Angeles; spent four years at the University of California at Berkeley, became involved in the civil rights movement from 1961; arrested and jailed many times during these years; member Executive Committee of Berkeley Free Speech Movement; worked in Martin Luther King's SCLC, 1965–6; worked on the voter registration campaign in the south; attended a class on women at the University of Chicago which sparked her interest, 1967; apprentice journalist in Chicago, experienced so many discriminatory barriers; went to graduate school, gained a PhD in political science from the University of Chicago, 1973 and a law degree from New York University School of Law in 1982; involved in forming the Chicago Westside Group, one of the original WLGs in the US, 1967; founder of an early WLM newsletter, the *Voice of the Women's Liberation Movement*; edited it from 1968–9; the coining and use of the term WLM is attributed largely to her; one of the important facets of the WLM was the challenge it made to traditional forms of organization, an important contribution to this thinking came from Freeman, whose publication analysed this issue of democracy in the WLM; *The Politics of Women's Liberation* won the 1975 American Political Science Association prize for the best scholarly work on women and politics; member of NOW; lives and works in New York as a lawyer and writer describing herself as 'a guerilla scholar and unaffiliated agitator' (1998).

p. The Bitch Manifesto; *The Tyranny of Structurelessness* in *The Second Wave*, vol. 2, no 1, 1971; *The Politics of Women's Liberation* (1975); *Women: A Feminist Perspective* (1975); *Social Movements of the Sixties and Seventies* (1983); *On the Origins of the WLM from a Strictly Personal Perspective* in Rahel Blau DuPlessis and Ann Swinton (1998).

s. Campbell and Coote (1982); Tuttle (1986); Schneir (1995); DuPlessis and Swinton (1998).

FRIEDAN, Betty Naomi Goldstein (US feminist theorist) *b.* 1921.

Credited with writing the book which was the catalyst for the WLM and the so-called 'problem which has no name'; seeking to discover if other women graduates who were now housewives were suffering from the same dissatisfaction as herself, she distributed a questionnaire to other Smith graduates in 1957; consequently, she wrote the classic text examining housewives' vicarious living and society's discrimination; she was involved in starting NOW in 1966 and was its President until 1969, campaigning for the ERA; she organized the Women's Strike for Equality on 26 August 1970 which was effective in 40 American cities with 50,000 women striking in New York, the ERA was passed days before the strike; she was subsequently accused of selling out with the ideas expressed in *The Second Stage*.

p. The Feminine Mystique (1963); *It Changed My Life: Writings on the Women's Movement* (1976); *The Second Stage* (1981); *The Fountain of Age* (1993).

s. Cullen-DuPont (1996).

GARNER, Helen (Australian feminist writer) *b.* 1942.

Born in Geelong; BA Hons from Melbourne University; taught in Melbourne but lost her job because of her honest response to her students on sexual matters, 1972; writer and actor with the Women's Theatre Group, Melbourne, mid-1970s; worked as a magazine journalist in the 1970s, before turning to writing short stories and novels; also occupied several university writer-in-residences; for her first novel, *Monkey Grip*, she won the National Book Council Award in 1978, it was turned into a film in 1982.

p. Monkey Grip (1977); *Honour and Other People's Children: Two Stories* (1980); *Moving Out* (with Jennifer Giles, 1984); *Children's Bach* (1984); *Postcards from Surfers* (1985); *Two Friends* (screenplay, 1986); *Cosmo Cosmolino* (1993); *The Last Days of Chez Nous* (1993); *The First Stone* (1995); *True Stories* (1996); *My Hard Heart* (1998).

s. Buck (1992); Arnold and Morris (1994); Chambers (1996); Caine (1998); *Who's Who in Australia* (2000).

GEORGE, Jennie (Australian trade unionist) *b.* 1947.

Born in a displaced persons' camp in Italy of Russian parents; she gained a scholarship to Sydney University, taking a BA and DipEd; secondary school teacher, from 1969; General Secretary of the NSW Teachers' Federation, 1980–82, becoming President from 1986–9; she was the first woman elected to the ACTU Executive in 1983; another first when she was elected as Vice President of ACTU in 1987; in ACTU she campaigned for childcare, equal representation for women in politics and the TU movement; Assistant National Director of TU Training Authority, 1989–91; Assistant Secretary ACTU, 1991–5; President from 1995; delegate for the Australian Republican Movement to the Constitutional Convention, 1997.

s. Arnold and Morris (1994); Caine (1998); *Who's Who in Australia* (2000).

GILL, Tess (UK feminist lawyer).

Read Politics and History at the University of Manchester; worked in a radical law firm on matrimonial and trade union cases; with Anna Coote (see entry) took the wine bar, El Vino, to the Court of Appeal for its discriminatory practice towards women, 1981.

p. Women's Rights: A Practical Guide (with Anna Coote, 1974); *Battered Women: How to Use the Law* (1975); *Women's Rights in the Workplace* (1983).

s. Coote and Gill (1974).

GILLIGAN, Carol (US feminist psychologist) *b.* 1936.

Took her BA from Swarthmore College, 1958, her MA from Radcliffe in 1960 and her doctorate from Harvard, 1964; credited with revisioning women's psychological development with her first book, *In a Different Voice*, in which she reviews the myth of 'women's inferiority' in the work of male psychologists; taught at Harvard, Rutgers and, in the UK, at Cambridge; was *Ms.* Magazine's, 'Woman of the Year' in 1984.

p. In a Different Voice: Psychological Theory and Women's Development (1982); *Making Connections: The Relational Worlds of Adolescent Girls at Emma Willard School* (1991); *Meeting at the Crossroads: Women's Psychology and Girls' Development* (1992).

s. Cullen-DuPont (1996).

GINSBERG, Ruth Bader (US lawyer) *b.* 1933.

Born in New York; it was her mother's hard work which paid for her college education; studied pre-law at Cornell University, then attended Harvard and Columbia Law Schools; she experienced great difficulty in obtaining her first job as a lawyer; worked and studied law in Sweden before becoming a Law Professor at Rutgers; worked on the landmark legal case where 14th Amendment protection was extended to women for the first time (Reed v. Reed), 1971; Director of the Women's Rights Project, 1972; went on to win five out of six strategic law cases for women in the Supreme Court; only the second woman to become a Supreme Court Judge, 1993.

p. Sex-Based Discrimination (et al., 1974).

s. Cullen-DuPont (1996); *Who's Who in America* (1998).

GOULD, Joyce (UK LP officer) *b.* 1932.

Attended Cowper Street Primary School, Roundhay High School; Bradford Technical College Dispenser, 1952–65; LP Assistant Regional Organizer, 1969–75; LP Assistant National Agent and Chief Woman's Officer, 1975–85; Secretary NJCWWO, 1975–85; Vice President Socialist International Women, 1978–86; LP Director of Organization, 1985–93; Opposition Spokesperson on women's affairs, 1995–7; particularly worked for women in the areas of single parent families, widows and taxation.

p. Women and Health (ed. 1979); *Women's Organizations in the Labour Party* (1982); pamphlets on feminism, socialism and sexism, women's right to work, violence in society, women's rights and welfare.

s. Who's Who (1999).

GREER, Germaine (Australian feminist academic) *b.* 1939.

Born in Melbourne; educated at a convent, first degree in French and English from Melbourne University, 1959; after gaining an MA in Sydney, she took her PhD at the University of Cambridge in Shakespearean comedy; wrote for the radical underground paper, *Oz*, 1967; lecturer at Warwick University, 1967–73; achieved prominence with her radical first book, *The Female Eunuch*, with its emphasis on women's need for sexual liberation; Director of the Centre for the Study of Women's Literature, Oklahoma, 1979; freelance writer, lecturer and media personality; currently Professor of English and Comparative Literature, University of Warwick; has her own press, Stump Cross Books specializing in women poets.

p. The Female Eunuch (1970); *The Obstacle Race* (1979); *Sex and Destiny: The Politics of Human Fertility* (1984); *Shakespeare* (1985); *Kissing the Rod: An Anthology of Seventeenth Century Women's Verse* (1988); *Uncollected Verse of Aphra Benn* (ed. 1989); *Daddy We Hardly Knew You* (1989); *The Change: Women, Ageing and the Menopause* (1991); *Slipshod Sibyls: Recognition, Rejection and the Woman Poet* (1995); *The Whole Woman* (1999).

s. Greer (1970); Uglow (1989); Chambers (1996); Caine (1998); University of Warwick website.

HEATHFIELD, Betty (UK/trade unionist).

Founder member of NWO; one of the spokeswomen and organizers of the women's support campaign during the miners' strike, 1984–5; associated with the

Derbyshire Women's Action Group; led the women's action group on the picket lines; worked as a national speaker, fundraising for the miners.

s. Stead (1987).

HEWITT, Patricia (UK rights and social policy activist, MP) *b.* 1948.

Educated in Canberra Grammar School and the Australian National University, Newnham College, Cambridge; Public Relations Officer, Age Concern, 1971–3; Women's Rights Officer NCCL, 1973–4; General Secretary NCCL, 1974–83; National Labour Women's Committee, 1979–83; unsuccessful LP PPC, Leicester East, 1983; Policy Coordinator to the Leader of the Opposition, 1988–9; Deputy Director Institute for Public Policy Research, 1989–94; Associate, Newnham College, 1984–97; LP MP Leicester West, from 1997; Economic Secretary HM Treasury, from 1998.

p. books – *Your Rights* (1973); *Danger! Women at Work* (ed. 1974); *Civil Liberties* (1977); *The Privacy Report* (1977); *Your Rights at Work* (1978); *The Abuse of Power* (1981); *Your Second Baby* (1990); *About Time: The Revolution in Work and Family Life* (1993); pamphlets – *Income Tax and Sex Discrimination* (nd c.1975); *Rights for Women: A Guide to the Sex Discrimination Act, the Equal Pay Act, Maternity Leave, Pensions Schemes and Unfair Dismissal* (1975).

s. Sisterwrite Catalogue 1981–2.

HOBBS, May (UK women's activist).

Born in Hoxton, evacuated to Somerset during WW2; after the war her parents had her unofficially adopted; on leaving secondary modern school she had a series of factory jobs; after marriage and having children, worked as a cleaner; it was her experiences with private landlords which politicized her; joined the LP in the 1960s; started the Cleaners' Action Group and the Night Cleaners Campaign in 1970 in an attempt to get office cleaners unionized by joining the TGWU; approached the International Socialists for support and was invited to a meeting of the Dalston WLG after which the campaign was supported by the WLM and students; continued to campaign for the Sex Discrimination Act, the homeless and the rights of young mothers and their children.

p. Born to Struggle (1973).

s. Hobbs (1973); *Red Rag*, no 6; Coote and Gill (1982).

hooks, bell (real name, Gloria Watkins, US writer and academic) *b.* 1952.

Born in Kentucky; her work concentrates on issues of feminism, race and class; taught English, African/American and Women's Studies at Oberlin College, Yale, now Distinguished Professor of English, City College, New York; her first book in 1981 was one of the most significant texts in the process of challenging white, middle-class women's domination of the WLM with the concept of the diversity of women's experience.

p. Ain't I a Woman: Black Women and Feminism (1981); *Feminist Theory: From Margin to Center* (1984); *Outlaw Culture: Resisting Representations*; *Talking Back: Thinking Feminist, Thinking Black* (1990); *Yearning: Race, Gender, and Cultural Politics*; *Breaking Bread: Insurgent Black Intellectual Life* (with Cornel West, 1992); *Black Looks: Race and Representation* (1992); *Sisters of the Yam: Black Women and Self-Recovery* (1993); *Teaching to Transgress: Education as the Practice of Freedom*

(1994); *Bone Black: Memories of Girlhood* (1997); *Wounds of Passion: A Writing Life* (1998); *Remembered Rapture* (1999).
  s. Tuttle (1986); Hooks (1993; 1999).

HUTT, Jane (UK community activist and politician) *b.* 1949.
  Born in Epsom; educated Sussex and Kenya; attended Universities of Kent, London (LSE) and Bristol, BA Hons, MSc; community worker from 1970; activist in the Welsh WLM; Co-ordinator of Welsh Women's Aid 1978–88; involved in Welsh Women's Assembly; Director of Chwarae Teg (EO organization); LP Councillor, South Glamorgan County Council, 1981–93; AM Vale of Glamorgan, from May 1999; Assembly Secretary for Health and Social Services from 1999; Chairwoman of the Assembly Committee on Equality of Opportunity.
  s. http://news.bbc.co.uk/hi/english/static/uk/wales13108.stm from Avril Rolph.

JACKSON, Stevi (UK activist and academic).
  Took a BA from Kent University, B. Phil from York; lived in Cardiff, active in the Cardiff Women's Centre and the South Wales Rape Crisis Centre; lecturer at the Polytechnic of Wales, researched into adolescent girls' view of their sexuality; currently, Professor and Director Centre for Women's Studies, University of York.
  p. On the Social Construction of Female Sexuality (1978); *Childhood and Sexuality* (1982); *Women's Studies: A Reader* (co-ed., 1993); *Theorizing Heterosexuality: Gender, Power and Pleasure* (1994); *The Politics of Domestic Consumption: Critical Readings* (ed. with Shaun Moores, 1995); *Christine Delphy* (1996); *Feminism and Sexuality: A Reader* (ed. with Sue Scott, 1996); *Contemporary Feminist Theories* (1998); *Concerning Heterosexuality* (1999).
  s. Friedman and Sarah (1982); Jackson (1999); staff.htm at www.york.ac.uk.

JAMES, Selma (UK activist) *b.* 1930.
  Born in US; member of a Trotskyist youth group, 1945; came to London in 1955; worked as a freelance audio-typist for the BBC, 1970; a prominent campaigner in Britain in the WLM, instrumental in founding several organizations and in fighting for continued funding for the King's Cross Women's Centre where these organizations had their base; established Wages for Housework Campaign, 1970 and the English Collective of Prostitutes, 1975; involved in setting up Women Against Rape, 1976.
  p. A Woman's Place (1952); *The Power and the Subversion of the Community* (1972); *Strangers and Sisters: Women, Race and Immigration* (1982); *The Ladies and the Mammies: Jane Austen and Jean Rhys* (1983).
  s. Tuttle (1986); Wandor (1990).

JEFFREYS, Sheila (Australian revolutionary feminist and writer).
  Lesbian separatist, involved in the WLM from the 1973, written many influential texts; member of Leeds Revolutionary Feminists; member London Lesbian History Group; active in campaigns against male violence, founder member of the London WAVAW in 1980; involved in establishing the London Lesbian Archive; currently teaches lesbian and gay politics at the University of Melbourne's Department of Political Science.

p. The Need for Revolutionary Feminism (pamphlet, 1977); 'Political Lesbianism: The Case Against Heterosexuality' in *Love Your Enemy: The Debate between Heterosexual Feminism and Political Lesbianism* (Leeds Revolutionary Feminists, 1981); *The Spinster and Her Enemies: Feminism and Sexuality 1880–1930* (1985); *The Sexuality Debates* (1987); *Not a Passing Phase: Reclaiming Lesbians in History 1840–1985* (1989); *Anticlimax* (1990); *The Lesbian Heresy* (1993).

s. Campbell and Coote (1982); Jeffreys (1987); Lesbian History Group (1989); Purvis (1995).

KENNY, Mary (Irish journalist) *b.* 1944.

Born in Dublin; worked as a journalist since 1965; for five years on the London *Evening Standard*; the foundations of her feminism originated in her experiences on a visit to the USA in 1967 and as a reporter covering the student riots in Paris, 1968; returned to Dublin as women's editor of the *Irish Press*, during which time she wrote honestly on the problems of Irish society and gained a reputation as a feminist and women's champion, from 1969; the 'casserole of exasperation' (Kenny, 1997) she felt with regard to women's position in Ireland led her to become one of the founder members of IWLM, 1970; CR meetings held in her flat at Ballsbridge; returned to London as features editor of the *Evening Standard*, 1971; one of the protesters who travelled on the 'contraceptive train' from Dublin to Belfast, 1972; the birth of her first son in 1974 led to a revision in her perceptions with regard to women's lives; European correspondent of the *Evening Standard*; freelance writer, broadcaster and journalist, regular contributor to *The Tablet*.

p. Woman X Two (1978); *Why Christianity Works* (1981); *Abortion: The Whole Story* (1986); *A Mood for Love and Other Stories* (1989); *Goodbye to Catholic Ireland* (1997).

s. Rose (1975); Kenny (1978, 1997).

KENNEDY, Mary (UK activist and academic) *b.* 1931.

Degree in History from Royal Holloway College, University of London; researcher in the FO, Bank of London and South America; part-time Latin American correspondent for the *New Statesman*, *The Tablet*, *The Statist*, 1962–8; lecturer in History, Ealing Technical College, 1964–8; WLM activist from the early 1970s in London; member of the London N7 Group which evolved from a CR group to research on homeworking, subsequently published and sent to the then Secretary of State for Employment, Michael Foot; worked on childcare issues around the WLM demand for 24-hour nurseries with Val Charlton (see entry); Development Officer, London WEA, 1977–80; lecturer/senior lecturer in Women's Studies and History, Birkbeck College, developed the Women's Studies programme and initiated the MA/MSc in Gender, Culture and Society, 1980–93; member of various working groups on extending feminist educational access for women – initiating self-defence classes for ILEA, founder member UCACE women's education group, member NIACE women's education programme, co-founder and member of the OWEG, co-chair WSN, currently chair of the IWCC.

p. Revolution in Perspective: People Seeking Change (1972); *Homeworkers in North London* (with Emily Hope, Anne de Winter) in *Dependence and Exploitation in Work and Marriage*, Diana Leonard Barker and Sheila Allen (1976); *The Paris Commune* (children's history, 1976); *New Futures: Changing Women's Education* (with Mary

Hughes, 1985); ? in *Gender & Expertise* (ed. Maureen McNeil, 1987); piece in *Out of the Margins: Women's Studies in the Nineties* (ed. Jane Aaron and Sylvia Walby, 1991); *Making Connections: Women's Studies, Women's Movements, Women's Lives* (ed. with Cathy Lubelska, Val Walsh, 1993).

s. interview.

KOEDT, Anne (US feminist activist and artist).

Pioneer of the WLM in America; member of NYRW; member of The Feminists; co-founder with Shulamith Firestone (see entry) of the NYRF; author of one of the earliest and most influential WLM tracts on the nature of women's sexual experience.

p. Notes From the First Year (ed. with Firestone, 1968); 'The Myth of the Vaginal Orgasm' in *Notes From the Second Year* (1970); 'Lesbianism and Feminism' in *Notes From the Third Year* (1971); *Radical Feminism* (ed. with E. Levine, A. Rapone, 1973).

s. Kramarae and Treichler (1985); Schneir (1995).

KROLL, Una (UK, ordination of women) *b.* 1925.

Educated at St Paul's Girls' School, Malvern Girls' College, Girton College, Cambridge, qualified as a doctor, the London Hospital; House Officer, 1951–3; overseas medical service in Africa (1953–60), met her future husband, a minister working as a missionary; returning to Britain, attempted to buy a cooker to discover she was not allowed to sign the hire purchase agreement, only her husband could do this, even though he was unemployed and she was a practising doctor, the injustice of this and subsequent experience of the poverty of many of her women patients resulted in her WLM activism; fought to be ordained as a minister herself for 30 years, surrendered that ambition to work for the campaign for women's ordination and to concentrate on her work as an Anglican deaconess with battered, homeless and single-parent women, decided this after continued harrassment and abuse from people opposed to the ordination campaign had badly affected her health; committed to the wider aims of WLM, particularly economic independence for women, stood as the first Women's Rights candidate in the general election of 1974; worked as a general practitioner, 1960–81; clinical medical officer, 1981–5; senior clinical MO, 1985–8; worked as a deaconess, 1970–88; an ordained deacon, 1988; Sister in the Society of the Sacred Cross, 1991–4; eventually achieved her long ambition to became a priest, Church of Wales, 1997.

p. Transcendental Meditation: A Signpost to the World (1974); *Flesh of my Flesh: A Christian View on Sexism* (1975); *Lament for a Lost Enemy: Study of Reconciliation* (1976); *What the Church Should be Saying to Homosexuals* (1979); *Sexual Counselling* (1980); *The Spiritual Exercise Book* (1985); *Growing Older* (1988); *In Touch with Healing* (1991); *Vocation to Resistance* (1995); *Trees of Life* (1997).

s. Daily Telegraph, 21 July 1977; *Wimbledon News*, 4 August 1978; *Who's Who*, 1999.

LOCKWOOD, Betty, Baroness of Dewsbury (22 January 1924–) LP Women's Officer; *do.* Arthur & Edith Alice Lockwood; *e.* Eastborough Girls' School, Dewsbury, Ruskin College, Oxford; *m.* Lt. Col. Cedric Hall, 1978; *a.* 6 Sycamore Drive, Addingham, Ilkley (1998).

Chief Woman Officer and Assistant National Agent, LP, 1967–75; Editor *Labour Woman*, 1967–71; member Department of Employment Advisory Committee on Women's Employment, 1969–83; Chair Mary Macarthur Educational Trust, 1971–94; Chair EOC, 1975–83; Vice Chair ICSDW, 1969–75; Chair Advisory Committee to the EC on EOWM, 1982–3; President Hillcroft College for Women, 1987–95; on the governing bodies of many universities; a Deputy Speaker, House of Lords from 1989; President Mary Macarthur Holiday Trust, from 1990.

p. Part-Time and Temporary Employment, report of the Select Committee in the EC, 1990.

s. Who's Who (1998).

LORDE, Audre (US radical feminist activist and poet) 1934–92.

She identified the fallacy of the American WLM , which universalized women's oppression as being that of the majority white Movement, thereby excluding all women of colour; she argued for the diversity of black lesbian experience and fought for the recognition of black women's positive contribution to the Movement; Professor of English at Hunter College, 1980; in the early 1980s she was involved in creating Kitchen Table: Women of Color Press with Barbara Smith (see entry); died from cancer.

p. The First Cities (1968); *Cables to Rage* (1970); *From a Land Where Other People Live* (1973); *New York Head Shop and Museum* (1975); *Coal* (1976); *Between Ourselves* (1976); *The Black Unicorn* (1978); *The Cancer Journals* (1980); '*The Master's Tools Will Never Dismantle the Master's House*' and '*An Open Letter to Mary Daly*' in *This Bridge Called My Back: Writings by Radical Women of Color* (1981); *Chosen Poems* (1982); *Zami – A New Spelling of My Name* (1982); *Sister Outsider: Essays and Speeches* (1984); *A Burst of Light* (1989); *Undersong: Chosen Poems, Old and New, Revised* (1992); *The Marvellous Arithmetics of Distance* (1993).

s. Kramarae and Treichler (1985); Tuttle (1986); Humm (1989); Schneir (1995); Penguin (1996).

McCAFFERTY, Nell (Irish journalist and writer) *b.* 1944.

Born in Derry City's Bogside; degree from Queens University, Belfast; after taking time out to travel, returned to Derry and became active in the Derry LP and the civil rights movement; moved to Dublin to write for *The Irish Times*, 1970; became involved in the Irish WLM in the early 1970s; her writing regarded as being of the 'eyewitness' school, having 'increased the oxygen in this community' (Boland's preface, McCafferty, 1984); became a freelance journalist and writer; reviewed the newspapers on weekly RTE television in *The Women's Programme*; her first play, *A Worm in the Heart* was performed in Dublin and London.

p. The Best of Nell: A Selection of Writings over Fourteen Years (1984); *Women in Focus: Contemporary Irish Women's Lives* (1986); *Goodnight Sisters: Selected Writings* vol. 2 (1987); *In the Eyes of the Law* (1987); *Peegy Deery: A Derry Family at War* (1988); *A Worm in the Heart* (1990).

s. McCafferty (1984); Buck (1994).

McCARTAN, Joyce (Irish community and peace campaigner) 1929–96.

Born in Banbridge, a Protestant; her mother died when she was seven, as the only girl she was expected to take over looking after the rest of the family; left school at fourteen, ran away to Belfast and worked in a draper's shop; married a Catholic; became involved in the BWIG from 1974, encouraging other women to become involved and use its services; non-sectarian women's and human rights campaigner; the first demonstration she organized was against Margaret Thatcher's cuts in the provision of free school milk, she took a cow along to Belfast City Hall; went on from there to start the WIDIC in the Lower Ormeau Road, Belfast to help women from both communities, 1987; the WIDIC took over the premises below their office to open the Lamplighter, a fish and chip shop, to provide some employment and a meeting place for Catholic and Protestant women; awarded the MBE and an honorary doctorate from Queen's University, Belfast, in recognition of her work for the community and the peace process; 14 members of her family had been killed during 'the Troubles', including her 17 year old son; wrote in her autobiography, 'To remain true to all you believe in, including your family, and yet be challenging the system the whole time, is something very difficult to achieve. That's why we call ourselves family feminists.'

p. A Battler All My Life (1995).

s. McCartan (1995); *Guardian*, 1 March 1996.

MACKINNON, Catharine (US activist and lawyer) *b.* 1946.

Took a first degree from Smith College, 1969, a law degree at Yale, 1977, and her PhD in political science from Yale, 1987; attacked the legal system for its attitudes and treatment of women as victims of crime; through challenging the courts, she has been instrumental in making sexual harassment an offence under sex discrimination law; worked with Andrea Dworkin (see entry) on outlawing pornography; her most recent work has examined the legislative perspective of women's rights as human rights, including rape cases from the Bosnian war, representing women and children pro bono seeking justice under international law; Professor of Law, University of Michigan Law School from 1990, also Visiting Professor of Law at Chicago Law School.

p. Sexual Harassment of Working Women (1979); *Women as Women in Law: On Exceptionality* (1982); *Feminism Unmodified: Discourses on Life and Law* (1986); *Pornography and Civil Rights: A New Day for Women's Equality* (with Andrea Dworkin, 1988); *Toward a Feminist Theory of the State* (1989); *Only Words* (1993); *In Harm's Way: The Pornography Civil Rights Hearings* (with A. Dworkin, 1998); 'Sex Equality' in *Feminism and Politics* (ed. Anne Phillips, 1998).

s. Cullen-DuPont (1996); Phillips (1998).

McWILLIAMS, Monica (Irish academic).

Activist and researcher of the WLM in Northern Ireland; recent research into domestic violence in NI for the DHSS; currently lecturer in Social Policy and Women's Studies, Senior Course Tutor at Jordanstown, University of Ulster.

p. 'Poverty in Northern Ireland' in *Poverty in Ireland* (ed. E. Hanna, 1987); 'Women's Paid Work and the Sexual Division of Labour' in *Women, Employment and Social Policy in Northern Ireland* (eds C. Davies and E. McLaughlin, 1991); 'The

Church, the State and the Women's Movement in Northern Ireland' in *Irish Women's Studies Reader* (ed. Ailbhe Smyth, 1993).
   s. Smyth (1993).

MAHER, Mary (Irish journalist).
   Editor of *Women First*, the revamped women's page of *The Irish Times* which tackled issues relating to the political, social and economic position of Irish women and the discriminations they faced instead of the traditional domestic content; one of the founder members of the IWLM, 1970.
   s. Rose (1975).

MAITLAND, Sara (UK writer and theologian) *b.* 1950.
   Brought up in Scotland; graduate of St Anne's College, Oxford with an English degree; writer and freelance journalist; involved in the WLM with *Women's Report* and Women's Aid since 1970; since 1978 an Anglo-Catholic feminist socialist; her work explores Christian thinking in line with feminism and the problems engendered; co-founder of the Feminist Writers Group with Zoe Fairbairns (see entry), Michele Roberts (see entry) and Michelene Wandor (see entry).
   p. Tales I Tell My Mother (with Z. Fairbairns, M. Roberts, M. Wandor, 1978); *Daughter of Jerusalem* (1979); *Telling Tales* (1983); *Walking on the Water: Women Talking about Spirituality* (ed. with Jo Garcia, 1983); *Virgin Territory* (1984); *Vesta Tilley* (1986); *A Book of Spells* (1986); *Arky Types* (with M. Wandor, 1987); *Very Heaven: Looking Back at the Sixties* (ed. 1988); *The Rushdie File* (ed. with Lisa Appignanesi, 1989); *Three Times Table* (1990).
   s. Guardian, 17 July 1988; Maitland (1988); Buck (1992).

MILLETT, Kate (US activist, author and artist) *b.* 1934.
   Born in St Paul, Minnesota; studied at the Universities of Minnesota and St Hilda's College, Oxford; spent two years in Japan as a sculptor, 1961–3; subsequently taught English at Barnard College; initially involved in the civil rights movement, subsequently joined the WLM; involved in the foundation of NOW; Lecturer in Literature and Philosophy and a recognized sculptor; activist in the WLM in Columbia University; agitator travelling around college campuses; *Sexual Politics* is a seminal work on the cultural politics of women's oppression; one of the first women to come out on her bisexuality; her later autobiographical books were noted for their honesty; travelled to Iran to work for women's rights and was deported, 1979; the pressure of working as a writer, sculptor and activist resulted in a complete breakdown of which she later wrote; also made a documentary film examining three women, *Three Lives* (1970/71).
   p. Token Learning (1967); *Sexual Politics* (1970); *The Prostitution Papers* (1971); *Flying* (1974); *Sita* (1977); *The Basement: Meditations on a Human Sacrifice* (1979); *Going to Iran* (1981); *The Loony-Bin Trip* (1990); *Politics of Cruelty* (1993).
   s. Millett (1970); Tuttle (1986); Schneir (1995); Cullen-DuPont (1996); Penguin (1998).

MITCHELL, Juliet (New Zealand/UK feminist psychoanalyst) *b.* 1940.
   According to Coote and Campbell she was 'the first major exponent of socialist feminism' credited with tackling the radical left and its attitudes toward women and

the women's cause in 1966 with her groundbreaking essay, *The Longest Revolution* published in *New Left Review*, it advanced a synthesis between socialism and feminism; read English at St Anne's College, Oxford; lectured in English Literature at Leeds and Reading universities; on the editorial board of *New Left Review* and *Social Praxis* and was a member of the LWLW; taught one of the first Women's Studies courses in Britain, 'The Role of Women in Society', at the Anti-University in London in the summer of 1968; lecturer in Gender and Society at Cambridge University; Fellow of Jesus College, Cambridge; A.D. White Professor-at-Large at Cornell University.

p. 'Women: The Longest Revolution' in *New Left Review* (1966); *Women's Liberation and the New Politics* (1969); *Woman's Estate* (1971); *Psychoanalysis and Feminism* (1974); *The Rights and Wrongs of Women* (with A. Oakley, 1976); *Feminine Sexuality, Jacques Lacan and the Ecole Freudienne* (ed. with Jacqueline Rose, 1982); *Women: The Longest Revolution* (1984); *Before I Was I: Psychoanalysis and the Imagination* (ed. with Michael Parsons, 1986); *Selected Melanie Klein* (ed. 1986).

s. Mitchell (1974); Coote and Campbell (1982); Tuttle (1986); Humm (1989); Oakley and Mitchell (1997).

MORGAN, Robin (US radical feminist writer and editor) *b.* 1941.

Born in Florida and grew up in Mount Vernon, NY; graduate of the University of Columbia; left-wing political activist for seven years before becoming involved in the WLM; her first feminist strike was in *Goodbye to All That*, an analysis of her first-hand experience of the sexism inherent in the civil rights and peace movements; Morgan was a founding member of NYRW, WITCH and WAP; she was a contributing editor to *Ms.* Magazine from 1977–89 when it folded, on its re-emergence she became its Editor from 1990–93.

p. 'Goodbye to All That' in *Rat* (1970) and *Ain't I A Woman* (25 September, 1971); *Sisterhood is Powerful: An Anthology of Writings from the Women's Liberation Movement* (1970); *Monster: Poems* (1972); *Lady of the Beasts: Poems* (1976); *Going Too Far: The Personal Chronicles of a Feminist* (1978); *Depth Perception: New Poems and a Masque* (1982); *The Anatomy of Freedom: Feminism, Physics, and Global Politics* (1982); *Sisterhood is Global: The International Women's Movement Anthology* (1984); *Dry Your Smile* (1987); *The Demon Lover: On the Sexuality of Terrorism* (1989); *The Word of a Woman: Feminist Dispatches 1968–92*.

s. Morgan (1970); Kramarae and Treichler (1985); Cullen-DuPont (1996).

MORGAN, Sally (Australian Aboriginal rights activist and writer) *b.* 1951.

With Aboriginal ancestry, she was born in Perth; graduated from the University of Western Australia in psychology, 1974; took a post-graduate diploma in counselling; won the Human Rights and EOC award for literature for her first two books; chosen as Western Australian Citizen of the Year, 1989; her paintings concentrate on women and Aboriginal themes and she first exhibited her paintings in 1987; member of the Aboriginal Arts Committee of the Australian Council, 1989; Professorial Fellow and Head of the Centre for Indigenous Art and History, University of Western Australia from 1996.

p. *My Place* (1987); *Wanamurraganya* (1989); *A Collection of Children's Stories* (1990); *Flying Emu* (1991).

s. Arnold and Morris (1994); *Who's Who in Australia* (2000).

MULLARNEY, Máire (Irish family planning activist) *b.* 1921.

Brought up between Ireland and Gibraltar, attending various Loreto convents; trained as a nurse at the Royal City of Dublin Hospital, went on to study physiotherapy; when her 11 children were established, she starting writing articles on early learning from her own experience and observation, successfully submitted to *The Irish Times* which began her career as a journalist; member of the Irish Theological Association; member of Reform, which opposed the corporal punishment of children; aware, again from her personal experience of the desperate need for birth control and contraceptive information, involved with five others in establishing a limited company, the Fertility Guidance Company, one of two women who instigated the first family planning clinic in Dublin in 1969 to provide advice and information (later prescriptions); lectured at women's clubs on family planning; became involved in the Esperanto Movement; founding member of the Ecology Party in Ireland, stood for election to the Dáil as a Green candidate for Dublin South East, 1982; Education spokesperson for the Green Party; elected to Dublin County Council, 1991.

p. Anything School Can Do, You Can Do Better (1983); *Esperanto for Hope* (1988); *Early Reading: A Guide for Parents* (1990); *What About Me? A Woman for Whom 'One Damn Cause' Led to Another* (1992).

s. Rose (1975); Mullarney (1992).

NORTON, Eleanor Holmes (US lawyer).

Norton had to attend segregated schools and colleges, later taking an MA in American Studies and a law degree at Yale University; she became the assistant legal director of the American Civil Liberties Union, specializing in freedom-of-speech cases, 1965–70; from 1970, Chair of the New York City Commission on Human Rights, she was particularly committed to women's rights and attained many significant rights for working women; she became the first woman Chair of the Equal Employment Opportunity Commission, 1977; Law Professor at Georgetown University, Law Centre, 1982–90; District of Columbia delegate to the House of Representatives from 1990.

s. Cullen-DuPont (1996).

OAKLEY, Ann (UK feminist academic) *b.* 1944.

A Londoner who studied at Chiswick Polytechnic and Somerville College, Oxford and gained her PhD at the University of London; her doctoral dissertation on the issue of housework within a feminist perspective inspired her influential publications and developed an innovative analysis of women's domestic role; Research Officer Bedford College, 1974; Consultant to the National Perinatal Epidemiology Unit, Churchill Hospital, Oxford, 1979; Professor of Sociology and Social Policy and Director in the Policy Studies Unit on health and education at the Institute of Education, University of London; more recently she has developed a career as a novelist.

p. Sex, Gender and Society (1972); *The Sociology of Housework* (1974); *Housewife* (1974); *The Rights and Wrongs of Women* (with Juliet Mitchell, 1976); *Becoming a Mother* (1979); *Women Confined* (1980); *Taking It Like a Woman* (1984); *Telling the Truth About Jerusalem* (1986); *Essays on Women, Medicine and Health* (1993); *Man and Wife: Richard and Kay Titmus, My Parents' Early Years* (1997); *Who's Afraid of Feminism: Seeing through the Backlash* (1997).

s. Tuttle (1986); Button (1995).

O'CONNOR, Sandra Day (US lawyer) *b.* 1930.

Born El Paso, Texas; BA Economics, 1950 and an LLB, 1952 from Stanford University; Deputy Attorney California, then established her own law firm in Arizona; appointed to the Governor's Committee on Marriage and the Family, 1965 and Assistant Attorney General of Arizona until 1969; as a member of the Arizona State Senate she voted for the ERA's ratification, 1969–74; US Supreme Court Justice from 1981; inaugurate the National Woman's Hall of Fame, 1995.

s. Cullen-DuPont (1996); *Who's Who in America* (1998).

PARMAR, Pratibha (UK activist, media).

Active in black and women's groups from the mid-1970s; member of the Bradford Black Collective; worked with young Asian women in Leicester and London; member of the Black Women Talk publishing collective; member of the Late Start film cooperative; writer, part-time lecturer.

p. 'Gender, Race and Class: Asian Women in Resistance' in *The Empire Strikes Back* (CCCS, 1982); 'Stepping Forward: Work with Asian Young Women' in *Gen 1* (with N. Mirza, 1983); *Many Voices, One Chant* (ed. with Valerie Amos, Gail Lewis, Amina Mama, 1984); 'Becoming Visible: Black Lesbian Discussions' in *Feminist Review* (with Gail Lewis, Carmen Williams, Shaila Shah, 1984); *Challenging Imperial Feminism* (with Valerie Amos, 1984); *Through the Break: Women in Personal Crisis* (with Pearlie McNeil, Marie McShea, 1986); 'Gender, Race and Power' in *Multi-Racist Britain* (1988); *Lesbians Talk (Safer) Sex* (with Sue O'Sullivan, 1992); *Queer Looks: Perspectives on Lesbian and Gay Film and Video* (with Martha Gever, John Greyson, 1993); *Warrior Marks: Female Genital Mutilation and the Sexual Blinding of Women* (with Alice Walker, 1993).

s. Feminist Review (Autumn 1984); Bodleian Catalogue.

PATEL, Pragna (UK activist).

An active member of the SBS since 1982; founded the first black women's centre in West London; a founding member of WAF; studied law.

p. Charting the Journey (et al., 1988); *Against the Grain* (et al., SBS, 1990).

s. Grewal (1988).

PETTIT, Ann (UK peace activist) *b.* 1947.

Brought up in Surrey; accompanied her father on CND marches as a child; gained a BSc, 1968; part of a squatters' campaign in East London in the late 1960s; teacher; involved with the WLM; disillusioned with the WLM, became more interested in the ecology movement, moved to Dyfed in Wales; with others formed CANC; she conceived the idea of the 'Women for Life on Earth Peace March' to Greenham Common, 1981.

s. Liddington (1989).

PIZZEY, Erin (UK activist) *b.* 1939.

Educated at St Anthony's, Leweston Manor, Dorset; established the country's very first refuge for 'battered' women and their children to provide them with a place to recover from their ordeal and plan to rebuild their lives; opened in 1971, Chiswick Women's Aid in London was the start of a network of Women's Aid hostels throughout Britain and Ireland and a movement to tackle domestic violence;

through her work she brought the issue into the mainstream, however, she antago-
nized many in the Women's Aid network by her attempts at dominating the
network; her 1983 book claiming that many battered women sought violence as they
were addicted to it caused her final rift, resulting in public demonstrations against
what was seen as her betrayal of the feminist position on domestic violence.

p. Scream Quietly or the Neighbours Will Hear (1974): *Infernal Child* (autobiog.,
1978); *Prone to Violence* (1982); *Wild Child* (autobiog., 1996); twelve novels.

s. Campbell and Coote (1982); *Spare Rib*, Issue 127, February 1983; *Who's Who*,
1999.

REID, Elizabeth (Australian senator and international adviser/director) *b.* 1942.

Born in South Australia she took an LLB at the University of Adelaide before
becoming a lawyer; WEL activist; appointed as the first 'femocrat', the first ever
adviser on women's issues to a Prime Minister (Gough Whitlam) in the world,
1973; oversaw Australia's International Women's Year events, 1975; delegate leader
to the Mexico World International Women's Year conference, 1975; resigned as
PM's adviser because of the disabling effect of the controversy surrounding her
role, 1975; adviser to Princess Ashraf Pahlavi of Iran, 1975–7; founder and director
of the Asian and Pacific Centre for Women and Development, 1977–9; UN principal
officer for the World Conference of the Decade for Women, 1980; consultant on
women and development, Zaire, 1981; later, UN HIV and Development programme director; a Liberal, chosen to represent the ACT in the Senate, 1981, and
then elected in 1983; member of the Senate Legislative and General Purposes
Standing Committee for Education and the Arts, 1981–3; Department Government
Whip in the Senate, 1982–3; Opposition Whip in the Senate, 1987.

s. Bowker-Saur (1991); Caine (1998).

RICH, Adrienne (US poet and lesbian feminist theorist) *b.* 1929.

Born in Baltimore; attended Radcliffe College; originally known as a prize-
winning poet, her writing began to explore feminist themes from 1963 with
Snapshots; became involved in the civil rights movement in 1966; at the ceremony
for winning the 1974 National Book Award for poetry, she accepted it on behalf of the
other two women poets nominated, Audre Lorde (see entry) and Alice Walker (see
entry), and for all other women who had been silenced; her most noted contribution
to feminist theory was her concept of the lesbian continuum or the woman-identified
experience; involved in lesbian and gay rights campaigns; also had an academic
career teaching at City College, new York and Douglas College; joint editor of the
Sinister Wisdom journal.

p. A Change of World (1951); *The Diamond Cutters and Other Poems* (1955);
Snapshots of a Daughter-in-Law (1963); *Leaflets: Poems 1965–8* (1969); *The Will to
Change* (1971); *Diving in to the Wreck* (1973); *Of Woman Born: Motherhood as
Experience and Institution* (1976); *Dream of a Common Language: Poems 1974–7*
(1978); *On Lies, Secrets and Silence: Selected Prose, 1966–78* (1979); *Compulsory
Heterosexuality and Lesbian Existence* (1980); *A Wild Patience Has Taken Me This Far*
(1981); *Blood, Bread and Poetry: Selected Prose, 1979–86* (1986); *Your Native Land,
Your Life* (1986); *An Atlas of the Difficult World: Poems 1988–91* (1991).

s. Campbell and Coote (1982); Tuttle (1986); Buck (1994); Schneir (1995);
Cullen-DuPont (1996); Penguin (1996).

RICHARDSON, Josephine (Jo) (UK feminist MP) 1923–94.

Born in Newcastle upon Tyne; educated at Southend High School for Girls; left school at fifteen with no qualifications; started work as a short-hand typist, later secretary to Ian Mikardo, Labour MP, as a result became involved in left-wing politics; one of her main concerns was championing the rights of poor, working-class women; member Keep Left Group, Bevan Group, Secretary Tribune Group, 1948–78; Labour councillor for Hornsey; Chairperson Tribune Group 1978–9; Vice President CND; member MSF, APEX; LP MP for Barking 1974–94; member LP NEC, 1979–91; introduced the non-contributory Invalidity Pension Bill to end discrimination against women, 1981; fought for the concept of a Ministry for Women within a Labour government, opposition spokesperson on women's rights, 1983–92; sponsored a bill to abolish the co-habitation rule, 1975; introduced the Domestic Violence Bill as a PMB, 1976; fought off the anti-abortion Corrie Bill, 1979–80; piloted the Sex Equality Bill through its second reading, 1983; led opposition against Alton's anti-abortion bill, late 1980s; complained about the discrimination against women's groups by the Warnock Committee, 1984; sought to have abortion legislation extended to include Northern Ireland, introduced a motion in the Commons insisting that under-16 girls should still receive confidential contraception advice, spoke on the need for more women judges, campaigned for more rape crisis centres and a review of judicial procedure with regard to rape; helped defeat Ann Widdecombe's (Tory MP) anti-abortion Bill, 1989; died, prematurely, February 1994.

p. *A New Ministry for Women* (1991); *Practice Nurses and the Small Practice Project of City and East London FHSA: An Evaluation* (with Julie George, 1993).

s. *Guardian*, 15 November 1983, *Guardian*, 27 July 1988; Roth (1991); *Who's Who* (1994).

ROBERTS, Michele (UK poet and novelist) b. 1949.

Half-English, half-French; read English at Somerville College, Oxford; trained as a librarian; worked in Britain and abroad, worked as a computer clerk; involved in the WLM since 1971; poetry editor of *Spare Rib*, 1975–7 and of *City Limits*, 1981–3; influential on the development of contemporary poetry in the UK; co-founder with Sara Maitland (see entry) and Zoe Fairbairns (see entry) of the Feminist Writers' Group; Visiting Fellow of Creative Writing University of East Anglia.

p. *Cutlasses and Earrings* (ed. with Michelene Wandor, 1976); *A Piece of the Night* (1978); *Licking the Bed Clean* (1978); *Tales I Tell My Mother* (with Sara Maitland, Zoe Fairbairns, Michelene Wandor, 1978); *Smile, Smile, Smile, Smile* (1980); *Touch Papers* (with Judith Kazantis, Michelene Wandor, 1982); *The Visitation* (1983); *The Wild Girl* (1984); *The Mirror of the Mother: Selected Poems 1975–85* (1986); *The Book of Mrs Noah* (1987); *Psyche and the Hurricane* (1991); *Daughters of the House* (1993); *During Mother's Absence* (1993); *The Place of Imagination* (1994); *All the Selves I Was: New and Selected Poems* (1995); *Flesh and Blood* (1995); *God's House* (1996); *Impossible Saints* (1997); *Fair Exchange* (1999); *In the Red Kitchen* (1999).

s. Buck (1992); Virago (1993).

ROBINSON, Mary (Irish human rights lawyer and politician) *b.* 1944.

Gained BA, LLB from Trinity College, Dublin, LLM at Harvard Law School; called to the Irish Bar, 1967; Middle Temple, 1973; Reid Professor of Constitutional and Criminal Law, Trinity College, Dublin, 1969–75; supporter of the WLM; assisted in establishing WPA, 1970; attended some IWLM meetings in Mary Kenny's (see entry) flat; involved in trying to bring legal remedies about for women's rights in contraception and divorce; lectured on European Community Law, 1975–90; elected to Seanad Eireann as a Senator, 1969–89, worked as Chair Social Affairs Sub-Committee 1977–87, Legal Affairs Committee, 1987–9; repeatedly attempted to have a Bill passed to enable the Senate to allow advice and control of contraceptives; President Cherish, 1973–90; elected President of Ireland, 1990–97, distinguished her presidency by her specific encouragement and inclusion of women and women's groups in Ireland affording them a high profile in public life; Honorary Fellow Hertford College, Oxford 1993; became UN High Commissioner for Human Rights, 1997.

p. Intellectual Property: Papers from the ICEL Conference, April 1989 (1989); *Creating a European Economic Space: Legal Aspects of EC-EFTA Relations: Papers from the Dublin Conference, October 1989* (1990); *A Voice for Somalia* (1992); *Women and the Law in Ireland* (in Smyth, 1993); *Sustainable Development: But for Whom?* (1994); *Realizing Human Rights: 'Take Hold of It Boldly and Duly': The Romanus Lecture for 1997* (1998).

s. Rose (1975); Smyth (1993); Kenny (1997); *Who's Who*, 1999.

ROWBOTHAM, Sheila (UK socialist feminist historian) *b.* 1943.

An activist in the WLM since the 1960s, member of the WLW; one of the most influential and prolific theorists of the WLM in the UK; born in Leeds; educated at a Methodist school, graduated from St Hilda's College, Oxford (1961–4) and the University of London; taught in a comprehensive school, technical, FE colleges and with the WEA; her contribution to pioneering women's history has been especially important; in addition to her books, has a large body of work in journals, magazines and the press; editorial board of the radical paper, *Black Dwarf*; visiting university lecturer in Europe, the US and Canada; member of GLC Popular Planning Unit until 1986; Research Adviser of the UN University, currently, Research Fellow in the Sociology Department at the University of Manchester and involved with the International Centre for Labour History.

p. books – *Women, Resistance and Revolution* (1972); *Woman's Consciousness, Man's World* (1973); *Hidden From History: 300 Years of Women's Oppression and the Fight Against It* (1973); *Dutiful Daughters: Women Talk About Their Lives* (with J. McCrindle, 1977); *Socialism and the New Life: The Personal and Sexual Politics of Edward Carpenter and Havelock Ellis* (with Jeffrey Weeks, 1977); *A New World for Women: Stella Browne, Socialist Feminist* (1977); *Beyond the Fragments: Feminism and the Making of Socialism* (with L. Segal and H. Wainwright, 1979); *Dreams and Dilemmas: Collected Writings* (1983); *Friends of Alice Wheeldon* (1986); *The Past is Before Us: Feminism in Action Since the 1960s* (1989); *Women in Movement: Feminism and Social Action* (1992); *Homeworkers Worldwide* (1993); *Dignity and Daily Bread: New Forms of Economic Organization Among Poor Women* (ed. with Swasti Mitter, 1994); *Women Encounter Technology: Changing Patterns of Employment in the Third World* (ed. with S. Mitter, 1995); *A Century of Women: The History of Women in*

Britain and the United States (1997); *Threads Through Time: Writings on History and Autobiography* (1999); pamphlets – *Women's Liberation and the New Politics* (1969).
   s. Rowbotham (1972, 1973, 1989, 1992, 1997); Bodleian Catalogue.

RYAN, Edna (Australian trade union activist) 1904–97.
   Ryan was born in Ultimo, NSW; left school at 15 to become a local government clerk; a CP activist from 1927 working on welfare issues for women and children until expelled from the Party in 1931; actively involved as office holder in ALP from 1935; member LWCOC; WEA organizer, as part of the 1949 summer school, she initiated a mother and children school; elected to Fairfield Council, Sydney, 1956–65; first woman President of the MEU, 1962; trained women trade unionists; campaigned for equal pay and succeeded in extending existing legislation for teachers to women clerical workers; the first woman President of the Local Government Officers' Association, 1965–74; after retiring from local government she became active in the WEL from 1973 working on various equal pay and allied campaigns; her publications resulted in her becoming an honorary associate of the Industrial Relations Department of Sydney University from 1987; from 1991 she worked on research relating to superannuation and wage bargaining for women in Canberra; she refused the Order of Australia award.
   p. Gentle Invaders: Australian Women in the Workforce 1788–1974 (with Anne Conlon, 1975); *Two Thirds of a Man* (1984).
   s. Arnold and Morris (1994); Caine (1998).

RYAN, Susan (Australian Senator) *b.* 1942.
   Born in Sydney; gained a BA and MA from Sydney University; member ALP; whilst in New York, inspired by the American WLM; worked on education and employment in the Women's Movement; she worked as a school teacher then a tutor at the Canberra College of Advanced Education; founding member of the WEL, Canberra, before becoming a member of the ACT legislative assembly, 1974–5; Education Officer at the Secretariat for International Women's Year, 1975; member LP Federal Policy Committee on Women, 1976; spokesperson on Women's Affairs, 1979–83; first woman cabinet minister in a federal ALP; Minister for Education, 1983–7 and Minister assisting the Prime Minister on the Status of Women, 1983–8; Special Minister of State, 1987–8 involved in the passing of the Sex Discrimination and Affirmative Action Acts; resigned in 1988; involved in publishing and chief executive of the Association of Superannuation Funds.
   s. Arnold and Morris (1994); Caine (1998).

SANDLER, Bernice (US women's rights activist).
   Born in New York, gained a BA at Brooklyn College, 1948, an MA from CCNY, 1950 and an EdD in 1969; worked largely as a teacher; head of the Action Committee for Federal Contract Compliance with the Women's Equity Action League, 1970–71; deputy director Women's Action programme, 1971; director of the project on status and education of the Women's Association of American Colleges, 1971–91; Senior Associate Centre for Women Policy Studies, 1991–4; senior scholar in residence, National Association Women in Education, Washington, from 1994.
   p. Chilly Climate for Women reports.
   s. Who's Who in America (1998).

SARACHILD, Kathie, a.k.a. Kathie Amatniek (US radical feminist).

One of the founders of the Redstockings; as Amatneik, she gave the 'Funeral Oration for Traditional Womanhood' at a NYRW demonstration at Arlington Cemetary during an anti-war demonstration in 1968; the maxim, Sisterhood is Powerful was originated by her for a pamphlet written for this demonstration; Editor of *Woman's World*.

p. 'Feminist Consciousness Raising and "Organizing"' in *Voices From Women's Liberation* (1970); 'Funeral Oration for Traditional Womanhood' in *Voices From Women's Liberation* (1970); 'Consciousness-Raising: A Radical Weapon' in *Feminist Revolution* (1973); 'Psychological Terrorism' in *Feminist Revolution* (1974); 'The Power of History' in *Feminist Revolution* (1975); 'Who are We? The Redstockings' Position on Names' in *Feminist Revolution* (1975).

s. Tanner (1970); *Spare Rib* (no 79, February 1979); Kramarae and Treichler (1985); Tuttle (1986); Cullen-DuPont (1996).

SCAFE, Suzanne (UK black community education) *b.* 1954.

Born in Jamaica; English teacher in Jamaica and London; taught and co-ordinated a black supplementary school in Brixton, South London; member of the Committee of Women for Progress in Jamaica; member of the Brixton Black Women's Group; Lecturer at Brixton College for Further Education, 1989.

p. *The Heart of the Race: Black Women's Lives in Britain* (1985); *Teaching Black Literature* (1989).

s. above publications.

SEGAL, Lynne (Australian activist and academic).

Born in Sydney; PhD on theories and practices of experimental psychology, Sydney University; came to live in Islington, London 1972; lecturer Middlesex Polytechnic; involved in the WLM in London, in the *Red Rag* collective, establishment of an early Women's Centre and women's health group, York Way, Holloway Prison Support Group, many other welfare and education campaigns; LP member, Socialist Society; member *Feminist Review* collective; member Feminist Anthology Collective; currently Professor of Psychology and Gender, Birkbeck College, University of London.

p. *Beyond the Fragments: Feminism and the Making of Socialism* (with Sheila Rowbotham, Hilary Wainwright, 1980); *What is to be Done about the Family?* (ed. 1983); *Is the Future Female? Troubled Thoughts on Contemporary Feminism* (1987); *Straight Sex: The Politics of Pleasure* (1994); *New Sexual Agendas* (1997); *Why Feminism? Gender, Psychology, Politics* (1999).

s. *Red Rag*, no 1, 1973; Segal (1987).

SLOAN, Margaret (US black feminist activist).

At *Ms.* Magazine, a contributing editor; Sloan was the first Chair of the NBFO.

p. 'Black Feminism: A New Mandate' in *Ms.* (1974).

s. Schneir (1995).

SMITH, Barbara (US black activist).

Began working as an activist in the early 1970s; one of the founder members of the CRC.

p. Home Girls: A Black Feminist Anthology (ed. 1983).

s. Schneir (1995).

SMYTH, Ailbhe (Irish activist and academic).

Involved in the Irish WLM from its inception particularly concerned with abortion and reproductive rights campaigns, citizenship and women's education; currently Director of the WERRC, University College, Dublin co-ordinating the BA, MA and Adult Education Women's Studies; co-editor of *Women's Studies International Forum*.

p. Feminism in Ireland (1988); *Wildish Things: An Anthology of New Irish Women's Writing* (1989); *The Abortion Papers* (1992); *Irish Women's Studies Reader* (ed. 1993).

s. Ailbhe (1993).

SPENDER, Dale (Australian feminist academic and writer) *b.* 1943.

Born in Newcastle, NSW; gained BA DipEd from Sydney University, MA from University NSW, a LittB from University of NE; teacher at Meadowbank Boys' High School, where 'I became a feminist' (www autobiog.), then Dapto High School; MA University of NSW (Wollongong) in Australian literature and sociology and a LittB University of New England; the only woman education staff member at James Cook University; involved in the Townsville branch of the WEL; came to Britain in 1975, PhD at London University; lecturer at University of London, 1976–85; activist in women's groups in the UK; executive member Fawcett Society (1983–7); returned to Australia in the late 1980s, honorary fellow University of Queensland; editor of the *Women's Studies International Forum* journal; series editor Penguin Australian Women's Library; involved in starting Women's International Knowledge: Encyclopaedia and Database; highly influential for her original work on the sexism inherent in language use and the domination of men in knowledge production leading to her work on the retrieval of the work and ideas of women writers throughout history.

p. The Spitting Image (with Garth Boomer, 1976); *Man Made Language* (1980); *Learning to Lose* (ed. 1980); *Men's Studies Modified: The Impact of Feminism on the Academic Disciplines* (1981); *Invisible Women: The Schooling Scandal* (1982); *Women of Ideas and What Men Have Done to Them* (1982); *Feminist Theorists* (1983); *There's Always Been a Women's Movement this Century* (1983); *Time & Tide Wait for No Man* (1984); *Scribbling Sisters* (with Lynne Spender, 1984); *For the Record: The Making and Meaning of Feminist Knowledge* (1985); *How the Vote was Won and Other Suffragette Plays* (with Carole Hayman, 1985); *Mothers of the Novel: 100 Good Women Writers Before Jane Austen* (1986); *Reflecting Men at Twice Their Natural Size* (1987); *The Education Papers* (1987); *Writing a New World: Two Centuries of Australian Women's Writing* (1988); *Penguin Anthology of Australian Women's Writing* (1988); *Anthology of British Women Writers* (with Janet Todd, 1989); *The Writing or the Sex? Or, Why You Don't Have To Read Women's Writing To know It's No Good* (1989); *Heroines: A Contemporary Anthology of Australian Women Writers* (1991); *The Diary of Elizabeth Pepys* (1991); *Life Lines: Australian Women's Letters and Diaries 1788–1840* (1992); *Living by the Pen: Early British Women Writers* (1992); *The Knowledge Explosion: Generations of Feminist Scholarship* (ed. Cheris Kramarae, 1992); *Weddings and Wives* (1994); *Nattering on the Net: Women, Power and Cyberspace* (1995).

s. Spender (1984); Caine (1998); Who's Who in Australia (2000); www.espc.com.au/dspender/intro/intro.html and intro/books.html.

STEINEM, Gloria (US feminist activist and editor) *b.* 1934.

Graduated with a degree in government from Smith College, 1956 and pursued a career in journalism; in 1968 she went to a Redstockings meeting and subsequently joined the WLM; regarded by some as one of the key activists in the US and by others as a media feminist; toured the US for many years with black women speakers (Dorothy Pitman Hughes, Florynce Kennedy and Margaret Sloan) in an attempt to encourage greater racial diversity in the WLM; assisted Betty Friedan (see entry) with the Women's Strike for Equality, 1970; in 1972, she founded *Ms.* Magazine and was its Editor, financial crises have caused it to close, be sold and re-open several times since; co-founder of the WAA; founding member of the CLUW; member of the NWPC NAC.

p. Outrageous Acts and Everyday Rebellions (1983); *Marilyn: Norma Jeane* (1986); *Revolution from Within: A Book of Self-Esteem* (1992); *Moving Beyond Words* (1994).

s. Schneir (1995); Cullen-DuPont (1996).

STOTT, Mary (UK journalist) *b.* 1907.

Born in the Midlands; proof reader and reporter *Leicester Mail*, 1924; women's editor *Leicester Mail*, 1926; women's editor *Bolton Evening News*; discrimination she suffered as a woman in journalism ignited her interest in feminism; member Bolton WCA; thrilled to be one of the women who voted for the first time in the general election of 1928, voting for the LP she wore a red dress; Editor of women's and children's publications, Co-operative Press, Manchester, 1933–45; during WW2 worked on the *Co-operative News* as leader writer, refused the editorship because of her gender, left the paper; discrimination continued at the *Manchester Evening News* where as the news sub-editor she was refused promotion, left in 1950; became known for her Editorship of the *Guardian* women's page, especially for the number of action groups often instigated by its articles and resulting correspondence, 1957–72; 'recruited' into the Women in Media campaign by Jill Tweedie (see entry); active member of the FS and many other equality campaigning groups.

p. Forgetting's No Excuse (1975); *Organization Woman: the Story of the National Union of Townswomen's Guilds* (1978); *Ageing for Beginners* (1981); *Before I Go... Reflections on my Life and Times* (1985); *Women Talking, An Anthology from the Guardian's Women's Page 1922–53 and 1957–71* (ed. 1987).

s. Guardian, 20 March, 23 March 1985; *Everywoman*, no 4, June 1985; *Bolton Evening News*, 21 March 1987, 21 March 1987; *Guardian*, 8 June 1987.

SYKES, Roberta (Bobbi) (Australian writer and Aboriginal rights activist) *b.* 1943.

Sykes was born in Queensland; leaving school at 14 she studied secretarial skills, briefly trained as a nurse and worked in factories; involved in Aboriginal activism from the early 1970s, first Executive Secretary of the Aboriginal Tent Embassy, held in the grounds of Parliament House, Canberra, 1972; studied education at Harvard and took her PhD, 1984; founded the Black Women's Action in Education Foundation to enable indigenous Australian women to attend Harvard University in the USA; worked for the rights of Aboriginal women although she did not participate in the Women's Movement believing it to be only engaged in white women's issues; winner of the Australian Human Rights medal, 1994; *Snake Cradle* won the Age Book of the Year, 1997.

p. Black Power in Australia (with Neville Bonner, 1975), *Love Poems and Other Revolutionary Actions* (1979); *Incentive, Achievement and Community* (1986); *Black Majority* (1989); *Murawina: Australian Women of High Achievement* (1994); *Snake Cradle* (1997).

s. Buck (1992); Arnold and Morris (1994); *Who's Who of Australia* (2000).

TWEEDIE, Jill (UK journalist) 1936–93.

Born in Cairo; educated at eight girls schools and Le Chateau du Lac finishing school for one year; became a copywriter, 1953; went to live in Canada, copywriting and radio work, Montreal, 1953–4; freelancer in London, 1965; columnist, *Daily Sketch*, 1967; assistant women's page editor, *Sunday Telegraph*, 1968–9; her prominence as a feminist journalist and supporter of the WLM emerged in her writing as a columnist for the *Guardian* from 1969–88; also a TV and radio broadcaster, scriptwriter; voted Woman Journalist of the Year, 1971; Granada TV Award, 1972; died from motor neurone disease.

p. In the Name of Love (1979); *It's Only Me* (1980); *Letters of a Fainthearted Feminist* (1982); *More from Martha* (1983); *Bliss* (1984); *Internal Affairs* (1986); *Eating Children: Young Dreams and Early Nightmares* (autobiog., 1993).

s. Tweedie (1993); *Who's Who* (1993); *The Annual Obituary 1993* (1994).

WAINWRIGHT, Hilary (UK academic).

Socialist feminist involved in the WLM from its origin; member of the GLC's Economic Policy Group, working with trade unionists and community groups on employment initiatives.

p. The Workers Report on Vickers; *The Lucas Plan: A New Trade Unionism in the Making?*; *Beyond the Fragments* (with Sheila Rowbotham, Lynne Segal, 1979).

s. Bodleian Catalogue.

WALKER, Alice (US author and activist) *b.* 1944.

Born in Georgia; educated at Spelman College, Atlanta and Sarah Lawrence College, New York; poet, novelist, short-story and essay writer, who won the Pulitzer Prize for her novel, *The Color Purple*, but has also been awarded a vast number of literary prizes and awards for her writing; after graduating she became involved in the Civil Rights Movement in the 1960s; much of her work addresses issues relating to black women's oppression and the term 'womanist' is recognized as being originated by Walker; became a contributing Editor to *Ms.* Magazine, from 1974 and *Freedomways*, a black freedom movement journal; teacher of women's and black studies; her latest work deals with FGM.

p. Once (1968); *The Third Life of Grange Copeland* (1970); *Revolutionary Petunias and other Poems* (1973); *In Love and Trouble: Stories of Black Women* (1973); *The Life of Thomas Lodge* (1974); *Langston Hughes: American Poet* (1973); *Meridian* (1976); *Goodnight, Willie Lee, I'll See You in the Morning* (1976); *I Live Myself When I'm Laughing… and then Again When I am Looking Mean and Impressive, a Zora Neale Hurston Reader* (ed. 1979); *You Can't Keep a Good Woman Down* (1981); *The Color Purple* (1982); *In Search of Our Mothers' Gardens: Womanist Prose* (1983); *Horses Make a Landscape*

More Beautiful (1984); *Possessing the Secret of Joy* (1992); *Warrior Marks: Female Genital Mutilation and the Sexual Blinding of Women* (with Pratibha Parmer, 1993).
s. Evans (1984); Cullen-DuPont (1996).

WALLACE, Michele (US black feminist activist, writer and teacher) *b.* 1952.
Attended Howard University, 1969; became a Black feminist at 18; spent some time with Barbara Ann Teer's New Age National Black Theatre; founded WSABL, c.1970; took a BA in English; had an essay published by Kathie Sarachild (see entry); her first book was a controversial attack on the sexism inherent in the Black Power movement; founding member of the NBFO, 1974; organizer of the Sojourner Truth festival of the Arts, 1976; wrote for *Village Voice*; became the media's representative black woman feminist after the publication of her second book; lamented the fact that despite much hard work, by the mid-1970s there was still no separate, definable black Women's Movement; teacher of Black Studies, Creative Literature and English; Laurie New Jersey Chair of Women's Studies at Douglas College, 1996–7; Associate Professor of English, CCNY and CUNY Graduate Centre; doctoral thesis on *A Genealogy of Race in American Cinema 1889–1919* in the late 1990s.
p. Black Women and White Women (an essay, 1971); 'On the National Black Feminist Organization' in *Feminist Revolution* (1975); *Black Macho and the Myth of the Superwoman* (1978, new edition, 1990); *Invisible Blues* (1990); *Black Popular Culture* (1992); '*To Hell and Back: On the Road with Black Feminism in the 1960s and 1970s*' in *DuPlessis* (1998).
s. Tuttle (1986); Schneir (1995); DuPlessis (1998).

WANDOR, Michelene (UK playwright) *b.* 1940.
Born in London; gained an English degree from Newnham College, Cambridge; involved in the WLM since the 1960s; poetry editor and theatre critic for *Time Out* magazine since 1971; articles and reviews for *Spare Rib*; largely known for her plays, also poetry, short stories; her contribution towards the establishment of a feminist theatre has been made not only through her writing but also in her work to promote women's theatre groups and in her critiques of the entrenched misogyny of the British theatre.
p. The Day After Yesterday (1972); *The Body Politic: Writings from the WLM in Britain 1969–72* (ed. 1972); *Spilt Milk* (1973); *To Die Among Friends* (1974); *Sink Songs: Feminist Plays* (with Dinah Brooke, 1975); *Cutlasses and Earrings* (ed. with Michele Roberts, 1976); *Care and Control* (1977); *Floorshow* (with Caryl Churchill, Bryony Lavery, 1977); *Aid Thy Neighbour* (1978); *Correspondence* (1979); *Strike While the Iron is Hot: Three Plays on Sexual Politics* (1980); *Carry On, Understudies* (1981); *Touch Papers* (with Judith Kazantzis, 1982); *Guests in the Body* (1986); *Look Back in Gender* (1987); *Arky Types* (with Sara Maitland); *Upbeat* (1988); *Once a Feminist* (1990).
s. Tuttle (1986); Buck (1992).

WILLIS, Ellen (US radical feminist activist and journalist).
Co-founder of the first WLM group in New York, NYRW and subsequently involved in forming the Redstockings; wrote for the *New Yorker* and *Rolling Stone*; senior editor and columnist at *Village Voice*; writer on culture and politics; Associate Professor of Journalism, New York University from 1992.

p. Up From Radicalism; Beginning to See the Light: Sex, Hope and Rock-and-Roll (1981–1993); 'Toward a Feminist Sexual Revolution' in *Social Text*, vol. 7, Fall, no 3 (1982); 'Feminism, Moralism and Pornography' in *Desire: The Politics of Sexuality* (A. Snitow et al., 1984).

s. Kramarae and Treichler (1985); Willis (1993); Cullen-DuPont (1996).

WILSON, Amrit (UK activist, writer, academic) *b.* 1941.

Born in Calcutta; lived in Bengal and Northern India, came to Britain as a student, 1961; her first profession was as a research chemist; freelance journalist interested in black women's experiences and women's rights, writing for the *Guardian*, *TES*, *Spare Rib*, *New Society* from 1974; editor of War on Want's journal, *Poverty & Power*; her first book was a milestone in exploring the diversity of women's lives and discrimination in the UK; currently Senior Lecturer in Women's Studies/South East Asian Studies at the University of Luton.

p. Finding a Voice: Asian Women in Britain (1978); *But My Cows Aren't Going to England: A Study in How Families are Divided* (with Lal Sushma, 1986); *The Challenge Road: Women and the Eritrean Revolution* (1991); *US Foreign Policy and Revolution: The Creation of Tanzania* (1989).

WILSON, Elizabeth (UK academic) *b.* 1936.

Born in Devon; attended St Paul's Girls' School, St Anne's College, Oxford, read English; became a publisher's secretary in London, and later a psychiatric social worker; active in the WLM, GLF and left-wing politics from 1970; member editorial board of the *Feminist Review*; lecturer at the Polytechnic of North London.

p. Women and the Welfare State (1977); *Only Halfway to Paradise: Women in Britain 1945–68* (1980); *Mirror Writing: An Autobiography* (1982); *Adorned in Dreams: Fashion and Modernity* (1985); *Hidden Agendas: Theory, Politics and Experiences in the Women's Movement* (with Angela Weir, 1986); *Prisms of Glass* (1986); *Hallucinations: Life in the Post Modern City* (1988); *Through the Looking Glass: A History of Dress from 1860 to the Present Day* (1989); *The Sphinx in the City: Urban Life, the Control of Disorder and Women* (1991); *Chic Thrills: A Fashion Reader* (with Juliet Ash, 1992); *Poisoned Hearts* (1995).

s. Feminist Review Reader (1987); Wilson (1982).

WISE, Audrey (UK socialist feminist Trade Unionist and MP) *b.* 1935.

Educated at Rutherford High School; trained as a shorthand typist; spoke as a representative from USDAW at the first NWLC, 1970; Labour MP Coventry South West, 1974–9; contested Woolwich, 1983; member LP NEC 1982–7; LP MP Preston from 1987; President USDAW, 1991–7; member War on Want, CND, Labour Action for Peace, Nicaraguan Solidarity, Soil Association; lists women as a special interest.

p. Women and the Struggle for Workers' Control (1973); *Eyewitness in Revolutionary Portugal* (1975).

s. Campbell and Coote (1982); *Who's Who* (1999).

ORGANIZATIONS

ACAC – Action Campaign for Abortion and Contraception, 1971 (UK)
Preliminary discussions for this group were held on the 8 November 1970 at the WNCC's weekend meeting. Subsequently, a campaign committee was formed in London. It was to be a single-issue, militant group.

Aims: 'To involve the millions of women who are affected by this question, particularly women of the working-class. To obtain a totally free contraceptive and abortion service under the NHS.'

s. *Women's Struggle*, vol. 1, no 4, 1971.

AIM – Action, Information, Motivation, 1972 (Ireland)
Frustrated with the endless debates and the extreme left-wing positions of the IWLM, Nuala Fennell (see entry) left the IWLM and formed AIM. Fennell wanted to achieve practical improvements for working women in Ireland whose lives needed changing. This pressure group directed its efforts at legislative reform concerned with the family and marital breakdown. It was reformist, rather than revolutionary. The Dublin AIM group formed the Irish Women's Aid Committee and opened the first hostel for 'battered' wives in Ireland.

p. *Education is Everybody's Business* (1979); *Modern Marriage: A Fresh Approach* (1983).

s. Rose (1975); Smyth (1993); Mahon (1996).

AWWW – Asian Women Writers' Workshop, 1984 (UK)
Formed in London with the intention of supporting new Asian women writers who were working in seclusion, in terms of their gender, the writing process and their cultural isolation. All the members' writing was produced as part of a workshop process where work is read and discussed by all the members.

p. *Right of Way: Prose and Poetry from the AWWW* (1988).

s. AWWW (1988).

BBWC – Brixton Black Women's Centre (UK)
Its aim was to assist and aid black women in that community. It did this in many practical ways through welfare rights information, a referral service, health group, making meeting space available, open days analysing black women's life and oppressions, children's projects in the school holidays and library provision.

s. *Feminist Review*, no 17, July 1984.

BWC – Belfast Women's Collective, 1977–80 (UK)
Formed after the disbanding of the Socialist Women's Group; broad-based coalition of women; had their own publication, *Women's Action*; women from the Collective became involved in other activities such as women's studies classes, Women in Media group, Action on Debt campaign, Women's Law and Research Group, Northern Ireland Abortion Campaign, Workers' Research Unit; these groups overtook the Collective's action and it was wound up in 1980.
    s. Feminist Anthology Collective (1981).

CHERISH, c.1972 (Ireland)
A self-help pressure group established by single-mothers. '…from the outset radical and outspoken, no doubt because the experience it set out to deal with had for so long been denied as a reality in women's lives in Ireland'.
    p. Singled Out (1983).
    s. Smyth (1993).

CLUW – Coalition of Labour Union Women, 1974 (US)
Started in Chicago principally by Dorothy Haener, Edith Van Horne and Olga Mader, United Auto Workers members, and Addie Wyatt from the Meatcutters Union.
    Aims:
1. Increase affirmative action on the job and women's participation in their unions at every level.
2. Work for passage of legislation important to women workers.
3. Encourage women's involvement in the political process, including election to office.
4. Organize the millions of unorganized women workers in this country, without which the labour movement cannot grow.
    s. Cullen-DuPont (1996).

COW – Cinema of Women, 1979 (UK)
Distribution collective for feminist film and video in order to challenge the traditional distribution network which did not enable feminist films to be seen. Also as part of the concept of WLM to produce and distribute work within a feminist-centred environment.
    s. Tuttle (1986).

CRC – Combahee River Collective, 1974 (US)
It began in Boston, taking its name from one of the raids to free slaves in 1863 carried out by the escaped slave, Harriet Tubman (suffragist, freedom-fighter); its members had previously worked in the Civil Rights Movement, the New Left and various women's groups; during the 1970s, it organized seven networking retreats for black feminists; in its famous *Statement* it declared it was 'actively committed to struggling against racial, sexual, heterosexual, and class oppression'.
    p. 'The Combahee River Collective Statement' in *The Vintage Book of Feminism* (1995).
    s. Schneir (1995); Cullen-DuPont (1996).

CRG – Consciousness-Raising Groups
A concept first introduced in America by the group NYRW, in the late 1960s, this method became a distinguishing feature of the WLM. In the initial stages of women's participation in the WLM, small women-only groups would meet together in their community. Women coming together to discuss their lives as women, without men, was a first 'revolutionary' act. CRGs would share and discuss their feelings, experiences and perceptions about being a woman in that place and time. This collective sharing was a means of exploring, learning and understanding in order to develop a feminist consciousness of how 'the personal is political'. This was a first step to political activity.

CSW – Council for the Status of Women, 1972 (Ireland)
Formed as a watchdog to guarantee the implementation of the recommendations of the Interim Report of the National Commission on the Status of Women (Beere Report, named after Dr Thekla Beere, only woman secretary of a civil service department, Secretary of Dept of Transport and Power) to ensure the realization of legal reform. It intended to function as a co-ordinating agency to which women's groups would affiliate. In October women from the IHA wrote to the press inviting other women's groups to come together and form the CSW.
  Aims:
  1. The implementation of the Beere report, de jure and de facto.
  2. To address discrimination cases as they emerged.
  3. To educate the public for women's role as equal citizens, ensuring their civil and political rights and to tackle societal prejudice against women.
    p. Irish Women Speak Out: A Plan of Action from the National Women's Forum (1981); *Women at Home: A Report on Nationwide Get-Togethers of Women* (nd); *Women in Rural Ireland: A Report of Get-Togethers Held in 1982* (1982).
    s. Tweedy (1992).

CWG – Coleraine Women's Group, 1974 (Ireland)
Initiated by women at the University campus as a CRG, it developed into a campaigning group as women from a housing estate became involved. It campaigned for the extension of British sex discrimination legislation to include NI. A petition, protest telegrams were sent to Westminster, demanding inclusion. A successful campaign brought the Sex Discrimination Order for NI in 1976. Focused on abortion, battered women, rape, maintenance payments to divorced and separated women, concentrating on legislative improvements. In 1977 CWG became Coleraine Women's Aid.
    s. Evason (1991).

ECP – English Collective of Prostitutes, 1975 (UK)
Started by Selma James (see entry) and based in the King's Cross Women's Centre. Its aim as a pressure group was to recognize prostitution as an employment where women's needs, such as special health care, must be addressed. It was giving visibility to women that society ignored.
    p. For Prostitutes, Against Prostitution (1975); *A–Z for Working Girls: A Guide to the Rules of the Game* (nd); 'Letter to Sir Michael Havers, the Attorney-General, 13 April 1981' in *Kanter, Hannah et al.* (eds).

EOC – Equal Opportunity Commission, 1975 (UK)
A government body established by the SDA :
1. To work work towards the elimination of discrimination.
2. To promote equality of opportunity between men and women generally.
3. To keep under review the EPA and the SDA and to suggest amendments.
The EOC supports test cases on discrimination issues taken to law.
Produces leaflets, reports, statistics.
s. Cowley (nd c.1986).

EEOC – Equal Employment Opportunity Commission, 1972 (US)
A government body whose remit is to enforce the battery of discrimination legislation on the statute book.
Aims: 'To seek full and effective relief for each and every victim of employment discrimination, whether sought in court or in conciliation agreements before litigation, and to provide remedies designed to correct the discrimination and prevent its recurrence.'
However, its achievements with regard to those cases dealing with sex discrimination has been poor and the delays in dealing with cases, enormous.
s. Cullen-DuPont (1996).

FAWCETT SOCIETY (see Part 1 for development) (UK)
The Society stands for equal rights and responsibilities between men and women as citizens, the removal of all inequalities and discrimination based on sex in law, practice and custom and the promotion of equal opportunities in all spheres.
p. Women's Report.
s. Cowley (nd c.1986).

THE FEMINISTS, 1968–early 1970s (US)
Originally known as the October 17 Movement to mark the day the three founders walked out of a NOW meeting. Became an influential radical New York City group. There were no leaders, but Ti-Grace Atkinson (see entry) came to be regarded by the media as such and was castigated by the group for this 'star' behaviour, she left in 1970. They advocated celibacy and predicted that eventually babies would be produced in test-tubes. Dedicated to challenging class and power structures they aimed:
To develop a theoretical analysis of the situation of women.
To devise a new, non-oppressive organizational structure.
There were stringent rules:
1. Only one third of the membership was allowed to live with a man.
2. Alliances with other groups or individuals was discouraged.
3. Attendance at meetings was compulsory.
Their influence dwindled and they became a small core group.
s. Carden (1974); Freeman (1975); Tuttle (1986).

FEMINIST BOOKS, 1974 (UK)
An independent publishing house created by four women. It was run as a non-profit making concern, carrying out all the processes themselves. Any profits would be used to publish further WLM writing. They offered authors control over their work

by participating in the production and distribution of their work, as well as being able to join the editorial board. Their first publication was Lee Comer's *Wedlocked Women*.

s. *Red Rag*, no 7; Comer (1974).

FEMINIST REVIEW, 1979 (UK)

After a series of 'open' meetings, a collective of nineteen women formed to produce a socialist feminist journal. 'All of us seek to bring our feminism into our various job experiences.' This collective was supplemented by other women who were unable to join the collective.

Aims:

To develop the theory of WL and debate the political perspectives and strategy of the Movement.

To be a forum for work in progress and current research and debates in Women's Studies.

'We hope that *Feminist Review* will act as a vehicle to unite research and theory with political practice.'

s. *Feminist Review*, no 1, 1979.

GLCWC – Greater London Council Women's Committee, 1982–6 (UK)

It was the first Women's Committee to be established in Britain. Its aim was to ensure equal opportunities practice throughout the GLC and an improvement in service provision for the women of London as well as supporting and grant-aiding unprecedented development of women's services and projects, 500 projects with £11 million in 1985–6. It was particularly active in promoting social justice opportunities for black, disabled, lesbian and working class women who suffered a greater level of discimination in their domestic and public lives. The Committee's work was facilitated through numerous specialist sub-committees with co-opted members from women's interest groups throughout the GLC area. The Chairperson of the WC was Valerie Wise, daughter of the LP MP, Audrey Wise (see entry). The GLC Women's Bulletin was launched in July 1982 as a vehicle for recording and disseminating the Committee's work to London's women. Its motto, *GLC – Working for Women*. The Committee was dissolved when the Tory Prime Minister, Margaret Thatcher abolished the GLC.

p. *GLC Women's Bulletin*, July 1982–6; *The London Women's Handbook* (1986).

s. Personal knowledge; *GLC Women's Bulletin*, July 1982.

GREENHAM WOMEN, 1981 (UK)

Ann Pettit, Lynne Whittemore, Angela Phillips and Carmen Kutler organized a 'Women for Life on Earth Peace March 1981' when 40 women, four men and three children set off on 27 August 1981 to walk from Cardiff in South Wales to the American cruise missile base at Newbury, Berkshire. When they arrived in early September four of the women chained themselves to the fence, a vigil began, and the peace camp was initiated. Greenham Women became a massed organization with a London office and camps at all gates of the base sustained by donations of money and resources by an endless stream of visitors and supporters.

s. Liddington (1989).

IWLM – Irish Women's Liberation Movement, 1970 (Ireland)
Originated with a group of women, mostly journalists, who started meeting at
Margaret Gaj's resturant in Dublin to discuss their discontents, which developed
into CRG meetings As many of the protagonists were journalists, such as Mary
Kenny (see entry), Nell McCafferty (see entry), Nuala Fennell (see entry), Mary
Maher (see entry), they were able to gain publicity for the Movement. *The Late Late
Show* dedicated a programme to the IWLM in March 1971, as a result, a thousand
women attended a mass meeting a few weeks later. Earlier in 1971 the group had
published their aims in a manifesto, *Chains or Change? The Civil Wrongs of Irish
Women*:

1. One family, one house.
2. Equal rights in the law.
3. Equal pay now; removal of the marriage bar.
4. Justice for widows, deserted wives, unmarried mothers.
5. Equal educational opportunities.
6. Contraception – a human right.

After a period of demonstrations, campaigns and direct action, the Movement
'fissured' (Kenny 1997) into groups such as Irishwomen United, the Women's
Political Association, AIM.
   s. Smyth (1993); Tweedy (1992); Kenny (1997).

IU – Irishwomen United, 1975 (Ireland)
A more radical group evolving in the wake of the IWLM. This was a coalition of
women from several other groups such as Revolutionary Struggle, People's
Democracy, the Movement for a Socialist Republic and lesbian activists- largely
professional and trade union women. It produced its own paper, *Banshee*. Its
demands were:

1. The removal of all legal and bureaucratic obstacles to equality.
2. Free legal contraception.
3. The recognition of motherhood and parenthood as a social function with
   special provisions.
4. Equality in education – state-financed, secular, co-educational schools with
   full community control at all levels.
5. The male rate for the job where men and women are working together.
6. State provision of funds and premises for the establishment of women's
   centres in major population areas to be controlled by the women themsleves.
7. The right of all women to a self-determined sexuality.
   s. Smyth (1993).

LEEDS REVOLUTIONARY FEMINISTS (UK)
Produced a controversial conference paper, *Political Lesbianism: The Case Against
Heterosexuality*, claiming that heterosexual women could not be true feminists as they
were conjoining with the enemy; it introduced the concept of political lesbianism as
the way forward for the WLM; this accusation marked one of the divisive moments
of the WLM, first published in 1979 in *WIRES 81*; the full debate was published
as *Love Your Enemy? The Debate Between Heterosexual Feminism and Political
Lesbianism* (1981).

LIL – Liberation for Irish Lesbians, 1978 (Ireland)
Lesbianism as an issue in the Movement first came under discussion in the IU's journal, *Banshee*, no 3; lesbian feminists were members of IU but the issue was not publicly debated until they formed their own group; the first Women's Conference on Lesbianism was held in Dublin on 1 May 1978 with 81 participants from Ireland and abroad, at a follow-up meeting in September LIL was formed and it campaigned for a Women's Centre; when it was given space in the gay men's centre in Fownes Street, Dublin LIL established a Lesbian Line; LIL worked with feminist IWLM women for a Women's Centre, opened 1982; as part of the Dublin Lesbian and Gay Collective, campaigned against police harassment, 1982; LIL was affiliated to the Anti-Amendment campaign to defend the Abortion Referendum.
    p. Out for Ourselves (1986).
    s. Women's Studies International Forum, vol. 11, no 4, 1988; Smyth (1993).

LONDON RAPE CRISIS CENTRE, 1975 (UK)
The initial meeting to discuss action on rape was held in November 1974 with approximately 40 women; rented a house from the Department of the Environment, secured advance funding and moved into the Centre in November 1975.
    Aims:
1. To provide emergency legal, medical and emotional counselling by having a 24–hour phone service.
2. To provide a supportive, calm and sympathetic environment for the woman.
3. To train women to be able to cope with the problems of women who have been raped.
4. To set up a co-ordinated group of contacts in different geographical areas who would be willing to personally meet and counsel women and accompany them to hospital/police/doctor and court.
5. To research the pattern and incidence of rape locally and nationally.
6. To publish information and educational material to destroy the current myths about rape.
7. To liaise with those community services which come into contact with women who have been raped.

    s. Feminist Anthology Collective (1981).

NAC – National Abortion Campaign, 1975 (UK)
Originally established as a pressure group to coordinate the campaign against the James White Abortion Amendment Bill. It resulted from 800 women lobbying Parliament on 7 February. It was organized as a national federation of local groups campaigning for 'Abortion – A Woman's Right to Choose'. In the face of continuing threats to women's right to choose, the group continued:
    To ensure that all women can choose whether or not to continue with a pregnancy.
    To ensure that all women who need abortions can get them on the NHS.
    s. Red Rag, no 9, June 1975; Cowley (nd c.1986).

NBFO – National Black Feminist Organization, 1973–c.1978 (US)
After a black women's gathering in May 1973, the group was formed in August with Margaret Sloan (see entry) as its first Chair; it held its first conference in November

with over 400 participants; it wanted to deal with the arts, the black lesbian, domestic workers, drug addiction, the media, prisons, rape, reproductive freedom and welfare; it had groups in over ten cities with an approximate membership of 2000; it was criticized by the Combahee River Collective as having a 'bourgeois-feminist stance'; one of its members, Michele Wallace, wrote an account of the organization and its difficulties.

p. 'National Black Feminist Organization Statement of Purpose' in *The Vintage Book of Feminism* (1995); 'On the National Black Feminist Organization' in *Feminist Revolution* (1975–78).

s. Schneir (1995).

NIAC – Northern Ireland Abortion Campaign, 1980–84 (Ireland)
'The first group to really break the silence' – a crucial contribution to the campaign. The group's first act to gain publicity was to send coat hangers and fake airline tickets to every British MP saying, 'These are the two ways in which NI women get abortions'. Concerned themselves with education and lobbying. The campaign was continued by the NI Association for Law Reform on Abortion.

s. Evason (1991).

NORTHERN IRELAND WOMEN'S AID FEDERATION (Ireland)
Belfast WA established in 1974 along traditional structures and ideas as members were social workers involved with women and children's welfare. Contact with WA in England and Scotland from 1975 developed a feminist perspective which caused rifts within the organizations, resolved in favour of the radical feminists. Derry WA combined women from trade union and labour movement and housing campaigns with those involved in other women's issues. A women's studies course at Magee College provided the common ground for the formation of Derry Women's Action/Socialist Group in 1976. From 1977–82 DWA worked to establish a refuge, under great financial stress. They were instrumental in the formation of the NIWAF as well as community politics, setting up the Foyle Day Care Association for childcare provision. Coleraine WA emerged from the CWG in 1977, the Triangle Women's Housing Association founded by them in 1978 and a refuge in 1979.

s. Evason (1991).

NIWRM – Northern Ireland Women's Rights Movement, 1975 (Ireland)
A 'Women in Society' film weekend at Queen's University, Belfast promoted its establishment. The issue of the extension of British sex discrimination legislation to NI resulted in follow-up sessions which attracted more women from the socialist, civil rights and trade union movement. The nature of the membership ensured that traditional structures were adopted, including membership open to men. The group worked on a Women's Charter for NI which included:
1. Equal opportunities in education, training and work.
2. Equal pay for work of equal value.
3. Improved family planning services.
4. Maternity leave and childcare facilities.

The tensions between factions in the group emerged 1976–7, the radical feminist women from Women's Aid demanded that women's liberation values and structures should replace the equal opportunity focus, they left the group. The Socialist

Women's Group members also left, dissatisfied with the lack of recognition of socilaism as a prime mover in women's liberation. The NIWRM continued to campaign and research the needs of working women such as low pay, childcare. It opened the Belfast Women's Centre in 1980. Additional to campaigning, it has undertaken considerable research into discrimination issues.

p. The Female Line (mid-1980s).

s. Evason (1991).

NWO – National Women's Organization, 1984 (UK)
A result of the Miners' Strike which began on 9 March 1984 and finished 3 March 1985; founded at a national conference of women's action groups in Chesterfield 10–11 November 1984.

Aims:
1. To consolidate the NWO and ensure victory for the NUM in their present struggle; to prevent pit closures and protect mining communities for the future.
2. To further strengthen the organization of women's groups which has been built up during the 1984 miner's strike.
3. To develop a relationship between the NUM and the Women's Organization at all levels.
4. To campaign on issues which affect mining communities, particularly peace, jobs, health and education.
5. To promote and develop education for working-class women.
6. To publicize the activities of the NWO at all levels.

s. Stead (1987).

NOW – National Organization for Women, 1966 (US)
Largest US women's group; founded by Betty Friedan (see entry) and other women; originated as a response to the failure of the EEOC to enforce the sex discrimination conditions of the 1964 Civil Rights Act (Title VII). It has in the region of 260,000 members.

Aims: 'To take the actions needed to bring women into the mainstream of American society *now*, exercising all the priviliges and responsibilities in truly equal partnership with men.'

s. Cullen-DuPont (1996).

NAC – National Abortion Campaign, 1975
The organization has been open to men but with a women-only management committee. Its aim was the defence of the 1967 Abortion Act which was under persistent attack. As part of the WLM, its remit was to champion women's right to choice and control of their bodies.

p. All About NAC (1991); *A Celebration of 25 Years of Safe, Legal Abortion* (1992).

s. Griffin (1995).

NWPC – National Women's Political Caucus, 1970 (US)
Initiated chiefly by Bella Abzug (see entry), Shirley Chisholm (see entry), Betty Friedan (see entry) and Gloria Steinem (see entry).

Aims: To increase women's participation in government.

To enable women to stand for office it provides training programmes and helps with funding; it has also started a special training programme for women of colour.
    s. Cullen-DuPont (1996).

NYRF – New York Radical Feminists, 1969 (US)
One of the breakaway groups formed by some members from the NYRW and The Feminists, Anna Koedt (see entry) and Shulamith Firestone (see entry) among them. It grew rapidly, the membership divided into small 'brigades'. Members in new 'brigades' spent three months in CR, a further three months in reading and discussion, only then was full membership conferred. The organization seemed to disband, reforming in 1972. It backed two 'speak-outs' about rape and in 1974, with the NBFO, jointly organized a 'speak-out' on sexual abuse and rape.
    s. Carden (1974); Tuttle (1986); Schneir (1995).

NYRW – New York Radical Women, 1967 (US)
This was the first WLG in New York, founded by Pam Allen, Shulamith Firestone (see entry), Robin Morgan (see entry) and Ellen Willis, it was originally known as just Radical Women. It was a breakaway group from the Stanton-Anthony Brigade. It introduced the concept of consciousness-raising into the WLM. It produced its own journal, *Notes From the First Year, 1968, a Journal of Radical Feminism*, ditto second and third years; in *Notes From the First Year*, Firestone laid out the lessons to be learned from the failures of the previous women's movements; staged protests which attracted the media; in the spirit of groups of the time they disbanded after two years.
    Aims:
    1. Never compromise basic principles for political expediency.
    2. Agitation for specific freedoms is worthless without the preliminary raising of consciousness necessary to utilize these freedoms fully.
    3. Put your own interests first, then proceed to make alliances with other oppressed groups. Demand a piece of that revolutionary pie before you put your life on the line.
    When differences among the membership developed, the group dissolved as those members formed new groups.
    s. Tanner (1970); Schneir (1995); Cullen-DuPont (1996).

ONLYWOMEN PRESS, 1974 (UK)
'A women's liberation publishing and printing group, producing work by and for women as part of creating a feminist communication network and, ultimately, a feminist revolution.'
    Radical lesbian feminist collective in an exclusively women-only operation. They published the Leeds Revolutionary Feminists (see entry) debate as *Love Your Enemy?*
    s. Onlywomen (1982); Tuttle (1986).

OWAAD – Organization of Women of Asian and African Descent, 1978–82 (UK)
Attempted to provide a forum for black women from different backgrounds and political affiliations. It was established by some African women from the African Students' Union. Its intention was an umbrella group to enable black women from

all over Britain to come together. At the first conference in 1979, 250 attended to discuss the oppression of black women in areas such as health, immigration and the law. It was involved in action such as demonstration at Heathrow against virginity tests on Asian women. As the organization developed, sub-committees were formed to address the specific needs of the groups. The strains of dealing with the divergences of so many black groups together with the energy needed as women additionally supported the struggles in their own countries, resulted in growing dissent, especially in areas such as sexuality. The fourth conference on Black Feminism highlighted these splits and the organization folded.

p. OWAAD Newsletter.
s. 'Black Women Organizing' in *Feminist Review*, no 17, July 1984.

OWG – Older Women's Group, 1979, 1980–90 (UK)
Founded by Zelda Curtis in London by placing an advertisement in the magazine, *Spare Rib*. After several years in the WLM Curtis realized that the issues relating to older women's lives were not part of the WLM's agenda which was dominated by young women. OWG started out as a CRG. As it developed Curtis spent considerable time as a speaker disseminating ideas about older women's lives and the difficulties they faced. The Group also made a film for BBC's Open Space series called 'Invisible Women'.

s. Feminist Review, no 31, Spring 1989.

POW – Pictures of Women, 1982.
This was a cooperative of women working in the media with the aim of compensating for the proliferation of sexist images in the media. They wanted to demonstrate how women were 'regulated, manipulated, constructed and defined' by men. They began their campaign with a six-part television series on Channel 4.

s. Outwrite, issue 21, January 1984.

RECLAIM THE NIGHT, 1977 (UK)
To counteract women's fear of male violence, both a symbolic and practical campaign to enable women to take back their space in the world of public spaces and travel anywhere, alone or together without fear of intimidation, harassment or attack. To gain control over their lives. The first Reclaim the Night marches in Britain took place on the evening of 12 November 1977 in London, Manchester, Leeds, Newcastle and York. The movement then spread throughout the country and simultaneous events would occur throughout Britain's towns and cities with women marching holding some form of light – candles, flaming torches, singing and chanting. The second march in London was on 7 July 1978. On the night of 31 October 1978, the third event marching through Soho in London, after an incident outside a porn cinema, women were attacked by the police and 16 women were arrested, five had to be treated in hospital. The marches still continue.

s. Feminist Anthology Collective (1981); Tuttle (1986).

RED RAG, 1973–80 (UK)
A magazine 'of liberation' produced by a Marxist collective of women in the WLM in London. 'We will offer in *Red Rag* our Marxist explanation of why women are oppressed and how that oppression can be fought and overcome.' Sally Alexander

(see entry), Bea Campbell (see entry), Val Charlton (see entry), Alison Fell (see entry), Sheila Rowbotham (see entry), Lynne Segal (see entry) and Michelene Wandor (see entry) were among the early members. Not all the women in the Collective were CP members, many being socialist feminists, the two strands of women having met within the WLM. By August 1980 with a Conservative government in power, the WLM splintering, the pressures of time and financial problems, *Red Rag* closed, 'For the past two years *Red Rag* has been struggling with itself and with some of the intractable political knots both inside feminism and in our relationship to socialism.'

   s. Red Rag, nos. 1, 4, and August 1980.

REDSTOCKINGS, 1969–71 (US)
Begun by Shulamith Firestone (see entry) and Ellen Willis, the name created by Firestone was a revolutionary adaptation of the eighteenth century abusive term for learned women, 'bluestockings'; the terms descriptive of WLM's methods and philosophy, 'sisterhood is powerful' and 'the personal is political' originated with the Redstockings; their Manifesto became a key document; its first action was to picket the New York state abortion reform hearings because there were 12 men and one nun on the Board.

   p. 'Redstockings Manifesto' in *The Vintage Book of Feminism* (1995).

   s. Scheir (1995); Cullen-DuPont (1996).

RWU – Rights for Women Unit of the NCCL, 1973 (UK)
Established to defend and extend women's rights. In the forefront of significant campaigns, produced literature for such campaigns, published pamphlets on new issues eg. sexual harassment, advice and support service for women, making amendments to legislation, action programmes.

   s. Sedley and Benn (1982).

ROW – Rights of Women, 1975 (UK)
'A feminist legal project... which informs women of their rights and promotes the interests of women in relation to the law.'

   It originated to campaign for the fifth of the seven WLM demands, namely the legal and financial independence of women. It worked with other groups such as the YBAW group and the Rape in Marriage campaign; it has had numerous important successes such as defending attacks on the Abortion Act, child benefits, amendments to the SDA and getting rape in marriage on the statute book.

   p. Lesbian Mothers on Trial (1984); *A Guide to the Children Act, 1989* (1992); *ROW Bulletin.*

   s. Griffin (1995).

SAPPHO, 1974–6 (Ireland)
Operating in Belfast, this consisted of a small group of women functioning as a discussion group. Succeeded by Lesbians in Belfast (1977) a feminist group with major responsibility for organizing the Belfast All Ireland Women's Conference in 1977. From a proliferation of small lesbian CRGs, Lesbian Line, a support line emerged in 1978.

   s. Evason (1991).

SHEBA FEMINIST PUBLISHERS, 1980 (UK)

A racially mixed feminist publishing co-operative. It sought to provide a forum principally for the writings of black, working class, lesbian and first-time women writers . It wanted its list to consist of fiction, non-fiction and poetry, together with anti-sexist and ant-racist work for children.

s. Sheba publicity statement.

SBS – Southall Black Sisters, 1979 (UK)

A secular black feminist women's campaigning, advice and support group in Southall, South London; founded in response to Asian and Afro-Caribbean women's experience of the male-domination of local radical organizations in the anti-racist movement; the first group to 'break the silence' on violence against women in the Asian community by highlighting those deaths through such direct actions as demonstrating outside the male perpetrators' houses; become skilled in campaigning for and succeeding with cases relating to violence against women and the results of racist immigration laws; involved in forming WAF; works with Justice for Women; celebrating its 21st anniversary in 2000 it has a resource centre which supports, counsels, informs and advises those women in its community suffering from domestic violence.

p. *Against the Grain: A Celebration of Survival and Struggle* (1990); *Domestic Violence and Asian Women* (1993).

s. GLC (1984); Griffin (1995); *Feminist Review*, no 64, Spring 2000.

SHREW, 1969–77 (UK)

Appeared from July 1969, an early WLM newspaper with a large distribution network. Designed to act as the voice of the WLM, production of the issues revolved around the London WLW with a new group taking responsibility each time. Its largest circulation was in the region of 5000, regularly appearing until 1974. As with many such publications, production became increasingly erratic and finished in 1977.

s. Tuttle (1986).

SPARE RIB, 1972–94 (UK)

A feminist magazine launched in June 1972, first edition in July, founded and edited by Rosie Boycott, with Marsha Rowe. Boycott was a pure mathematics graduate from Kent University with brief experience of working on *Friends* magazine. 'It was startling to realize that we could not buy any publication which discussed what we felt to be vital issues… What we can do is reflect the questions, ideas and hope that is growing out of our awareness of ourselves…'.

Rowe and others working on the magazine wanted it to become a collective to reflect the WLM's political practices, but Boycott wanted to sustain the traditional 'management' style. In 1973 she left the magazine. *Spare Rib* reached its zenith in the 1980s with a 25,000 circulation. It developed through many changes in personnel in the collective, through lesbian and black politics until it closed through financial difficulties.

s. *Spare Rib*, 1 July 1972; Tuttle (1986); Boycott (1988).

THE 300 GROUP, 1980 (UK)

Founded by Lesley Abdela (see entry) in September 1980.

To encourage and train women of any political party or as yet unaffiliated to stand for elected office at local council, Westminster or European level. The name derives from the intention to get 300 women into the House of Commons as MPs.

s. Cowley (nd c.1986).

VIRAGO (woman warrior), 1973 (UK)

Women's publishing company started by Carmen Callil (see entry) with Ursula Owen as its first editor. The significance of Virago was in establishing a company to encourage, support and publish feminist texts which otherwise would have remained unseen; it also republished out-of-print women's literature, relaunching the significant amount of women's writing which had become 'hidden' and 'lost'; the company was immensely successful and provided the impetus not only for other feminist publishing ventures but for the publishing of feminist work by mainstream publishers who went on to develop feminist lists; it had an advisory panel comprising WLM activists, academics and writers; Virago became part of the Chatto, Bodley Head and Cape Group, 1982. In 1987 there was a management buy-out and the company was returned to being an independent publisher, but later became part of Little, Brown.

s. Virago (1993).

WAC – Women's Action Committee, 1980 (UK)

WAC of the Campaign for Labour Party Democracy, whose Secretary was Ann Pettifor. Its objective was, 'To campaign for action, including positive discrimination, to ensure that women are fully represented at every level of party life, and thereby to strengthen the fight for a fundamental shift in the balance of power in favour of women as well as working men.' WAC was attempting to redress the lack of power of women members who had no voice in the policy and decision-making processes of the LP.

p. Women Discover Your Strength (1983).

s. WAC membership application form.

WACC – Women's Abortion and Contraceptive Campaign, 1972 (UK)

The Skegness WLM Conference in October 1971 was the starting point for a national abortion and contraception campaign. This was followed by 'actions in solidarity' with women globally who were suffering under legal constraints with regard to these issues. The London Abortion Action Group met in January 1972 and established WAAC .

Demands:

1. Free, safe and reliable contraception available to every woman on the NHS.
2. Abortion – a woman's right to choose: any woman who is unwilling to continue her pregnancy should have the undisputed right to a free and safe abortion.
3. No forced sterilization: pressure should not be put on any woman to accept sterilization as a condition for abortion.

There was a network of WAAC groups nationwide for campaigning, self-examination, pregnancy testing.

s. Red Rag, no 11.

WAGES FOR HOUSEWORK CAMPAIGN, 1970 (UK)
Instigated by Selma James (see entry), conducted through the Power of Women Collective. 'Wages for Housework – All Women are Workers'. The analysis has been made that capitalism would be unable to function without the unpaid servicing performed by legions of women at home and this campaign aimed to get economic recompense for those women. However, many in the WLM saw this argument as a reactionary one playing into the hands of those forces who wish to keep women confined to the private role of domestic servicing. The campaign created antagonism and division within the WLM.

   s. Tuttle (1986).

A WOMAN'S PLACE, 1977 (UK)
Opened in London by women squatters, and run as a collective. With GLC funding from 1982 it expanded its operations with six employed workers plus the volunteers who provided an information and resources service to women, nationally and internationally. It was able to provide free meeting space for women's groups and housed a feminist bookshop at Hungerford House, Victoria Embankment.

   s. Tuttle (1986).

WAP – Women Against Pornography, 1979 (US)
Founded by Susan Brownmiller (see entry). It supplies speakers, conducts protests and has its own publication, *Women Against Pornography – Newsreport*.

   Aim: Dissemination that pornography is 'about the degradation, objectification, and brutalization of women'.

   s. Cullen-DuPont (1996).

WAVAW – Women Against Violence Against Women c. early 1980s (UK)
A national coalition of regional groups campaigning against all forms of violent bahaviour against women, whilst researching the issues relating to male domination and violence. The first conference was attended by a thousand women in London, 1981. Campaigns concern issues such as rape in marriage, street lighting, child abuse, self-defence, pornography.

   s. Tuttle (1986).

WEL – Women's Electoral Lobby, 1972 (Australia)
The first WEL group was started in Melbourne by Beatrice Faust, an abortion law reform activist. Her intention was to highlight WLM demands within the political forum by canvassing federal election candidates on women's issues. By the end of 1972 there were WEL groups over almost all of Australia with in excess of two thousand members. The results of questionnaires were publicized, exposing the ignorance and neglect of women's issues in mainstream politics. Results were submitted to government. WEL Australia was founded in 1978, an umbrella of the network of groups countrywide.

   s. Caine (1998).

WIRES – Women's Information, Referral and Enquiry Service, 1975 (UK)
Originally based in Leeds, it moved to different cities every couple of years.

   Aims: To provide an information service with comprehensive files of groups, campaigns, contacts, etc.

WITCH

To provide a newsletter to keep local groups and areas in touch with each other's activities.

Provided a *WIRES Newsletter*.

s. Cowley (nd c.1986); Tuttle (1986).

WITCH – Women's International Terrorist Conspiracy from Hell, 1968 (US)
This was a breakaway group from NYRW, its first 'coven' being in New York. It was also known as Women Inspired to Commit Herstory or Women Intent on Toppling Consumer Holidays. It had branches in several US cities. Its tactic was to 'hex' those events and institutions regarded as being perpetrators of sexist discrimination and conditioning such as the stock exchange, the United Fruit Company and bridal fairs.

s. Schneir (1995); Cullen-DuPont (1996).

WLNCC – Women's Liberation National Coordinating Committee, 1970.
'Recognizing that at the present stage of the development of the women's liberation movement in Britain, a united national women's organization with common pro-gramme does not exist. But in fact there are many women's groups in different parts of the country with differing concepts, approaches and objectives regarding women's liberation.

Recognizing that only by involving the masses of women and building a united, national women's organization with common objectives will it be possible to effect a basic change in society to realize women's liberation.

In view of the above, it is agreed that the WNCC is based upon the following principles:

1. The CC should be open to all women's groups and organizations with two representatives each.
2. The independence and equality of all groups is recognized.
3. The CC shall take necessary steps to disseminate information to promote better understanding of the viewpoints of various groups and their activities and facilitate towards unity and broadening of women's liberation struggle.
4. Upholding the principle of democracy and equality, the CC shall take its decisions by mutual agreement.
5. No decision shall be binding on any group that does not agree with it.
6. To promote unity, step by step, the CC will help not only mutual discussion regarding women's problems and role in society but will positively encourage united action among them on issues about which there is agreement.
7. If a number of groups, by mutual agreement, decide to take united action on any issue, such a decision is not binding on others who are not a party to it.
8. Real co-ordination, to be effective, should be not only in words but also in deeds if a united women's liberation movement is to be achieved.
9. To promote the aims of women's liberation and to achieve better under-standing of women's problems, the CC shall periodically organize national conferences and help local conferences of women.

Additions:

1. No joint or co-ordinating meeting can be called without prior consultations and agreement by all participant groups on time, place and form of meeting.
2. Publicity for any meeting must state clearly the names of the groups orga-nizing the meeting.

p: publications;   s: sources

3. Agreement must be reached between groups on the question of inviting press to meetings.

4. No reference to other groups, or to alleged 'divisions' within Women's Liberation must be made in any interview with the press. Women should talk about the work of their own group or about the position of women. We hammer out our differences between ourselves, not within the columns of the bourgeois press.

Paper: Women's Struggle.

s. *Women's Struggle*, vol. 1, no 4, 1971.

WLM – Women's Liberation Movement, c.1970 (UK)

Officially recognized as having come into being at the first National Women's Liberation Conference, February 1970 where the first four demands were formulated. The sixth demand was proposed by the Brighton WLG at the Birmingham NWL Conference, 1978.

The seven demands:

1. Equal pay.
2. Equal education and job opportunities.
3. Free contraception and abortion on demand.
4. Free 24–hour nurseries, under community control.
5. Legal and financial independence.
6. An end to discrimination against lesbians.
7. Freedom from intimidation by the threat or use of violence or sexual coercion, regardless of marital status. An end to the laws, assumptions and institutions that perpetuate male dominance and men's aggression towards women.

s. Feminist Anthology Collective (1981).

WMAG – Women's Media Action Group (UK)

Campaign for the elimination of sexism and stereotyping in the media portrayal of women. Publication, *Women's Media Action.*

s. Cowley (nd c.1986).

WPA – Women's Political Association, 1970 (Ireland)

Founded in Dublin by Margaret Waugh. The situation in Northern Ireland caused her to wonder if more politically active women could have an influence. Her intention was to encourage more women to enter politics, to this end she contacted Mary Robinson (see entry) and originally the Women's Progressive Association was formed, later renamed. It aimed to:

1. Educate members to be politically and socially aware.
2. Encourage women to join established political parties and become candidates for local and general elections.
3. Give them sufficient confidence to become politically active on committees.

By 1974, five WPA members were elected in local elections.

s. Mahon (1996).

WOMEN'S PRESS, 1978 (UK)

Started by Stephanie Dowrick, who was its managing director from 1978–81. It was 'dedicated to publishing incisive feminist fiction and non-fiction by outstanding women writers from all around the world'. It also established a Women's Press Bookclub for discounted publications and a special list for young women, Livewire. By 1988 it had achieved a £1.5 million turnover with a list of 60 titles a year.

s. Guardian, 13 April 1988; WP publicity.

WRRC – Women's Reproductive Rights Information Centre (UK)
Runs the international contraception, abortion and sterilization campaign.

To provide information and support on all issues related to women's right to decide if and when to have children, including pregnancy testing, contraception, abortion rights, sterilization, 'morning after' contraception, reproductive technology and infertility.

s. Cowley (nd c.1986).

WSP – Women Strike for Peace, 1962 (US)
Formed by Bella Abzug (see entry) and Dagmar Wilson as an international pacifist organization. It has worked against the McCarthy trials, the Vietnam war and nuclear weapons. Its monthly publication is *WSP – Legislative Alert*.

s. Cullen-DuPont (1996).

WOMEN'S STUDIES INTERNATIONAL QUARTERLY (Forum), 1978 (UK)
'A multidisciplinary journal for the rapid publication of research communications and review articles in Women's Studies', edited by Dale Spender (see entry); later became the WSI Forum 'to aid the distribution and exchange of feminist research in the multidisciplinary, international area of women's studies and in feminist research in other disciplines. The policy of the journal is to establish a feminist forum for discussion and debate.'

s. WSIQ vol. 1 1978; WSIF http://www.elsevier.co.jp/inca/publications/store/3/6/1/361.pub.htt.

APPENDIX 1

CHRONOLOGY OF UK EMANCIPATORY LEGISLATION 1918–84

This list represents legislative reforms which have contributed towards the emancipation of women and child welfare protection in Britain during the stated period. Many of these reforms were inititiated by women's groups or steered through Parliament by women, however this is not exclusively the case. This does not represent a complete list of such legislation.

1918

Representation of the People Act – women over thirty with a property qualification or over thirty and married to a ratepayer, were able to vote for the first time.

Parliament (Qualification of Women) Act – enabled women over 21 to stand for Parliament (even though women between 21 and 30 had no vote).

Maternity and Child Welfare Act – the establishment of infant welfare centres.

Registration of Midwives Amending Act – this adjusted the 1902 legislation.

Affiliation Orders (Increase of Maximum Payment) Act – increased the weekly payment to be made for an illegitimate child from five to ten shillings by the father.

1919

Sex Disqualification (Removal) Act – enabling women to enter the legal profession, women householders to serve on juries, women to become magistrates, extended entrance to the Civil Service.

Nurses Registration Act – the compulsory registration of practising nurses.

Maintenance Orders (Facilities for Enforcement) Act, 1920 – women could recover amounts from maintenance orders from those men who lived elsewhere in the Empire.

1920

Married Women's Property (Scotland) Act – rights available in England and Wales were now available in Scotland.

1921

Deceased Husband's Brother Act – equalizing the situation whereby a woman could now marry her deceased husband's brother (it was legal for men to marry their deceased wife's sister).

1922

Criminal Law Amendment Act – raising the age of sexual consent in indecent assault cases from 13 to 16.

Infanticide Act – women accused would no longer be charged with murder where postnatal distress could be proved.

Married Women (Maintenance) Act – under a separation order a woman was entitled to a maximum of forty shillings, and ten shillings per child.

Law of Property Act – equal inheritance rights to one another's property for wife and husband; also equal rights to inheritance of intestate children's property.

1923

Matrimonial Causes Act – equalizing divorce.

Bastardy Act – increased the amount to be paid by the affiliation order.

Intoxicating Liquor Act – prevented sales of alcohol to those under eighteen.

1925

Guardianship of Infants Act – awarding the mother equal rights and responsibilities toward her children with the father.

Summary Jurisdiction (Separation and Maintenance) Act – the grounds on which male or female marriage partners could obtain a separation were extended to cover cruelty, habitual drunkenness, enforced co-habitation by a partner with a venereal disease.

Widows, Orphans and Old Age (Contributory Pensions) Act – awarded child allowances for widows and further allowances in cases where both parents had died.

Criminal Justice Act – to abolish the presumption that offences committed by a wife in the presence of her husband are committed under coercion.

1926

Registration of Midwives and Maternity Acts – to regulate this provision by registration and inspection.

Legitimacy Act – to legitimize children born out of wedlock when parents subsequently marry.

Adoption of Children Act – formalizing adoption through court procedures.

1927

Nursing Homes Registration Act- to extend the safeguards for women and infants.

1928

Representation of the People (Equal Franchise) Act – enabling women to vote on the same grounds as men.

1929

Age of Marriage Act – raised the age of marriage for males and females to 16.

Infant Life (Preservation) Act – concerned with the grey area between murder and abortion in the protection of the baby during birth, it also justified abortion after the 28th week of pregnancy if the mother's life was in danger.

Children (Employment Abroad) Act – improved the protection of children up to 18.

Bastardy (Witness Process) Act – to enable magistrates to compel the attendance of witnesses at affiliation hearings, closing a legal loophole.

Illegitimate Children (Scotland) Act – enabling unmarried mothers to claim improved financial allowances.

1931

Sentence of Death (Expectant Mothers) Act – abolished the passing of the death sentence on pregnant women.

1932

Children and Young Persons Act – regulated child employment.

1933

British Nationality and Status of Aliens Act – enabled women who did not acquire their husband's nationality to retain their own, avoiding statelessness.

Children and Young Persons Act – protected young people up to 17 from 'exposure to moral danger'.

1935

Law Reform (Married Women and Tortfeasors*) Act – to amend the capacity, property and liabilities of married women so that a married woman would be treated as a single woman with respect to liability for her property .

1936

Midwives Act – every expectant mother was entitled to attendance by a trained mid-wife and a doctor, if required, paid for by the local authority.

1938

Inheritance (Family Provision) Act – prevented the disinheritance of spouses (usually wives) and dependent children.

1945

Family Allowances Act – provided for the payment of child allowances to mothers.

1948

British Nationality Act – enabling a woman to retain her British nationality unless she legally changed it.

1949

Married Women (Restraint Upon Anticipation) Act – to equalize, to render inoperative any restrictions upon anticipation or alienation attached to the enjoyment of property by a woman.

---

* Tort: 'It is a civil wrong independent of contract: it gives rise to an action for damages irrespective of any agreement not to do the act complained of. Torts include such wrongs as assault, battery... trespass... defamation of character.' (Williams and Glanville, *Learning the Law*, London, 1982, Stevens and Sons).

1950

Criminal Law (Amendment) Act – amending an 1885 Act to bring prostitutes within the law and protect them against abuse and abduction.

1954

Children and Young Persons (Harmful Publications) Act – to restrict the import of
morally damaging materials.

1958

Maintenance Orders (Attachment of Income) Act – for arrears of maintenance to
women to be deducted direct from earnings with a court order.

Parliament (Qualification of Peeresses) Act – women who were life peers were
admitted to the House of Lords.

Matrimonial Causes (Property and Maintenance) Act – regarding the time for making maintenance orders or alimony; the avoidance of disposition to defeat a wife's
claim for financial relief; provision for a former wife from the deceased former
husband's estate.

1962

Law Reform (Husband and Wife) Act – to amend the law with respect to civil proceedings between husband and wife to give them the same right of action in tort*
against each other as if they were not married.

1963

Public Lavatories (Turnstiles) Act – to abolish the use of turnstiles and payment for
access to women's public lavatories.

Peerage Act – enabled women who were peeresses in their own right to sit and vote
for the first time in the House of Lords.

1964

Married Women's Property Act – the right of the wife to an equal share of any
money regarded as 'housekeeping' money and property derived from a housekeeping allowance in the case of a dispute.

1967

Abortion Law (Amendment) Act – legalized the provision of abortions within
certain parameters of time and medical consent.

1969

Family Law Reform Act – relating to property rights of illegitimate children; provision for the use of blood tests to determine paternity; the evidence required to
establish legitimacy; provision for entering the name of the father on registration
of an illegitimate child.

1970

Equal Pay Act – to entitle women to be paid the same as a man when she is doing
the same or broadly similar work in the same employment.

Matrimonial Proceedings and Property Act – maintenance provision pending suit in cases of divorce, etc.; in divorce, financial provision for parties to the marriage and children of the family; transfer of property in divorce; neglect to provide maintenance; protection for children in divorce; abolishing the right to claim restitution of conjugal rights.

1971

Finance Act – allowed for the separate taxation of a married woman's earnings.

1975

Sex Discrimination Act – made it unlawful to discriminate, directly or indirectly on the grounds of sex in housing, employment and training, education and the provision of goods, facilities and services.

Employment Protection Act – ensuring statutory paid maternity leave and outlawing unfair dismissal for pregnant women.

Social Security (Pensions) Act – enabled women to earn a full pension in their own right.

1976

Domestic Violence Act – in the event of violence against them, to enable married or unmarried women to apply for an injunction against the the man concerned to leave the home.

Sexual Offences (Amendment) Act – to improve the privacy of rape victims during trials.

1978

Employment Protection (Consolidation) Act – improved maternity employment protection, re. payment and job protection.

1981

Matrimonial Homes (Family Protection) Act – to protect the right of both wife and husband to occupy the home and to resist eviction by their partner.

Armed Forces Act – completing the assimilation for all purposes of statute law of the women's services administered by the Defence Council.

1983

Equal Pay (Amendment) Act – to entitle women to be paid the same as men when they are employed on work of equal value.

1984

Matrimonial and Family Proceedings Act – to prevent petition for divorce within one year of marriage; decrees of nullity; welfare of children under 18 re. orders for financial relief after divorce; orders for financial relief in cases of neglect to maintain previous agreements; financial assistance where divorce obtained overseas and jurisdiction of the court; duty to notify change of address on persons liable to make payments under maintenance orders.

APPENDIX 2
CLUBS

For the history of women's clubs and extensive detail on these clubs refer to the 'Clubs' section in Crawford (1999). This list contains some of the clubs of which women in the 1914–67 section were members.

Albemarle – established 1874, social club, mixed, 37 Dover Street, London W1

Cowdray – established 1922, social club principally for nurses, medical and other professional women, 20 Cavendish Square, London W1

Efficiency – business and professional women, 60–61 South Molton Street, London W1

Emerson – established 1911, mixed, 19 Buckingham Street, London WC2

Forum – established 1919, for women of professional and social standing interested in the Arts, Science Travel, etc., 6 Grosvenor Place, London SW1

Halcyon – social, for professional women, 13 Cork Street, London W1

International Women's Franchise – established 1910, mixed, feminist library, 9 Grafton Street, London W1

Ladies' Army and Navy – established 1902, relations of naval and military officers, 27 St James's Place, London SW1

Ladies' Carlton – social and political, 5 Grosvenor Place, London SW1

Ladies' Empire – established 1902, social, Grosvenor Street, London W1

Lyceum – established 1904, literature, art, science and music, women from the educational world, 128 Piccadilly, London W1

1917 Club – established 1917 partly in response to the Russian Revolution; open to Radicals and radically-minded Liberals, bohemian atmosphere, largely peopled by the 'Labour Left' with Ramsay MacDonald as its first President, Gerrard Street, London W1

Overseas League – Park Place, St James's, London SW1

Pen – established 1921, writers, protect freedom of speech, 7 Dilke Street, London SW3

Pioneer – established 1892, women of advanced views, temperance, motto – 'They say. What they say. Let them say', 9 Park Place, London SW1

Soroptimist – Bush Lane House, Cannon Street, London EC4

St Andrew's House – 31a Mortimer Street, London W1

Three Arts – established 1911, women engaged in the arts, painting and sculpture, music, drama and literature, 19a Marylebone Road, London NW1

Three Counties – established 1914, social, limited number of professional women accepted on special subscription, 67a New Street, Birmingham

University Women's (originally University Club for Ladies) – established 1887, university and medical, George Street, Hanover Square, London W1, then 2 Audley Square, South Audley Street, London W1

Victoria – established 1894, town club for country ladies, 145 Victoria Street, London SW1, then 36 Grosvenor Place, London SW1

VAD Ladies'- 28 Cavendish Square, London W1

Women's Automobile and Sports' Association – established 1930, residential for sportswomen of all interests, 17 Buckingham Palace Gardens, London SW1.

Women's United Services – established 1920, residential for professional women, 23–4 Courtfield Gardens, London SW5

Writers' – established 1892, literary and journalistic, 10 Norfolk Street, Strand, London WC2

s. The Lady's Who's Who (London, 1919, The International Art and Publishing Co); Gates (1923); *Women's Who's Who, 1934–5*; *The Lady's Who's Who* (1939); *Dictionary of Labour Biography*, vol. 5; Fry (1992); Crawford (1999).

BIBLIOGRAPHY

The extent of secondary material now available to the feminist history researcher is an exciting post-1970s progression. However, recent developments in book-selling, with even traditional academic bookshops operating pile 'em high and sell 'em cheap marketing, are having an effect on access. The lifespan of a text in terms of its availability for purchase based on volume sales determines its likelihood of reaching libraries; coupled with diminishing resources available for university and public libraries, this means that although feminist research is increasing, availability may be problematic. The economic position of women does not ensure volume sales. Sales are further jeopardized by the continuing marginalization of feminist history in the academic cannon. Difficulty in obtaining texts was most evident with the books on Irish women's history. There is a fascinating and extensive literature, but its availability, especially in Britain, is limited. It is still the case that without the Fawcett Library's extensive and eclectic stock, many avenues for feminist historical research, even of the past forty years, are difficult to access. The Feminist Library in London, although struggling to survive, has an extensive holding of WLM texts and the Feminist Archive in Bristol is a further specialist source for WLM archives. Catalogue searches for extant material can also increasingly be achieved via the internet.

For reference books covering the entire period of this book, Caine and Cullen-DuPont for the Australian and American movements respectively, are vast in the breadth of their research. Whilst Crawford (1999) is a treasure-trove for the 1866–1914 period, with some material covering 1914–28. The *British Biographical Index* is an essential tool for the beginning of the period, the scale of the trawl undertaken for neglected women and men is impressive. Both Banks' volumes which pioneered the biographical hunt for women activists are significant starting points. Of the out-of-print period reference volumes, all the *Who's Who* type are vital, such as *Suffrage* (1913), *Labour* (1924–7), *Hutchinson* (1934) and *Lady's* (1938–9).

In relation to texts addressing the 1914–60 years, Pugh (1992) and, especially Brookes (1967), contain significant amounts of detail in relation to parliamentary issues and women participants. Moving on to Irish women, both North and South, early and later period, there is an abundance of excellent material once you have located it. Luddy (1995a) and Smyth (1993) are two essential starting points.

There is no shortage of material for studying the WLM in America or Britain.

The writings of the period were abundant, much is still in print or being reprinted. The extensive writings of Rowbotham offer key insights into this period for researchers. Within the past decade a reassessment of the late 1960s and 70s activism is producing a retrospective analysis of its achievements, methods and experiences in many new publications and conferences. The current enthusiasm for autobiography also yields further material, in this category, DuPlessis et al. (1998) is enlightening. The *Tuttle Encyclopaedia* (1986) and *Kramarae Dictionary* (1985) are dense with information, ideas and leads. Schneir's (1995) collection of WLM texts has been comprehensively edited to include biographical notes and background information which contextualize the papers.

With regard to primary sources used, references for organizational and private papers, newspapers, ephemera and special collections are all included after each entry. Apart from special collections, the majority of research on such primary material was undertaken at the Fawcett Library at the London Guildhall University, the TUC Collection at the University of North London and the Bodleian Library in Oxford.

Alberti, Johanna, *Beyond Suffrage, Feminists in War & Peace 1914–28* (London, 1989, Macmillan)

Alberti, Johanna, *Eleanor Rathbone* (London, 1996, Sage)

Alexander, Sally, *Introduction* in *Round About a Pound a Week*, Maud Pember Reeves (London, 1979, Virago)

Alexander, Sally, *Becoming a Woman* (London, 1994, Virago)

Appleyard, Rollo, *Charles Parsons, His Life and Works* (London, 1933, Constable)

Archdale, Helen Elizabeth, *Indiscretions of a Headmistress* (Sydney, 1972, Angus & Robertson)

Arnold, J and Morris, D (eds), *Monash Biographical Dictionary of Twentieth Century Australia* (Victoria, Australia, 1994, Reed Reference Publishing)

Asian Women Writers' Workshop, *Right of Way* (London, 1988, The Women's Press)

Astor, Michael, *Tribal Feeling* (London, 1963, John Murray)

Bank, David and McDonald, Theresa, *British Biographical Index* (Munich, 1998, Saur)

Banks, Olive, *The Biographical Dictionary of British Feminists*, vol. 1, *1800–1930* (Brighton, 1985, Harvester Wheatsheaf)

Banks, Olive, *The Biographical Dictionary of British Feminists*, vol. 2: *A Supplement, 1900–45* (New York, 1990, New York University Press)

Banks, Olive, *Faces of Feminism* (Oxford, 1981, Martin Robertson)

Barrow, Margaret, *Women 1870–1928: A Select Guide to Printed and Archival Sources in the UK* (New York, 1981, Mansell)

Baylen, Joseph O. and Gossman, Norbert J. (eds), *Biographical Dictionary of British Radicals*, vol. 3, *1870–1914* (US, 1988, Harvester)

Beale, Jenny, *Women in Ireland* (London, 1986, Macmillan)

Beaumont, Caitriona, 'Gender, Citizenship and the State in Ireland, 1922–90' in S. Brewster et al. (eds), *Ireland in Proximity: History, Gender Space* (London, 1999, Routledge)

Beddoe, Deirdre, *Back to Home and Duty: Women Between the Wars 1918–39* (London, 1989, Pandora)

Beddoe, Deirdre, *Discovering Women's History* (London, 1983, Pandora)

Bellamy, J.M. and Saville, J., *Dictionary of Labour Biography*, vols 1–8 (London, 1972–87, Macmillan)

Benn, Melissa and Sedley, Ann, *Sexual Harassment at Work* (London, 1982, NCCL)

Blake, Lord and Nicholls, C.S. (eds), *The Dictionary of National Biography 1971–1980* (London, 1986, OUP)

Blake, Lord and Nicholls, C.S. (eds), *The Dictionary of National Biography 1981–85* (London, 1990, OUP)

Boase, Wendy, *The Sky's the Limit* (London, 1979, Osprey)

Boston, Sarah, *Women Workers and the Trade Unions* (London, 1980, Davis-Poynter)

Boycott, Rosie, *A Nice Girl Like Me* (London, 1984, Chatto & Windus)

Braddock, Jack and Bessie, *The Braddocks* (London, 1963, Macdonald)

Brakeman, Lynne, *Chronology of Women Worldwide: People, Places and Events that Changed Women's History* (Detroit, 1997, Gale)

Branson, Noreen, *The History of the Communist Party in Britain 1927–41* (London, 1985, Lawrence & Wishart)

Branson, Noreen, *The History of the Communist Party in Britain 1941–51* (London, 1997, Lawrence & Wishart)

Brittain, *Vera, Lady Into Woman: A History of Women from Victoria to Elizabeth II* (London, 1953, Andrew Dakers)

Brookes, Pamela, *Women at Westminster* (London, 1967, Peter Davies)

Bryan, Beverley, Dadzie, Stella and Scafe, Suzanne, *The Heart of the Race: Black Women's Lives in Britain* (London, 1985, Virago)

Buck, Claire (ed.), *Guide to Women's Literature throughout the World* (London, 1992, Bloomsbury Publishing)

Burton, Elaine, *What of the Women: A Study of Women in Wartime* (London, 1941, Frederick Muller)

Burton, Elaine, *And Your Verdict?* (London, 1942, Frederick Muller)

Button, John, *The Radicalism Handbook: A Complete Guide to the Radical Movement in the Twentieth Century* (London, 1995, Cassell)

Caine, Barbara (ed.), *Australian Feminism: A Companion* (Melbourne, 1998, Oxford University Press)

Carden, Maren Lockwood, *The New Feminist Movement* (New York, 1974, Russell Sage Foundation)

Chevins, Hugh, 'Anne Loughlin' in *An International Women's Year Tribute* (Milton Keynes, 1975, NUTGW)

Clancy, Mary, 'Aspects of Women's Contribution to the Oireachtas Debate in the Irish Free State, 1922–37' in Maria Luddy and Cliona Murphy (eds), *Women Surviving: Studies in Irish Women's History in the 19th and 20th Centuries* (Dublin, 1990, Poolbeg)

Collette, Christine, *For Labour and For Women: The Women's Labour League 1906–18* (Manchester, 1989, MUP)

Collins, Louise Mooney and Mabunda, Lorna Mpho, *The Annual Obituary* (Detroit/London, 1994, Washington)

Collis, Maurice, *Nancy Astor, an Informal Biography* (London, 1966, Faber & Faber)

Colville, Cynthia, *A Crowded Life* (London, 1963, Evans Bros)

Colquhoun, Maureen, *A Woman in the House* (Shoreham-by-Sea, 1980, SNA Books)

Cooper, Davina, *Sexing the City: Lesbian & Gay Politics Within the Activist State* (London, 1994, Rivers Oram Press)

Coote, Anna and Campbell, Beatrix, *Sweet Freedom: The Struggle for Women's Liberation* (London, 1982, Picador)

Coote, Anna and Pattullo, Polly, *Power & Prejudice: Women & Politics* (London, 1990, Weidenfeld & Nicholson)

Courtney, Janet E., *The Women of My Time* (London, 1934, Lovat Dickson)

Cousins, James and Margaret, *We Two Together* (Madras, 1950, Talbot)

Cowley, Ruth, *What About Women?* (Manchester, nd, Fanfare Press)

Crawford, Anne et al., *The Europa Biographical Dictionary of British Women* (London, 1983, Europa Publications)

Crawford, Elizabeth, *The Women's Suffrage Movement: A Reference Guide 1866–1928* (London, 1999, UCL Press)

Crone, Joni, *Lesbian Feminism in Ireland* in Women's Studies International Forum, vol. ii, no 4, 1988

Cullen-DuPont, Kathryn, *The Encyclopedia of Women's History in America* (New York, 1996, Facts on File Inc.)

Deneke, Helen, *Grace Hadow* (London, 1946, Oxford University Press)

Dictionary of Quaker Biography (unpub. Library of Society of Friends)

Doughan, David and Gordon, Peter, *Dictionary of British Women's Organizations 1850–1960* (London, 2000, Woburn Press)

Doughan, David and Sanchez, Denise, *Feminist Periodicals 1885–1984* (Brighton, 1984, Harvester Press)

Douie, Vera, *The Lesser Half* (London, 1943, WPPA)

Douie, Vera, *Daughters of Britain* (Oxford, 1949, George Ronald)

Dublin Lesbian and Gay Collective, *Out for Ourselves* (Dublin, 1986, Women's Community Press)

DuPlessis, Rachel Blau and Snitow, Ann, *The Feminist Memoir Project: Voices from Women's Liberation* (New York, 1998, Three Rivers Press)

Edwards, Joseph and Pethick Lawrence, F.W., *The Reformers' Year Book* (London, 1908, Labour Party)

Eoff, Shirley, *Viscountess Rhondda: Equalitarian Feminist* (Ohio, 1991, Ohio State University Press)

Evans, Mari, *Black Women Writers* (London, 1983, Pluto)

Evason, Eileen, *Against the Grain: The Contemporary Women's Movement in Northern Ireland* (Dublin, 1991, Attic Press)

Fawcett Society and Women's Lobby, *Women's Report*, vol. i–vol. iii (London, 1972)

Feminist Anthology Collective, *No Turning Back: Writings from the WLM 1975–80* (London, 1981, The Women's Press)

Feminist Review, 17, July 1984.

Feminist Review, Sexuality: A Reader (London, 1987, Virago)

Feminist Review, 31, Spring 1989.

Fenwick, Gillian, *Women and the Dictionary of National Biography: a Guide to DNB Volumes 1885–1985 and 'Missing Persons'* (Aldershot, 1994, Scolar Press)

Ferree, Myra Marx and Martin, Patricia Yancey (eds), *Feminist Organizations: Harvest of the New Women's Movement* (Philadelphia, 1995, Temple University Press)

Fox, R.M., *Louie Bennett, Her Life & Times* (Dublin, 1958, Talbot Press)

Freeman, Jo, *The Politics of Women's Liberation* (New York, 1975, David McKay Co. Inc.)

Friedman, Scarlet and Sarah, Elizabeth, *On the Problem of Men* (London, 1982, Women's Press)

Fry, Ruth, *Maud and Amber* (Christchurch, New Zealand, 1992, Canterbury UP)

Gaffin, Jean and Thoms, David, *Caring & Sharing: The Centenary History of the Co-operative Women's Guild* (Manchester, 1983, Co-operative Union)

Gates, G. Evelyn, *Woman's Year Book 1923–4* (London, 1923, Women Publishers)

Gibbon, Monk, *Netta* (London, 1960, Routledge & Kegan Paul)

Glendenning, Victoria, *Rebecca West* (London, 1998, Penguin)

Glick, Daphne, *The National Council of Women of Great Britain, the First One Hundred Years* (London, 1995, NCW)

Golemba, Beverley E., *Lesser-Known Women: A Biographical Dictionary* (Colorado, 1992, Lynne Rienner)

Graves, Pamela M., *Labour Women: Women in British Working-Class Politics 1918–39* (Cambridge, 1994, CUP)

Grewal, Shabnam (ed.), *Charting the Journey: Writings by Black and Third World Women* (London, 1988, Sheba)

Griffin, Gabriele (ed.), *Feminist Activism in the 1990s* (London, 1995, Taylor & Francis)

Harrison, Brian, *Prudent Revolutionaries: Portraits of British Feminists Between the Wars* (Oxford, 1987, Clarendon Press)

Hartnoll, Phyllis, *The Oxford Companion to the Theatre* (Oxford, 1988, OUP)

Helmond, Marij van, *Votes for Women: The Events on Merseyside 1870–1928* (Liverpool, 1992, National Museums & Galleries on Merseyside)

Higgs, Mary, *Where Shall She Live? The Homelessness of the Woman Worker* (London, 1910, P.S. King & Son)

HMSO, *Index to the Statutes: A–K & L–Z* (London, 1992)

HMSO, *Public General Acts, 1918–84* (London)

Hobbs, May, *Born to Struggle* (London, 1973, Quartet Books)

Hodge, Esther, *A Woman-Oriented Woman* (Sydney, 1989, Gooday Publishers)

Holledge, Julie, *Innocent Flowers: Women in the Edwardian Theatre* (London, 1981, Virago)

Holtby, Winifred, *Women and a Changing Civilisation* (London, 1934, John Lane, Bodley Head)

Holland, Joy, *Feminist Action* (London, 1984, Battle Axe Books)

Hopkinson, Diana, *Family Inheritance: A Life of Eva Hubback* (London, 1954, Staples Press)

Hubback, Eva M., 'The Family Allowances Movement 1924–48' in Rathbone, Eleanor, *Family Allowances: A New Edition of The Disinherited Family* (London, 1949, Allen & Unwin)

Hughes, Mary and Kennedy, Mary, *New Futures: Changing Women's Education* (London, 1985, Routledge & Kegan Paul)

Humm, Maggie, *The Dictionary of Feminist Theory* (London, 1989, Harvester Wheatsheaf)

Hutchinson Woman's Who's Who (London, 1934, Hutchinson)

Irish Women's Diary & Guide Book, 1983–4 (Dublin, 1983/1984, Irish Feminist Information Publications)

Irish WLM, *Chain or Change? The Civil Wrongs of Irish Women* (Dublin, 1971, Dublin Founding Group)

Izzard, Molly, *A Heroine in Her Time* (London, 1969, Macmillan)

Jenkins, Inez, *The History of the Women's Institute Movement of England and Wales* (Oxford, 1953, OUP)

Jeremy, David J., *Dictionary of Business Biography, a biographical dictonary of business leaders active in Britain in the period 1860–1980* (London, 1984–6, Butterworth)

Kanner, Barbara Penny, *Women in Context: Two Hundred Years of British Women Autobiographers* (New York, 1997, G.K. Hall & Co.)

Kean, Hilda, *Deeds Not Words* (London, 1990, Pluto Press)

Keir Cazalet, Thelma, *From the Wings* (London, 1967, The Bodley Head)

Kenny, Mary, *Goodbye to Catholic Ireland: A Social, Personal & Cultural History from the Fall of Parnell to the Realm of Mary Robinson* (London, 1997, Sinclair Stevenson)

Koedt, Anne et al., *Radical Feminism* (New York, 1973, Quadrangle)

Kramarae, Cheris and Treichler, Paula A., *A Feminist Dictionary* (London, 1985, Pandora)

Labour Who's Who (London, 1924 and 1927, Labour Publishing Company)

The Lady's Who's Who 1938–9 (London, Pallas Publishing Co.)

Law, Cheryl, *Suffrage and Power: The Women's Movement, 1918–28* (London, 1997, I.B. Tauris)

Lerner, Gardner, *The Majority Finds its Past* (Oxford, 1979, OUP)

Lesbian History Group, *Not a Passing Phase: Reclaiming Lesbians in History 1840–1985* (London, The Women's Press)

Levine, June, *Sisters: The Personal Story of an Irish Feminist* (Dublin, 1983, Ward River Press)

Liddington, Jill, *The Long Road to Greenham: Feminism & Anti-Militarism in Britain Since 1820* (London, 1989, Virago)

Linklater, E., *An Unhusbanded Life, Charlotte Despard* (London, 1980, Hutchinson)

Luddy, Maria (a), *Women in Ireland, 1800–1918* (Cork, 1995, Cork University Press)

Luddy, Maria (b), *Hanna Sheehy Skeffington* (Dublin, 1995, Historical Association of Ireland)

Mahon, Evelyn, 'Women's Rights and Catholicism in Ireland' in Monica Threlfall (ed.), *Mapping the Women's Movement*, (London, 1996, Verso)

Maitland, Sara, *Very Heaven: Looking Back at the 1960s* (London, 1988, Virago)

Mann, Jean, *A Woman in Parliament* (London, 1962, Odhams Press)

Manning, Leah, *A Life for Education: An Autobiography* (London, 1970, Victor Gollancz)

Martindale, Hilda, *From One Generation to Another: A Book of Memoirs, 1839–1944* (London, 1944, George Allen & Unwin)

Masters, Anthony, *Nancy Astor, A Life* (London, 1981, Weidenfeld & Nicolson)

Mathews, Vera Laughton, *Blue Tapestry* (London, 1948, Hollis & Carter)

May, E.H., *Women Speaking*, vol. 1, no 5 (London, 1960)

McCartan, Joyce, *A Battler All My Life* (London, 1994, Fount)

Messenger, Rosalind, *The Doors of Opportunity: A Biography of Dame Caroline Haslett* (London, 1967, Femina Books)

Middleton, Lucy (ed.), *Women in the Labour Movement* (London, 1977, Croom Helm)

Mitchell, Juliet and Oakley, Ann, *Who's Afraid of Feminism?* (London, 1997, Hamish Hamilton)

Morgan, Robin, *Sisterhood is Powerful* (New York, 1970, Vintage Books)

Moseley, Sydney A., *Broadcasting in My Time* (London, 1935, Rich & Cowan)

Mullarney, Máire, *What About Me?* (Dublin, 1992, Townhouse)

Mulvihill, Margaret, *Charlotte Despard, A Biography* (London, 1989, Pandora)

NCW, *The First Sixty Years, 1895–1955* (London, 1955, NCW)

Nicholls, C.S. et al., *Dictionary of National Biography Missing Persons* (Oxford, 1994, OUP)

Nicholson, Linda, *The Second Wave* (London, 1997, Routledge)

Northcroft, D.M., *British Women MPs* (London, nd 1922?, WFL)

Offen, Karen, Pierson, Ruth Roach and Rendall, Jane (eds), *Writing Women's History: International Perspectives* (London, 1991, Macmillan)

Onlywoman Press, *Love Your Enemy?* (London, 1981)

Oram, Alison, *Women Teachers and Feminist Politics* (Manchester, 1996, Manchester University Press)

Oxford, Margot (ed.), *Myself When Young by Famous Women of Today* (London, 1938, Frederick Muller)

Owens, Rosemary, *Did Your Granny Have a Hammer? A History of the Irish Suffrage Movement 1876–1922* (Dublin, 1985, Attic Press)

Owens, Rosemary, *Votes for Women: Irish Women's Struggle for the Vote* (Dublin, nd, Owens, R. and Sheehy, A.)

Parker, Peter, *Ackerley: A Life of J.R. Ackerley* (London, 1989, Constable)

Parnell, Nancy Stewart, *The Way of Florence Barry* (London, 1965, SJSPA)

Parry, Melanie (ed.), *Chambers Biographical Dictionary of Women* (Edinburgh, 1996, Chambers)

Penguin Biographical Dictionary of Women (London, 1998, Penguin Reference)

Peters, Julie and Wolper, Andrea, *Women's Rights, Human Rights* (London, 1995, Routledge)

Phillips, Melanie, *The Divided House* (London, 1980, Sidgwick & Jackson)

Phipps, Emily, *History of the NUWT* (London, 1928, NUWT)

Pugh, Martin, *Women and the Women's Movement in Britain 1914–59* (London, 1992, Macmillan)

Purvis, June (ed.), *Women's History Britain, 1850–1945* (London, 1995, UCL Press)

Rathbone, Eleanor, *Family Allowances: A New Edition of the Disinherited Family* (London, 1949, Allen & Unwin)

Redstockings, *Feminist Revolution* (New York, 1975–8, Random House)

Reiss, Erna, *The Rights & Duties of Englishwomen* (London, 1934, Sherratt & Hughes)

Richardson, Mary R., *Laugh a Defiance* (London, 1953, Weidenfeld & Nicholson)

The Roll of Honour for Women: An Annual Biographical Record of Women of the World Who Have Worked for the Public Good (London, 1906, The Gentlewoman)

Rose, Catherine, *The Female Experience: The Story of the Woman Movement in Ireland* (Galway, 1975, Arlen House)

Rowbotham, Sheila, *Hidden From History: 300 Years of Women's Oppression and the Fight Against It* (London, 1973, Pluto Press)

Rowbotham, Sheila, *Dreams & Dilemmas* (London, 1983, Virago)

Rowbotham, Sheila, *The Past is Before Us* (London, 1989, Penguin Books)

Russell, Dora, *The Tamarisk Tree* (London, 1977, Virago)

Ryan, Louise, *Irish Feminism and the Vote: An Anthology of the Irish Citizen Newspaper 1912–20* (Dublin, 1996, Folens)

Scafe, Susan, *Teaching Black Literature* (London, 1989, Virago)

Schneir, Miriam, *The Vintage Book of Feminism* (London, 1995, Vintage)

Scott, Richenda C., *Elizabeth Cadbury* (London, 1955, George G. Harrap & Co.)

Segal, Lynne, *Is the Future Female?* (London, 1987, Virago)

Sharp, Evelyn, *Hertha Ayrton: A Memoir 1854–1923* (London, 1926, E. Arnold)

Shorney, David, *Teachers in Training: A History of Avery Hill College* (London, 1989, Thames Polytechnic)

Siddiqui, Hannana, 'Black Women's Activism: Coming of Age?' in *Feminist Review*, no 64, Spring 2000

Simey, Margaret, *Charity Rediscovered: A Study of Philanthropic Effort in Nineteenth Century Liverpool* (Liverpool, 1992, Liverpool University Press)

Simms, Madeleine and Hindell, Keith, *Abortion Law Reformed* (London, 1971, Peter Owen)

Sisterwrite, *Sisterwrite Catalogue 1981–2* (London, 1982, Sisterwrite Bookshop)

Smyth, Ailbhe, *Irish Women's Studies Reader* (Dublin, 1993, Attic Press)

Spare Rib, no 79 (London, February 1979)

Stambler, Sookie (ed.), *Women's Liberation: Blueprint for the Future* (New York, 1970, Ace Books)

Status of Women Committee, *Particulars of Organizations Working for the Equal Status of Women as Citizens* (London, nd c.1946, SWC)

Stead, Jean, *Never the Same Again: Women and the Miners' Strike* (London, 1987, The Women's Press)

Stenton, M. and Lees, S., *Who's Who of British Members of Parliament*, vol. 3 (Sussex, 1979, Harvester Press), vol. 4 (Sussex, 1981, Harvester Press)

Stocks, Mary, *Eleanor Rathbone* (London, 1949, Victor Gollancz)

Stott, Mary, *Organization Woman: The Story of the NUTG* (London, 1978, Heinemann)

Strachey, Ray, *Millicent Garrett Fawcett* (London, 1931, John Murray)

Strachey, Ray, *Our Freedom and Its Results* (London, 1936, Hogarth Press)

Strachey, Ray, *Careers and Openings for Women* (London, 1937, Faber & Faber)

Summerfield, Penny, *Women Workers in the Second World War, Production and Patriarchy in Conflict* (London, 1987, Routledge)

Summerskill, Edith, *A Woman's World* (London, 1967, Heinemann)

Swanwick, Helena, *I Have Been Young* (London, 1935, Victor Gollancz)

Sykes, Christopher, *Nancy, The Life of Lady Astor* (London, 1972, Collins)

Tanner, Leslie B., *Voices From Women's Liberation* (New York, 1970, Signet)

Thomas, Margaret Haig, *This Was My World* (London, 1933, Macmillan)

Thompson, Dorothy, *Over Our Dead Bodies: Women Against the Bomb* (London, 1983, Virago)

Thompson, Laurence, *The Enthusiasts: a Biography of John and Katharine Bruce Glasier* (London, 1971, Gollancz)

Toole, Millie, *Mrs Bessie Braddock* (London, 1957, Robert Hale)

Tooley, Sarah H., *Ladies of Liverpool* (Liverpool, 1895)

Trager, James, *The Women's Chronology: A Year-by-Year Record, from Prehistory to the Present* (London, 1994, Aurum Press)

Tredgold, Arderne, *Lucy Frances Nettlefold* (London, 1968, privately)

TUC, *Women in the Trade Union Movement* (London, 1955, TUC)

TUC, *Industrial Newsletter for Women* (London, 1937–58, TUC)

TUC Reports (London, TUC)

Tuttle, Lisa, *Encyclopaedia of Feminism* (London, 1986, Longman)

Tweedy, Hilda, *A Link in the Chain: The Story of the Irish Housewives' Association 1942–92* (Dublin, 1992, Attic Press)

Uglow, Jennifer S., *The Continuum Dictionary of Women's Biography* (New York, 1989, Continuum)

Uglow, Jennifer S., *The Macmillan Dictionary of Women's Biography* (London, 1999, Macmillan)

Vallance, Elizabeth, *Women in the House* (London, 1979, Athlone Press)

Vernon, Betty D., *Ellen Wilkinson* (London, 1982, Croom Helm)

Virago, *A Virago Keepsake* (London, 1993, Virago)

Wallace, Malcolm, *Single or Return: The History of the TSSA* (London, 1996, TSSA)

Wandor, Michelene, *The Body Politic* (London, 1972, Stage 1)

Wandor, Michelene, *Once A Feminist* (London, 1990, Virago)

Ward, Margaret, *Unmanageable Revolutionaries* (London, 1983, Dingle/Pluto Press)

Ward, Margaret, *Hannah Sheehy Skeffington: A Life* (Cork, 1997, Attic Press)

WCG, *Notes on Its History, Organization, and Work* (1932, WCG)

Wearing, J.P., *The London Stage: A Calendar of Plays and Players*, vols 1900–07, 1910–19, 1920–29 (N.J. and London, Metuchen, 1981, 1982, 1984, The Scarecrow Press)

Weaver, J.R.H. (ed.), *The Dictionary of National Biography 1922–1930* (London, 1937, OUP)

Whately, Monica, *Dorothy Evans and the SPG: The Story of a Militant* (London, 1945, SPG)

Evelyne White, *Winifred Holtby as I Knew Her* (1938)

Wickham Legg, L.G. (ed.), *The Dictionary of National Biography 1931-1940* (London, 1949, OUP)

Wickham Legg, L.G. & Wiliams, E.T. (eds), *The Dictionary of National Biography 1941–1950* (London, 1959, OUP)

Williams, E.T. and Palmer, Helen M. (eds), *The Dictionary of National Biography 1951–1960* (London, 1971, OUP)

Williams, E.T. and Nicholls, C.S. (eds), *The Dictionary of National Biography 1961–1970* (London, 1981, OUP)

Willis, Ellen, *Beginning to See the Light* (Hanover/London, 1992, Wesleyan University Press)

Wilson, Elizabeth, *Mirror Writing: An Autobiography* (London, 1982, Virago)

WLNCC, *Women's Struggle*, vol. 1, no 4 (London, 1971, WLNCC)

Wood, Ethel M., *Mainly for Men* (London, 1943, Victor Gollancz)

WWCAWF, *Woman To-Day*, vol. 1, no 1 (London, 1936–37, WWCAWF)

Who's Who (1929) (London, A & C Black)

Who's Who in Australia (Melbourne, 1980, Information Australia)

Who's Who in Australia 2000 (Melbourne, 1999, Information Australia)
Who Was Who, vols 1–8 (London, A & C Black)
Who's Who in the Theatre (London, 1922, Pitman)
Who's Who in Wales (London, 1933–7, Belgravia Publications)
Who's Who of Women in World Politics (London, 1991, Bowker-Saur)
Women's Who's Who 1934–5 (London, 1934, Shaw Publishing Co.)

CD Rom
The Times Perspectives, *Women's Rights: The Story So Far* (London, 1996, News
Multimedia)

Website
History of Feminism, Second Wave: Articles – http://www.nau.edu/wst/access/
2ndwav/2ndart.html

GLOSSARY

This is a list of acronyms which appear in the text. The date for inauguration has been given in all cases where it could be traced.

AA	Associate in Arts
AAM	Anti-Apartheid Movement
ACAC	Action Campaign for Abortion and Contraception
ACT	Australian Capital Territory
ACTU	Australian Council of Trade Unions
ACW	Associated Countrywomen of the World
ADAPT	Association for Deserted and Alone Parents (Irish)
AEWHA	All England Women's Hockey Association
AFL	Actresses' Franchise League 1908
AGS	Assistant General Secretary
AIM	Action, Information, Motivation 1972 (Irish)
AKA	also known as
ALP	Australian Labour Party
ALRA	Abortion Law Reform Association 1936
AM	Assembly Member
AMCWC	Association of Maternity and Child Welfare Centres 1911
AMIAE	Associate Member of the Institute of Automobile Engineers
AMSH*	Association for Moral and Social Hygiene 1915
APEX	Association of Professional, Executive, Clerical & Computer Staff
APSA	American Political Science Association
ARCSc	Associate of the Royal College of Science
ASW	Association of Service Women 1920
ATDS	Association of Teachers of Domestic Subjects 1896
ATS	Auxiliary Territorial Service
AUCE	Amalgamated Union of Co-operative Employees
AUWT	Association of University Women Teachers
AWKS	Association of Women Clerks and Secretaries 1903
BA (Hons)	Bachelor of Arts Degree (Honours)
BAWC	British–American Women's Crusade

* indicates organizational name change: see end of section

BBC	British Broadcasting Corporation
BC	Borough Council
BCL*	British Commonwealth League 1925
BDWCU*	British Dominions Women Citizens' Union 1919
BDWSU*	British Dominions Woman Suffrage Union 1914
BFBPW	British Federation of Business and Professional Women 1935
BFI	British Film Institute
BFMW	British Federation of Medical Women
BFUW	British Federation of University Women 1907
BG	Board of Guardians
BHA	British Housewives Association 1925
BLWS	British Legion Women's Section 1921
BMA	British Medical Association
BMAC	British Medical Association Committee
BMWF	British Medical Women's Federation (see MWF)
BPhil	Bachelor of Philosophy
BPWC	Business & Professional Women's Club
BS	Batchelor of Surgery
BSc	Batchelor of Science
BUF	British Union of Fascists
BUGC	Birmingham University Girls Clubs
BWIG	Belfast Women's Information Group 1974
BWIL	British Women's International League
BWILPF	British Women's International League for Peace and Freedom 1915
BWSS*	Belfast Women's Suffrage Society
CACE	Central Advisory Council for Education
CANC	Carmarthen Anti-Nuclear Campaign 1980
CAWU	Clerical and Administrative Workers Union 1941
CB	Companion of the Bath
CBC	Society for Constructive Birth Control 1921
CBE	Commander of the Order of the British Empire
CC	Coordinating Committee
CCL*	Commonwealth Countries League
CCNS	Central Committee for National Service
CCNSWS	Central Committee of the National Society for Women's Suffrage
CCWI	Central Council of the Women of Ireland
CCWO	Consultative Committee of Women's Organizations 1921
CCWO	Consultative Committee of Women's Organizations 1921
CCWS	Central Committee for Women's Suffrage
CCWTE	Central Committee of Women's Training & Employment, WWI
CD (ACTS)	Contagious Diseases Acts 1864, 1866, 1869
CoE	Council of Europe
CEBSCA	Central Employment Bureau and Students' Careers Association 1898

CEMA	Council for the Encouragement of Music & the Arts
CEMS	Centre for Extra-Mural Studies
CH	Companion of Honour
CI	Lady of the Imperial Order of the Crown of India
CIE	Companion of the Order of the Indian Empire
CIEE	Council of the Institute of Electrical Engineers
CLA Bill	Criminal Law Amendment Bill 1917
CLP	Constituency Labour Party
CLPD	Campaign for Labour Party Democracy
CLUW	Coalition of Labour Union Women (US) 1974
CLWS	Church League for Women's Suffrage 1909
CM	Master in Surgery
CMB	Central Midwives Board
CMW	Council of Married Women 1952
CND	Campaign for Nuclear Disarmament
COORD	Coordinating Committee in Defence of the Abortion Act c.1975
CP	Communist Party
CPW	Communist Party Women
CR	Consciousness-Raising
CRC	Combahee River Collective (US) 1974
CRWLN	Council for the Representation of Women in the League of Nations 1919
CS	Civil Service
CSA	Civil Service Alliance 1916
CSCA	Civil Service Clerical Association
CSEU	Confederation of Shipbuilding and Engineering Unions
CSSA	Civil Service Sorting Assistants
CSU	Christian Social Union
CSW	Council for the Status of Women 1972
CSWS	Central Society for Women's Suffrage 1900
CUFS	Cambridge University Fabian Society
CUWFA	Conservative and Unionist Women's Franchise Association 1911
CWCS	Council of Women Civil Servants 1920
CWG/WCG	Co-operative Women's Guild
CWL	Catholic Women's League 1906
CWP	Committee of Women Power 1940
CWRA	Conservative Women's Reform Association 1908
CWSS*	Catholic Women's Suffrage Society 1911
CWTE	Committee for Women's Training and Employment
DBE	Dame Commander British Empire
DCO	Dame Commander of the Order
DCVO	Dame Commander of the Royal Victorian Order
DD	Doctor of Divinity
DHSS	Department of Health and Social Security
Dip. Ed.	Diploma in Education

DLB	Dictionary of Labour Biography
DLitt	Doctor of Letters
DORA	Defence of the Realm Act, 1914
DPH	Diploma in Public Health
DSc	Doctor of Science
DSO	Distinguished Service Order
DWU	Domestic Workers' Union
EAW*/ESW	Electrical Association/Society for Women 1924
EC	European Commission
ECP	English Collective of Prostitutes 1975
EdD	Educational Doctorate
ELFS*	East London Federation of Suffragettes 1914
EO	Equal Opportunities
EOC	Equal Opportunities Commission 1975
EOWM	Equal Opportunities Women and Men
EPA	Equal Pay Act, 1970 (UK)
EPCC	Equal Pay Campaign Committee 1944–56
EPRDCC	Equal Political Rights Demonstration Coordinating Committee, 1926
ERA	Equal Rights Amendment (US)
ERC	Equal Rights Committee
ERCCA	Equal Rights in Clubs Campaign for Action 1979
ERGECC	Equal Rights General Election Campaign Committee
ERI	Equal Rights International 1929
ESP	Extra-Sensory Perception
ESU	English Speaking Union
FANY	First Aid Nursing Yeomanry
FCO	Foreign & Commonwealth Office
FCLWS	Free Church League for Women's Suffrage 1910
FCSU	Forward Cymric Suffrage Union 1912
FCWC	Free Church Women's Council
FE	Further Education
FEC*	Family Endowment Committee 1917
FECl*	Family Endowment Council 1918
FES*	Family Endowment Society 1924
FGM	Female Genital Mutilation
FIL	Fellow of the Institute of Linguistics
FIPS	Fellow of the Incorporated Phonographic Society
FISA	Fellow of the Incorporated Secretaries' Association
FLS	Fellow of the Linnaean Society
FMW	Federation of Medical Women
FO	Foreign Office
FOR	Fellowship of Reconciliation 1914
FPA*	Family Planning Association 1939
FRCM	Fellow of Royal College of Music
FRCOG	Fellow of Royal College of Obstetrics & Gynaecology

FRS	Fellow of Royal Society
FRSL	Fellow of Royal Society of Literature
FRSM	Fellow of Royal Society of Medicine
FRSP	Fellow of the Royal Society of Physicians
FS	Fabian Society
FS*	Fawcett Society (see LSWS) 1953
FSW	Feminist Studio Workshop (US)
FWCS	Federation of Women Civil Servants 1913
FWG	Fabian Women's Group 1908
FWGC	Federation of Working Girls' Clubs
FWI/NFWI	Federation of Women's Institutes
GBE	Dame Grand Cross British Empire
GC	General Council
GFTU	General Federation of Trade Unions
GGC	Guild of Girl Citizens
GLC	Greater London Council
GLCWC	Greater London Council Women's Committee
GLF	Gay Liberation Front
GMC	General Medical Council
(GMW)	General & Municipal Workers
GMWU	General and Municipal Workers Union
GPO	General Post Office
GP	General Practitioner – Medical Doctor
HCC	Health & Cleanliness Council
HON	Honourable (in a title)/Honorary (in a degree)
HVA	Health Visitors Association
HW/HWJ	History Workshop/Journal
IAAM	Irish Anti-Apartheid Movement
IAF	International Abolitionist Federation
IAW	International Alliance of Women
IAWSEC	International Alliance of Women for Suffrage and Equal Citizenship 1926
ICCL	Irish Council for Civil Liberties
ICSDW	International Council Social Democratic Women
ICW	International Council of Women 1888
ICWG	International Co-operative Women's Guild 1921
ICWSA	Irish Catholic Women' Suffrage Association 1915
IEE	Institute of Electrical Engineers
IFBPW	International Federation of Britsh and Professional Women 1930
IFUW	International Federation of University Women 1919
IFWW	International Federation of Women Workers
IHA	Irish Housewives Association 1946
IHC	Irish Housewives Committee 1942
ILEA	Inner London Education Authority

ILO	International Labour Organization
ILP	International Labour Party 1893
INH	Inghinidhe Wa Héireann 1900
INSET	In-Service Educational Training
INW	Industrial Newsletter for Women
IRA	Irish Republican Army
IRS	Inland Revenue Service
ISF	Irishwomen's Suffrage Federation 1911
ITA	Independent Television Authority
IU	International Understanding
IWA	Independent Women's Association 1917
IWA	Indian Women's Association 1917
IWCA*	Irish Women's Citizens' Association 1923
IWCC	Islington Women's Counselling Centre
IWCG	International Women's Co-operative Guild 1921
IWCLGA*	Irish Women's Citizens and Local Government Association 1918
IWCSA	Irish Women's Catholic Suffrage Association 1915
IWD	International Women's Day (1st) 1910
IWEDO	International Women's Environment and Development Organization (US)
IWFC	International Women's Franchise Club
IWFL	Irish Women's Franchise League 1908
IWG	Islington Women's Group
IWIL	Irish Women's International League
IWLM	Irish Women's Liberation Movement 1970
IWPL	change to RWPDL Republican Women's Prisoners' Defence League
IWRL	Irish Women's Reform League 1911
IWSA	International Woman Suffrage Alliance 1902
IWSA	International Woman Suffrage Alliance
IWSG	International Women's Service Groups
IWSLGA*	Irish Women's Suffrage and Local Government Association 1876
IWSPU*	Independent Women's Social and Political Union 1916
IWWC	Islington Women's Counselling Centre
IWWU	Irish Women Workers' Union 1911
IWY	International Women's Year 1975
JBL	Josephine Butler League
JP	Justice of the Peace
KCSI	Knight Commander of the Star of India
LAMW	London Association of Medical Women
LBE	London Board of Education
LCC	London County Coucil
LCCWTU	London County Council Women Teachers' Union

LCG	London City & Guilds
LCM	League of the Church Militant 1919
LDA	Liverpool Dressmakers' Association
LGSS	London Graduates' Suffrage Society
LGUWS	London Graduates Union for Women's Suffrage 1909
LittB	Bachelor of Letters
LLA	Lady Literate in the Arts
LLB	Bachelor of Laws
LLD	Doctor of Laws
LLL	Ladies Land League 1880
LLM	Master of Laws
LM	Licentiate in Midwifery
LMH	Lady Margaret Hall
LN	League of Nations 1919–45
LNSASRV	Ladies' National Society for the Abolition of the State Regulation of Vice
LNSWS*	London and National Society for Women's Service 1926
LNU	League of Nations Union
LP	Labour Party 1906
LPWS*	Labour Party Women's Sections 1918
LRC	Labour Representation Committee
LRCP (&I)	Licenciate of the Royal College of Physicians
LRCS	Licenciate of the Royal College of Surgeons
LSE	London School of Economics
LSMW	London School of Medicine for Women
LSWS	London Society for Women's Service
LSWS*	London Society for Women's Suffrage 1907
LSWS*	London Society for Women's Service 1919
LWCOC	Labour Women's Central Organizing Committee (Australia)
LWFS	Liverpool Women's Franchise Society
LWLW	London Women's Liberation Workshop c.1970
LWSS	Liverpool Women's Suffrage Society
LWW	Labour's Who's Who
MA	Master of Arts
MB	Bachelor of Medicine
MBE	Member British Empire
MCC	Middlesex County Council
MD	Doctor of Medicine
MEU	Municipal Employers Union
MF	Miners Federation
MIA	Mothers in Action
MIEE	Member of the Institute of Electrical Engineers
MJI	Member of the Institute of Journalists
MLRL	Marriage Law Reform League
MMLWS	Manchester Men's League for Women's Suffrage
MO	Medical Officer
MOL	Ministry of Labour and National Service

MOW	Movement for the Ordination of Women
MP	Member of Parliament
MRI	Member of the Royal Institutions
MS	Master of Surgery
MSB	Marylebone Sanitary Board
MSF	Union of Manufacturing, Science, Finance
MU	Mothers' Union 1876
MWA	Married Women's Association 1938
MWF	Medical Women's Federation 1916
MWIA	Medical Women's International Association
NAC	National Abortion Campaign
NAPIM	National Association for the Prevention of Infant Mortality
NATO	North Atlantic Treaty Organisation
NAUL	National Amalgamated Union of Labour
NAUSAWC	National Amalgamated Union of Shop Assistants, Warehousemen and Clerks
NAWCS	National Association of Women Civil Servants
NBCC*	National Birth Control Council 1930
NBFO	National Black Feminist Organization (US) 1973
NBTF	National Birthday Trust Fund
NBWC	National Baby Welfare Council
NBWTAU	National British Women's Total Abstinence Union
NCCL	National Council for Civil Liberties 1934
NCEC	National Council for Equal Citizenship 1932
NCGC	National Council of Girls' Clubs 1926
NCL	National Church League
NCM	National Clean Milk
NCMCW	National Council of Mother and Child Welfare
NCLW	National Conference Labour Women
NCSS	National Council of Social Service
NCT	National Chamber of Trade
NCUMC	National Council for the Unmarried Mother and her Child 1918
NCW	National Council of Women 1895
NEAC	New English Art Club
NEC	National Executive Committee
NESWS	North East Society for Women's Suffrage
NEWSS	North of England Women's Suffrage Society 1897
NFBPWC	National Federation of Business and Professional Women's Clubs
NFMW	National Federation of Medical Women
NFTG	National Federation of Townswomen's Guilds
NFWI/FWI	National Federation Women's Institutes 1915
NFWT*	National Federation of Women Teachers 1906
NFWW*	National Federation of Women Workers 1906–20
NGO	Non-Governmental Organization
NHI	National Health Insurance

NHS	National Health Service 1945
NI	Northern Ireland
NIACE	National Institute for Adult and Continuing Education
NIH	National Institute of Houseworkers 1946
NIPWSS	National Industrial and Professional Women's Suffrage Society 1905
NJACWER	National Joint Action Campaign for Women's Equal Rights 1969
NJCWWO	National Joint Committee Working Women's Organizations* 1941
NJU	National Union of Journalists
NMW	No More War Movement
NOGC	National Organization of Girls' Clubs 1911
NOW	National Organization of Women (US) 1966
NPC	National Peace Council 1904
NSPCC	National Society for the Protection of Children
NSW	New South Wales
NTUC	National Trade Union Club
NUC	National Union of Clerks
NUDAW	National Union of Distributive and Allied Workers
NUEI	National Union of Educational Institutes
NUGC	National Union of Guilds for Citizenship 1932
NUGMW	National Union of General and Municipal Workers
NUGW	National Union of General Workers
NUJ	National Union of Journalists
NUJEWP	National Union of Journalists Equality Working Party early 1970s
NUM	National Union of Mineworkers
NUSA	National Union of Shop Assistants
NUSEC*	National Union of Societies for Equal Citizenship 1919
NUSS	Northern Union of Suffrage Societies
NUSW	National Union of Scientific Workers
NUT	National Union of Teachers
NUTG	National Union of Townswomen's Guilds 1932
NUTGW	National Union of Tailor and Garment Workers
NUWSS*	National Union of Women's Suffrage Societies 1897
NUWT*	National Union of Women Teachers 1920
NUWW*	National Union of Women Workers 1895
NWAC	National Women's Advisory Council
NWC	National Women's Conference (US) 1977
NWCA	National Women Citizens' Associations 1918
NWCC	National Women's Coordinating Committee 1970
NWLC	National Women's Liberation Conference (1st) 1970
NWLF*	National Women's Liberal Federation 1919
NWO	National Women's Organisation 1984
NWPC	National Women's Political Caucus (US) 1970
NYRF	New York Radical Feminists (US) 196
NYRW	New York Radical Women (US) 1967

* indicates organizational name change: see end of section

NZ	New Zealand
OBE	Order British Empire
ODC	Open Door Council 1926
ODI	Open Door International 1926
OUWSS	Oxford University Women's Suffrage Society
OW(E)G	Older Women's (Education) Group
OWAAD	Organization of Women of Asian and African Descent
OWP	Older Women's Project
OWSS	Oxford Women's Suffrage Society
PAG	Prisoner's Action Group (Australia)
PEN	Poets, Playwrights, Essayists, Editors & Novelists 1921
PL	Primrose League 1883
PLC	Poor Law Commission
PMB	Private Members Bill
PNEU	Parents National Educational Union
POW	Pictures of Women (US)
POWCA	Post Office Women's Clerk Association
PPC	Prospective Parliamentary Candidate
PPS	Parliamentary Private Secretary
PPU	Peace Pledge Union 1935
QC	Queen's Counsel (Barrister)
QMAAC	Queen Mary Women's Army Auxiliary Corps
RAMC	Royal Army Medical Corps
RBA	Royal Society of British Artists
RC	Royal Commission
RCA	Railway Clerks Association
RFC	Royal Flying Corps
RFH	Royal Free Hospital
RI	Republic of Ireland
RN	Royal Navy
RRC	Lady of Royal Red Cross
RSA	Royal Society of Arts
RSI	Royal Sanitary Institute
RTE	Radio Telefis Eireann
RUI	Royal University of Ireland
RWG	Railway Women's Guild
SAU	Shop Assistants' Union
SBS	Southall Black Sisters
SC	Suffragette Crusaders
SCBCRP	Society for Constructive Birth Control and Racial Progress (usually known as CBC) 1921
SCF	Save the Children Fund
SCLC	Southern Christian Leadership Conference

SCLWS	Scottish Churches League for Women's Suffrage
SCWCA	Scottish Council of Women Citizens' Associations 1919
SCWG	Scottish Co-operative Women's Guild 1892
SCWT	Scottish Council for Women's Trades
SDA	Sex Discrimination Act 1975 (UK)
SDF	Social Democratic Federation
SDP	Social Democratic Party
SEC	Society for Equal Citizenship
SECWCA/SECWA	Society for Equal Citizenship and for Women Citizens Associations
SF	Suffragette Fellowship 1926
SFSU	Scottish Farm Servants Union 1913
SFWSS	Scottish Federation of Women's Suffrage Societies
SI	Sanitary Inspector
SJCIWO*/SJC/ SJCWIO	Standing Joint Committee of Industrial Women's Organizations 1916
SJIA	St Joan International Alliance
SJSPA*	St Joan Social and Political Alliance 1923
SMOH	Society of Medical Officers of Health
SOSBW	Society for Overseas Settlement of British Women 1920–62
SPBCC*	Society for Provision of Birth Control Clinics 1921/22
SPG	Six Point Group 1921
SRN	State Registered Nurse
SS	Social Security
SUWSU	Scottish Universities Woman Suffrage Union
SWLF	Scottish Women's Liberal Federation
SWJ	Society of Women Journalists 1895
SWS	Society for Women's Suffrage
SWIC	Socialist Women's International Committee
SWM	Society for Women in the Ministry
SWSPU*	Suffragettes of the Women's Social and Political Union 1916
SWWJ	Society of Women Writers and Journalists 1894
TC	Trades Council
TG	Townswomen's Guild
TGWU	Tailors and Garment Workers Union
TGWU	Transport and General Workers Union
ThD	Doctor of Theology
TLL	Teacher's Labour League
TOS	Theosophical Order of Service
TSSA	Transport & Salaried Staffs' Association
TU	Trade Union
TUC	Trade Union Congress
TUC WAC	Trade Union Congress Women's Advisory Committee
UCACE	University Committee on Adult and Continuing Education
UCL	University College London
UCWW	Unions Catering for Women Workers

     * indicates organizational name change: see end of section

UDC	Union of Democratic Control
UJW	Union of Jewish Women 1902
UN	United Nations
UNA	United Nations Association
UNO	United Nations Organisation
UPOWWS	Union of Post Office Workers Women's Section 1919
US	United Suffragists 1914–18
USDAW	Union of Shop, Distributive and Allied Workers
UWC	University Women's Club
UWR	University Women's Review
UWW	Union of Women Workers
VAD	Voluntary Aid Detachment
WA	Women's Aid
WAA	Women's Action Alliance (US)
WAAC	Women's Army Auxiliary Corps
WAAC	Women's Abortion and Contraception Campaign
WAC	Women's Action Committee of the CLPD 1980
WAC-CP	Women's Action Committee of the Communist Party
WAF	Women's Aid Federation
WAF	Women Against Fundamentalism
WAHC	Women's Advisory Housing Council
WAP	Women Against Pornography (US) 1979
WAS	Women's Auxiliary Service 1914
WASA	Women's Automobile and Sports Association
WAVAW	Women's Against Violence Against Women 1980
WAWF	Women's Committee Against War and Fascism 1934
WBB	Women Behind Bars (Australia)
WBCG	Workers' Birth Control Group 1924
WBCG	Workers Birth Control Group 1924
WC	Women's Committee
WCA	Women Citizens Association (incorrect in glossary)
WCA	Women Citizens Association
WCAWF	Women's Committee Against War & Fascism 1934
WCC	Women's Consultative Committee of the Ministry of Labour 1941
WCG/CWG	Women's Co-operative Guild 1883
WCNTTLC	Women's Committee Northern Territory Trades and Labour Council (Australia)
WCS	Women Clerks and Secretaries
WEA*EAW	Women's Electrical Association
WEC	Women's Election Committee 1920
WEC	Women's Emergency Corps 1914
WEL	Women's Electoral Lobby (Australia)
WERCC	Women's Equal Rights Campaign Committee
WES	Women's Engineering Society 1919
WES	Women's Engineering Society 1919

WEU	Western European Union
WFGA	Women's Farm and Garden Association 1899
WFH	Wages for Housework 1970
WFL*	Women's Freedom League 1907
WFPC	Women's Foreign Policy Council (US)
WFS	Women's Franchise Society
WFW	Women For Westminster
WGA	Women Graduates' Association (Irish)
WGC	Women's Gas Council
WGCGA	Women Graduates and Candidate Graduates Association (Irish) 1902
WGE	Women's Guild of Empire
WGEU	Women's Group of the Ethical Union
WGSU	Women Graduates of the Scottish Universities
WHVCF	Women's Housing and Village Council Federation
WI	Women's Institute
WIC	Women's Industrial Council 1894
WIDIC	Women's Information Drop-In Centre late 1970s
WIL*	Women's Industrial League 1918
WILPF	Women's International League for Peace & Freedom 1915
WITCH	Women's International Terrorist Conspiracy from Hell (US) c.1968
WL	Women's Liberation
WLA	Women's Liberation Association
WLF*	Women's Liberal Federation 1886
WLG	Working Ladies Guild
WLG	Womens Liberation Group
WLGS	Women's Local Government Society 1888–1925
WLL	Women's Labour League 1906–18
WLM	Women's Liberation Movement
WLUA	Women's Liberal Unionist Association 1886
WNAC	Women's National Advisory Committee
WNCC	Women's National Coordinating Committee
WNLA*	Women's National Liberal Association 1892
WNLF	Women's National liberation Foundation 1919
WP*	Women's Party 1918
WPA	Women's Political Association 1970
WPC	Woman Power Committee 1944
WPDL	Women Prisoners Defence League 1922
WPH	Women's Pioneer Housing 1920
WPHOA*	Women Public Health Officers Association 1896
WPL	Women's Political League 1918
WPPA	Women's Publicity Planning Association 1939
WPS	Women's Printing Society 1897
WRAF	Women's Royal Air Force
WRNS	Women's Royal Navy Service
WRRC	Women's Research and Resources Centre 1970s
WRU	Women's Rights Unit

     * indicates organizational name change: see end of section

WS	Women's Sections
WSABL	Women Students and Artists for Black Liberation
WSF*	Workers' Suffrage Federation 1916
WSI (short for WSIHVA) Association 1836	Women's Sanitary Inspectors and Health Visitors'
WSIA	Women Sanitary Inspectors' Association
WSIHVA*	Women Sanitary Inspectors and Health Visitors Association 1896
WSISS	Women Sanitary Inspectors Suffrage Society
WSL	Women's Service Library
WSN	Women's Studies Network
WSP	Women's Strike for Peace (US) 1962
WSPL	Women's Social and (Progressive) Political League (Irish) 1937
WSPU	Women's Social and Political Union 1903
WSPU*	Women's Social and Political Union 1903
WSS	Women's Soroptomist Society
WSSS	Women Students' Suffrage Society
WST	Women's Service Trust
WSU	Women's Service Union
WTAT	Wholesale Tailoring and Allied Trades
WTFU	Women Teachers' Franchise Union
WTRL	Women's Tax Resistance League
WTU	Women Trade Union
WTUA	Women Trade Union Association
WTUC	Women's Trade Union Council
WTUL*	Women's Trade Union League 1874–1920
WU	Workers' Union
WUO	Women's Unionist Organization 1918
WVS	Women's Voluntary Service
WUA	Women's Unionist Association
WW1	First World War 1914–18
WW2	Second World War 1939–45
WWEC	Workers' War Emergency Committee
WWG*	Women Workers' Group (of the TUC) 1921
WWO*	Working Women's Organizations 1941
WWU	Warehouse Workers Union
WWSL	Women Writers' Suffrage League 1908
YBAW	Why Be A Wife
YS	Young Suffragists 1926
YWCA	Young Women's Christian Association 1855

Organizational name changes

AMSH: the British branch of the International Abolitionist Federation, founded by Josephine Butler in 1875; successor to the Ladies' National Association for the Abolition of State Regulation of Vice and for the Promotion of Social Purity, founded by J.B. in 1870.

APOWC: became part of the Federation of Civil Service Clerks in 1913, which was later FWCS.

BCL: is now the Commonwealth Countries League.

BDWSU: became the BDWCU in April 1919.

BWSS: became the WPL in February 1918.

CWSS: became the SJSPA in October 1923.

EAW: originally known as the Women's Electrical Association, WEA. This caused confusion with the Workers' Education Association, so the name was changed.

ELFS: became the WSF in March 1916. Then in June 1920 the WSF was renamed the Communist Party (British Section of the Third International).

FEC: begun in October 1917, became the FECl after the Autumn of 1918 and then the FES in 1924.

IWSLGA: became the IWCLGA in November 1918, then the IWCA, 1923, finally incorporated into the IHA, 1947.

IWSPU: this and the SWSPU were breakaway factions of the WSPU.

LPWS: came into existence in June 1918 from the WLL, as a result of the LP's new constitution.

LSWS: became the LSW Service in February 1919; became the LNSWS February 1926; 1953 the LNSWS renamed the Fawcett Society.

NBCC: became the FPA in 1939

NFWT: became the NUWT at its Bath Conference 1920.

NFWW: became the Women Workers' Section of the National Union of General Workers in 1920.

NUWSS: became the NUSEC in March 1919.

NUWW: its governing body was the NCW; in October 1918 it merged with the NCW and ceased to exist as a separate entity.

SJCIWO: became the National Joint Committee of Working Women's Organizations from 1941.

SPBCC: originated in 1921 as the Walworth Women's Advisory Clinic.

WFL: broke away from the WSPU in September 1907.

WLF: split in their ranks in 1892 over suffrage with the formation of the WNLA who were not interested in the suffrage question. WLF and the WNLA merged in April 1919.

WP: formed from the WSPU in November 1917.

WSIHVA: became the WPHOA.

WTUL: became the Women Workers' Group operating through the Women's Department of the General Council of the TUC.